McGILL IN HISTORY

McGILL IN HISTORY

Edited by

BRIAN LEWIS, DON NERBAS,
and MELISSA N. SHAW

McGill-Queen's University Press
Montreal & Kingston • London • Chicago

ISBN 978-0-2280-2592-4 (cloth)
ISBN 978-0-2280-2593-1 (ePDF)
ISBN 978-0-2280-2594-8 (ePUB)

Legal deposit fourth quarter 2025
Bibliothèque et Archives nationales du Québec

Printed in Canada on acid-free paper that is 100% ancient-forest-free, containing 100% sustainable, recycled fibre, and processed chlorine-free.

This book has been published with the help of a grant from the Federation for the Humanities and Social Sciences, through the Awards to Scholarly Publications Program, using funds provided by the Social Sciences and Humanities Research Council of Canada. Funding was also received from the Equity Team, Office of the Provost and Executive Vice-President (Academic), McGill University.

Funded by the Government of Canada | Financé par le gouvernement du Canada | Canada | Canada Council for the Arts | Conseil des arts du Canada

We acknowledge the support of the Canada Council for the Arts.

Nous remercions le Conseil des arts du Canada de son soutien.

McGill-Queen's University Press in Montreal is on land which long served as a site of meeting and exchange amongst Indigenous Peoples, including the Haudenosaunee and Anishinabeg nations. In Kingston it is situated on the territory of the Haudenosaunee and Anishinaabek. We acknowledge and thank the diverse Indigenous Peoples whose footsteps have marked these territories on which peoples of the world now gather.

Library and Archives Canada Cataloguing in Publication

Title: McGill in history / edited by Brian Lewis, Don Nerbas, and Melissa N. Shaw.

Names: Lewis, Brian, 1965- editor | Nerbas, Don, 1980- editor | Shaw, Melissa N., editor.

Description: Includes bibliographical references and index.

Identifiers: Canadiana (print) 20250196468 | Canadiana (ebook) 20250196522 | ISBN 9780228025924 (cloth) | ISBN 9780228025948 (ePUB) | ISBN 9780228025931 (ePDF)

Subjects: LCSH: McGill University—Historiography.

Classification: LCC LE3.M22 M325 2025 | DDC 378.714/28—dc23

This book was typeset by Marquis Interscript in 10.5/13 Sabon.
Copyediting by Gwendolyn Schulman.

McGill-Queen's University Press
Suite 1720, 1010 Sherbrooke St West, Montreal, QC, H3A 2R7

Authorized safety representative in the EU: Mare Nostrum Group BV, Mauritskade 21D, 1091 GC Amsterdam, the Netherlands, gpsr@mare-nostrum.co.uk

Contents

Figures

Acknowledgments

The editors would like to acknowledge the McGill historians of Canada – Catherine Desbarats, Elsbeth Heaman, Suzanne Morton, the late Jarrett Rudy, David Wright, and John Zucchi – who were part of the discussions ultimately resulting in this volume. We also appreciate the contributors/attendees at the "McGill in History" colloquium in the spring of 2022 for their insights and stimulating conversation. In addition, we would like to thank Gérald Cadet (director of the McGill Bicentennial) and his staff for their consistent support and encouragement. Not least, we are grateful to Angela Campbell and Tynan Jarrett in the Office of the Provost for enabling a generous grant from McGill University for this project.

McGILL IN HISTORY

Introduction

BRIAN LEWIS, DON NERBAS,

AND MELISSA N. SHAW

The presence of James McGill, namesake of McGill University, was marked on university campus by a statue just beyond the Roddick Gates. In a North American environment shaped by the murder of George Floyd, the rise of the Black Lives Matter movement, and growing recognition of the persistence of an insidious white supremacy, student-led calls for the removal of the McGill statue were mounting by 2021. A Scottish-born merchant who rose to prominence in post-Conquest Quebec society to become a public figure and landowner of considerable significance, James McGill provided the bequest that allowed for the establishment of the university two hundred years earlier.[1] He also owned and profited from the sale of enslaved Black and Indigenous people.[2] The Black Students' Network of McGill disseminated the hashtag #TAKEJAMESDOWN in the summer of 2020 and critical editorials accumulated. In the summer of 2021, after repeated vandalism, the McGill statue was removed from public view.[3]

The previous summer, Tomas Jirousek had graduated with an honours degree in political science and as valedictorian for the Faculty of Arts. A member of the Kainai First Nation in southern Alberta, Jirousek had led the successful campaign to rename the varsity men's sports teams. "A couple of decades ago, my grandparents wouldn't have been allowed to go to a university like McGill without losing their status. I've been reflecting on that a lot over the past couple days," noted Jirousek.[4] That a racial epithet, Redmen, could persist as an element of McGill "tradition" until 2019, when Principal Suzanne Fortier announced that the name would be dropped, is telling.

The cases of the James McGill statue and the Redmen name were examples of how legacies of slavery and settler colonialism continued to play out at the university. Official accounts of the university's history had offered limited perspective on the histories that animated student-led protests. Institutional university histories are indeed often presented in isolation from the mainstream of history and historiography. In this mode, the history of a university serves as a chronicle of institutional development and progress – an insider's story intended to inform and please.[5] Stanley Brice Frost's two-volume history of McGill, published in 1980 and 1984, is an admirable work that continues to be drawn upon by many scholars. A careful reader of this volume will indeed note that Frost's history is widely cited throughout; it is an important contribution that continues to serve as an essential resource. But the Frost history is also marked by the limitations of the university-history genre, a chronicle of institutional evolution removed from the historiographical questions and methodologies that were influencing history departments of the period.[6] The Frost project was in fact, as Brian Young notes, supported by McGill's administration in the 1970s instead of an alternate proposal from McGill's Department of History for a long-term research project on the university's history.[7]

This volume sets out to reassert a renewed version of the project proposed by the Department of History decades ago. The volume has also been aided by a shift in attitude at the university. Following the example of other institutions, McGill University has thrown support behind initiatives to facilitate critical investigations of its own history, including the institution's connections to slavery and colonialism.[8] Yet, it is important to note that scholars at McGill – and scholarship about McGill – had moved ahead before the university's initiative. In 2020, professor of art history Charmaine Nelson co-authored a report on James McGill and the university's relationship to slavery with students from her undergraduate seminar. The report not only detailed James McGill's known history as an enslaver, it also critiqued upper administration's ongoing reluctance to support a full investigation of the institution's connections to slavery.[9] Meanwhile, since 2016, Professor Suzanne Morton, a member of the Department of History and Classical Studies, has offered an undergraduate seminar on the history of McGill as part of her regular teaching rotation. The seminar has generated original research on diverse aspects of the university's history, some of which is drawn upon in this volume. Additionally, Morton conducted her own research to produce two informative historical pamphlets in 2019 – *Indigenous McGill* and *Black McGill* – as well as a widely viewed YouTube video on the origins of the Redmen name at McGill during an important moment in the debate on renaming.[10] These unofficial faculty initiatives around the time of the university's bicentennial were significant, and they played a role in creating an environment that encouraged the university to reckon with McGill's history in a more fulsome manner.

The title of this volume, *McGill in History*, captures its primary purpose. It places the university's history in a societal context to consider how McGill, as an institution, was implicated in dominant power structures and ideologies. As a site of knowledge production, cultural authority, and power, McGill University cannot be understood in isolation from the wider Atlantic world and colonial expansionism from which it emerged in the nineteenth century. These historical forces also connected the university to the ascendency of an Anglo-Protestant bourgeoisie in a majority French-Canadian and Catholic city. At the close of the nineteenth century, McGill was at the centre of an elite residential district, the Square Mile, that had grown fabulously rich from the rise of a Canadian political economy. The inequities of this social order were thus expressed in the urban landscape itself.[11] McGill's place in this turn-of-the-century world – which affirmed the economic, cultural, social, racial, and linguistic inequities of empire and colonialism – needs to be registered if we are to attempt to understand the twentieth-century developments that changed the character of the university and the spectres that continue to haunt it.

Following James McGill's founding bequest, McGill University remained a privately funded university during the nineteenth and early twentieth centuries. The university's greatest individual benefactor was tobacco magnate William C. Macdonald (1831–1917), namesake of the Macdonald Engineering Building and founder of what would become Imperial Tobacco.[12] The names connected with McGill buildings reveal links to other nineteenth-century commodities: Redpath (sugar), Morrice (cotton textiles), Molson (beer), and McLennan (coal). Railways were also central to Canada's industrial political economy of the late nineteenth century and drew wealth into the Square Mile that helped create powerful McGill boosters. With his cousin and Bank of Montreal president George Stephen, Donald A. Smith was among the small syndicate that founded the Canadian Pacific Railway (CPR); his image driving the last spike of the transcontinental railway at Craigellachie in 1885 remains iconic today. A long-serving university chancellor (1889–1914) responsible for the establishment of McGill's women's college, Royal Victoria College, Smith was one of McGill's greatest benefactors. He was also made a peer in the British House of Lords, Lord Strathcona and Mount Royal, in 1897.[13] Six years after Strathcona's death, in 1920, CPR president Edward Beatty was appointed McGill chancellor, a position he would hold until he died in 1943. During a period that spanned over half a century (1889–1943) – with the exception of an essentially wartime interlude – a founder and then president of the CPR served as chancellor.[14]

As a privately funded university, McGill relied upon wealthy patrons to expand and sustain its operations. And during the Great Depression of the 1930s, Chancellor Beatty continued to champion the private university as an institution free from government interference. However, beginning in 1939, public money was committed to McGill.[15] By this time, the Square Mile world that had given rise to McGill was experiencing relative political and economic decline, and in the mid-twentieth century, public investment in universities became a state priority. These twin developments ensured that McGill's future would be that of a public institution in Quebec. This transition brought new questions to the fore during the era of Quebec's Quiet Revolution, as Jean-Philippe Warren shows in his chapter on Operation McGill français. Precisely because of the university's international connectedness and place within Quebec society, McGill was powerfully linked to a wider world and exposed to its diversity. The option of conservative isolationism and retreat behind the Roddick Gates was radically diminished during the twentieth century. McGill was a unique site of political contestation and negotiation.

McGill in History brings together diverse episodes to trace elements of the university's history across two centuries. It does not claim to be a definitive or comprehensive account of the university's history. Nor does it provide a forensic accounting of the university's connection to slavery.[16] These studies remain to be fully carried out. This book, rather, seeks to place McGill's history in an ongoing scholarly conversation by incorporating diverse historiographies and perspectives. The chapters that follow present new research and provide essential historical context needed to overcome the limitations of the siloed university history.

It should not come as a surprise that McGill has already been written about in many different historical contexts. This work can be organized according to faculties and disciplines: law,[17] medicine,[18] natural history and science,[19] engineering,[20] social sciences,[21] social work,[22] and so on. Given the university's broader importance in a changing social order, existing literature on the university's history can also be organized according to critical themes and subjects, such as anti-Black racism and slavery,[23] settler colonialism,[24] empire and international affairs,[25] business and elite influence,[26] and social reform.[27] *McGill in History* builds upon these literatures connected to the university's history to offer a distinct contribution to the history of higher education in Quebec and Canada.[28] In so doing, it seeks both to broaden the historical frame of critical university studies and to demonstrate the utility of the university as an archetype for the study of power in modern society.[29]

The first portion of the volume centres on James McGill and his environments and legacies in Scotland and Quebec. Stephen Mullen's chapter details McGill's upbringing in Glasgow and his student days at Old College (now the University of Glasgow) in the mid-eighteenth century, before he departed for Montreal around 1766. Young James would have been surrounded by the culture of colonial commerce in the city and at the college – by the Atlantic-world entrepreneurs who dominated the local economy and society and the sons of slave-owning planters who arrived each school year from America and the Caribbean. But the college was also at the heart of the Scottish Enlightenment and the pioneering attacks on the institution of slavery by leading philosophers like Francis Hutcheson. What McGill thought about this clash between the economics of chattel slavery and the philosophical movement for its abolition is unknown, but his later ownership of enslaved people in Montreal suggests that the abolitionist critiques had little impact on him. In light of this, Mullen's chapter concludes with a discussion of James McGill's legacy and how he has been memorialized in Scotland, especially at the University of Glasgow.

Andrew Mackillop's chapter further explores the political, economic, social, and intellectual influences shaping James McGill's attitudes and thinking. It argues that both his philanthropy and his role as an enslaver can be seen as facets of a "provincial" worldview shaped by the mixing of his Scottish and Quebec backgrounds. Growing up in Scotland in the aftermath of the 1745 Jacobite rising and spending his life in two "provincial" societies – dedicated to social "improvement" and marked by economic specialization within an integrated empire – inculcated a strong belief in social order, the rule of law, and the defence of property. This served to justify some of the defining traits in his life: his loyalism during the American Revolution, his civic activism in areas such as the militia and the development of educational provision, and his treatment of Indigenous and African-descended people as chattel property.

Brian Young's contribution, the third chapter reflecting on James McGill and his legacy, discusses the considerable distance between the man depicted in the university's official history and reality. Its first theme examines the university's founding document, James McGill's will, including its intentions and the subsequent dispute over its settlement. The second theme considers the significance of his wealth – largely in the form of landed property – and his marriage into the Catholic Desrivières family, prominent members of the Quebec francophone bourgeoisie, who (with the help of James McGill's money) established a three-generation landed dynasty in the province's Eastern Townships. The third theme discusses the university's construction of a "founding history," only begun in the 1970s in the wake of student unrest and nationalist turmoil, which represented him as a very different figure: a Montreal entrepreneur with commercial and individualistic instincts aligned with presentist university values.

The university existed thanks to a land and money bequest from James McGill, but this was insufficient to cover debts and ambitions by the mid-nineteenth century. Brian Gettler's chapter details the attempts by the chancellor and the Board of Governors of McGill University to secure an endowment from the government. The breakthrough came in 1860 after the Crown transferred authority over the Indian Department to the Province of Canada, and with it the management of the Indian Fund. This fund, held in trust by the Crown, was generated by the sale and lease of First Nations lands and resources, and was invested by the Colonial Office in London to earn interest and prevent loss of value due to inflation. But, as critics feared, local control over Indigenous affairs brought with it the temptation by local politicians to plunder the fund. As soon as the reserve became available, the Province of Canada brokered a loan to McGill for £40,000. While the university reimbursed the fund's capital outlay a short while later, McGill greatly profited from Indigenous dispossession in receiving the loan, which helped transform the college into a thriving institution.

The McGill of the late nineteenth century built by such resources and the wealth of moneyed benefactors is the subject of Don Nerbas's chapter on Willie McDonald. Willie was the nineteen-year-old son of

Senator William McDonald of the Cape Breton coal town of Glace Bay, and he spent the 1896–97 academic year at McGill taking courses in applied science (engineering) and endeavouring to accumulate social and cultural capital. His letters home, preserved in the senator's personal papers, reveal in detail his impressions of student life, including his expenses, his lodging arrangements, his religious practices, his social networking, his invitations to call on grandee families of the Square Mile, and his leisure pursuits. The letters also uncover a masculine, bourgeois student culture that was exceptionally unruly and violent, including reports of skirmishes with police and, in another instance, a fight in the Arts Building between first- and second-year students that, at least Willie believed, had resulted in a student's death. In an era of high imperialism, such rowdy behaviour could be mobilized to political purpose, as would be suggested a few years later when McGill students, inflamed by jingoist sentiments of imperial loyalism, ran riot in the streets of Montreal during the South African War.

Turn-of-the-century McGill was the product of a dramatic expansion interconnected with the rise of industrial capitalism in Canada. The development of the curriculum and the composition of the student body reflected McGill's role in a fast-changing industrial society. This produced new debates and tensions in the twentieth century. Elsbeth Heaman's chapter takes us into the early twentieth century and a deep dive into the emerging discipline of economics, questions of national and racial identity, and student culture at McGill. It begins with a lecture to second-year arts students by Professor Stephen Leacock in 1910 on the subject "What Is Money?" – a controversial topic subject to intense debates over such questions as whether money was "endogenous" or "exogenous." But the lecture was disrupted by an "attack" by first-year students, written up in the *McGill Annual* by undergraduate Jacob Viner, a Montrealer of Romanian-Jewish descent. This sets up a discussion not only of antisemitism at McGill but also of the decades-long debate between the conservative, imperialist, protectionist Leacock, and Viner, who in his later career at the University of Chicago became one of the foremost money theorists of the day. The chapter frames the analysis by adapting the endogenous/exogenous distinction to apply not only to money but also to the university and the city.

By the interwar period, McGill had secured a reputation as Canada's leading university in science and medicine, but the social sciences lagged behind. Marlene Shore's chapter explains how the university took steps to develop sociology, economics, and psychology in these decades, perceiving them to be socially useful. But, since McGill was a private university in the country's financial capital with a board of governors drawn from Montreal's largest businesses, top-down ideas based on a robust utilitarian tradition and religiously infused notions of "national efficiency" conflicted with faculty desires for academic freedom. The resulting storm in the 1930s marginalized the social sciences and laid bare a deeper Canadian problem: the weak reputation of the country's thinkers and cultural producers. Shore's study of interwar McGill demonstrates how powerfully new ideas in the social sciences were buffeted by the university's policies and the degree to which ideas are subject to erasure through the strategies employed to control them.

Moving into the period of the Second World War, Tess Elsworthy's chapter discusses one of the most shameful but little-examined episodes in McGill's history: the senate ban on the admission of all students "of Japanese racial origin" in October 1943. One such student already enrolled was subsequently expelled but at least seven continued to take classes. The Canadian government had exiled all Japanese Canadians from the Pacific coast soon after Pearl Harbor, including students at the University of British Columbia, but no other Canadian university passed such a blatantly racist policy. The exclusion was highly contentious on campus, with spirited anti-racist resistance from the students' society, professors, the registrar, many members of senate, alumni, and Japanese Canadian students and activists. And although the policy was repealed in 1945 once the war crisis was over, the board of governors still made efforts to stall its official termination.

A refugee from Nazi Germany, Heinz Lehmann would make a major contribution as a member of McGill's Department of Psychiatry in the 1950s, although his work has since been overshadowed by the notorious MKULTRA scandal, the CIA-funded covert mind control program associated with Donald Ewen Cameron. Andrea Tone's chapter demonstrates Lehmann's enduring impact on practitioners and patients through his clinical trial of the drug chlorpromazine in 1953 at the Verdun Protestant Hospital (today's Douglas Mental Health University Institute). Lehmann's determination that chlorpromazine contained but did not cure the symptoms of serious mental illnesses mainstreamed pharmacotherapy and gave rise to the global deinstitutionalization of patients. Lehmann was pivotal in cementing McGill Psychiatry's reputation as one of the world's leading centres for pharmacology and neuropsychiatry.

Propelled by the momentum of the Quiet Revolution, a coalition of nationalist forces – incorporating worker and student movements – protested against McGill in Operation McGill français in March 1969, believing that McGill served as a bastion of the wealthy, elitist, Anglo-Saxon establishment. Jean-Philippe Warren's chapter focuses on this rally, intended to change the language of instruction and operation at the university. The protesters shared a belief that the dire socio-economic position of francophone workers and inadequate provision for francophone students could only be achieved through the liberation of Quebec from a colonial subjugation connected to McGill itself. The slogan "McGill français" seemed to be an especially effective way of uniting students and workers in a program of national liberation. The chapter investigates the local, national, and international factors contributing to the rally's success and explores its immediate and more far-reaching effects on McGill and on Quebec society as a whole.

The final chapter, by Brian Lewis, brings us up to date, with a discussion of the LGBTQ+ history of McGill. It traces the fragments of a queer presence at the university before Stonewall, but its main focus is on the burst of gay liberationist energy from the 1970s to the present, beginning with the rise of GAY (later Queer McGill), the first anglophone gay organization in Quebec. This initial response to and contribution towards the changing social and political environment was led by students and a limited number of faculty and staff in the face of homophobia, intolerance, indifference, or incomprehension from the university administration. This started to change around the turn of the millennium when McGill began to rebrand itself in a transition from hostility to unease to tolerance to inclusion. The chapter investigates the reasons for this transformation and captures the voices of the participants in the struggle for fostering a more inclusive and accepting McGill.

Wendell Nii Laryea Adjetey, a historian of the African diaspora, supplies the epilogue, a poignant reflection on the university's past and present derived from Adjetey's scholarly expertise on the history of Pan-African liberation movements. While the pro-Palestinian encampment installed on campus from April to July 2024 called attention to McGill's position in world affairs, for Adjetey it also recalls certain aspects of McGill's recent past during the Cold War era. Through two examples – McGill professor and ballistics engineer Gerald Bull, and the MKULTRA program – Adjetey captures McGill's role in a Cold War geopolitics predicated on the reproduction of anti-Black racism and colonialism. Bull's efforts to design weapons for the defeat of anticolonial struggles in Africa and of Pan-Africanism across the Atlantic World suggest, moreover, that the legacies of James McGill's Atlantic World are not as distant from our present times as is often thought.

McGill in History seeks to open new vistas into the past of McGill University, ones that place the evolution of an institution in relation to its wider historical context. Moving away from narration of the university's history as a unified account of progress and achievement, this volume is kaleidoscopic in its overall approach and effect: it brings together diverse historical expertise through investigation of distinct episodes and themes connected to the university's history. *McGill in History* spans two centuries through the prisms of different historiographies and methodologies but does not make claim to comprehensiveness. Certitude is undermined by registering the immensity and complexity of the past. It is an acknowledgment that, we believe, is necessary for critical reflection and evaluation of the university's history. Ultimately, there is no single story or polemical lesson to tell.

McGill University has been a site of knowledge production and competing ideas and aims that have evolved with the reconfiguration of the university and its place in the world. The paradoxes and contradictions of the university's history derive from that larger history. Which historical tendencies and trajectories will be most consequential in shaping the university's future? That is unclear. As before, a diverse ecosystem of people – administrators, faculty, staff, students, government officials, and the public – will decide that. Knowing something of the past will, we hope, guide those efforts towards socially responsible outcomes.

NOTES

1 John Irwin Cooper and James Woycke, *James McGill of Montreal: Citizen of the Atlantic World* (Ottawa: Borealis Press, 2003), 69; Maysie Steel MacSporran, "James McGill: A Critical Biographical Study" (MA thesis, McGill University, 1930), 24, 44; F.J. Shepherd, "The First Medical School in Canada: Its History and Founders, with Some Personal Reminiscences," *Canadian Medical Association Journal* 15, no. 4 (1925): 418, 420, 424; Cyrus MacMillan, *McGill and Its Story: 1821–1921* (London: J. Lane, 1921), 152; Craig Steven Wilder, *Ebony & Ivy: Race,*

Slavery, and the Troubled History of America's Universities (New York: Bloomsbury Press, 2013), 373n31.

2 Charmaine Nelson, *Slavery, Geography and Empire in Nineteenth-Century Marine Landscapes of Montreal and Jamaica* (London and New York: Routledge, Taylor & Francis Group, 2016), 92; Frank Mackey, *Done with Slavery: The Black Fact in Montreal, 1760–1840* (Montreal and Kingston: McGill-Queen's University Press, 2010), 74, 85; Stanley Brice Frost, *James McGill of Montreal* (Montreal and Kingston: McGill-Queen's University Press, 1995), 64.

3 "Statue of University Namesake and Slave-Owner James McGill Removed After Most-Recent Bout of Vandalism," CTV News Montreal, 10 July 2021 (updated 21 July 2021), accessed 22 March 2024, https://montreal.ctvnews.ca/statue-of-university-namesake-and-slave-owner-james-mcgill-removed-after-most-recent-bout-of-vandalism-1.5504661.

4 Ka'nhehsí:io Deer, "First Nations Student Honoured as McGill Valedictorian After Leading Fight Against 'Redmen' Team Name," CBC News, 22 June 2020, accessed 19 March 2024, https://www.cbc.ca/news/indigenous/first-nations-valedictorian-mcgill-1.5619676.

5 The limitations of "institutional biographies" are also noted in Paul Axelrod and John G. Reid, "Introduction," in *Youth, University, and Canadian Society: Essays in the Social History of Education*, ed. Paul Axelrod and John G. Reid (Montreal and Kingston: McGill-Queen's University Press, 1989), xi–xii.

6 See Stanley Brice Frost, *McGill University: For the Advancement of Learning, Volume I, 1801–1895* (Montreal and Kingston: McGill-Queen's University Press, 1980); and *McGill University: For the Advance of Learning, Volume II, 1895–1971* (Montreal and Kingston: McGill-Queen's University Press, 1984). Frost also wrote biographies of Principal Cyril James and James McGill: *The Man in the Ivory Tower: F. Cyril James of McGill* (Montreal and Kingston: McGill-Queen's University Press, 1991) and *James McGill of Montreal.*

7 See chapter 3.

8 Marissa J. Fuentes and Deborah Gray White, eds, *Scarlet and Black: Slavery and Dispossession in Rutgers History* (New Brunswick: Rutgers University Press, 2020); Wilder, *Ebony & Ivy*; Lindsey K. Walters, "Slavery and the American University: Discourses of Retrospective Justice at Harvard and Brown," *Slavery & Abolition* 38, no. 4 (2017): 719–44; Jennifer Schuessler, "Confronting Academia's Ties to Slavery," *New York Times, 5 March 2017; Report on Lord Dalhousie's History on Slavery and Race* (Scholarly Panel to Examine Lord Dalhousie's History on Slavery

and Race, Dalhousie University, 2019, Chair: Dr Afua Cooper); Shirley Tillotson, "How (and How Much) King's College Benefitted from Slavery in the West Indies, 1789–1854," 6 May 2019 (and small corrections 30 January 2020), King's & Slavery: A Scholarly Inquiry, University of Kings College, accessed 27 November 2024, https://ukings.ca/wp-content/uploads/2021/01/202001TillotsonKingsSlaveryIndirectConnections_Secure.pdf; Karolyn Smardz Frost and David W. States, "King's College, Nova Scotia: Direct Connections with Slavery," 21 April 2021, King's & Slavery: A Scholarly Inquiry, University of King's College, accessed 27 November 2024, https://ukings.ca/wp-content/uploads/2021/10/KINGS-Slavery-Report-October-12-2021-FINAL.pdf; Melissa. N. Shaw, "Historical Legacies, Black Canadian Slavery, and Institutional Histories," in *Black Perspectives*, African American Intellectual History Society, 22 September 2022, accessed 27 November 2024, https://www.aaihs.org/historical-legacies-black-canadian-slavery-institutional-histories/.

9 Charmaine A. Nelson and Student Authors, *Slavery and McGill: Bicentennial Recommendations* (2020), accessed 27 November 2024, https://blackmaplemagazine.com/wp-content/uploads/2022/09/bicentenary-recommendations.pdf.

10 Suzanne Morton, "Colour, Colonialism and the McGill Redmen: A Short History" (January 2019), accessed 27 November 2024, https://youtu.be/qfReCSFu5Xg?feature=shared; Suzanne Morton, *Indigenous McGill* (2019), https://www.mcgill.ca/indigenous/files/indigenous/indigenous_mcgill_october_2019_0.pdf, and *Black McGill* (2019), https://www.mcgill.ca/antiblackracism/files/antiblackracism/black_mcgill_may_2021.pdf.

11 See Dimitry Anastakis, Elizabeth Kirkland, and Don Nerbas, eds, *Montreal's Square Mile: The Making and Transformation of a Colonial Metropole* (Toronto: University of Toronto Press, 2024).

12 William Fong, *Sir William C. Macdonald: A Biography* (Montreal and Kingston: McGill-Queen's University Press, 2007); MacMillan, *McGill and Its Story*, 238–39 and 259–60.

13 Alexander Reford, "SMITH, DONALD ALEXANDER, 1st Baron STRATHCONA and MOUNT ROYAL," *Dictionary of Canadian Biography*, vol. 14 (University of Toronto/Université Laval, 1998), accessed 22 March 2024, http://www.biographi.ca/en/bio/smith_donald_alexander_14E.html; MacMillan, *McGill and Its Story*, 239, 241, 258–9; David L. Johnston, "The Legacy of Peter Redpath," *Fontanus* 9 (1996): 24; Alexandria Pierce, "Imperialist Intent – Colonial Response: The Art Collection and Cultural Milieu of Lord Strathcona in Nineteenth-Century Montreal" (PhD diss., McGill University, 2002); Shepherd, "The First Medical School in Canada," 421, 425.

14 William Macdonald (1914–1917) and then Prime Minister Robert Borden (1918–1920) served as chancellor between the tenures of Smith and Beatty.

15 Frost, *McGill University*, 2:199–200, 209 (fn. 17).

16 For examples, see *Report on Lord Dalhousie's History on Slavery and Race*; Stephen Mullen and Simon Newman, *Slavery, Abolition and the University of Glasgow: Report and Recommendations of the University of Glasgow History of Slavery Steering Committee* (September 2018); Sven Beckert, Katherine Stevens, and the students of the Harvard and Slavery Research Seminar, *Harvard and Slavery: Seeking a Forgotten History* (2011); *Slavery and Justice: Report of the Brown University Steering Committee on Slavery and Justice* (2006).

17 Ian C. Pilarczyk, Angela Fernandez, and Brian Young, eds, *Law, Life, and the Teaching of Legal History: Essays in Honour of G. Blaine Baker* (Montreal and Kingston: McGill-Queen's University Press, 2022); Brian Young, *The Politics of Codification: The Lower Canadian Civil Code of 1866* (Montreal and Kingston: McGill-Queen's University Press, 1994), esp. 66–97.

18 Joseph Hanaway and Richard L. Cruess, *McGill Medicine, Volume 1: The First Half Century, 1829–1885* (Montreal and Kingston: McGill-Queen's University Press, 1996); Joseph Hanaway, Richard L. Cruess, and James Darragh, *McGill Medicine, Volume 2, 1885–1936* (Montreal and Kingston: McGill-Queen's University Press, 2006).

19 Suzanne Zeller, *Early Victorian Science and the Idea of a Transcontinental Nation* (Toronto: University of Toronto Press, 1987); A.B. McKillop, *A Disciplined Intelligence: Critical Inquiry and Canadian Thought in the Victorian Era* (Montreal and Kingston: McGill-Queen's University Press, 1979).

20 Peter Collins, *Notes on the Centenary of the Faculty of Engineering of McGill University: Its Origin and Growth* (1971). See also J. Rodney Millard, *The Master Spirit of the Age: Canadian Engineers and the Politics of Professionalism, 1887–1922* (Toronto: University of Toronto Press, 1988).

21 Marlene Shore, *The Science of Social Redemption: McGill, the Chicago School, and the Origins of Social Science Research in Canada* (Toronto: University of Toronto Press, 1987).

22 Suzanne Morton, *Wisdom, Justice, and Charity: Canadian Social Welfare through the Life of Jane B. Wisdom, 1884–1975* (Toronto: University of Toronto Press, 2014).

23 rosalind hampton, *Black Racialization and Resistance at an Elite University* (Toronto: University of Toronto Press, 2020). See also Delice

Mugabo, "'A Spirit of Disobedience': Black Women Freedom Runners and the Collective Practice of Abolition" (PhD diss., CUNY, 2024); Shaw, "Historical Legacies"; Jacqueline Riddle, "Uncovering Slavery and Empire: Six Views of Montréal in 1830," in *Legacies Denied: Unearthing the Visual Culture of Canadian Slavery*, ed. Charmaine Nelson (Montreal: C.A. Nelson, 2013); Nelson, *Slavery, Geography and Empire*; Afua Cooper, *The Hanging of Angélique: The Untold Story of Canadian Slavery and the Burning of Old Montréal* (Toronto: HarperCollins, 2006).

24 See, for instance, chapter 4 in this collection. For broader and recent historiographical treatment of settler colonialism, see Fred Burrill, "The Settler Order Framework: Rethinking Canadian Working-Class History," *Labour / Le Travail* 83 (Spring 2019): 173–98; Amy Fung, "Is Settler Colonialism Just Another Study of Whiteness?" *Canadian Ethnic Studies* 53, no. 2 (2021): 115–31; Dallas Jokic, "Cultivating the Soil of White Nationalism: Settler Violence and Whiteness as Territory," *Journal of Critical Race Inquiry* 7, no. 2 (2020): 1–21.

25 The barring of Black students from McGill's Faculty of Medicine during the First World War is examined within the context of Canada-Caribbean relations in Paula Hastings, *Dominion Over Palm and Pine: A History of Canadian Aspirations in the British Caribbean* (Montreal and Kingston: McGill-Queen's University Press, 2022), 116–18, 120, 125; Megan Brankley Abbas, "McGill University as a 'Midwife for the Islamic Reformation,'" in *Whose Islam? The Western University and Modern Islamic Thought in Indonesia* (Stanford: Stanford University Press, 2021), 52–91.

26 Jessica van Horssen, *A Town Called Asbestos: Environmental Contamination, Health, and Resilience in a Resource Community* (Vancouver: UBC Press, 2016), 51–5 and 150–62; Shore, *Science of Social Redemption*; Don Nerbas, *Dominion of Capital: The Politics of Canadian Big Business and the Crisis of the Canadian Bourgeoisie, 1914–1947* (Toronto: University of Toronto Press, 2013), 148–51; Young, *Politics of Codification.*

27 Shore, *The Science of Social Redemption*; Morton, *Wisdom, Justice, and Charity.*

28 Axelrod and Reid, eds, *Youth, University, and Canadian Society*; Paul Stortz and E. Lisa Panayotidis, eds, *Historical Identities: The Professoriate in Canada* (Toronto: University of Toronto Press, 2006); E. Lisa Panayotidis and Paul Stortz, eds, *Women in Higher Education, 1850–1970: International Perspectives* (New York: Routledge, 2016).

29 Darvarian L. Baldwin's examination of the modern university's impact on its urban surroundings notes a failure to "examine the consequences of schools embracing an increasing for-profit approach" through a "corporate mode" that "includes the financially predatory relationship between universities and their own students." Stefan M. Bradley's *Upending the Ivory Tower* delves deeper into this relationship by studying Black Power movement student protests at Ivy League schools in the USA from 1940 to the 1970s. However, protest politics in academia are not limited to student involvement. Longstanding debates on history as a profession – including the relationship between history and memory in historical understandings of slavery, as discussed by Ira Berlin – have impacted methodological approaches. Most recently, the debate has hinged on historians' role in producing scholarship that speaks to "present-day" issues and ideologies. Adhering to the enlightenment notion that history is an objectified science rather than a craft, some have invested in gatekeeping a discipline violently premised on a biased canon that has sanctified, sustained, and cloaked histories of oppressors and their oppression as a benign and justified history of winners over losers. Historians, often descendants and benefactors of these "winners," explain the stories of oppressors succeeding in their exploitation and marginalization of the oppressed as an objective "telling" of how power works without explaining who has and still bears the costs and consequences of them reaping the spoils of their ill-gotten gains. As Keisha N. Blain points out, "Telling 'neutral' historical accounts of egregious practices such as slavery and lynching serves a fundamental purpose – to excuse injustices of the present and thereby maintain systems of oppression. It is a form of purposeful amnesia designed to empower oppressors." While being accused of ruining the profession with "presentism," those telling counternarratives to the supposedly benign practices of "neutral" history-making bear a particular weight and responsibility. This weight is "especially great for members of marginalized groups." Historians from these groups, operating in "a white-dominated world and academy," must grapple with these historical contingencies and continuities. To survive places designed to exclude them as an objective fact of competency, they have a heightened awareness of the dubious notion of neutrality and meritocracy. See Darvarian L. Baldwin, *In the Shadow of the Ivory Tower: How Universities Are Plundering Our Cities* (New York: Bold Type Books, 2021), 13; Stefan M. Bradley, *Upending the Ivory Tower: Civil Rights, Black Power, and the Ivy League* (New York: NYU Press, 2018); Ira Berlin, "American Slavery and Memory and the Search

for Social Justice," *Journal of American History* 90, no. 4 (March 2004): 1251–68; Keisha N. Blain, "Black Historians Know There's No Such Thing as Objective History," *New Republic*, 9 September 2022, accessed 27 November 2024, https://newrepublic.com/article/167680/presentism-history-debate-black-scholarship; and Jennifer Schuessler, "As Historians Gather, No Truce in the History Wars," *New York Times*, 8 January 2023, accessed 27 November 2024, https://www.nytimes.com/2023/01/08/arts/american-historical-association-james-sweet.html.

I

McGill's Glasgow

City, University, Atlantic Slavery, and Abolition, 1744–66

STEPHEN MULLEN

McGill University in Montreal, Quebec, Canada, was founded via the bequest of James McGill (1744–1813). Born in Glasgow, Scotland, he matriculated at Old College (now the University of Glasgow) in 1756. Emigrating to North America around 1760, he arrived in Montreal six years later.[1] On the University of Glasgow's 450th anniversary in 1901, McGill University acknowledged this origin story in a congratulatory address (in Latin), which claimed that McGill's memory of his alma mater, "the sweet Argos" (bright one), shaped his commitment to establishing a similar institution:

> Since we are not much different in race, institution, and academic studies, so we are more closely related by a kind of bond of kinship with our grandfather, because he was born in Glasgow, more than a hundred and fifty years ago, that of ours the founder, James McGill, whose memory we will still continue with a grateful heart and with the utmost zeal; who, though unequally divided by the equal space of the Atlantic, even when he was dying remembered the sweet Argos, and wished to establish in his new home an Academy which would bear the appearance of your University in particular. It is fitting, then, to proclaim that we have received from our ancestors that shining ember through him, which may never be darkened or disappear in these lands![2]

Throughout the twentieth century, James McGill not only exemplified the institutional attachments between Old College and McGill University, but also the migratory and intellectual connections between Scotland and Canada. Given McGill's elevated standing in both institutions and nations for most of the last two centuries, this chapter seeks to understand more about the familial, commercial, institutional, and intellectual environments from which he emerged. In particular, this chapter examines Glasgow and its university's connections with Atlantic slavery and abolition between 1744 and 1766, as well as how these associations have been memorialized in Scotland and Canada. James McGill's development is situated in a city that was at once a thriving hub of transatlantic commerce and an incipient hotbed of abolitionism. This chapter argues that McGill was exposed on a regular basis at Old College to the profits of Atlantic slavery, and his conduct afterwards was more in line with enslavers than with abolitionists. However, while many Old College alumni repatriated slavery-derived capital from colonial societies to the institution, McGill's status as a permanent emigrant meant his wealth improved White settler colonizing society instead. In doing so, McGill's strategy of emulating his alma mater institutionalized colonial inequalities that have consequences to the present day.

FAMILY ORIGINS

While James McGill's connections to the Atlantic slavery economy in Montreal have gradually come into focus, relatively little is known about his Glasgow origins, and much of what is known comes from family memoirs.[3] J.I. Cooper's entry in the *Dictionary of Canadian Biography* – based on a broad survey of antiquarian biographies – notes that the McGill family originated in Ayrshire on the west coast of Scotland.[4] By the opening of the eighteenth century, the family resided in Glasgow. The McGills became distinguished citizens and married into prominent trade families. James McGill's grandfather, also James McGill, married Janet Craig in Glasgow on 7 April 1716.[5] His father-in-law, James Craig, was a hammerman, and McGill matriculated with Glasgow's Burgess and Guild Brethren in September 1716.[6] "Men of the hammer" comprised different trades and crafts, such as blacksmiths, goldsmiths, lorimers, ironmongers, saddlers, cutlers, buckle-makers, and armourers. Admission as a burgess (also known as a "freeman") was an exclusive legal privilege that allowed individuals to carry out a trade or mercantile business. There were several requisites for membership; individuals had to enrol and take an oath, demonstrate the capacity to produce good work, and be resident in the burgh. Payment of entry money varied based on the status of entrants; both son and sons-in-law of members took advantage of lower entry fees. Thus, James McGill's marriage to Janet Craig in 1716 provided an easier route to burgess status and this helped establish a family dynasty of hammermen.[7]

James McGill II was born on 7 April 1717. Like his father, he registered as a hammerman burgess and guild brethren on 12 September 1741.[8] He was thus well established by the time he married Margaret Gibson on 16 May 1742.[9] Their first child, Janet, was born in 1743. The second child and first boy, James McGill III, was born on 6 October 1744, and registered on 14 October in the Old Parish Register (Glasgow), the Church of Scotland register of births and baptisms.[10] James McGill III, who would have a further seven brothers and sisters,[11] took a different route from his direct forefathers.

McGILL'S EDUCATION

This latter James McGill, founder of McGill University, was said to have attended the Grammar School of Glasgow, likely around 1751.[12] A predecessor of the Grammar School existed before 1450, and would come to be associated with Glasgow Cathedral and nearby Old College. Surviving records provide insights into the grammar system up to 1794. The school week was seven days, with twelve hours of teaching, from 6 a.m. to 6 p.m., on weekdays. Saturdays were set aside for "disputts." Sunday was reserved for religious teaching. It seems unlikely these young scholars attended religious service in the cathedral on the Sabbath, since "the seats in the Kirk not being able to conteane them." In 1685, the regents of Old College inspected the Grammar School and commented on the curriculum. Scholars who entered the Grammar School were expected to learn Latin for five years. The first year involved learning the "common rudiments" of Latin. The second, third, and fourth years involved examining grammar and syntax, and specialist texts in the final year. "Speciall care" was taken that scholars "speak nothing but Latin" at the Grammar School. If scholars successfully completed all levels, they could matriculate in the humanity class at Old College. By the late eighteenth century, the curriculum had evolved to include the "elements of Geography" alongside Latin.[13]

Few sources survive to comprehensively illustrate the activities of students in the Grammar School of Glasgow, yet much can be deduced about James McGill's formative years. He likely attended from 1751, aged seven, and after a successful five years, left for nearby Old College. Since he matriculated in the humanity class at Old College in 1756, he was proficient in written Latin, and would also have been able to converse daily. Beyond the curriculum, attendance at the Grammar School exposed McGill to Glasgow's colonial elite. Every February, scholars convened in the common hall to publicly gift a "Candlemas Offering" to the rector and masters. An offering of under five shillings received no remarks, but a gift equalling that sum received a rector's response "Vivat" (Let Him Live) and all scholars stamped their feet once. An offering of ten shillings received the response "Florest" (Let Him Flourish) and two stamps of the feet. An offering of fifteen shillings received the response "Floreat bis" (Let Him Twice Flourish) with three stamps of the feet. An offering of twenty shillings received the response "Floreat ter" (Let Him Thrice Flourish) with four stamps of the feet. A gift of one guinea (twenty-one shillings) and above received the response "Gloriat" (Let Him Be Glorious) with six stamps of the feet. The individual providing the highest offering was declared the victor, and he was "hailed by the whole Scholars with thunders of applause." The sons of Mr McDowall, an absentee West India merchant-proprietor in Glasgow, and of Mr Spiers of Elderslie, one of Glasgow's famous Virginia merchants, were the "victors of their day."[14] James McDowall, son of William McDowall, matriculated at Old College in 1752 and was therefore likely to have been a senior Grammar School scholar around the time McGill arrived.[15] By the time McGill entered Old College in the mid-1750s, he was acutely aware of the public approbation, elevated rank and status afforded to sons of enslavers in Scottish society.

One of seven ancient universities in Great Britain, Old College (now the University of Glasgow) was established in 1451 by a papal bull awarded by Pope Nicholas V. From around the 1640s, Glasgow was transformed into a bustling commercial hub with an integrated Atlantic economy, including sugar houses and rope-works. The parliamentary union with England in 1707 provided Scots with legal access to what became the British Empire. While Scottish merchants had relatively limited involvement with "triangular trade" voyages, they monopolized the Atlantic trades in produce grown by enslaved people in the Americas.[16] Glasgow's "tobacco lords" came to dominate the trade in the Chesapeake-grown crop. The period 1740 to 1790, when McGill was in the city, was Glasgow's classical age of tobacco.[17] After the American War of Independence, the city's merchants refocused on the West Indies, and ushered in the city's sugar era, c. 1790–1838.[18] The import of sugar, rum, and especially cotton promoted Scotland's industrial revolution, as large swathes of the population were employed in textile manufacturing, which was dependent on Atlantic markets.

The influx of slavery-derived wealth also transformed many institutions in the West of Scotland. Scots who acquired great slavery fortunes often donated to the University of Glasgow. David Brown, a tobacco merchant in Somerset County, Maryland, bequeathed £100 sterling to Old College on his death in 1697 to establish Brown's Bursary.[19] Many other Scots repatriated colonial wealth after parliamentary union. Alexander Macfarlane, for example, was a large-scale planter in Jamaica, owning 5,605 acres of land (mainly sugar plantations) and 791 enslaved people. On his death in August 1755, he bequeathed astronomical instruments – amongst the best in Europe at that time – to Old College.[20] This donation led Old College to establish, with the aid of the city, the MacFarlane Observatory in 1760.[21] Thus, by the time James McGill matriculated at Old College in 1756, Atlantic slavery and its commerce underpinned the rapid transformation of Scotland and Glasgow. Indeed, throughout his four years at Old College, donations from individuals with colonial fortunes were already reshaping university infrastructure.

James McGill's 1756 matriculation record at Old College reads (in Latin): "JACOBUS M'GILL filius natu maximus Jacobi Mercatoris Glasguensis" (James eldest son of James, merchant in Glasgow).[22] James McGill matriculated aged twelve, and while young by modern standards, this was a typical age then. His brother, Andrew, later to become his partner in Montreal, matriculated later, in 1765.[23] Matriculation fees at Glasgow were much lower than those charged at Oxbridge.[24] Even so, that McGill and his brother matriculated at all confirms the family's middling background. Prior to the mid-nineteenth century, few students matriculated. Most students simply took private classes with tutors who issued them with attendance certificates, although the 1858 Universities (Scotland) Act made matriculation compulsory.[25] Based upon the matriculation record, J.I. Cooper noted that the "McGills had risen from tradesmen to traders" and claimed the family had by then shifted from the trades to more lucrative mercantile pursuits.[26] However, if the family business ever exclusively focused on commerce (and this seems unlikely), this was not a permanent shift. McGill's father remained in the hammermen business in Stockwell Street into the 1780s.[27]

On matriculation, James McGill would have been presented with a library ticket (a privilege that cost ten shillings in the mid-nineteenth century), testifying that he was "Civis Universitatis Glasguensis." After matriculating as a "civis," scholars presented themselves to a professor, paid the fees, and exchanged the library ticket for a class ticket. Teaching would have taken place in each professor's study. Students who entered Old College generally took junior humanity and middle Greek (the *Provectiores*).[28] James McGill matriculated under the supervision of Reverend George Muirhead, professor of Oriental languages at Old College from 1753. He was appointed chair of humanity (Latin) in December 1754, just before McGill's arrival, and was a noted member of the Glasgow Literary Society.[29] As a matriculated student of humanity, James McGill wore a scarlet gown (toga). Younger students wore cloth caps and senior scholars silk hats. One visitor to Glasgow noted many unkempt students: "The habit of the students gave me surprise. They were scarlet gowns, reaching only to their knees. Most I saw were very dirty, some very ragged and all of very coarse cloth."[30]

Old College was once a residential home for students, but this ended when the use of the common table was abandoned in 1694. Residency was no longer compulsory by 1704, when just forty of the university's two hundred to three hundred regents and students continued to reside in the college.[31] Since James McGill's family lived less than one mile away, in Stockwell Street, it seems unlikely he would have taken up lodgings within Old College. However, his life changed in other ways, since he would have been subject to strict regulations – as laid out in the *Leges* – governing behaviour in the city and university. Students were banned from playing dice, billiards, or cards, and could not visit the theatre before April, and after then only with permission of their professor. Students were also prohibited from smoking and entering tobacco stores or local taverns, and they could not attend drinking parties. Students were required to maintain certain behavioural standards: act gravely, quietly, and courteously (*pie, modeste, atque comiter*). The punishment for misconduct was severe: for those under eighteen, expulsion and floggings. For those over eighteen, fines and even imprisonment.[32]

Between 1740 and 1839, Old College's matriculated students were increasingly drawn from industrial and commercial backgrounds, while growing numbers of alumni entered teaching, law, and medicine.[33] The irony is that McGill's pathway operated in reverse; rather than training him for professional occupations, his father worked in local industry and the educated McGill emigrated and took up occupations centred around Atlantic commerce. Perhaps the status of scholarly peers appealed. Through most of the eighteenth century, Old College was an imperial space where sons of colonial merchants, planters, and enslavers freely mixed with the sons of local tradesmen and gentry alike.

Despite the perceived status as an institution unfit to educate budding merchants (see below), it remained a prestigious seat of learning, which explains why many of their sons still attended. Between 1736 and 1838, around 130 sons of merchants and planters resident in the West Indies attended Old College (about 1 per cent of all matriculated students).[34] Some of McGill's direct contemporaries hailed from the Caribbean. Thomas White, eldest son of Hugo White, a merchant in Jamaica, matriculated in 1755.[35] McGill also attended at the same time as the sons of Glasgow's most famous colonial merchants, absentee planters and enslavers. James Dunlop, son of "tobacco lord" Colin Dunlop, matriculated in 1753.[36] Henry Horsburgh, son of Alexander Horsburgh, the surgeon and the supercargo of the *Hannover*, one of Glasgow's very few triangular trade voyages, matriculated in 1754.[37] Alexander and James Milliken, sons of Renfrewshire planter James Milliken, who owned estates and enslaved people in St Kitts, also matriculated in 1754.[38] These contemporaries would have been aware of each other and while McGill's conversations are impossible to trace, sons of the West India interest in Glasgow were notorious pro-slavery advocates who sometimes resorted to violence to advance their cause.[39]

EXPOSURE TO SLAVERY AND ABOLITIONIST IDEALS AT OLD COLLEGE

The proximity of Old College to the commercial hub of Glasgow further exposed the young James McGill to the vicarious influence of enslavers and their privileged offspring. The university was located close to the Town Hall at Glasgow cross (later the site of the Tontine Coffee House). In the 1750s, scarlet-cloaked "tobacco lords" with powdered wigs and gold-tipped canes paraded on the city's only paved promenade, as if they "alone of all had the right to pace the *Plainstanes*."[40] Many of these merchants also owned Black children, who were often put to work as servants in great houses. While slavery was not legally codified in Scotland as it was in the American colonies and the West Indies, many enslaved people were forced to travel to Scotland with enslavers who had acquired them under colonial slave codes.[41] Black people had an undecided legal status in Scotland up to 1778, when the Joseph Knight case decreed that slavery was inconsistent with Scots law. Before this famous decision in the Court of Session, newspapers were filled with examples of Black runaways escaping across Scotland. During McGill's formative years in Glasgow (1744–1760), advertisements were placed in Scottish newspapers every two years, on average, with enslavers hoping to reclaim their "property." In 1758, when McGill was at Old College, an advertisement appeared in a Glasgow newspaper with an owner desperate to reclaim a Black boy the same age as him:

> Run away,
>
> About 15 or 16 days ago, from Mrs. Campbell of Askomils, in Inveraray. A BLACK BOY, about 14 years of age; he was dressed in a dark brown coat, with yellow lining and yellow metal buttons, and breeches of the same colour, a drugget vest, strip'd with blue, red and white, and short black curly hair.
>
> Whoever will apprehend him, and send information to Mess. Campbell & Connel, merchants in Glasgow, shall have a sufficient reward, and all charges paid.[42]

Thus, while slavery was never codified in Scotland, it was an everyday feature of Scottish society. For enslavers such as Mrs Campbell of Askomill in Inverary, it was routine legal practice to employ merchants in Glasgow to publicly recapture their "lost property." How such proximity affected young McGill's *mentalité* is difficult – if not impossible – to know. Nonetheless, exposure to those enmeshed in Atlantic slavery, the profits and status it provided, as well as the public act of reclaiming Black people as "property" would have been regular features of the broader environment known by many Old College students, McGill among them.

At the same time as Atlantic commerce and slavery shaped the development of the West of Scotland, Old College philosophers wrote tracts that critiqued the system of chattel slavery and the British

Empire more broadly. In 1808, celebrated abolitionist Thomas Clarkson noted: "It is a great honour in the University of Glasgow, that it should have produced, before any public agitation of the question, three professors, all of whom bore their public testimony against this cruel trade [in enslaved people]."[43] These three professors were Francis Hutcheson, Adam Smith, and John Millar. A major figure in the Scottish Enlightenment, Francis Hutcheson (1694–1746) was professor of moral philosophy at Old College between 1730 and his death. His lectures in the 1730s provided the foundation for *A System of Moral Philosophy in Three Books* (1755), which provided a moral critique of the practice of slavery.[44] This was published posthumously in 1755, the year before McGill matriculated at Old College.

According to one of Hutcheson's biographers, *A System of Moral Philosophy* was "widely used in Scottish and American universities in the eighteenth century."[45] Hutcheson's volumes were certainly available to students at Old College and were borrowed from the library seventeen times between 1756 and 1760. McGill's contemporaries, such as James Morehead, borrowed it in 1757. The volumes became increasingly popular the next year.[46] However, James McGill did not borrow *A System of Moral Philosophy*, nor any other book from the eighteenth-century Old College library, though his brother Andrew was apparently more studious after his arrival in 1765.[47] Yet, the Hutchesonian critiques of slavery were very influential. Adam Smith attended Old College in the late 1730s and attended Hutcheson's classes. During McGill's time at Old College, Adam Smith was professor of logic, then professor of moral philosophy at Old College (from 1751 to 1764). Smith later published *An Inquiry into the Nature and Causes of the Wealth of Nations* (1776) and made the powerful argument that the British Empire was an economic drain and that chattel slavery, as an economic system, was inefficient. Smith also taught John Millar at Old College and he continued the anti-slavery tradition.[48] *A System of Moral Philosophy* later became globally influential. However, the anti-slavery teaching environment and publications apparently had little impact on McGill and how he conducted himself after he departed Glasgow.

It has long been argued that James McGill's family suffered a financial event that compelled him to leave Old College and emigrate to North America in 1760. In April 1956, Dr F. Cyril James, principal and vice-chancellor of McGill University, made this claim in a speech at the opening of McGill Primary School in Pollok, Glasgow:

"[McGill was] able to enter the great University of Glasgow, but his family was unable to keep him there long enough to win a degree. He and his brother, like many other Scottish lads in that period, decided to seek the opportunities of a new life on the great continent."[49] However, as noted above, few students matriculated at Old College prior to the mid-nineteenth century, and even fewer graduated. Graduation was not the formal rite of passage it is today or in Cyril James's time, and McGill's non-graduation was typical rather than exceptional. The romanticized narrative according to which James McGill was compelled to migrate by his family's economic conditions in Scotland was a more palatable origin story than the reality, which is that he chose to pursue exploitative opportunities in North America. With the appropriate background, education, and financial support, James McGill became the quintessential Scottish settler-colonizer.

James McGill left Old College around 1760 and is next recorded in Montreal in 1766. Stanley Brice Frost referred to a lacuna in evidence for these six years and conjectured that McGill's Old College education allowed him to take up mercantile positions in the Carolinas.[50] However, by the mid-eighteenth century, Old College's arts curriculum was publicly described as unsuitable to educate the youth of a prominent commercial city. In 1761, Reverend William Thom, minister of Govan, noted that it had been founded to instruct theologians, and by then the arts curriculum was "of little use to the lawyer or physician, and still less to the merchant or gentleman."[51] It seems almost certain that before leaving for North America, McGill undertook commercial training. A newspaper advertisement in Glasgow in early 1762 provides insights into the new forms of practical learning provided in a private academy: "by which means the youth committed to their care will be instructed in every branch of literature, proper for the merchant, the mechanic, the marine and the farmer." Classes included "writing and flourishing; arithmetic and book keeping ... practical geometry, plain and spherical trigonometry with their application in land surveying, longimetry, altimetry, navigation, geography, astronomy, fortification, gunnery and dialling; a separate class in geography; algebra; Euclid's Elements either in Latin or in English; the French language, and Italian and Spanish."[52] Only this type of practical learning in Glasgow – which provided the best commercial training in Scotland at the time – would have fully prepared James McGill for life as a colonial merchant in the Americas.

MCGILL AND THE ATLANTIC SLAVERY ECONOMY

Scottish emigration to British North America was both sustained and large-scale. In the eighteenth century, pioneering Scottish settlers laid the foundations for large-scale migration, and more Scots travelled to Canada than any other colony or nation before 1847.[53] Overall, it has been estimated that 180,000 Scots emigrated to Canada before 1870, with those from the Scottish Highlands more numerous than Lowlanders.[54]

James McGill was one such migrant. As noted, Frost suggested McGill initially took up mercantile positions in the Carolinas in the early 1760s before his eventual arrival in Quebec, confirmed as a British possession in the Treaty of Paris in 1763. McGill is recorded as passing through Montreal to Michilimackinac in 1766. He operated as a fur trader, first working for a fellow Scot, William Grant, and then setting out on his own account from 1767. With the onset of hostilities brought about by the American War of Independence (1775–83), McGill settled in Montreal as a merchant, diversifying into the Atlantic trades and establishing new partnerships.[55] A commercial journal for the firm Todd, McGill and Company reveals that from 1798 to 1800, the firm shipped goods such as hides and grain to the West Indies in return for rum, sugar, and tobacco.[56]

In his 1995 biography of McGill, Frost acknowledged that McGill must have been "very familiar" with chattel slavery; in 1788, James McGill purchased an enslaved woman, Sarah. The system of slavery in Canada was not unlike that in Scotland before 1778, and since it was not illegal, the practice continued. However, the proximity of British North America to slave societies meant the practice was more extensive and widespread compared with Scotland.[57] Charmaine Nelson's recent work has revealed new details of McGill's mercantile affairs and ownership of people of Indigenous (*panis*) and African descent. Ownership of more than two enslaved people was considered exceptional in Montreal. McGill owned at least five people, mainly for household duties. This included an unknown *panis* who was buried at the age of ten in 1778. Nelson suggests that since the two Indigenous people enslaved by McGill were both baptized in the year of death, McGill might have advocated baptism only once they became sick. These deaths may have also shaped his decision to purchase people of African descent.[58] In this way, James McGill came to emulate the great colonial merchants and planters of Glasgow, owning enslaved people for his household and acquiring a large fortune derived, in part, from slavery and its commerce.

James McGill died in 1813 and was by then, according to Frost, "reputed to be the richest man in Canada." On his death, he was worth approximately £160,000. Had he returned, this would have ranked him amongst Great Britain's wealthiest men – a fortune of £100,000 was considered nationally significant.[59] For comparison, £160,000 sterling in 1813 is equivalent to £134 million in 2021 (relative to the worth of average UK earnings).[60] Was chattel slavery and its commerce a minor or major contributing factor to McGill's wealth accumulation? According to Frost, McGill's primary interests were in the fur trade and eventually the colonial trades. McGill lessened his involvement with the fur trade from 1805, and he "continued in trade, less actively in his senior years, until his death" in the firm that by then specialized in Atlantic commerce. McGill also diversified into multiple concerns; Todd, McGill and Co. exported timber to London in 1796, and he was invested in "imports and exports, land dealings, [and] the embryo functions of banking."[61] Since McGill's earlier commercial records (before the 1790s) do not seem to have survived, it is impossible to ascertain the significance of slavery to his various concerns, but the Atlantic mercantile business looks to have been fundamental after 1798 at least. It is fair to describe McGill as part of Montreal's wealthy mercantile elite with substantial property holdings. Atlantic slavery and its commerce were not the exclusive source in the accumulation of his fortune, and by extension the founding of what became McGill, but he was thoroughly enmeshed at all levels in the transatlantic slavery economy as a West India merchant and enslaver.

In life, James McGill was very generous to family in both Montreal and Glasgow, including a loan of £1,500 to his father in 1773–74. In death, he similarly attended to the needs of family and wider settler society. He donated £200 each to public institutions in Glasgow: the Royal Infirmary and Glasgow Asylum. Frost's assessment of McGill's inheritance transmission strategies reveals that most of his wealth remained in Canada: his two main heirs each received £60,000. In addition to £10,000 in monies, James McGill donated his forty-six-acre Burnside estate to establish the Royal Institution for the Advancement of Learning, with one of its colleges to be named "McGill College." Frost estimated the McGill College bequest was worth £20,000.[62] This was a huge bequest, equivalent to £16.8 million in 2021 (relative to the worth of average UK earnings).[63] McGill's donation was larger than any single slavery-derived donation to the University of Glasgow in the colonial era (with the exception of the Bellahouston bequest).[64] While James McGill attended Old College and must have been aware of the bequests that were derived, at least in part, from slavery, he chose to emulate rather than enrich his alma mater with the colonial profits he had acquired. While many Scots were transients in slavery economies, especially sojourners to the British West Indies, McGill became a permanent emigrant, and used his wealth to improve the settler-colonial society in which he was thoroughly established.

RECKONING WITH MCGILL'S LEGACY

Until fairly recently, James McGill has been celebrated in official and institutional records in Scotland and Canada. This trend is exemplified in Scotland's register of births and baptisms, the Old Parish Register, which permanently celebrates James McGill's role as a philanthropist. As noted above, his birth was recorded on 14 October 1744 in the Old Parish Register (Glasgow), the Church of Scotland register. Handwritten marginalia – probably from the nineteenth century – next to McGill's entry simply notes "McGill University," thus venerating one of Scotland's most famous emigrants in the national register of baptisms.[65] The notation is illustrative of the process by which McGill's colonial activities, including ownership of enslaved people, have been elided while McGill the man has been positively celebrated as the benefactor of a famous university.

In the twentieth century, James McGill personified the migratory and intellectual connections between Scotland and Canada. When Cyril James addressed McGill Primary School in Glasgow in April 1956, he represented McGill as the quintessential learned adventurer: "James McGill carried with him from Glasgow to the new world a vivid memory of the Scottish tradition of education and a keen sense of the part that educated men and women can play in the growth of Canada and the development of the modern world."[66] The positive memorialization of the McGill connection remains in modern Glasgow. A plaque in Stockwell Street commemorates the place of James McGill's birth in 1744.[67]

McGill's connections to slavery are also largely absent or minimized in biographical treatments of his life.[68] While Frost did acknowledge McGill's ownership of enslaved people in *James McGill of*

Montreal (1995), he ended the book with an almost apologetic tone: "James McGill was a man of the eighteenth century, not of the twentieth."[69] Yet, McGill's legacy has come under scrutiny by academics, institutions, and the wider public in recent years. Charmaine Nelson's 2016 book provided new insights into the people of Indigenous (*panis*) and African descent owned by McGill, thus shifting perspectives from the enslaver to the enslaved.[70] In advance of the bicentenary of McGill University, Nelson's report *Slavery and McGill University: Bicentenary Recommendations* (2020) unravelled James McGill's connections to the Atlantic slavery economy after he emigrated to Montreal. While Nelson noted an absence of "leadership and support" for McGill University's investigation of slavery within the institution, students helped to research and write the report.[71] By July 2021, in the aftermath of the global Black Lives Matter movement, a statue of James McGill on McGill campus was removed after repeated vandalism and a 5,000-strong petition calling for it to go.[72]

While James McGill's fall from grace in Montreal has been dramatic, there have been no similar calls for any removals in Glasgow. Indeed, until recently, he remained one of Old College's most celebrated alumni. William Innes Addison, registrar of the University of Glasgow from 1911, painstakingly compiled Old College matriculant records, which were published as *The Matriculation Albums of the University of Glasgow from 1728 to 1858* (Glasgow, 1913). Addison undertook additional research and the seminal text includes biographical details that remain the starting point for research on Old College alumni. James McGill's entry in 1756 is as follows:

> Born at Glasgow, 6th October 1744. Went to Canada before the American Revolution. Engaged sometime in the north-west fur trade, thereafter Merchant in Montreal in partnership with his brother Andrew. For many years a Member of the Lower Canadian Parliament for West Montreal, and afterwards a Member of the Legislative and Executive Councils. Lieutenant-Colonel, subsequently Colonel, of the Montreal City Militia, and Brigadier-General, 1812. Principal Founder of M'Gill University. Died at Montreal, 19th December 1813.[73]

While accurate, Addison's imperially myopic approach set the institutional tone on James McGill (and other alumni). A plaque on the wall of the undercroft at the University of Glasgow's Gilmorehill campus notes, "This memorial stone is placed here by McGill University in honour of James McGill (1744–1813) student in arts of the University of Glasgow trader soldier and statesman in Canada and founder of McGill University Montreal."[74] Thus, he remains celebrated in the University of Glasgow's most picturesque civic space. However, *The University of Glasgow Story* – an online dictionary of the university's most famous alumni – has recently been updated to reflect McGill's connections to the Atlantic slavery economy: "As a Montréal-based merchant, he traded in Caribbean tropical, slave produced, plantation goods. McGill also became a slave owner in Montréal, including purchasing an enslaved woman named Sally in 1788, and helped other wealthy individuals procure slaves."[75] This digital acknowledgment is consistent with the University of Glasgow's approach to recognizing the institution and its alumni's historic connections with slavery. Despite the University of Glasgow's well-publicized reparative justice strategy – launched in response to the report that examined its institutional connections with Atlantic slavery in 2018 – the plaque remains in place in the Gilmorehill campus.[76] These contrasting institutional approaches highlight a transatlantic paradox. McGill University has been hesitant in its approach to institutional introspection regarding its historic connections with slavery, yet removed the McGill statue from campus. The University of Glasgow has attempted to atone for its historic connections with Atlantic slavery through a reparative justice strategy, yet simultaneously celebrates an alumnus who went on to become an enslaver in Montreal, Canada.

CONCLUSION

In June 2012, McGill University celebrated its 190th anniversary, which provided the platform for another transatlantic partnership between institutions. At a ceremony in May 2012, Professor Anton Muscatelli, principal and vice-chancellor of the University of Glasgow, was awarded an honorary doctorate. Professor Heather Munroe-Blum, McGill's principal and vice-chancellor, was effusive about the connections: "James McGill was motivated to found this university by a sense of curiosity and a spirit of social responsibility instilled in him as a young man in Scotland."[77]

This chapter examines McGill's background and underlines how his associations with Atlantic slavery in Glasgow shaped this "spirit

Figure 1.1 James McGill plaque, Gilmorehill campus, University of Glasgow

of social responsibility." It illuminates the familial, commercial, institutional, and intellectual environments from which James McGill emerged, and situates him in the context of two separate processes. First, the city of Glasgow's rise was predicated upon the perpetuation of Atlantic slavery and the profits it generated through commerce, trade, and manufacturing. McGill's attendance at the Glasgow Grammar School and Old College, as well as the close proximity to colonial merchants, would likely have exposed him to pro-slavery views and influences. Second, while the development of Old College was underpinned by the profits of slavery, James McGill was educated amidst the Glasgow Enlightenment. Francis Hutcheson died before McGill's attendance, but his work was published the year before McGill matriculated. He would also have been exposed to Hutcheson's philosophical ideas and moral critiques that arguably underpinned the abolition movement in 1787. But McGill was not persuaded by the Hutchesonian moral critiques of slavery. Instead, he emigrated and became a colonial merchant and enslaver of some repute. The University of Glasgow produced very few abolitionists, but it received many dozens of matriculants from the British West Indies who then went on to become colonial merchants and planters across the British Atlantic world.

McGill's trajectory operated in reverse, transitioning from industry in Glasgow to colonial pursuits across the British Empire. The University of Glasgow is an exemplar of how the profits from slavery improved British institutions in the mid-eighteenth century, and James McGill replicated this process, in colonial form. His social responsibility ultimately lay with White settler colonizing society. He helped establish an institution in the image of his alma mater: both institutions served the needs of White imperialists, disbursing wealth derived from Black slavery to White communities, thus perpetuating imperial inequalities established in the colonial era into the twenty-first century.

NOTES

1 Stanley Brice Frost, *James McGill of Montreal* (Montreal and Kingston: McGill-Queen's University Press, 1995), 11.

2 University of Glasgow Archives (herafter UofGA) GB 248 DC 184/123, File, Congratulatory Address from the McGill University, Montreal, April 1901.

3 For example, Frost's biography *James McGill of Montreal* devotes less than ten pages to Glasgow origins, largely compiled from the work of family historian John Michael McGill.

4 J.I. Cooper, "MCGILL, JAMES," in *Dictionary of Canadian Biography*, vol. 5 (University of Toronto/Université Laval, 2003–), accessed 7 April 2023, http://www.biographi.ca/en/bio/mcgill_james_5E.html.

5 National Records of Scotland (hereafter NRS), Old Parish Registers Marriages 644/ 1 (Glasgow), 181. Note that the surname was then listed as "McGil."

6 J. Anderson, ed., *The Burgesses and Guild Brethren of Glasgow, 1573–1750* (Edinburgh: J. Skinner, 1925), 321.

7 Harry Lumsden and P. Henderson Aitken, *The Hammermen of Glasgow: A Study Typical of Scottish Life and Organisation* (Paisley, 1912), xviii, 2, 9.

8 Anderson, ed., *Burgesses and Guild Brethren*, 441.
9 NRS, Old Parish Registers Marriages 644/ 1 (Glasgow), 78. Note that the surname was by then listed as the more familiar "McGill."
10 NRS, Old Parish Registers Births 644/1, Glasgow, James McGill, 1744.
11 Frost, *McGill of Montreal*, 7.
12 Frost, *McGill of Montreal*, 8.
13 James Cleland, ed., *Historical Account of the Grammar School of Glasgow* (Glasgow: Khull and Blackie, 1825), 10–14, 17.
14 Cleland, ed., *Historical Account of the Grammar School*, 17.
15 W. Innes Addison, *The Matriculation Albums of the University of Glasgow, From 1728 to 1858* (Glasgow: J. Maclehose and Sons, 1913), 47.
16 Mark Duffill, "The Africa Trade from the Ports of Scotland, 1706–66," *Slavery & Abolition* 25, no. 3 (December 2004): 102–22.
17 T.M. Devine, "The Golden Age of Tobacco," in *Glasgow, vol. 1, Beginnings to 1830*, eds T.M. Devine and G. Jackson (Manchester: Manchester University Press, 1995), 139–84.
18 Stephen Mullen, *The Glasgow Sugar Aristocracy: Scotland and Caribbean Slavery, 1775–1838* (London: University of London Press, 2022).
19 *Deeds Instituting Bursaries, Scholarships, and Other Foundations, in the College and University of Glasgow* (Glasgow: Maitland Club, 1850), 130–1; Clayton Torrence, *Old Somerset on the Eastern Shore of Maryland* (Baltimore: Regional Publishing Company, 1966), 363–5.
20 "Alexander Macfarlane," *Legacies of British Slavery database*, accessed 25 July 2023, http://wwwdepts-live.ucl.ac.uk/lbs/person/view/2146644157.
21 J.D. Mackie, *The University of Glasgow* (Glasgow: Jackson, Son and Co., 1954), 222.
22 Addison, *Matriculation Albums*, 55.
23 Addison, *Matriculation Albums*, 77.
24 Paul L. Robertson, "The Finances of the University of Glasgow before 1914," *History of Education Quarterly* 16, no. 4 (Winter 1976): 458, 475.
25 David Murray, *Memories of the Old College of Glasgow: Some Chapters in the History of the University* (Glasgow: Jackson, Wylie and Co., 1927), 277.
26 Cooper, "MCGILL, JAMES." Stanley Brice Frost concurs with this conclusion. See Frost, *McGill of Montreal*, 9.
27 In September 1773, for example, Robert Scott was a serving apprentice hammerman with James McGill in Glasgow. See Anderson, ed., *Burgesses and Guild Brethren*, 82. In 1783–84, "James McGill, hammerman" was

still a listed business in Stockwell Street. See *John Tait's Directory for the City of Glasgow*, 1783–84 (1784), 50.

28 Murray, *Memories of the Old College*, 275–9.

29 Richard B. Sher, "Muirhead, George (bap. 1715, d. 1773), Church of Scotland Minister and Classical Scholar," *Oxford Dictionary of National Biography* (hereafter ODNB), 23 September 2004; accessed 25 July 2023, https://www.oxforddnb.com/display/10.1093/ref:odnb/9780198614128.001.0001/odnb-9780198614128-e-19504?rskey=qItuFF&result=1363.

30 Murray, *Memories of the Old College*, 473, 476.

31 Murray, *Memories of the Old College*, 97.

32 Murray, *Memories of the Old College*, 479–84.

33 W.M. Mathew, "The Origins and Occupations of Glasgow Students, 1740–1839," *Past & Present* 33 (April 1966): 75, 78, 85; Paul L. Robertson, "The Development of an Urban University: Glasgow, 1860–1914," *History of Education Quarterly* 30, no. 1 (Spring 1990): 47–78.

34 Stephen Mullen, "British Universities and Transatlantic Slavery: the University of Glasgow Case," *History Workshop Journal* 91, no. 1 (Spring 2021): 214.

35 Addison, *Matriculation Albums*, 53.

36 Addison, *Matriculation Albums*, 49.

37 Addison, *Matriculation Albums*, 51.

38 Addison, *Matriculation Albums*, 51.

39 Stephen Mullen, "Proslavery Collaborations Between British Outport and Metropole: The Rise of the Glasgow–West India Interest, 1775–1838," *Journal of Imperial and Commonwealth History* 51, no. 4 (2023): 25.

40 John Strang, *Glasgow and Its Clubs: Or Glimpses of the Condition, Manners, Characters, and Oddities of the City, During the Past and Present Centuries* (London and Glasgow: R. Griffin and Co., 1857), 25.

41 S. Mullen, C. Mundell, and S. Newman, "Black Runaways in Eighteenth-Century Britain," in *Britain's Black Past*, ed. G. Gerzina (Liverpool: Liverpool University Press, 2020), 81–99.

42 *Glasgow Courant*, 4 September 1758, 4. See *Runaway Slaves in Britain: bondage, freedom and race in the eighteenth century*, accessed 30 November 2024, https://www.runaways.gla.ac.uk/database/display/?rid=49.

43 Thomas Clarkson, *History of the Rise, Progress, and Accomplishment of the Abolition of the African Slave Trade by the British Parliament* (London: John W. Parker, 1839), 76.

44 Alison Webster, "The Contribution of the Scottish Enlightenment to the Abandonment of the Institution of Slavery," *European Legacy* 8, no. 4 (2003): 481.

45 James Moore, "Hutcheson, Francis (1694–1746), Moral Philosopher," ODNB, 23 September 2004, accessed 12 July 2023, https://www.oxforddnb.com/display/10.1093/ref:odnb/9780198614128.001.0001/odnb-9780198614128-e-14273.

46 *Eighteenth Century Borrowing From the University of Glasgow*, accessed 12 May 2023, https://18c-borrowing.glasgow.ac.uk/results/?type=booktitle&letter=S&btid=8.

47 *Eighteenth Century Borrowing From the University of Glasgow*, Student: McGill, accessed 12 May 2023, https://18c-borrowing.glasgow.ac.uk/results/?type=search&searchBookTitle=&searchAuthor=&searchStudent=McGill&searchProfessor=&searchDateFrom=&searchDateTo=.

48 Iain Whyte, *Scotland and the Abolition of Black Slavery, 1756–1838* (Edinburgh: Edinburgh University Press, 2006), 82, 91; Fred Ablondi, "Millar on Slavery," *Journal of Scottish Philosophy* 7, no. 2 (Autumn 2009): 163–75.

49 UofGA, GB 248 DC 008/629, Correspondence, 1953–1961, F. Cyril James, "The Tradition of McGill," 24 April 1956.

50 Frost, *McGill of Montreal*, 9–11.

51 William Thom, *The Works of the Rev. William Thom, Late Minister of Govan, Consisting of Sermons, Tracts, Letters* (Glasgow: James Dymock, 1799), 263–302; Donald J. Withrington "Education and Society in the Eighteenth Century," in *Scotland in the Age of Improvement*, ed. N.T. Phillipson (Edinburgh: Edinburgh University Press, 1996), 181.

52 *Glasgow Journal* (no. 1073, 18–25 February 1762) quoted in Withrington, "Education and Society," 197–8.

53 Marjory Harper, "Exiles or Entrepreneurs? Snapshots of the Scots in Canada," in *A Kingdom of the Mind: How the Scots Helped Make Canada*, eds Peter E. Rider and Heather McNab (Montreal and Kingston: McGill-Queen's University Press, 2006), 22–3.

54 Stephen J. Hornsby, "Patterns of Scottish emigration to Canada, 1750–1870," *Journal of Historical Geography* 18, no. 4 (October 1992): 397–416.

55 Frost, *McGill of Montreal*, 9–12, 15–28.

56 Frost, *McGill of Montreal*, 24, 64–6.

57 Frost, *McGill of Montreal*, 63–4.

58 Charmaine Nelson, *Slavery, Geography and Empire in Nineteenth-Century Marine Landscapes of Montreal and Jamaica* (Oxford and New York: Routledge, 2016), 85–92.

59 Stanley Brice Frost, "McGill, James (1744–1813), Fur Trader and Politician in Canada," *ODNB*, 23 September 2004, accessed 26 July 2023, https://www.oxforddnb.com/display/10.1093/ref:odnb/9780198614128.001.0001/odnb-9780198614128-e-49239; W.D. Rubinstein, *Who Were the Rich? A Biographical Directory of British Wealth-Holders, Vol. I: 1809–1839* (London: The Social Affairs Unit, 2009), 13, 17.

60 Lawrence H. Officer and Samuel H. Williamson, "Five Ways to Compute the Relative Value of a UK Pound Amount, 1270 to Present," *MeasuringWorth*, 2023, accessed 23 July 2023, https://www.measuringworth.com/calculators/ukcompare/result.php?year_source=1813&amount=160000&year_result=2023.

61 Frost, "McGill, James"; Frost, *McGill of Montreal*, 67–8.

62 Frost, *McGill of Montreal*, 24, 151; *Extract from the Will of the Late Hon. James McGill, with the Charter of the University of McGill College* (Montreal: Lovell and Gibson, 1843); Frost, "McGill, James."

63 Officer and Williamson, "Five Ways to Compute the Relative Value of a UK Pound Amount."

64 Mullen and Newman, *Slavery, Abolition and the University of Glasgow*, accessed 20 November 2020, https://www.gla.ac.uk/media/media_607547_en.pdf.

65 NRS, Old Parish Registers Births 644/ 1 Glasgow, James McGill, 1744.

66 UofGA, GB 248 DC 008/629, Correspondence, 1953–1961, F. Cyril James, "The Tradition of McGill," 24 April 1956.

67 "James McGill House Plaque Stockwell Street Glasgow," Wikipedia, accessed 13 May 2023, https://en.wikipedia.org/wiki/File:James_McGill_House_Plaque_Stockwell_Street_Glasgow.jpg.

68 For example, Cooper, "MCGILL, JAMES"; Frost, "McGill, James."

69 Frost, *McGill of Montreal*, 64.

70 Nelson, *Slavery, Geography and Empire*, 85–92.

71 Charmaine A. Nelson and Student Authors, *Slavery and McGill University: Bicentenary Recommendations* (2020), 5, accessed 13 April 2023, https://www.blackcanadianstudies.com/Recommendations_and_Report.pdf.

72 "Statue of University Namesake and Slave-Owner James McGill Removed After Most-Recent Bout of Vandalism," CTV News, Montreal, accessed 7 May 2023, https://montreal.ctvnews.ca/

statue-of-university-namesake-and-slave-owner-james-mcgill-removed-after-most-recent-bout-of-vandalism-1.5504661.

73 Addison, *Matriculation Albums*, 55.

74 "James McGill Plaque – University of Glasgow Undercroft," Wikipedia, accessed 7 May 2023, https://commons.wikimedia.org/wiki/File:James_McGill_Plaque_-_University_of_Glasgow_Undercroft.jpg.

75 "James McGill," *University of Glasgow International Story*, accessed 13 June 2023, https://internationalstory.gla.ac.uk/person/?id=WH25639.

76 Mullen and Newman, *Slavery, Abolition and the University of Glasgow*.

77 "McGill University Celebrates Long-Standing Ties with Glasgow," June 2012, accessed 24 May 2023, https://www.gla.ac.uk/myglasgow/news/archives/2012/june/headline_234408_en.html.

2

A North Atlantic "Provincial"

James McGill, Empire, "Property," and "Improvement"

ANDREW MACKILLOP

Reconsidering James McGill, his life, and his career carries with it a number of methodological and ethical issues. An excessive focus on the man himself and his commercial and civic world in later eighteenth- and early nineteenth-century Montreal risks centring a known enslaver while erasing or marginalizing the historical implications arising from a better awareness of those he exploited. This is one of the core messages to emerge from the 2020 research by Professor Charmaine A. Nelson, which critically reassessed McGill as an enslaver.[1]

The new perspectives opened up by such scholarship extend well beyond questions of how McGill University reassesses its founding figure and the nature of the wealth that enabled the institution's creation. By building on Professor Nelson's earlier scholarship on the legacies of enslavement in colonial Canada, it critiques narratives that erase the racial hierarchies and prejudices inherent in the development of British North America's settler-provinces up to the mid-nineteenth century.[2] While challenging Canadian national narratives of this period, Nelson's bicentennial project also raises key questions (and intellectually productive possibilities) for historians of Scotland and Scots during the pre-1830s era of British Atlantic colonialism and slavery. If Canadian historiography has been prone to glossing over the nation's relationship to racialized slavery, not least in explicit or implicit comparison to its southern neighbour, there is a good case to be made that the Scottish academy shared some intriguing similarities until the appearance of new research from the mid-2000s to 2015.[3] The tendency towards a "hierarchization of whiteness" that distanced both societies from their multi-faceted involvement in transatlantic slavery formed a marked characteristic of Canadian, Scottish, and Scottish-Canadian historical studies throughout most of the twentieth century.[4] These are still in the process of critical deconstruction in the academic and civic society realms.

What follows here is an effort to reframe James McGill in the context of these parallel and ongoing reappraisals in Canadian and Scottish national histories. The emphasis shifts from centring only select and seemingly "progressive" aspects of McGill's life to exploring the wider political, economic, civic, and cultural environments that shaped what might be described as his "North Atlantic provincial" worldview. This chapter does so by highlighting a number of key themes that shaped his life as a transatlantic Scottish migrant, anglophone businessman, militia officer, politician, and enslaver. These connective themes are his perception of properly constituted government; the importance of an active, loyal subject undertaking military service; his understanding of the centrality of "improvement" in provincial societies; and, finally, the enabling impact of education.

While obviously very different societies, Quebec and Scotland engaged with the institutions, practices, and ideologies of colonialism as self-consciously provincial parts of a wider British world. It is well known that both Glasgow and Montreal were profoundly shaped by their involvement in all aspects of Britain's transatlantic empire. Each city was located in a wider riverine complex that enabled access to a web of oceanic destinations. While Glasgow's axis ran on an east-west alignment, Montreal's links encompassed the continental interior through the fur trade as well as crucially important north-to-south connections with the slave colonies of the British Caribbean. The two port cities that shaped McGill and his worldview were important Atlantic World centres of trade enabled by racialized slavery. Beyond his own personal involvement in the enslavement of five individuals, commodities such as sugar, tobacco, and rum were absolutely central to McGill's business interests.[5] Both Scotland and Quebec were distinctively structured societies and rapidly developing economies that were especially reliant on export-orientated staples and associated migratory and labour needs. This drove an abiding provincial interest in the nature of stadial development and the sustainability of progress.[6] The dynamics of provincialism in the northern rim of Britain's transatlantic world provides one means of contextualizing McGill's involvement in the evolution of Quebec as a settler society while also enabling a holistic assessment that intertwines the Canadian and Scottish elements of his life and career.

~~~

It is uncontroversial to note that older biographical approaches valorize McGill, emphasizing his commercial acumen, sociability, and civic philanthropy.[7] This has remained a feature of the literature until relatively recently.[8] His Scottishness has played an important, even foundational part in the creation of McGill's historic persona and public memory of him. Hagiographical works did much to generate tropes of diasporic Scottishness, a notable example of which is William Jordan Rattray's multi-volume *The Scot in British North America*, published in the early to mid-1880s.[9] The privileging of McGill's origins served parallel but ultimately complementary agendas. In Montreal, Scottishness could act as a variant of anglophone culture and influence that at once buttressed but also multi-centred the hegemony of English influence. Meanwhile, back in Scotland, the foregrounding of his origins was part of a "wha's like us" attempt to distinguish Scotland's past from its dominant English counterpart. Placing an emphasis on the country's diaspora has been a means of generating a version of Scottish national history with some global significance or relevance beyond the country's own borders.[10]

The characterization of his Scottish origins and the possible influence these may have had on his time in Montreal have continued in this uncritical vein throughout the twentieth century. The representation of his connections to Scotland is exemplified by the plaque at 27 Stockwell Street (the site of the family home in Glasgow) and at the University of Glasgow.[11] The latter in particular deploys terminologies such as "student," "trader," and "statesman," which project noticeable celebratory stereotypes of the Scottish migrant. These serve to erase McGill's status as an enslaver and prominent settler-colonist whose status was heavily dependent on the exploitation of Indigenous resources and peoples as well as individuals of African descent.[12]

Rethinking McGill as a North Atlantic provincial is one way to challenge the narratives that use his Scottish background to foreground celebratory themes – such as commercial innovation, civic activism, and educational philanthropy – without acknowledging the colonial realities and racialized inequalities that shaped his life and
~~~

career. McGill lived in an age when ideas of "province" and "provincial" were common intellectual currency and a means of understanding the challenges and the potential of certain territories and societies. The terms were shorthand for places at great physical distance from metropolitan society, and that were marked by radically different geographies, climates, natural habitats, demography, and social order. In addition, such territories were characterized by rudimentary but expanding political and civic infrastructures and economies that required improvement and diversification. Provincial social structures often featured marked demographic imbalances between colonists and Indigenous or enslaved peoples and so exhibited stark cultural and increasingly racialized demarcations and inequalities.[13]

Alongside the notion of "province" as a dependent overseas territory and economy, the term could also denote parts of metropolitan Britain and Ireland. As Ned Landsman has so persuasively shown for long eighteenth-century Scotland in the Atlantic World, the British-Irish Isles had their own "provinces."[14] These were kingdoms (such as Ireland) or former kingdoms (Scotland) that had integrated into Anglo-Britain to a far greater extent than overseas territories, but had retained distinctive politics, religions, legal structures, economies, and urban/rural sectors. James McGill originated from and migrated to societies that corresponded closely to these characteristics.

Crucially, neither the overseas nor metropolitan versions of "provincial" necessarily denoted an unsophisticated, narrow-minded, insular society or culture: indeed, in McGill's era, ideas of "provincial" often had the opposite connotation. In confronting more systematically the nature of modern liberty while also seeking to enhance their economic function as an integrated part of the wider Empire, provincials could (and did) argue they provided an important diversification of both metropolitan Britain and its colonial expansion.[15] Typical of the stress placed on the nature and value of provinces was the assessment of Montreal by one of the many surveys of British North America produced prior to the outbreak of the American War of Independence: "They have hitherto raised no staple commodities to answer any great demands. Their trade with the Indians produces all their returns for that market ... Having mentioned Mont-Real, ... the inhabitants are said to be about five thousand. Yet the Indian fair, and the trade of the same kind (furs) which they drive more or less for the whole year, make it no inconsiderable place."[16] The same publication's assessment of Scotland placed similar emphasis on a reliance on primary staples such as barley, cattle, and fish but also on the potential for major economic expansion.

Alongside such contributions was a belief that the provinces had to think in new and innovative ways about the management and sustainability of rapid economic change and its impact on the social and moral order.[17] Enlightenment-era political economists drew on classical ideas of the role of Rome's provinces to represent certain territories as the source of vital staple products and key modes of exchange. They were also reserves of human virtue that acted as a natural counter to any degenerative tendencies at the imperial metropole. Materially less affluent but also not yet weakened by excessive luxury, the provinces were seen to bring other strengths that complemented or reinforced the Empire's centre. These included martial culture, religious idealism, and a commitment to educational attainment as a means of societal development. Typical of this provincial patriotism is a letter to the *Scots Magazine* in 1765, only a few years after McGill migrated to North America. It noted: "Let our southern English brethren rant at us for the lead we now take in war and in commerce, in the arts and the sciences ... The richest part of England is ... given to luxury and bad living."[18]

Through his education and his later access to the transatlantic circulation of printed materials, McGill would have been familiar with these modes of thinking.[19] Such conceptualizations of society and their actual and potential contributions to the wider British world provide a rubric for rethinking McGill as a "North Atlantic provincial." This framing reduces the great physical distance and stark environmental, economic, and cultural differences between later eighteenth- and early nineteenth-century Glasgow and Montreal. It is also a version of society that can be used to explore McGill's espousal of the need for conspicuous civic and military engagement, educational philanthropy, and the right to reduce people to the status of property. Viewed through the prisms of government, economy, and those forms of social order most likely to ensure "improvement," his Scottish and Quebec provinciality becomes intertwined.

An aspect of McGill's life where this comparability and mutually influencing dynamic can be seen clearly is in the realm of constitutional instability, military invasion, and resultant cultures of loyalty to the British political order. His experience of insurrection – or, given his constitutional inclinations, what he would see as "unnatural rebellion" – was a major connective thread between his Glasgow and

Montreal experiences. The beginning, middle, and end of his life involved either the reality or the threat of invasion and occupation by armed forces intent on implementing a significantly different constitutional, although not social, order.[20] Although the initial Jacobite assault on the Scottish Lowlands in the early autumn of 1745 targeted Edinburgh, the correspondence of Glasgow's lord provost, Andrew Cochrane, reveals an acute sense of proximity to threatening, alien Highlanders, and of the city having no practical means of defence. Added to this was the chilling effect on trade arising from Jacobite demands for a £15,000 tax contribution and "by stop of trade ... as the unavoidable consequence of an intestine war."[21] The 1745 rising hardened McGill's home city's identification with Presbyterianism and its loyalty to a unionist order that protected economic privileges along with legal and religious pluralism.[22] In a well-known sermon by the kirk minister associated with Glasgow University College, Reverend James How used the theme of the Israelites' journey from Egypt into the wilderness and their resulting discontent with Moses as an analogy for those Scots opposing the Hanoverian and unionist settlement.[23] This critique of Jacobitism drew on a wider and well understood political language and imagery. These ideas shaped the environment in which the young McGill would have formulated notions of properly constituted government, the obligations due from subjects, and under what conditions it was permissible or impermissible to oppose established authority. In an assessment of the last major rising in Scotland that would surely have echoed McGill's understanding of later events in 1775, How noted of the Jacobites:

> In their pretended zeal for the publick Good, they sigh out their Sorrows for Mismanagements, deplore the Dangers that hangs upon us, and endeavour to persuade the world, that every thing is out of order ... It is an easie matter to pretend a Zeal for, and a Love of our Country: This is, what all Parties and Faction, make a Pretence of, how much soever they are alienated in their minds ... Never yet was there any Insurrection against the lawful Magistrate, but that was prefaced with glorious Pretences, *The Liberty of the Subjects, and Freedom from heavy Burdens, &c.*[24]

In another sermon commemorating the first anniversary of Culloden, and similarly published in Glasgow, How reinforced the apparently irreligious nature of attacks on established government, taking as his text the book of Proverbs, chapter 17, verse 11: "An evil man seeketh only Rebellion."[25]

It is not known if McGill ever read these pamphlets or if they in any way shaped his reaction to the onset of the American invasion of the Province of Quebec thirty years later. What is beyond doubt is that he would have been brought up in a civic, religious, and educational environment where this understanding of the balance between government and subject formed an almost unchallenged orthodoxy. Ongoing connections to family and commercial society in Glasgow once he settled in Montreal would have served to reinforce such thinking.[26] Financial support to family and to Glasgow's medical and welfare institutions in his will certainly confirm that he remained well linked to his place of origin.[27] It is highly likely he would have been well aware of how his hometown reacted to the onset of the Revolution and resultant conflict. The early stages, from the campaign against the Stamp Act to the outbreak of the war, was marked by an ambiguous set of civic responses driven by a concern for commercial stability. However, the city's support for the British order was never seriously in doubt and hardened as the conflict expanded into a global war after 1778.[28]

McGill's noticeable loyalty to Britain would have been shaped largely and most immediately by the distinctive context in which Quebec and, more specifically, Montreal found themselves by 1775. Nevertheless, his politics in this period can also be understood as a provincial reaction to a spectrum of transatlantic instabilities rather than simply the influence of his Scottish origins or as a result of his status as a leading figure in colonial politics. Past and present blended in a transnational but markedly provincial experience of constitutional, religious, and military turmoil that would have had a profound impact on his sense of properly constituted political authority and the rights of the individual in relation to that authority. His Scottish upbringing imparted an awareness of the perceived link between unwarranted demands for liberty and chronic political instability. The kingdom faced a sequence of eight risings or attempted risings over eighty years from 1665 to 1745 – first Covenanting and then Jacobite.[29] As Reverend How's sermon indicates, this induced a striking degree of skepticism about what was perceived to be excessive demands for irresponsible, destabilizing forms of liberty. Rather than an emphasis on universal political rights, an ideology of property and the legal protection of property became ever more embedded in ideas of what formed the basis of legitimate politics. As Adam Ferguson put it while explaining the stadial development of societies, "It must appear very evident, that property is a matter of progress."[30]

It is difficult to exaggerate the central place of property in concepts of how society should be structured and developed. As was true across the rest of Britain and Ireland, property defined who voted. But in pre-1832 Scotland, it produced the narrowest electorate in the British and Irish Isles, generating in turn a distinctive culture of patronage and clientage politics.[31] The potential for property owning was far more open-ended in a settler-colonist society like Quebec. Beyond the infinitely greater access to land through the displacement of Indigenous peoples, the boundaries of "property" extended to legally enforceable and socially mandated claims on human beings. Yet if the boundaries of "property" were configured in some profoundly differently ways, McGill's patrician and reactionary politics still chimed with understandings in *ancien régime* Scotland of what constituted the public realm and its gradations of liberty. A strong hint of this can be found in the sermon preached at the Presbyterian Church in Montreal on 28 April 1793 by Reverend John Young, a sermon it is likely McGill heard or read in its subsequent pamphlet form. In reacting to yet another seemingly destabilizing sequence of events, this time in France, Young articulated the post-1783 belief in the virtuous balance of religious and legal liberties that defined the seemingly sustainable hierarchies inherent in the British constitutional order. He exhorted his congregation to "Pray for the best of sovereigns, who is indeed a nurturing Father to our churches, and rejoice in a most excellent constitution by which every man's civil and religious liberty is secured. Especially we of this highly favoured Province have the greatest reason to be thankful."[32]

Young's talk of "everyman's civil liberty" jars with the well understood role of enslavement in Montreal's economy and social order. The circulation of such ideas underlines how understandings of property ensured provincial as well as metropolitan societies evolved notions of freedom and liberty based on legal and increasing racial advantages, as opposed to natural, universal rights. In this world of hierarchical liberties, enslavement acted as an affirmation of the legally privileged forms of freedom available to and defended by McGill, his family, and his associates. This world of gradations in freedom meant the right to enslave sat alongside a range of other privileges that were all the more important given the fragile and changing character of Quebec society. These ranged from the guaranteed rights of Protestants and Catholics to freedom of worship, access to British or French legal systems and courts, and the right to an elected assembly for the purposes of agreeing on taxation and other government measures.[33] To McGill and his contemporaries, property was absolutely foundational to a form of ordered politics that managed "liberty" in ways that would determine Quebec's future trajectory.

Beyond the importance of a distinctly provincial sense of the need for ordered, hierarchical liberty, there were other aspects of McGill's transatlantic connections that shaped his attitudes and actions. Glasgow and Montreal shared strikingly similar military and associated civic experiences in 1745 and 1775. The lack of a meaningful number of regular Crown forces, not least as a result of government efforts to prioritize the metropoles of Edinburgh and Quebec, proved to be an issue on both occasions.[34] The urgent need to augment local defence and demonstrate political loyalty meant that involvement in militias played a noticeably prominent role throughout McGill's life. Glasgow raised the largest militia regiment of any Scottish city during the last Jacobite rising. Over 800 men from this unit formed part of the government's reserve at the Battle of Falkirkmuir, fought on 17 January 1746. As was common at the time, the Glasgow regiment was viewed by the regular army as poorly trained and equipped. Its primary function was to make up numbers and to act as a clear manifestation of the city's loyalty. Despite this, some commentaries on the battle, the largest of the last Jacobite rising, argued that Glasgow's militia stood their ground well after some regular forces collapsed.[35]

Thirty years later, McGill was involved in similar efforts to use a city militia to defend the established political order. This was part of a wider pattern that involved the province's merchant elite using involvement in military service to establish political profile and leverage.[36] If hardly exceptional in this respect, McGill made adroit use of the mercantile-to-military dynamic. Although later known for his time as colonel of Montreal's militia during the outbreak of the War of 1812, his most active phase of service was in the autumn and early winter of 1775.[37] On 25 September of that year, an American force under Colonel Ethan Allan was defeated at the Battle of Pointe Longue, an engagement in which Montreal's militia played a significant role. General Richard Montgomery's subsequent invasion was larger and more successful, leading to the fall of Montreal on 12–13 November 1775.[38] McGill would have been active among the Montreal units participating in both these campaigns.

Military service complemented his commercial prominence and helped pave the way for a more substantive role in civic and wider provincial politics. His actions in this respect conformed to the stereotype of the virtuous, active citizen that formed such a central trope in the campaign for a Scottish militia. The controversy was arguably the key political issue in Scotland when McGill was a young man.[39] The unwillingness of the British parliament to establish the institution north of the border was seen as a major breach of the Union. Scotland's press in the late 1750s and early 1760s, just as McGill attended university, was replete with debates on the matter.[40] The idealization of military participation as active citizenship clearly influenced McGill: of all the civic roles he undertook once established in Montreal, one of the earliest, most conspicuous, and persistent was his role in Quebec's militia.

The link between military service and the fashioning of a "virtuous" political self was not the only continuity from his place of origin.[41] Beyond informing his conservative provincial politics and long record of militia service, there were other lessons McGill drew from the experience of his hometown during the 1745 rising that find striking resonances in his later actions. Having been largely bypassed during the Jacobite takeover of the Scottish Lowlands in the early autumn of 1745, Glasgow was occupied by approximately 3,600 troops loyal to the Stuarts in late December 1745. How the city's leadership reacted to this event would have been relayed to McGill during his formative years. In the absence of any Crown representative, it was the burgh magistrates who negotiated with the Jacobite high command in the last week of December 1745 for the provision of clothing and free quarter while attempting to minimize other exactions of money and materiel. An even more obvious resonance that contextualizes McGill's willingness to negotiate the articles of Montreal's capitulation on 12 November 1775 was the effort by four Glasgow merchants to treat with the Jacobites in September 1745 and "to make the best terms ... for saving the city, its Trade and Inhabitants."[42] In both instances, civic leadership came from the commercial elite and involved the prioritization of existing legal privileges, property protection, the maintenance of trade, and the avoidance of conscription by the insurrectionists.[43] Exactly these priorities characterized the effort by Montreal loyalists when negotiating with the Americans.

Alongside obvious resonances in relation to dramatic events, such as the 1745 rising and the American War of Independence, was the generic aspiration in provincial societies to sustainable forms of "improvement." A key factor widely understood as shaping societal progress was the specific possibilities and challenges offered by the economically and culturally distinct hinterlands surrounding provincial port cities such as Glasgow and Montreal. In the case of the former, this was the Gaelic Highlands. Gaels had been a prominent human, linguistic, and economic presence in the city for centuries. When McGill matriculated at the university in 1756, he did so with sixty-eight other students, eight of whom were from Highland and Gaelic-speaking parts of Scotland.[44] Besides the influx of a linguistically distinctive population, many of whom then migrated along with McGill to colonial destinations, the north of Scotland supplied key primary staples such as cattle, kelp, and fish. These were all products strongly associated with the contribution of provincial economies to the wider colonial economy.[45] Glasgow and its Clyde ports dominated the West Highland fisheries, which in turn provided a key commodity that facilitated export and re-import trades from the Caribbean.[46] Rural and coastal hinterlands played a vital supply-chain role in the wider framework of transatlantic exchanges that had slavery-reliant production at its centre.

The parallels with Montreal's status as a regional metropole in a mutually influencing dynamic with its own socially and culturally "othered" hinterland are obvious. While the political economy of later eighteenth-century British colonialism is more usually associated with Adam Smith, it was another Scot, John Campbell, and his work, *A political survey of Britain*, that McGill is more likely to have known when shifting from personal involvement in the fur trade to an established business position in Montreal by the mid-1770s. Its analysis of the Province of Quebec exemplifies the sense of untapped potential associated with territories specialized in staple goods but that were also evolving more diverse economies. Campbell's political survey noted: "The present staples of Canada are furs, fish, oil and timber; but as every-thing is now in a thriving way, the Number of Inhabitants increases and the Commerce much more considerable than it was, there is no Doubt that Canada will become daily of greater Consequence to Britain."[47] This generally positive tone survived the post-1783 reassessment of British North America. In an important restatement of the role of territories like Scotland and Quebec in restabilizing the empire, it was noted of the latter: "The habitable part joins the American states, and was originally in the possession of the French, to whom it proved an expensive, unprofitable burden. It hath been no less so for Great Britain, but it is supposed very improvable, and is likely to become an important member of our empire."[48]

Campbell and Knox's praising of Quebec's potential found echoes in Scotland. In 1772, while rejecting accusations in the London press regarding Scotland's unstable and fragile economy, newspapers north of the border were filled with the characteristic emphasis on the interrelated forces of provincial virtue and economic expansion. On 3 July 1772, in a letter to *The Edinburgh Courant*, a merchant proclaimed "the improvement of North Britain in agriculture, in foreign and domestic trade, have been astonishing. History perhaps does not furnish an example of improvements so equally rapid."[49]

An important feature of these noticeably optimistic assessments of what might be termed Britain's North Atlantic provincial productivity was the emphasis on commodities rather than the people and labour systems that supplied them. This prioritization arose in part because of one of the great tensions and ambiguities in contemporary ideas of improvement, a tension exemplified by growing questions surrounding the defining place of enslavement in new commercial societies. Attempts to justify the practice relied on ancient or biblical precedence, moral differences within a framework of "savagery" and "civility," and an increasing reliance on conceptions of innate racial hierarchies.[50] The intensifying debate over the moral, economic, or racial basis of enslavement formed part of a much wider sense of anxiety around the future configuration of populations and the impact of growing human mobility.[51] Such questions formed a crucial context to the whole arc of McGill's life and career. The place of people in the new commercial society, be they enslaved or settler-colonial migrants, posed complicating and potentially destabilizing questions over the morality and sustainability of "improvement."[52] As a successful provincial merchant who relied heavily on enslaved or Indigenous labour and their associated products, McGill lay at the centre of this fundamental tension in contemporary thinking. He would have been all too aware of fears that rapid socio-economic development induced alarming population instability. A problem with "improvement" was to ensure it did not threaten itself in the medium or longer term. In the case of Scotland, this took the form of profound fears over the country's burgeoning levels of migration. A key feature of North British provincial culture was a perennial concern for the productive management of its relatively low population reserves, a defining demographic feature the country shared with Quebec.[53]

One solution to this issue was to enhance the productive value of populations and better improve their socio-economic utility. This increase in national wealth via people could be effected through better education. Again, his hometown provided important lessons in this regard. There is no need to elaborate on the educational context of Glasgow in this period; suffice to say McGill was brought up in an urban context that prided itself on the scale, achievements, and, above all, utility of its educational provision.[54] Few other national stereotypes of Scottish culture are as over-exposed as that of the country's education system. What is not in doubt, however, is that in the eighteenth century this was a widespread belief rather than a retrospective national stereotype. In yet another example of the projection of provincial virtue through the press, *The Scots Magazine* carried a letter in the mid-1760s claiming that "the English in general are unquestionably less instructed than the Scotch."[55] Education was seen as especially apt for provincial societies with economies heavily reliant on a smaller population base, a limited number of staple commodities, and an economy requiring rapid diversification. It is not just the specific civic context of his Glasgow background that explains McGill's well-known educational philanthropy in Montreal; it fits exactly with a well-entrenched, even conventional provincial emphasis on education as both a social disciplining mechanism for labour and a wider societal strategy.[56]

Viewing James McGill as a North Atlantic provincial risks neglecting the generic elements of his Enlightenment worldview and the corresponding sense of privilege he would have developed as a "white" and increasingly elite settler. Equally, his substantial north-to-south links with the Caribbean part of the British Atlantic must be seen as of equal, if not more, importance than the legacies of his west-to-east connections with Scotland. Yet in the realm of civic politics, provincial economy, and social ordering it is possible to discern clear overlaps and continuities with his Scottish origins. A defining feature of this provinciality was its internal ambiguities and tensions. Metropolitan culture and economy could be criticized as prone to luxury and corruption even as societies like Scotland and Quebec sought to refashion themselves in the metropole's image. The different dimensions were constitutive of the provincial "improvement" that McGill so obviously espoused, and reconciling them was seen as key to sustainable social development. This helps explain why his brutal exploitation of some individuals co-existed so seamlessly with a willingness to develop civic and educational institutions (in both Montreal and Glasgow) that would assist and develop others. He would not have recognized these actions as contradictory. His provincial worldview meant he almost certainly saw no tension whatsoever in these defining aspects of his life and career: politics, property, productivity, and people existed in a world of orderly, sustainable hierarchies. This was a world of managed and legally defined ideals and practices of liberty. Managing liberty and managing improvement meant privilege for some and enslavement for others. In such a society, McGill could both be an enslaver and, for directly related reasons, leave major legacies for future development through education of his new provincial home.

NOTES

1 Charmaine A. Nelson and Student Authors, *Slavery and McGill University: Bicentenary Recommendations* (2020), accessed 15 May 2023, https://blackmaplemagazine.com/wp-content/uploads/2022/09/bicentenary-recommendations.pdf.

2 Charmaine A. Nelson, *Slavery, Geography and Empire in Nineteenth-Century Marine Landscapes of Montreal and Jamaica* (London: Routledge/Taylor & Francis, 2016), 86–109.

3 For outputs that marked a new level of awareness of the extent and significance of slavery and enslavement-derived products in Scottish society, see David Hancock, *Citizens of the World: London Merchants and the Integration of the British Atlantic Community, 1735–1785* (Cambridge: Cambridge University Press, 1995), 25–278; Douglas Hamilton, *Scotland, The Caribbean and the Atlantic World, 1750–1820* (Manchester: Manchester University Press, 2005); T.M. Devine, ed., *Recovering Scotland's Slavery Past: The Caribbean Connection* (Edinburgh: Edinburgh University Press, 2015). For a review of historiographical trends in the treatment of the slavery theme by historians of Scotland between c. 1960 and c. 2020 see Stephen Mullen, "Centring Transatlantic Slavery in Scottish Historiography," *History Compass* 22, no. 1 (2020): 1–14, https://doi.org/10.1111/hic3.12707.

4 Nelson et al., *Slavery and McGill University*, 28.

5 For the vital importance of north-to-south as much as east-to-west connections in the consolidation of Britain's post-1783 Atlantic Empire, see Lucy Brown and Emma Ridsdal, "Critical Biography of James McGill, Slave Owner and West Indian Merchant," in Nelson et al., *Slavery and*

McGill University, 57–8; P.J. Marshall, *Remaking the British Atlantic: The United States and the British Empire after American Independence* (Oxford: Oxford University Press, 2012), 171–2.

6 For assessments of societal progress in Scotland and Quebec written at the time McGill would have been contemplating migration, see "Of the Riches of North Britain," in Robert Wallace, *Characteristics of the Present Political State of Great Britain* (London: A. Miller, 1758), 126–34; Ignotus, *Thoughts on Trade in General, Our West-Indian in Particular, Our Continental Colonies, Canada, Guadaloupe, and the Preliminary Articles of Peace. Addressed to the Community* (London: John Wilkie, 1763), 28–51. For the importance of staples as a driver of the early Canadian economy and so also of its society, see Harold A. Innis, *The Fur Trade in Canada: An Introduction to Canadian Economic History* (New Haven, CT: Yale University Press; London: Oxford University Press, 1930), 385–401.

7 J.W. Dawson, "James McGill and the University of McGill College," reprinted from *Barnard's American Journal of Education* (September 1859): 3–6; Cyrus MacMillan, *McGill and Its Story, 1821–1921* (London & New York: John Lane, 1921), 31–6; Stanley Brice Frost, *McGill University: For the Advancement of Learning, Volume I, 1801–1895* (Montreal and Kingston: McGill-Queen's University Press, 1980), 4–20.

8 Stanley Brice Frost, *James McGill of Montreal* (Montreal and Kingston: McGill-Queen's University Press, 1995), 5–11; Lewis W. Abbott, "James McGill (1744–1813)," *International Review of Scottish Studies* 12 (2008): 26–39.

9 William Jordan Rattray, *The Scot in British North America*, vols I–IV (Toronto: Maclear and Co., 1880–1884), 2:355.

10 For discussion of the use of diaspora histories to create a national history, see Catriona M.M. Macdonald, "Imagining the Scottish Diaspora: Emigration and Transnational Literature in the Late Modern Period," *Britain and the World* 5, no. 1 (2012): 12–42.

11 For a detailed plan of McGill's hometown seventeen or eighteen years after his departure in c. 1761 to North America, see John McArthur, *Plan of the City of Glasgow: Gorbells and Caltoun / From an Actual Survey by John McArthur ... Engraved by Alexr. Baille and James Lumsden etc.* (Glasgow, 1778), accessed 11 June 2023, https://maps.nls.uk/joins/2767.html.

12 "James McGill House Plaque Stockwell Street Glasgow," Wikipedia, accessed 26 March 2025, https://commons.wikimedia.org/wiki/

File:James_McGill_House_Plaque_Stockwell_Street_Glasgow.jpg; "James McGill Plaque – University of Glasgow Undercroft," Wikipedia, accessed 26 March 2025, https://commons.wikimedia.org/wiki/File:James_McGill_Plaque_-_University_of_Glasgow_Undercroft.jpg.

13 Bernard Bailyn and Philip D. Morgan, "Introduction," in *Strangers within the Realm: Cultural Margins of the First British Empire*, eds Bernard Bailyn and Philip D. Morgan (Chapel Hill and London: University of North Carolina Press, 1991), 20–31; Colin Kidd, "North Britishness and the Nature of Eighteenth-Century British Patriotisms," *The Historical Journal* 39, no. 2 (June 1996): 361–82; H.V. Bowen, *Elites, Enterprise and the Making of the British Overseas Empire, 1688–1775* (London: Palgrave Macmillan, 1996), 154–5.

14 Ned C. Landsman, "The Provinces and the Empire: Scotland, the American Colonies and the Development of British Provincial Identity," in *An Imperial State at War: Britain from 1689–1815*, ed. Lawrence Stone (London and New York: Routledge, 1994), 258–87; Ned Landsman, "The Legacy of British Union for the North American Colonies: Provincial Elites and the Problem of Imperial Union," in *A Union for Empire: Political Thought and the British Union of 1707*, ed. John Robertson (Cambridge: Cambridge University Press, 1995), 297–317; Ned C. Landsman, "Nation, Migration, and the Province in the First British Empire: Scotland and the Americas, 1600–1800," *American Historical Review* 104, no. 2 (April 1999): 463–75.

15 Kathleen Wilson, *The Sense of the People: Politics, Culture and Imperialism in England, 1715–1785* (Cambridge: Cambridge University Press, 1998), 13, 32–41.

16 Oliver Goldsmith, *The Present State of the British Empire in Europe, America, Africa and Asia. Containing a Concise Account of Our Possessions in Every Part of the Globe* (London: W. Griffin, 1768), 346–50 (quotation from 346–7). See also John Huddlestone Wynne, *A General History of the British Empire in America: Containing, an Historical, Political, and Commercial View of the English Settlements*, vols I–II (London: W. Richardson and L. Urquhart, 1770), 173–5.

17 James Livesey, *Civil Society and Empire: Ireland and Scotland in the Eighteenth-Century Atlantic World* (New Haven, CT, and London: Yale University Press, 2009), 154–76.

18 *The Scots Magazine* 27 (Edinburgh: Sands, Murray & Cochran, 1765), 134.

19 Richard B. Sher, *The Enlightenment & the Book: Scottish Authors & Their Publishers in Eighteenth-Century Britain, Ireland & America* (Chicago and London: Chicago University Press, 2006), 503–40.

20 *The Scots Magazine* 8 (Edinburgh: Sands, Murray & Cochran, 1746), 30; Mark R. Anderson, *The Battle for the Fourteenth Colony: America's War of Liberation in Canada, 1774–1776* (Hanover and London: University of New England Press, 2013), 120–38; Stanley Brice Frost, "James McGill and the War of 1812," *Fortanus* 7 (1994): 41–52.

21 James Smith, *The Cochrane Correspondence Regarding the Affairs of Glasgow, M.D.CC.XLV-VI* (Glasgow: Maitland Club, 1836), 10–12, 66–7; *A Loyal Address to the Citizens of Glasgow, Occasioned by the Present Rebellion* (Glasgow, 1745), 19.

22 Christopher Whatley, "Reformed Religion, Regime Change, Scottish Whigs and the Struggle for the 'Soul' of Scotland, c. 1688–c. 1788," *Scottish Historical Review* 92, no. 233 (April 2013): 66–99.

23 University of Glasgow Library, Sp Coll Mu42-e.35, James How, *A Sermon Preached in Black-Friears-Church Glasgow, December 6th, 1745; On Occasion of the Present Rebellion; to Which is Annex'd an Appendix, Directed to all the Jacobites in North-Britain* (Glasgow: John McCalum, 2nd edition, 1746), 1–48.

24 How, *A Sermon*, 12.

25 James How, *An Anniversary Sermon, in Commemoration of the Victory Obtained at the Battle of Culloden, by His Majesty's forces, Under the Command of His Royal Highness the Duke of Cumberland, Over the Rebels, April 16th, 1746. Preached in the Trone-Church, Glasgow, April 16th, 1747* (Glasgow, 1747), 5.

26 The extent to which McGill liaised with acquaintances in Scotland during the imperial crisis would benefit from further research.

27 The National Archive (hereafter TNA), Kew, PROB, 11/1559/533, fos 185–490.

28 For Glasgow's engagement with transatlantic politics, see Brad A. Jones, *Resisting Independence: Popular Loyalism in the Revolutionary British Atlantic* (Ithaca and London: Cornell University Press, 2021), 4–8, 46–9, 143–4.

29 Keith M. Brown, *Kingdom or Province? Scotland and the Regal Union, 1603–1715* (London: Bloomsbury, 1992), 112–96; Murray Pittock, *The Myth of the Jacobite Clans* (Edinburgh: Edinburgh University Press, 1995).

30 Adam Ferguson, *An Essay on the History of Civil Society* (Edinburgh: A. Kincaid & J. Bell, 1767), 129.

31 J.S. Shaw, *The Political History of Eighteenth-Century Scotland* (Basingstoke: Macmillan, 1999), 32; L.M. Cullen, "Scotland & Ireland, 1600–1800: Their Role in the Evolution of British Society," in *Scottish*

Society, 1500–1800, eds R.A. Houston and I.D. Whyte (Cambridge: Cambridge University Press, 1989), 231–43.

32 *A Sermon Preached in the Presbyterian Church of Montreal, April 28th 1793. By the Revd. John Young* (Montreal: F. Mesplet, 1793), 12.

33 Marshall, *Remaking the British Atlantic*, 167–75.

34 Smith, *The Cochrane Correspondence*, 14–15.

35 Jonathan Oates, *The Jacobite Campaigns: The British State at War* (London: Pickering and Chatto, 2011), 179.

36 See the 1775 petition of William Grant, merchant in Quebec, TNA, CO5/115, fo. 114.

37 Frost, *James McGill*, 128–4.

38 *A Narrative of Col. Ethan Allen's Captivity, From the Time of His Being Taken by the British, near Montreal, on the 25th day of September, in the Year 1775* (Boston, 1779), 7–8.

39 John Robertson, *The Scottish Enlightenment and the Militia Issue* (Edinburgh: John Donald, 1985), 90–1; Adam Ferguson, *Reflections Previous to the Establishment of a Militia* (London: R. and J. Dodsley, 1756), 1–58.

40 *The Scots Magazine* 22 (Edinburgh: Sands, Murray, and Cochrane, 1760), 44, 55, 168, 513; *The Scots Magazine* 25 (Edinburgh: Sands, Murray, and Cochrane, 1763), 67–8, 117, 253.

41 Richard B. Sher, "Adam Ferguson, Adam Smith, and the Problem of National Defense," *Journal of Modern History* 61, no. 2 (June 1989): 240–68.

42 Smith, *The Cochrane Correspondence*, 130–3.

43 ARTICLES OF CAPITULATION, *Made and Entered into Between* RICHARD MONTGOMERY, *Esquire, Brigadier General of the Continental Army, and the Citizens and Inhabitants of Montreal, Represented by the Subscribers, John Porteous, Pierre Panet, John Blake, Pierre Meziere, James Finlay, Saint George Dupree, James McGill, Louis Carrignant, Richard Huntly, Francois Mathiot, Edward William Grey, and Pierre Guy, Duly Elected for that Purpose*, accessed 18 July 2023, https://www.loc.gov/resource/bdsdcc.00501/?st=text.

44 W. Innes Addison, ed., *The Matriculation Albums of the University of Glasgow from 1728–1858* (Glasgow: Maclehose, 1913), 53–6.

45 John Campbell, *A Political Survey of Britain: Being a Series of Reflections on the Situation, Lands, Inhabitants, Revenues, Colonies, and Commerce of this Island*, vols I–II (London: Richardson and Urquhart, 1774),

1:225–6. Eric Richards, "Scotland and the Uses of the Atlantic Empire," in *Strangers within the Realm*, 67–114.

46 John Knox, *Observations on the Northern Fisheries: With a Discourse on the Expediency of Establishing Fishing Stations, or Small Towns, in the Highlands of Scotland, and the Hebride Islands* (London and Edinburgh: J. Walter & W. Gordon, 1786), 90. For the Highland's supply chain role in Glasgow's Atlantic Economy, see Stephen Mullen, *The Glasgow Sugar Aristocracy: Scotland and Caribbean Slavery, 1775–1838* (London: University of London Press, 2022), 30–1, 248–9.

47 Campbell, *A Political Survey of Britain*, 2:641.

48 John Knox, *A View of the British Empire, More Especially Scotland; With Some Proposals for the Improvement of that Country, the Extension of its Fisheries, and the Relief of the People* (London: J. Walter, 1784), xi.

49 *The Scots Magazine* 34 (Edinburgh: A. Murray & J. Cochran, 1772), 361.

50 Silvia Sebastiani, *The Scottish Enlightenment: Race, Gender, and the Limits of Progress*, trans. Jeremy Carden (New York: Palgrave Macmillan, 2013), 38–43; Onur Ulas Ince, "Between Commerce and Empire: David Hume, Colonial Slavery and Commercial Incivility," *History of Political Thought* 39, no. 1 (2018): 107–34.

51 Ted McCormick, *Human Empire: Mobility and Demographic Thought in the British Atlantic World, 1500–1800* (Cambridge: Cambridge University Press, 2022), 188–234.

52 Fredrik Albritton Jonsson, *Enlightenment's Frontier: The Scottish Highlands and the Origins of Environmentalism* (New Haven and London: Yale University Press, 2013), 12–16.

53 *A Candid Enquiry into the Causes of the Late and the Intended Migrations from Scotland. In a letter to J--------- R--------- Esq; Lanarkshire* (Glasgow: P. Tait, 1771), 1–68; TNA, CO42/16, fos. 8, 46, 77.

54 Mullen, *The Glasgow Sugar Aristocracy*, 41–3, 62–4.

55 *The Scots Magazine* 27 (Edinburgh: W. Sands, A. Murray & J. Cochran, 1765), 134.

56 Andrew Mackillop, "Poverty, Health and Imperial Wealth in Early Modern Scotland," in *Imperial Inequalities: The Politics of Economic Governance Across European Empires*, ed. Gurminder Bhambra and Julia McClure (Manchester: Manchester University Press, 2022), 157–76.

3

James McGill and Constructing the History of a University

BRIAN YOUNG

James McGill has physical presence on the university's front campus. In 1875, his remains were removed from Montreal's Protestant Cemetery for reinterment in a strategically placed tomb in front of the Arts Building. University historian Stanley Frost accorded mythical qualities to the site, writing that James McGill "lies in deep content beneath the tomb ... and as he hears the many voices of young students passing by, he smiles in his sleep."[1] The tomb has served to commemorate masculinity and military courage. For example, 1944 was the bicentennial of James McGill's birth. With major enlistment by McGill students in Canada's Second World War effort, the Canadian Grenadier Guards held a tomb-side ceremony honouring James McGill's patriotism and his service as colonel of the 1st Battalion of Montreal Militia. The tomb and the founder as a symbolic father figure are recalled in a student drinking song:

> James McGill, James, McGill
> Peacefully he slumbers there
> Blissful, though we're on a tear
> He's our father, oh yes, rather,
> James McGill![2]

The "Founder's Elm" stood near McGill's tomb. Dating from c. 1790, this massive tree was a campus icon until 1976 when it was felled by Dutch elm disease. Its base remains as a "memorial stump" in front of the School of Architecture and a slice of its trunk has been exhibited in the Redpath Museum.[3] In 1996, another front campus memorial to the founder was unveiled. This handsome life-size bronze statue, now removed, depicted James McGill striding towards the front gates, as the University historian put it, "to do good in Montreal."[4] In 1975, the university established the History of McGill Project and its director, Stanley Frost, produced a two-volume history of the university and a biography of James McGill. These works, instrumental in framing the university's founding legend, emphasize McGill's fur trading, entrepreneurial, and military career.

This contribution picks up on McGill University's intimate association with the personage and presumed ideology of its namesake and first benefactor. University emphasis on James McGill reaches back into the nineteenth century and intensified as a marketing device in the politically charged atmosphere of the 1970s. In their use of campus public space, university museums, official discourse, and sponsored publications, officials have successfully elevated founder James McGill to Canada's best-known university brand. I am interested in the implications of mating an eighteenth-century notable with the history of a twenty-first-century institution of higher learning.

My first section reconstructs the history of James McGill as a corrective to the mythology surrounding his life and the founding of the university. Using the archival sources of the legal historian, I examine the university's founding document, James McGill's will, pausing over the testator's intentions and the dispute over its settlement. Written in 1811, the will emphasizes McGill's profound attachment to his French Catholic family, the Desrivières. This is of significance since the university, first through the courts, then in the official history and biography, and finally in the construction of campus material culture, has obscured the role of family in the founder's life and heritage. This has permitted free rein to an image of both founder and university as individualistic, masculine, competitive, and entrepreneurial.

My second section, a venture into social history, develops the history of his family, the Desrivières, treating their place in the landed gentry and their intermarriages across Quebec's French Catholic elite. Here, I emphasize the importance of James McGill as a landed proprietor as opposed to his portrayal as a bold Scot fur trader and Protestant pillar of the commercial empire of the St Lawrence. McGill owned large land tracts, particularly in Quebec's Eastern Townships. What were the effects of this proprietorship on a rural region? For, while the university is a principal result of his urban landed bequests, it is important to evaluate the role of his rural properties in the history of colonization and institutionalization in southern Quebec. And if we turn to James McGill's succession strategy, his willing of half of a township assured the privileges of his family heirs over generations and into the 1890s.

If James McGill's will, its execution, and the early history of the university and his family, the Desrivières, are nineteenth century phenomena, my third theme is contemporary, examining why, in the late twentieth century, a mythology of James McGill as hero-entrepreneur was created. This section corresponds to my own lived experience as an historian at McGill after 1976. Characterized by paternalist governance when I arrived, McGill University transited steadily into a neoliberal saddle. This shift in ideology and administrative practice occurred in the aftermath of the McGill français movement (1969), the rise of Quebec's strong feminist movement, and the election in 1976 of a provincial government committed to independence. Challenged as to the university's social usefulness, McGill authorities reached to what they saw as a certain liberal ideological consensus around the personality of its founder, a Protestant Scot, military hero, and successful fur-trade entrepreneur.

JAMES MCGILL

Scottish-born, a student of the University of Glasgow, and an active trader in post-Conquest Montreal, James McGill lived permanently in the city after 1775. In these late eighteenth-century decades of the American and French revolutions and then the Napoleonic Wars, Montreal remained a French Catholic city but one in which its British minority, of which McGill was a prominent member, had dominant military, judicial, and economic power. Raised a Presbyterian, and an Anglican when he died, McGill, like several of his peers in the Scots merchant community, married into a prominent French Catholic family. In an Anglican ceremony in 1776, he married widow Charlotte Trottier Desrivières, Ursuline-educated and a member of the Guillimin family. Her first husband, Amable Trottier Desrivières, was a prominent fur trader, sometime partner of James McGill and, also, a slaveowner.[5] Known as an affectionate couple, McGill and the widow Desrivières did not have children together but she brought two young sons, raised as Catholics, into the marriage. "Fond of children," as his biographer J.I. Cooper put it, James McGill legally adopted both sons, François-Amable Desrivières and Thomas-Hippolyte Desrivières.[6]

François Amable (1764–1830) became a trusted business partner of his stepfather, was active in the construction of the Lachine Canal, and served both as warden of Trinity House and as commander of the First Militia Battalion; symbolically, James McGill left him his gold watch.[7] The younger Desrivières son, Thomas-Hippolyte, died in a duel in Jamaica in 1799, but his son, James McGill Trottier Desrivières, was a great favourite of his grandfather. Proud of his connection with the city's Scots elite, James McGill Trottier Desrivières gave each of his four sons the McGill name of their great-grandfather.[8]

In 1798, James McGill built Burnside, future site of the university, as a summer estate. Outside the city on the fertile flats below Mount Royal, it became a favoured family residence. His widow continued to live there and, on her death in 1818, son François-Amable and his family occupied Burnside as well as an adjoining estate. Besides his wealth in Montreal, James McGill was a major landowner in Upper and Lower Canada. In southern Quebec, his holdings in the Township of Stanbridge included vast forests, a navigable river, and the settlement potential of rich arable land. Accessible by Missisquoi Bay and Lake Champlain to American markets and to Montreal via the Richelieu River, the area would prosper thanks to a forest and dairy economy and rural industries powered by falls along the Pike River.

James McGill wrote his will, 9 January 1811 (apparently his second), and died two years later.[9] This essential document in the history of the university must be understood in the context of the colony's post-Conquest legal structures. One of the critical features of that legal regime was freedom of willing, a right granted under the Quebec Act of 1774 as an exception to the general application of the Custom of Paris. This assured individual autonomy to a testator like McGill over principles of family rights prioritized in the Custom.[10] As Judge George Pyke wrote in his judgment in the suit McGill University trustees brought against the Desrivières family, the Quebec Act had "changed" the ancient laws of France and Rome "for the preservation of estates in families" giving instead "entire freedom" to the individual to dispose of his property "without reserve, even to the prejudice of the heir at law." Nailing the lid on the coffin of customary family succession rights, Pyke continued that "the consideration to the claims of blood and nature must be left to the discretion of the testator alone."[11]

Also important in understanding the larger colonial context of James McGill's landed wealth was the establishment under the Constitutional Act of 1791 of freehold tenure on Lower Canadian lands outside the historic seigneuries of the St Lawrence Valley. As part of large patronage grants, British authorities ceded the Township of Stanbridge to Hugh Finlay who, in turn, ceded parts to Isaac Todd and James McGill. By acquiring Todd's share, McGill became proprietor of half of the township by 1801.

A final condition, essential to James McGill's bequest to establish a university and again a culturally sensitive issue, was passage of the Royal Institution for the Advancement of Learning Act (1801). An effort to encourage popular, and presumably secular, schools free from control by Catholic authorities, the act was of historic importance in repealing French feudal restrictions on mortmain, that is, the right of institutions (monasteries for example) to an inalienable possession of lands. Modelled on British legislation of 1788, the act allowed the Crown to establish charitable or educational corporations that could own and hold property in mortmain.[12] It was under this legal umbrella and the act's broad nomenclature for the "Advancement of Learning" that McGill University would be established.[13]

THE WILL AND THE COURTS

Drawn up in English in 1811 by lawyer James Stuart, McGill's will was a thirteen-page document. Reading the will, one is immediately struck by its attention to family: by one estimate, some 85 per cent of his estate was bequeathed to immediate members of his family.[14] "My dear wife Charlotte Guillimin" is mentioned six times in the will. She was to have usufruct of the McGill family home at the corner of Notre Dame Street and Place Jacques Cartier and of the Burnside summer estate (until construction of the university), and was accorded an annual annuity of £600. With the exception of his gold watch and a silver cup, she was to inherit McGill's moveable goods in their entirety, including his furniture, art works, livestock, and carriages.

His adopted stepson, described in the will as "her son Francis [*sic*] Desrivières," was named as McGill's principal heir. His name appears thirteen times, including designation as an executor and, with his nephew, as residuary legatee. This status was of critical significance in the subsequent legal struggle between university and family. For, if the will's conditions to establish a university were not fulfilled, the

Burnside property and the university start-up fund of £10,000 would revert to them. In addition to McGill's gold watch, Desrivières was to inherit the family home on the death of his mother as well as Burnside until erection of a university. At the core of his will, McGill named François Desrivières heir of his principal landed property, that is, the 32,400 acre tract in the Township of Stanbridge.[15] McGill also left him £11,000, a money bequest larger than that left to establish McGill University. As further protection, his stepson was specifically exonerated from any debts resulting from the liquidation of James and Andrew McGill & Company, a family business in which François Desrivières was a partner. The other principal family heir was grandson and namesake James McGill Trottier Desrivières. Named seven times in the will, he was to receive £5,000.

In addition to these major legacies to his immediate family, McGill's will included bequests of some £11,000 to a broad range of family members, mostly women and thereby assuring them livelihood in spinstership or widowhood. Principal among these was Charlotte Porteous, an adopted daughter who lived in the McGill household from 1785 until her death in 1812. She was bequeathed McGill's silver cup and £5,000.[16] Smaller bequests were made to Marguerite Desrivières, his daughter-in-law and the wife of François Desrivières (£500); Mrs Robert Reynolds (Thérèse Bouchette), widow of Thomas-Hippolyte Desrivières and mother of grandson James McGill Desrivières (£500); and Mrs William Hall, his wife's cousin (£250). Nor did he neglect his brother's family.[17] Friends and business partners in Montreal, Quebec, and England also received substantial bequests.[18] Several others, not explicitly family members, received minor bequests.[19] McGill made no expression of religious faith in his will and left no funeral or burial instructions. His bequests to social institutions were markedly ecumenical.[20]

Wealthy, one of Montreal's most distinguished citizens, and endowed with a strong sense of self, McGill encouraged perpetuation of his name. In his will, he imposed the condition that the university he funded was to bear his name. In the same vein, he made another bequest conditional to the taking of his name. James Cartwright, eldest son of his friend Richard Cartwright, was bequeathed tracts in six Upper Canadian townships. However, this legacy would only be delivered on condition that within two years of coming into possession of his land and tenants, James Cartwright was to "assume and take upon himself and use in all deeds and writings … the surname of McGill after his own surname and shall also take and bear the family arms of McGill as I the said James McGill do now bear." If young Cartwright did not fulfill this condition, the bequest was to revert to François Desrivières.[21]

A precise individual, McGill was surprisingly circumspect in his instructions for the university that was to bear his name. The will in fact gave no hint as to McGill's vision of higher education. Unlike, for example, American university benefactors Leland Stanford or Cornelius Vanderbilt, McGill did not establish the university during his lifetime, thus abdicating any direct role in determining its construction, religious orientation, or intellectual course.[22] The idea of establishing a university may have originated with McGill's participation on the commission examining disposition of the colony's Jesuit Estates or through urging from John Strachan.[23] McGill's instructions were brief: in return for the Burnside estate and £10,000, the trustees were to establish a university or college "for the purposes of Education and the advancement of learning in this Province with a competent number of professors and teachers to render such establishment effectual and beneficial ..."[24] Two conditions were imposed. The university was to bear his name and was to be erected within ten years of his death. Failing the deadline, the estate and the money legacy were to revert to family members named in his will as residual legatees.

McGill died 19 December 1813. In the first years after his death, his trustees were able to take little concrete action in establishing a university. For their part, the Desrivières continued to occupy the site. Until her death in April 1818, McGill's widow lived at Burnside and she was succeeded by son François Desrivières, who apparently lived there or on a nearby estate until his death in March 1830. A third generation, that of grandson Henri Desrivières, seems to have occupied Burnside into the 1830s.

The four trustees of the proposed university – different individuals from the executors of the will – gained only slow traction in establishing an institution of higher learning under the Royal Institution for the Advancement of Learning Act of 1801. For although elementary schools were opened under the legislation, formal establishment by the Crown of the Royal Institution's governing body stalled. Trustees of the Royal Institution were finally named in October 1818 and December 1819, and in August 1820 the Burnside estate was conveyed to the Royal Institution. When a Crown charter was finally accorded to McGill University on 31 March 1821, eight of the ten years stipulated in the will had passed.

The Desrivières encouraged these delays. By 1819 and in residence at Burnside, François Desrivières had begun posing legal obstacles to delivery of the Burnside estate.[25] Besides his obvious material interest in abortion of the university project, his opposition appears also have been rooted in his general suspicions as a member of the Catholic establishment of educational institutions established under the Royal Institution for the Advancement of Learning Act. Although the conflict moved rapidly to the courts, there was no evident ethnic hostility in this period between trustees and family. During the 1820s, the Desrivières continued to collaborate with Royal Institution trustees like John Richardson in elite activities such as the Lachine Canal project and as board members of the Montreal General Hospital. And, in a notable cross-cultural union in January 1820, James McGill Trottier Desrivières, French, Catholic, and a residual legatee of his grandfather's estate, married Caroline Frobisher, English and member of one of the colony's most prominent fur-trading families. [26]

By the early 1820s, trustees of the Royal Institution for the Advancement of Learning had initiated two lawsuits, one to force delivery of Burnside and the second to obtain the £10,000 bequest. In October 1822 and again in June 1823, Justice George Pyke ruled unequivocally in their favour, pointing to the sea change in willing rights accorded by the Quebec Act. Before 1774, "rule of law" under the Custom of Paris had "recognized no other heir than the héritier du sang or natural heir." These customary claims of "blood and of nature," Judge Pyke declared, had given way to an individual's "decided power" to dispose of his estate "as the owner may see fit."[27] Murray Greenwood points to these McGill lawsuits as fundamental in the deconstruction of "the linkage of family to its land," part of what he calls "the sloughing off of older concerns grounded in feudal and Roman Catholic morality, so as to promote autonomous individual will ..."[28] A law professor at McGill, Blaine Baker connected the bundle of rights around freedom of willing, freedom of land ownership, and freedom of contract, to construction of the liberal legal regime that would characterize post-Confederation Canada.[29]

Equally important in the history of the university, and in the larger history of public institutions in Quebec, was Judge Pyke's expansive interpretation of the power of a charitable or educational corporation. He accepted the Royal Institution's argument that "erection" – the term specified in James McGill's will – was not limited to a physical construction but was "equally applicable to a Corporation as to a building."[30] This broad definition was expanded in the appeal court judgment (1826). Confirming the lower court decision in favour of the Royal Institution was Judge James Kerr. Scottish born, called to the bar in England, and with reputation as an "insensitive chauvinist," Kerr was seen to have little sympathy for the "ancient law" of France.[31] Describing appellant Desrivières as "ungracious" and as the "guilt cause," he turned to English judgments concerning the Knight Templars and the Savoy Hospital as charitable corporations. These institutions, he wrote, although not actually founded or built, had through their charter "created a body politic and corporate."[32]

Denied in appeal in both of their suits, the Desrivières appealed to London and the highest court in the empire, the Judicial Committee of the Privy Council. In decisions in June 1828 and October 1835, the Desrivières lost. By then, they had surrendered the McGill estate. In 1836, Principal John Bethune seems to have moved his family into Burnside and in 1839 the cornerstone of the Arts Building was laid. By the late 1830s, the politics of nationalism had poisoned relations between the Desrivières and the English community around the university. Several Desrivières took up arms in the rebellions of 1837–38. McGill's grandson, François-Guillaume Desrivières, was imprisoned in 1837 and distant relative Rodolphe Desrivières was exiled to Bermuda.

COLONIZATION

James McGill's wealth, I have suggested, must be analyzed in the context of landed property and his estate, of which the university represented one bequest, inserted into a larger history of capitalism, colonization, and town-country relations in early nineteenth-century Quebec. The university's use of its bequest from James McGill is part then of a larger narrative that draws our attention to two generations of the Desrivières family and their utilization of James McGill's legacy in the Eastern Townships.

On his death in 1830, François-Amable Desrivières left James McGill's undeveloped and largely forested Stanbridge property to sons François-Guillaume and Henri. François-Guillaume moved to Stanbridge in 1833, began selling settlement lots, and initiated construction of a family manor house, Malmaison. In 1842, Henri, his wife Marie-Angélique Birranger dite Hay, and young son Willy left

Montreal for the McGill estate. James McGill's silver, family portraits, library, furniture, and remnants of his papers accompanied them.[33]

With the proprietors on site, colonization was rapid. The McGill property attracted settlers from bordering, overpopulated seigneuries along the Richelieu River, Irish famine immigrants, and a few Protestants of American origin from adjoining townships. This frontier demography posed issues of overlapping languages and religions and, particularly, the challenge of organizing institutions for a largely French seigneurial population in the cultural environment of freehold land tenure. Although the two brothers shared ownership, an ailing François-Guillaume left Henri Desrivières as principal promoter. At the dam and water power site adjacent to the manor house, a five-stone grist mill, sawmill (1842), tannery, and covered bridge (1843) were constructed. Logging became a major industry; in the winter of 1850 for example, 18,000 logs were drawn to the Desrivières mill and lumber yard. Enjoying prosperity, the family received its forty-five employees at their New Year's party in 1865: these included inside staff, their cook, nanny, maid, butler, and gardener, and from outside, their mill workers. By 1878, and exclusive of farmers, at least 175 people lived in the village of Malmaison working at the tannery, sawmills, or local manufactures.[34] Construction of three international railways across Desrivières lands transformed the local economy. In particular, opening of the Vermont and Montreal Junction Railway in 1864 and its "Desrivières Station," a short walk from Malmaison, brought visits from bishops, judges, and politicians.[35] Malmaison boasted an eight-acre vegetable garden, stables, a cottage, and ample meadows. Family members travelled to Montreal, Vermont, New York City, and Quebec City, and visited Frobisher, Masson, Mackenzie, or Taschereau family members in estates across Quebec.

As major landowners and local notables, but not seigneurs, the Desrivières were instrumental in the organization of local institutions. The municipality of Notre-Dame-des-Anges-de Stanbridge was established in 1848 and Henri Desrivières would serve as first mayor, first warden, and then prefect of the County of Missisquoi. His wife, Marie-Angélique Hay, was a tireless promoter of Catholic institutions. Her arrival in 1842 coincided with the establishment of a mission at Malmaison, which was elevated to parish status in 1845. She oversaw construction of a chapel in 1845 and, after its destruction by fire in 1846, its reconstruction in 1847.[36] By 1851, the parish numbered 450. Across from the manor, she organized the opening of a one-room schoolhouse (1863) and construction of a cemetery. The Desrivières enjoyed a privileged relationship with local clergy and the bishop in Saint-Hyacinthe. Doubling as parish priest and family chaplain, Abbé Bénoni Leclaire took up residence in 1847 in the Desrivières manor house, remaining there for thirty-two years.[37]

Thanks to their McGill legacy, the Desrivières prospered as landed gentry for a generation. François-Guillaume died childless in 1861, his brother, Henri, in 1865, and his wife, Marie-Angélique Hay, in 1875. Their children, Caroline and François-Guillaume (Willy), faced uncertain futures. By the 1870s, the family had subdivided and sold most of their acreage. The local economy, its agriculture and entrepreneurship, were diversifying. Industries along the Pike River – a tannery, biscuit factory, and grist mill – migrated to a better water-power site one kilometre upstream from Malmaison. It was here, in Notre-Dame-des-Anges-de-Stanbridge, that the new stone church and parish cemetery were built. Without land or profession, Caroline and Willy turned to elite marriage for livelihood. Caroline married an elderly judge, Thomas McCord, and moved to Quebec City. Willy, the great grandson of James McGill, was more problematic. Indebted, he finally married Eugénie Taschereau, daughter of a supreme court judge, and for a time, Taschereau money subsidized his horse racing and gambling. However, a fall from his horse in 1885 left him paralyzed.[38] On his death in 1893, his bankrupt widow was forced to sell Malmaison, its grounds, mill, and twenty-eight acres, all that remained of James McGill's legacy of 31,000 acres. James McGill's furniture and possessions were included with family goods sold at auction.[39]

Accompanied by her son, Henri Desrivières, Eugénie Taschereau moved back to Quebec City to lodge with her widowed sister-in-law, Caroline Desrivières. With the James McGill heritage connected to painful memory of his father's decadence and family collapse, Henri Desrivières's focus turned to the Taschereaus, and the status of his great uncle, Archbishop Elzéar-Alexandre Taschereau, and his uncle, provincial premier Louis-Alexandre Taschereau. Graced with these credentials, Henri Desrivières married into the family of Judge Auguste Tessier and his children into the prominent Beaudoin and Flynn families. Ironically, a sixth-generation descendant of James McGill's wife was Louise Beaudoin, the daughter of Judge Jean Beaudoin and of Louise Desrivières. A prominent supporter of Quebec independence, minister of culture and communications, and minister responsible for application of the Charter of the French Language, her relationship with English institutions like McGill University was frequently strained.[40] It seems that neither Beaudoin nor the university drew attention to the common connection of James McGill.

HISTORIOGRAPHY

In the study of Montreal's past by McGill academics, the 1970s and '80s were an extraordinary period. As part of his seminal study of the Indigenous peoples of Eastern Canada, and in a case study of what would become Burnside and then the McGill campus, Bruce Trigger, anthropologist at McGill, analyzed the Huron site Hochelaga.[41] In the History Department, one floor down in the Stephen Leacock Building from Anthropology, Louise Dechêne inspired a generation of graduate students in writing Quebec history. Her *Habitants et marchands de Montréal au XVIIe siècle* (1974) brought her rank as Canada's most eminent research historian.[42] In 1976, the Montreal Business History Project, a research collective on the history of Montreal, was founded in the History Department. In his study of the local trade in firewood (1988), Robert Sweeny, one of the project's founders, challenged the staple theory as the motor of Canadian history.[43] Across the period, works by McGill authors in political, legal, and gender history explored the university's history. Historian Carman Miller, for example, pointed to the complex role of Chancellor Charles Dewey Day in structuring nineteenth-century McGill University (1982).[44] In studies critical to understanding the university's particular legal history, John Brierley of the Faculty of Law analyzed Quebec's polyjural system of common and civil law (1979).[45] The emerging field of feminist history contributed to an understanding of McGill in the history of higher education. Jennifer Stoddart, a McGill graduate in law, was a member of the Collective Clio, which published the *L'Histoire des femmes au Québec depuis quatre siècles* (1982), and in the Faculty of Education, Margaret Gillett published a provocative history of women at McGill (1981).[46] Andrée Lévesque, a specialist in women's history, joined the History Department in 1984. She introduced one of Canada's first courses in the history of women and was a leader in tempering the university's pervasive male culture.[47] McGill's museums, archives, and rare book collections represented yet another aspect of the university's critical position in historical research. In 1968, for example, Stanley Triggs became curator of the university's Notman Photographic Archives, a world-class collection of 700,000 images. His commitment to making McGill collections accessible was clear: "What interests me is social history ... people."[48] The Notman Collection was lodged in the university's McCord Museum. In 1980, the university incorporated the museum as a public institution and with major help from private benefactors and state grants, the McCord Museum of Canadian History, now the McCord Stewart Museum, became emblematic of the richness of McGill's historical collections.

In this panoply on the history of Montreal and on McGill University in particular, the career of James McGill attracted only minor attention. Two MA theses, one written in 1930 and the other in 1993, treated McGill and his wife Charlotte Guillimin.[49] His biography in the *Dictionary of Canadian Biography* was written by J.I. Cooper, historian at McGill and a specialist of the history of Montreal. Published in 1983, Cooper's biography downplayed McGill's role as a fur trader, noting that his involvement in the fur trade peaked in 1782, three decades before his death. By 1790, his investment in the fur trade had fallen to £10,000, and by 1803 he had withdrawn entirely from the trade. Rather than giving importance to markets and trade in furs, Cooper emphasized McGill's significance as a land speculator, what he called "the manipulation of land," noting that his major assets were in real estate, investments in the United Kingdom, and mortgages.[50] Treating the McGill University endowment in a single paragraph, Cooper commented that James McGill was not "a theorist about education." While Cooper's biography did not mention slavery, other historians had placed James McGill among prominent Montrealers owning domestic slaves. In his *Dictionnaire des esclaves et de leurs propriétaires au Canada français* (1990), Marcel Trudel enumerated McGill's ownership of four Black and two Indigenous slaves.[51]

By the mid-1960s, McGill University had been swept into the turbulence of Quebec's Quiet Revolution, its nationalism, and its push for a strong regulatory state in education. In 1968, the Quebec government established the Conseil des universités, a challenge to the McGill vision of the university as a private and autonomous institution. The McGill français movement (1969) saw some 10,000 demonstrators at the campus's Roddick Gates demanding McGill's conversion into a French-speaking university. Ethnic turmoil intensified in the 1970s. In the debate leading to passage of the French

Language Charter (Bill 101), McGill's brief described the proposed law as "coercive" and "detrimental." Political pressures did not only emanate from without. In the Faculty of Arts, Marxist social scientists like Stanley Gray, Pauline Vaillancourt, and Marlene Dixon demanded radical reform and pummelled university administrators. Resigning in 1974, Marlene Dixon described herself as "brutalized" by "the McGill environment," its "repressive ideologies," "its corporate liberal ideology," and its "intimidation" of student leaders.[52] Over the following years, the university would face recurring public condemnation concerning racism, antisemitism, and the ethics of its military and medical research.[53]

Destabilized, McGill officials reached to history and, particularly, to the life of founder James McGill as a means of giving an ethical neoliberal anchor to the university. Lauren Berlant bitingly describes this as an institution's use of "issues of intimate life to normalize particular forms of knowledge and practice ..."[54] By 1975, the university was publicizing a timeline noting that McGill University's "long and colourful history stretches back to the birth of James McGill in 1744." In the McGill français crisis and charges that the university was an alien institution in Quebec, Vice-Principal Robert Shaw was able to draw on the founder's biculturalism: "Our interest in French Canada is not new." And countered with: "James McGill married a French Canadian."[55] As the university became less paternalistic and moved instead to neoliberal principles of competition, excellence, and research production, James McGill might stand as a model male entrepreneur who "knew that a solid amount of money and some tangible real estate could often achieve what lofty ideals can only dream."[56] In her principal's message celebrating McGill's 190th anniversary, Heather Munroe-Blum spoke to James McGill's presumed intellectual role in bringing together the ideals of the Scottish Enlightenment and the Canadian frontier. "The exploration of ideas ... and ... the serious examination of opinions running counter to one's own – was at the heart of [James McGill's] education."[57]

In 1975, the administration founded the History of McGill Project to undertake historical study on McGill University. The idea of a sponsored institutional history of McGill was sold to the board of governors by Principal Robert E. Bell. A physicist responsible for the development of nuclear research at McGill and then dean of the Faculty of Graduate Studies and Research, Bell was principal from 1970 to 1979. With several specialists in the history of Montreal and Quebec in the Department of History, Bell, in establishing the History of McGill Project, might have been expected to consult historians in his own shop, to lodge the project in the History Department, and to turn to one of the university's professional Canadian historians.[58] Surprised to learn that a history of the university was to be undertaken, History Department chair Michael Maxwell, accompanied by historians of Canada Carman Miller and John Thompson, met with Bell. They proposed funding of a ten-year graduate student project that would prepare archival and historiographical documentation for a study of the institution. Bell told them that, although sympathetic to professional historians, he had decided to use the History of McGill Project as a means of delicately removing Stanley Frost from his politically sensitive position as vice-principal, Administration.[59]

English born, with graduate degrees in divinity and title as a Methodist minister, Frost came to McGill in 1956 as professor of Old Testament studies. He served in the administration as dean of the Faculty of Divinity, dean of Graduate Studies and Research, and then as vice-principal, Administration from 1969.[60] An outspoken opponent of Quebec nationalism, Ministry of Education bureaucrats, and faculty unionism, Frost was well-known for what reformers described as his "reactionary diatribes."[61] Operating with administrative funds, independent of peer review, and publishing in-house at McGill-Queen's University Press, the History of McGill Project was housed in the university library across campus from social science departments in the Stephen Leacock Building.[62] The project's most important publications were Frost's two-volume institutional history of McGill, 1980, 1984, and his 1995 biography of James McGill.[63] The offices of the History of McGill Project also served as a wheelhouse in the promotion of the university's history. Frost was instrumental in founding the James McGill Society in 1975. Housed at the project and bringing together a broad gamut of historians, both professional and amateur, with the goal, as the society's constitution put it, "to defend and advocate on behalf of McGill University's history and heritage."[64] Frost remained director of the project until 2003 when he was replaced by Peter McNally.

In his approach to the place in Canadian history of family, gender, social class, and property, Frost's interpretation of James McGill was markedly out of step with research undertaken elsewhere in the university. Furthermore, Frost did not concur with J.I. Cooper's interpretation published three decades earlier in the *Dictionary of*

Canadian Biography. Instead, Frost integrated his James McGill into Donald Creighton's narrative of Protestant superiority and Scots entrepreneurship in the staple trades of the St Lawrence Valley.[65] The fur trade "was a new and risky venture," Frost wrote, "and those who responded were necessarily of an adventurous temperament ... They shared the freedom, the dangers, and the toil of the long canoe journey."[66] In Frost's account, the success of the founder, the university, and the host city was grounded implicitly in a shared British and Protestant culture, a common two-century destiny based implicitly on the superiority of Montreal's British and Protestant community.

Just as Principal Heather Munroe-Blum had linked James McGill to the Enlightenment and the intellectual tradition of the university, Frost telescoped the founder's entrepreneurial character with the emergence of the university's business school: "James McGill's Montreal had to be a trading city – and here in his college would emerge a fully fledged faculty of management."[67] Fundamental to this cult of a masculine and entrepreneurial vision of philanthropist and university was the disconnection of James McGill from his family. Frost wanted no part of McGill as head of a Catholic family or, as J.I. Cooper had put it, as a man "fond of children" and whose namesake, James McGill Trottier Desrivières, "would be the object of much solicitude at the end of McGill's life."[68] Frost's McGill was characterized by individualism and Protestantism, a man who "had no affectionate family to nourish his memory ... He had no children ... His wife's family, francophone and Catholic, despite being his fortunate heirs, had no natural affinity with their anglophone, Protestant benefactor, and the second and third generations quickly forgot him ..."[69]

CONCLUSION

In the past years, McGill University has undergone a complete about-face from Stanley Frost's depiction of James McGill as a one-dimensional entrepreneur who gave benevolent human face to the neoliberal university. On its website (2023), the university now points to the importance to James McGill of the Desrivières family, of his wife, and of his adopted stepsons. It is admitted that James McGill profited from an Atlantic trading system that included Caribbean slave plantations and that the university's founder owned five Black and Indigenous slaves. The university describes its own establishment as deriving in part from "James McGill's engagement in the colonial economic system and the transatlantic slave trade."[70] Faced with protests in 2021 against the evident hypocrisy of linking McGill as an ethical brand to that of a slaveowner, the university removed James McGill's front campus statue for what was described as "repair work."

This reversal points to the difficulties of assimilating the values of an eighteenth-century benefactor to those of a twenty-first-century university. McGill's political correctness in revising the history of its founder can perhaps be classified as simple cynicism and the ongoing use of history by the wily folks in university marketing. But, as we saw above, McGill University is deeply invested in academic history and in historical collections for which it acts as trustee: across multiple faculties there is research, publication, and teaching in the history of law, the history of medicine, the history of business, the history of science, and the history of architecture; the university hosts a broad range of historical collections that include the University Archives, Rare Books and Special Collections, the Osler Library of the History of Medicine, the Redpath Museum, and the McCord Stewart Museum; and, in its Faculty of Arts, the university hosts forty-seven professional historians (2023) in a thriving Department of History.[71] If the university has the will to continue subsidizing the research and writing of its own institutional history, the shape and methodology of this study must be broadened. As the university now explains on its website, James McGill and his university stand squarely as two elements in the extended history of Atlantic capitalism. The university as an institution and James McGill's career, family, capital, landed property, will, and the fate of his legacies are suggestive of interdisciplinary study – and why not by the university's own pool of specialists in law, finance, property, race, colonialism, and institutions. With increased commitment to its own rich history and to the institution's historical place in local and global communities, the university could actively intervene to protect its historical collections and to increase their access to researchers.

The histories of James McGill and of McGill University are of multilayered significance. Indeed, since the lawsuits of the 1820s over James McGill's will with their implications for the rights of the individual and corporation versus those of the customary family, the university has been a major player in the organization of civil society in Canada. And, while the university was being constructed as a Victorian institution on the grounds of James McGill's summer estate, his family, using their share of his landed property, influenced the colonization and institutional structures of a rural region in Quebec. From this perspective, James McGill and his university can be seen as part of a larger history of Quebec outside Montreal. In short, the multiple dots concerning James McGill's legacy remain to be connected.

NOTES

1 Stanley Brice Frost, *James McGill of Montreal* (Montreal and Kingston: McGill-Queen's University Press, 1995), 155.

2 Cited in Roderick MacLeod, "James McGill Monument – 1813," in *The Identity of English-Speaking Quebec in 100 Objects*, accessed c. November 2022, https://100objects.qahn.org/content/james-mcgill-monument-1813.

3 "Founder's Elm," Exhibit in the Redpath Museum, McGill University, 26 September 2016, Redpath Museum, accessed c. November 2022, https://commons.wikimedia.org/wiki/File:Founder%27s_elm,_planted_1790,_cut_down_1976_-_Redpath_Museum_-_McGill_University_-_Montreal,_Canada_-_DSC07759.jpg; "A Leafy Legacy,"' *McGill News (*Winter 2008), accessed 30 November 2024, https://mcgill-news-archives.mcgill.ca/news-archives/2001/summer/trees/index.html.

4 *McGill Reporter* (June 1996), accessed 30 November 2024, http://www.reporter-archive.mcgill.ca/Rep/r2818/garden.htm.

5 Margaret Anne Lindsay, "'Especially in this free Country': Webs of Empire, Slavery and the Fur Trade" (PhD diss., University of Manitoba, 2021), 59.

6 J.I. Cooper, "MCGILL, JAMES," in *Dictionary of Canadian Biography*, vol. 5 (University of Toronto/Université Laval, 1983), accessed 30 November 2024, https://www.biographi.ca/en/bio/mcgill_james_5E.html; Marie-Charlotte Guillimin also had two daughters, Marie-Josephe (1766) and Marie-Élizabeth (1767), both of whom apparently died before her marriage to McGill. Lynda Tanguay, "Madame James McGill (1747–1818): Marie-Charlotte Guillimin ou la vie d'une femme mondaine à Montréal au dix-huitième siècle" (MA thesis, McGill University, 1993), 98.

7 Maysie Steel MacSporran, "James McGill: A Critical Biographical Study" (MA thesis, McGill University, 1930), 306; Stanley B. Frost, "DESRIVIÈRES (Trottier Desrivières), FRANÇOIS (François-Amable, Francis) (baptized Amable-François)," in *Dictionary of Canadian Biography*, vol. 6 (University of Toronto/Université Laval, 1987), accessed 30 November 2024, https://www.biographi.ca/en/bio/desrivieres_francois_6E.html.

8 The four sons were named Jacques-François McGill Trottier Desrivières, James Frobisher McGill Desrivières, Joseph-Henri McGill Trottier Desrivières, and Théodore-Robert Roch Trottier McGill Desrivières. The Desrivières are a prominent family in the history of Quebec. In the Montreal region, their status brought marriage not only with James McGill but also into the Frobisher and Hay families. In Quebec City, their marriage alliances included the Taschereau, Tessier, Flynn, and Beaudoin families.

9 McGill University Archives, no. 1766/5/2, "Will of James McGill," 9 January 1811 (transcribed by Faith Wallis).

10 For freedom of willing in Quebec, see *André Morel, Limites de la liberté testamentaire dans le droit civil de la Province de Québec* (Paris: Libraire générale de droit et de jurisprudence, 1960).

11 *Reports of Cases Argued and Determined in the Court of King's Bench and in the Provincial Court of Appeals* (Quebec, 1834), 233–66.

12 Great Britain, 51 and 52 Vic, 1888, cap. 42, "Mortmain and Charitable Uses Act."

13 Lower Canada, 41 George III, cap.17 (1801), "An Act for the Establishment of Free Schools and the Advancement of Learning in this Province." James McGill was a member of the Legislative Assembly that passed this act.

14 Stanley Frost suggests that the endowment for the university represented one-eighth of his estate. See Frost, *James McGill of Montreal*, 154.

15 He was also to receive three lots in the Quebec suburb of Montreal, a mill in the Township of Barnston, and land on the ramparts of Montreal.

16 Her two brothers William and Andrew were each bequeathed £750. For the adoption of Charlotte Porteous, the orphan of his friend, see Lynda Tanguay, "Madame James McGill (1747–1918)," 72.

17 To fulfill the intentions of his brother's will, he set up a £7,000 trust fund to provide an annual £300 annuity for his brother's widow, Ann Wood (who had remarried with John Strachan); £50 annually for her mother, May Wood, as well as an annual annuity of £50 for her upkeep at the General Hospital of Quebec; and £20 annually for Agnes Craig of Glasgow.

18 James Cartwright, £250; John Porteous of Montreal, £250; John Brickwood of Croydon, England, £1,000; "my friend Robert Morrogh of Quebec," £1,000; and his children Robert and Mary Ann, each £250; Thomas Blackwood of Montreal, £500; Benjamin Beaubien of Montreal, £250.

19 Mrs Richardson, "wife of hospital inmate Mr. Richardson," £250; Miss Lisette Dumuesseau of Sault St Louis, £20 "annual annuity"; Sophia Réaume, "wife of Dezery," £150; Louisa Sutherland, daughter of Daniel Sutherland of Montreal, £150; servant Marie Marguerite Fouquet, £150;

Pierre Goulet, £100; "my godson" James Hamilton, £250; James Dunlop of Montreal, £25; John Gillespie of London, £25.

20 He bequeathed £200 to the poor Protestants of Montreal and "a like sum" to the poor Roman Catholics. He left £200 for the Hôtel-Dieu Hospital in Montreal and a similar amount to the Grey Nuns orphanage. He gave £200 to the Infirmary of Glasgow and £200 to the Asylum of Glasgow.

21 In October 1811, and before receiving his heritage, James Cartwright apparently died. "James Cartwright (abt. 1786–abt. 1811), WikiTree, accessed 30 November 2024, https://www.wikitree.com/wiki/Cartwright-2712.

22 In memory of his son, Leland Stanford established Stanford University in 1885 and it opened in 1891; he died in 1893. Vanderbilt University was established in 1873 and Cornelius Vanderbilt died in 1877.

23 G.M. Craig, "STRACHAN, JOHN," in *Dictionary of Canadian Biography*, vol. 9 (University of Toronto/Université Laval, 1976), accessed 30 November 2024, https://www.biographi.ca/en/bio/strachan_john_9E.html. Then an Anglican clergyman in Upper Canada, founder of the Cornwall Grammar School, and advocate of colleges that might train an Anglican elite, Strachan married Ann Wood, widow of James McGill's brother Andrew. Although named in the will as one of four trustees of the proposed university, Strachan does not appear to have been a force in the university's early history. The other trustees were John Richardson, James Reid, and James Dunlop.

24 "Will of James McGill," 12.

25 MacLeod, "James McGill Monument – 1813."

26 Their son James Frobisher Desrivières (b. 1832) would perpetuate the McGill name in two of his children, James McGill Desrivières and Louise Henriette McGill Desrivières.

27 "On Appeal from Montreal," François Desrivières Appellant and the Hon. John Richardson and others, Respondents, *Report of Cases argued and determined in the Court of King's Bench and in the Provincial Court of Appeals (Stuart's Reports) (Quebec: 1834)* 218–41; Frost notes that although Judge Louis-Charles Foucher heard the case with Pyke, the written judgment was by Pyke. See Frost, *McGill University: for the Advancement of Learning, Volume I, 1801–1895* (Montreal and Kingston: McGill-Queen's University Press, 1980), 53.

28 Murray Greenwood, "Lower Canada (Quebec): Transformation of Civil Law, from Higher Morality to Autonomous Will, 1774–1866," *Manitoba Law Journal* 132 (1995): 135, https://www.canlii.org/en/commentary/doc/1995CanLIIDocs135#!fragment, accessed 30 November 2024.

29 Cory Verbauwhede, "The Camel's Nose in the Constitutional Tent: Extrapolating from G. Blaine Baker's Thoughts on Late Nineteenth-Century Legal Liberalism and Elite Lawyer Resistance to the Canadian Welfare State," in *Law, Life, and the Teaching of Legal History: Essays in Honour of G. Blaine Baker*, eds Ian G. Pilarczyk, Angela Fernandez, and Brian Young (Montreal and Kingston: McGill-Queen's University Press, 2022), 464–5.

30 "On Appeal from Montreal," François Desrivières Appellant and the Hon. John Richardson and other, Respondents, *Report of Cases argued and determined in the Court of King's Bench and in the Provincial Court of Appeals (Stuart's Reports) (Quebec: Neilson & Cowan, 1834)*, 218–41.

31 Greenwood, "Transformation of Civil Law," 146.

32 Greenwood, "Transformation of Civil Law."

33 W.D. Lighthouse, "The Newly-Discovered 'James and Andrew McGill Journal, 1797,'" *Transactions of the Royal Society of Canada* 29, section 2 (1935), 43.

34 Marie-Angélique Hay, wife of Henri, kept a detailed diary for thirty years. Digitalized, the twenty-volume diary is held at McGill's Rare Book Room and in the McCord Museum of Canadian History. Entries for 8 March 1850, 1 January 1865.

35 The Stanbridge area was also served by the Portland and Boston Railway and the Lake Champlain and St Lawrence Junction Railway.

36 For the history of Malmaison and Notre-Dame-de-Stanbridge, see Jef Asnong, *Chronique de Pike River* (Brome-Missisquoi: La Soleillée, 2007); Abbé Isidore Desnoyers, *Histoire de la Paroisse Notre-Dame-des-Anges-de-Stanbridge, étude manuscrite* 1885 (Centre d'archives, Diocèse de Saint-Hyacinthe).

37 See Marie-Angélique Hay diary, multiple entries concerning Bénoni Leclaire and Église de Notre-Dame-des-Anges; "La famille Des Rivières-McGill," *Le Saint-Armand* 17, 3 (December 2019–January 2020), accessed 30 November 2024, https://journalstarmand.com/la-famille-des-rivieres-mcgill/.

38 *Bedford Times* (March 1893).

39 *Bedford Times*, n.d.; Lighthouse, "The Newly-Discovered 'James and Andrew McGill Journal, 1797,'" 43.

40 Martin Patriquin, "Louise Beaudoin (Interview)," in *The Canadian Encyclopaedia*, 15 December 2013, accessed 30 November 2024, https://www.thecanadianencyclopedia.ca/en/article/louise-beaudoin-interview.

41 Bruce Trigger and J.F. Pendergast, *Cartier's Hochelaga and the Dawson Site* (Montreal and Kingston: McGill-Queen's University Press, 1972).

42 Louise Dechêne, *Habitants et marchands de Montréal au XVIIe siècle* (Paris: Plon, 1974).

43 Robert Sweeny, *Les relations ville/campagne: Le cas du bois de chauffage* (Montreal: Groupe de recherche sur les milieux d'affaires de Montréal, 1988).

44 Carman Miller, "DAY, CHARLES DEWEY," in *Dictionary of Canadian Biography*, vol. 11 (University of Toronto/Université Laval, 1982), accessed 30 November 2024, https://www.biographi.ca/en/bio/day_charles_dewey_11E.html. See also Carman Miller, John Bland, Bruce Anderson, *A History of the McGill Faculty Club* (Montreal and Kingston: McGill-Queen's University Press, 1975).

45 John E.C. Brierley, "The Co-Existence of Legal Systems in Quebec: 'Free and Common Soccage' in Canada's 'pays de droit civil,'" *Les Cahiers de Droit* 20, nos 1–2 (1979): 277–87.

46 Micheline Dumont, Marie Lavigne, Michèle Jean, Jennifer Stoddart, *L'histoire des femmes au Québec depuis quatre siècles* (Montreal: Quinze, 1982); Gillett, *We Walked Very Warily: A History of Women at McGill* (Montreal: Eden Press, 1981).

47 For an example of Lévesque's early work, see *Virage à gauche interdit. Les communistes, les socialistes et leurs ennemis au Québec*, 1929–1939 (Montreal: Boréal, 1984).

48 George W. Lyon, "Stanley G. Triggs, Accompanying himself …," *Canadian Folk Music Bulletin* 30, no. 1 (1996): 6–8, accessed 30 November 2024, https://cfmb.icaap.org/content/30.1/BV30-1art3.pdf.

49 Macsporran, "James McGill"; Tanguay, "Madame James McGill."

50 Cooper, "MCGILL, JAMES."

51 Marcel Trudel, *Dictionnaire des esclaves et de leurs propriétaires au Canada français* (Lasalle, Quebec: Hurtubise HMH, 1990).

52 Marlene Dixon, *Things Which Are Done in Secret* (Montreal: Black Rose Books, 1976), 13, 29, 31; Stanley Gray, "Bienvenue à McGill," reprinted in the McGill *Student Handbook* (1969).

53 See for example, Pierre Anctil, *Le rendezvous manqué. Les Juifs de Montréal face au Québec de l'entre-deux-guerres* (Quebec City: IQUC, 1988); Dale Grant, *Wilderness of Mirrors: The Life of Gerald Bull* (Toronto: Prentice-Hall, 1991); Anne Collins, *In the Sleep Room: The Story of CIA Brainwashing Experiments in Canada* (Toronto: Key Porter Books, 1988).

54 Cited in Ann Brooks, *Genealogies of Emotions, Intimacies, and Desire Theories of Changes in Emotional Regimes from Medieval Society to Late Modernity* (New York and London: Routledge, 2017).

55 McGill *Student Handbook*, 24 March 1969, cited in Dixon, *Things Which Are Done in Secret*, 29.
56 Frost, *James McGill of Montreal*, 110.
57 McGill University, *Principal's Report* 2010–2011, accessed 30 November 2024, http://www.kiyokogotanda.com/uploads/2/1/9/8/21989822/princreport11_web_en.pdf.
58 The university hired four Canadianist historians in the years preceding foundation of the History of McGill Project: Carman Miller (1971), John Thompson (1971), Louise Dechêne (1973), and Richard Rice (1973).
59 Email, Carman Miller to author, 20 April 2022.
60 "Obituary of Stanley B. Frost," *McGill Reporter*, 30 July 2013, accessed 30 November 2024, https://reporter.mcgill.ca/stanley-b-frost-1913-2013/.
61 Dixon, *Things Which Are Done in Secret*, 37.
62 "The History of McGill Project," accessed 30 November 2024, https://historyofmcgillproject.mcgill.ca/about.html#.
63 Frost also published a biography of McGill principal F. Cyril James: *The Man in the Ivory Tower: Cyril James of McGill* (Montreal and Kingston: McGill-Queen's University Press, 1991).
64 "Constitution of the James McGill Society," accessed 30 November 2024, https://www.mcgill.ca/jms/files/jms/jms-constitution-20141117.pdf.
65 See Donald Creighton, *The Empire of the St. Lawrence* (Toronto: Macmillan, [1937] 1956); Donald Wright, *Donald Creighton: A Life in History* (Toronto: University of Toronto Press, 2015).
66 Frost, *McGill University*, 1:3–5.
67 Frost, *James McGill of Montreal*, 155.
68 Cooper, "MCGILL, JAMES."
69 Stanley Brice Frost, "'Much Given to Reading': A Literary Footnote on James McGill," *Fontanus* 9 (1996): 10.
70 "Who was James McGill? James McGill 1744–1813," McGill University website, accessed June 2023, https://www.mcgill.ca/about/history/who-was-james-mcgill.
71 McGill University, Department of History and Classical Studies website, accessed 20 June 2023, https://www.mcgill.ca/history/people-0/faculty-members; for the university's historical collections, see the *Report of the Heritage Advisory Committee* (2010), accessed 30 November 2024, https://www.mcgill.ca/historicalcollections/.

4

"To Relieve It from Present Embarrassments"

Fiduciary Colonialism in Service to McGill College

BRIAN GETTLER

In early March 1860, the chancellor and Board of Governors of McGill College sent a petition soliciting material support to the governor general of British North America. "Your Memorialists can only look to the Government, and the Provincial Parliament," they wrote, as they were in "absolute need of the Grant of a sum of not less than £10,000 for this Year to be applied towards the payment of the debt and the erection of buildings, and a sum of £1000 Yearly afterwards to enable them to meet the necessary expenditure in carrying on with efficiency the business of the University."[1] The Province of Canada, the colony made up of Upper and Lower Canada, what today are the southern portions of Ontario and Quebec respectively, concurred with McGill College, providing a loan later that same year for $40,000, the amount requested.[2] It did not do so, however, from its own funds, but from monies belonging to First Nations for which it had only just become responsible. In financing a loan in this way, politicians took advantage of the colony's position as trustee to save a cash-strapped settler institution despite questionable legality and little apparent reason to believe that the investment would yield financial returns for the trust.

Unlike many other institutions of higher learning in North America and throughout the British imperial world in the nineteenth century, McGill in 1860 was not a "land-grab university" – that is, it was not an institution "built not just *on* Indigenous land, but *with* Indigenous land." In the United States, these institutions, commonly called "land-grant universities," were, and in many cases still are, funded under the Morrill Act (1862) with endowments of land far larger and situated over a much wider geographical region than the relatively small area occupied by campuses. Universities that benefited from such endowments sold or leased lands in order to meet operating costs.[3] While less widespread, funding universities in this way in what is now Canada was not unheard of in the nineteenth century. In 1828, for example, King's College, precursor to the University of Toronto, received roughly 225,000 acres as material support from the money-poor but land-rich colony of Upper Canada. Historian Caitlin Harvey notes that the Board of Governors of McGill College yearned for similar treatment. They not only wanted the material support provided by monetary grants, they also "craved for McGill ... the perception of permanence that land offered."[4] In their 1860 petition, college officials made this explicit when asking the province to provide "such portion of the Public Lands as will form a permanent endowment sufficient for its future maintenance upon an extended scale of usefulness." The chancellor and board of governors portrayed the college as having been unfairly excluded from the benefits of the School Act of 1801. This law – under which the body that would oversee McGill College, the Royal Institution for the Advancement of Learning, received its letters patent in 1818 – promised funding for education from the revenues of "a suitable proportion of the lands of the Crown."[5] In light of this law, McGill claimed it deserved a land endowment at least as much as the University of Toronto did.

In 1860, the college's leadership made this argument while in an unenviable financial position. Established in 1821 with support from the estate of wealthy Montreal merchant and slaveholder James McGill, the college had long faced financial uncertainty, particularly from the mid-1840s.[6] When it appointed William Dawson its fifth principal in 1855, McGill's affairs were in a sorry state. The new principal discovered that getting to the college required climbing a "circuitous and ungraded cart-track, almost impassable at night" from the city of Montreal. Having done this, one came upon "two blocks of unfurnished and partly ruinous buildings" surrounded by unfenced grounds "pastured at will by herds of cattle" that passed for campus.[7] Over the Christmas holidays following his appointment, the principal travelled to Toronto to lobby Governor General Edmund Walker Head and the provincial secretary for Canada East, George-Étienne Cartier.[8] While unsuccessful in securing a grant for McGill, the trip allowed Dawson to reconnect with Head, one of those who recommended he be appointed principal, and to make the acquaintance of Cartier, a key politician in what would become Quebec until his death in 1873.[9] Dawson would call on these and other influential officials to provide funding through the 1850s and 1860s as Confederation drew nearer then passed and as he found increasingly worrisome the prospect of having to rely for support on the francophone-dominated assembly of the Province of Quebec.[10] Dawson and many of his colleagues were convinced that McGill could only secure equitable treatment through the Crown, the one actor they felt might adequately support an English-language college in Quebec. That an anglophone institution should be motivated to seek the Crown's assistance due to the perceived hostility of one ethnic minority and that support should ultimately arrive via executive appropriation of property belonging to several Indigenous nations is more than mere irony.

Although the 1860 petition argues that McGill was underfunded, the college received financial support that was comparable to and perhaps more generous than that received by francophone institutions of higher learning at the time.[11] However, the land endowment the college's leadership so desired had seemed wholly unlikely since at least the 1830s. In 1838, in the aftermath of armed rebellion sparked in part by perceived imperial overreach, a commission of inquiry into education in Canada found that the imperial Crown would never establish a permanent endowment because doing so would be "viewed with great jealousy by the Provincial Government." Rather than set aside lands for the college, the commissioners felt that the assembly would be a better source of support. Elected officials, however, proved far less accommodating than McGill would have liked, with the Assembly of the Province of Canada only providing financial support from the mid-1850s.[12] In 1854, the colony granted the college $8,000 towards the construction of a new building and a further $2,000 for general expenditures.[13] Two years later, the assembly created the Fund for Superior Education in Lower Canada from the Jesuit Estates, which gave the superintendent of education monies to distribute on the basis of number of students to high schools, academies, *collèges classiques*, and universities.[14] Officials at McGill continued to complain that funding was insufficient, however, with Dawson claiming in the mid-1860s that "all the moneys received by [the college] from public sources ... do not amount to one-fourth of the annual revenues of the University of Toronto, or one-tenth of the value of Mr. McGill's bequest."[15]

In addition to state support, however, McGill could also draw on a community of wealthy, English-speaking benefactors in Montreal who, from the second half of the nineteenth century, proved perfectly willing to provide funding for the university.[16] The first major private donation since James McGill's initial bequest came in 1860 when John, Thomas, and William Molson gave $20,000 – a sum they later doubled – to support the construction of a new wing for the Arts Building.[17] While most likely solicited from an earlier date, the Molsons' gift only arrived several months after the Province of Canada had approved McGill's request for a $40,000 loan.

Loans provided the final source of monies from which the college benefited during the period. In the years immediately following McGill's founding, state and college officials considered seeking significant advances on public funds on a number of occasions, though these projects ultimately amounted to nothing.[18] From the 1850s, however, McGill contracted a number of debts beginning with a $12,000 loan in 1853 from William Forsyth Grant, a former Quebec merchant, then residing in Scotland. This was the maximum amount the college could borrow under legislation then in effect.[19] Four years later, the assembly raised the ceiling on McGill's debt to $20,000.[20] Once this modification had been made, Chancellor Charles Dewey Day requested that the province provide $8,000 to help pay for the reconstruction of a building destroyed by fire in February 1856.[21] Cartier, who as attorney general of Canada East likely authored the updated loan legislation, recommended the colony advance this amount for a period of three years from "funds now or hereafter to be available for investment as the proceeds of the sale of public lands made to raise an income for Common School Education" or from "the Consolidated Revenue Fund."[22] While the province granted this loan at 6 per cent annual interest, it rapidly became apparent once again that the college's needs were greater than the amount it had borrowed.[23]

In February 1860, Chancellor Day travelled to Quebec to meet Governor Head in an attempt to secure more permanent funding for McGill. Day reported to Dawson that while Head "seemed disposed to interest himself in the matter," the governor "suggested the difficulty of singling out one Institution for Endowment when there are so many claimants." At their meeting, the chancellor presented copies of correspondence from the 1810s between then Colonial Secretary Bathurst and the duke of Richmond, the governor general, "authorizing the erection of Buildings out of the fund of the Jesuit Estates." Head then directed his civil secretary, Richard Theodore Pennefather, "to see if he could find those dispatches."[24] This may have been a critical meeting for what was to come, not only because Day presented evidence suggesting that high-ranking officials in the colonies and the metropole had favoured using the properties seized from the Jesuit Order following the Conquest to fund McGill at the outset, but also because Pennefather, who held the position of superintendent general of Indian Affairs as well, was in the room to hear it.

During his term as superintendent, Pennefather challenged standard practice when it came to investment from the Indian Fund. Shortly after taking over the position, he explained to the governor that these Indigenous-owned monies should be managed "as the proceeds of a private property to which the Government acts as Trustee." Pennefather argued that the colony's practice of using the Fund to support its institutions "inflicts great injury upon the Indian interests" and he insisted that "the Indians have a strong equitable claim against the Government for compensation on account of the loss sustained by the misapplication of their Funds."[25] Pennefather explicitly reminded Head of the English law of equity under which trustees had the obligation to invest funds in their care according to the principle of safety. A trust that declined in value could be taken as evidence that trustees had failed to respect this principle and were thus in breach of their duty.[26]

Settler misuse of First Nations' monies had a long history by this point, perhaps most notoriously in the investment of Haudenosaunee funds in the Grand River Navigation Company. In 1834 and 1835 alone, the three settlers who acted as trustees for the Haudenosaunee, also known as the Six Nations of the Grand River, pledged roughly $148,000 to acquire a three-quarters stake in the company. By 1838, the company's shares were recognized as virtually worthless.[27] Nevertheless, the trustees continued to make instalment payments on the stock and even purchased a few extra shares. By 1858, they had sunk $153,025 belonging to the Haudenosaunee in the company, an amount equivalent to more than 10 per cent of total Indian Fund investment at that point.[28] This case is an example of what historian of the United States Emilie Connolly calls "fiduciary colonialism" – "a mode of territorial acquisition and population management carried out through the expansion of administrative control over Native peoples' wealth."[29] While Pennefather challenged the worst forms of the practice, he did not call into question the use of Indigenous funds to support settler institutions that is typical of fiduciary colonialism.

The impending transfer to colonial control of the Indian Fund coincided with a notable shift in the management of the monies it held, of which the McGill loan is illustrative. However, the Province of Canada had first taken steps to use the Indian Fund to prop up a colonial institution several months earlier. In August 1859, six months before Day travelled to Quebec to meet the governor, Thomas Blackwell, the vice-president of the Grand Trunk Railway, wrote to Pennefather to suggest an investment since he "understood that it is in the contemplation of the government to recommend to parliament a different disposition of the funds held on account of the Indian tribes." As the company worked to complete the Victoria Bridge, Blackwell proposed taking on the Indian Fund's investment portfolio in exchange for the Grand Trunk's "bonds of the city of Toronto for £100,000, as well as a large amount of second preference bonds and other securities of undoubted character, which they are desirous to delay placing in the London market until the completion of the undertaking shall have given the company the benefit of the increased traffic which will undoubtedly immediately arise." In other words, the Grand Trunk wanted to avoid liquidating at a loss various securities it held. Blackwell offered to redirect the money the province paid the Grand Trunk for carrying mail to the Indian Fund until the debt was repaid.[30] Despite clear and longstanding evidence that the Grand Trunk offered little prospect for profit, the government adopted an order in council approving the proposal.[31]

While the vice-president of the Grand Trunk made the request for support, one of three ministers had informed Blackwell that Canada was planning "a different disposition" of the Indian Fund. From the sources, this was most likely the inspector general (finance minister), Alexander Tilloch Galt, who had been involved in the Grand Trunk's 1852 incorporation, had business dealings with it on multiple occasions, and clearly pursued policy that was favourable to the railway.[32] Beyond ensuring significant personal profit, Galt's pro-company stance was designed to ensure Montreal's role as the hub through which British goods, capital, and migrants would flow into the North American West.[33] Moreover, one of the other members of government with close ties to the railway later referred to the use of the Indian Fund explicitly as Galt's plan.[34] Cartier was another possibility. He was the Grand Trunk's legal advisor for Canada East since 1853 and, while not deeply involved in the company's financial management, he and Macdonald, his co-premier, were aware of its plans with respect to securities from June 1859 and took part in approving the Indian Fund-based financing scheme in August.[35] The final minister, John Ross, was not only Canada's receiver general; he was also the president of the Grand Trunk. Ross was absent, however, from the meeting of the Executive Council that authorized the scheme, and in the weeks that followed he seemed to prefer funding the railway from a different source than the Indian Fund.[36]

Whoever the driving force in government was, the plan to use the Indian Fund to support the Grand Trunk was unravelling by the end of September. Ross, in London to meet with the railway's main commercial underwriters – the merchant bankers Thomas Baring and George Carr Glyn – provided Galt with the details of a different funding scheme both he and the company's financial backers preferred, one that "is defensible in every shape *which your Indian arrangement is not*."[37] Shortly thereafter, Galt communicated to Baring the government's decision to pull the plug on the plan. He asked that the securities earmarked for transfer to the Grand Trunk "be returned to the Indian fund and the Order in Council based upon Mr. Blackwell's letter, rescinded."[38] When the Grand Trunk scheme fell through, the capital it was to have used became available for investment in McGill College.

McGill's involvement with fiduciary colonialism stems from the intense lobbying effort it launched with Day's February 1860 trip to Quebec. It continued with the petition the chancellor and board of governors sent in early March to the governor. Chancellor Day added a personal note in a cover letter for the petition, requesting that the provincial secretary exert his "friendly cooperation in promoting the object of it."[39] This was McGill's preferred option – a grant of funds or, better yet, an endowment of land. Still, if this proved impossible, the college would need other resources to stay afloat. To this end, Day informed Galt in a separate letter written the same day that, "the Governors would be pleased to obtain an advance of £10,000 upon such security as may be deemed Satisfactory."[40] Over a period of only a few weeks, the chancellor met with the governor to solicit assistance, submitted a written petition to make the case, and corresponded with the minister who controlled the public purse. He would continue to make use of his access to the halls of power when, at the end of March, Day met with George-Étienne Cartier, who by this point was leading the government of the Province of Canada alongside John A. Macdonald. Once more, Day pressed the college's case for financial assistance. However, it had become apparent that McGill would not receive a grant. As a result, the chancellor adjusted his efforts to focus on securing a loan of $40,000 while increasing the annual payment made by the superintendent of education to cover the interest on this loan.[41]

In June 1860, Galt formalized the government's support for the loan. He told the other members of the Executive Council that it would be "desirable" to relieve McGill in this way "from present embarrassments." The loan would not pose any risk, according to Galt, since "ample security can be given upon the landed estates of the Institution." Suggesting that Day had succeeded in the effort to increase the funds the government already supplied McGill each year, Galt noted that "the Interest on the loan can be further secured by a transfer of the annual appropriation from the Superior Education Fund, or so much thereof as may be necessary." Once McGill provided such security "to the Satisfaction of the Law Offices of the Crown," Galt recommended extending "a loan to the University of $40,000 from the uninvested monies belonging to the Indian Fund." Galt's recommendation was adopted under a 14 June 1860 order-in-council.[42]

This was the first time any participant in this conversation mentioned the Indian Fund in writing. However, the government was already well aware of these monies. A month earlier, on 19 May 1860, the governor reserved for royal assent An Act Respecting the Management of Indian Lands and Property. The law gave the governor in council the discretion to determine "how, and in what manner, and by whom, the moneys arising from sales of Indians Lands, and from the property held or to be held in trust for the Indians, shall be invested." In this sense, the terms of the McGill loan respected the law. However, the 1860 law did not receive royal assent until 30 June 1860, over two weeks after the order-in-council authorizing the loan. Moreover, the governor did not proclaim the law in the *Canada Gazette* until 13 October 1860, a full four months after the order-in-council authorizing the loan.[43]

When submitting the Indian Lands Management Act, the governor asked that it be given royal sanction as quickly as possible to ensure the smooth transfer of the Indian Department along with the administration of Indigenous lands and monies from the imperial to the colonial state, planned for 1 July 1860.[44] The bill was first introduced to the Legislative Council on 16 April by Philip VanKoughnet, the commissioner of Crown lands who, after the department shifted to colonial jurisdiction, was to become the chief superintendent of Indian Affairs.[45] At the precise moment, then, that the provincial government was considering a $40,000 loan to McGill, the assembly adopted a law giving it authority over the Indian Fund. In other words, while college leadership repeatedly pressed for public support, the Province of Canada initiated the use of the Indian Fund to this end. Moreover, it did so via an order-in-council before it technically had the right to do so.

After the Executive Council approved the loan in June, a Montreal notary worked for months in collaboration with McGill's board of governors and elected officials to hash out the details of the $40,000 loan.[46] This once more included Cartier, with Day promising "to hunt him & the other gouvernmentals until the tedious business is accomplished."[47] The loan was formally contracted by a second notary on 12 December 1860 and adhered to the terms set out in the order-in-council adopted in June that authorized the transaction.[48]

A week after the contract was signed, the monies were debited from the Indian Fund. McGill received the $40,000 from nine different First Nations accounts. Almost all of it – 91.3 per cent – arose from the sale of dispossessed lands in what is now Ontario, with the remaining amount originating in lands in Quebec. The Moravians of the Thames, whose account supplied $10,000, were the single largest contributor at a full 25 per cent, with Six Nations providing the third most at $8,000, or 20 per cent of the total. Five other accounts bore $1,000 or more each for a total of $21,640.16, or 54 per cent of the total loan. The largest of these, and the second in value overall, was the $9,504.78 from the Indian Land Management Fund, a collection of monies created by charging 10 per cent on all land sales for the purpose of covering the Indian Department's day-to-day expenses.[49] The remaining $359.84 – less than 0.1 per cent of the loan – was charged to two accounts, both belonging to communities in Lower Canada: Kanesetake ($345.44) and Odanak ($14.40).[50] In January, the Receiver General's Office produced a "Statement of Indian Investments" showing these investments had grown by $42,000 over the preceding year.[51] In other words, 95 per cent of Indian Fund monies invested in 1860 went to McGill.

The story of the loan has been told at and around McGill for years. Perhaps the most widely circulated version holds that the university never repaid the loan. While this has sparked interest among students and has contributed to at least one lawsuit from the Six Nations of the Grand River seeking repayment, the history of the loan has received virtually no scholarly attention.[52] McGill's administration, for its part, has repeatedly denied the claim it owes First Nations anything as a result of the loan. In this case, the university appears to be correct, even if it has never provided a convincing demonstration itself. The explanation comes down to an 1861 change in policy that, while not settling McGill's debt, did transfer it from the Indian Fund to the Province of Canada.

In January 1861, less than a month after the transfer of funds, the Executive Council moved to put an end to the system of investment that had allowed for the McGill loan. It passed an order-in-council declaring that, from the end of the calendar year, the receiver general would "assume for account of the Province all the Investments which he may hold for account of the Indian Department," dealing with them and all cash balances "as the Investments &c belonging to other Special or Trust Funds." This was to be done following norms established in November 1859 for the management of all of the trust funds for which Canada was responsible with the exception, at the time, of the Indian Fund.[53] In other words, rather than making discrete investments as had been done until that point, the Province of Canada would "grant annuities charged on the Consolidated Revenue." The idea was to avoid the possibility that different securities, attributed to different First Nations accounts, might return different rates of interest while also ending the risk of questionable investment that might lead to a "loss to the Trust, as has already occurred in the case of the Grand River Navigation stock." While the Executive Council first outlined these changes in August 1859, they were not implemented until 1861.[54]

While no single document demonstrates on its own the restoration of capital to First Nations accounts, that this did indeed occur is suggested by several disparate pieces of evidence. First, the ledgers of the Indian Department include entries detailing both the withdrawal of a total of $40,000 from the several accounts mentioned above in December 1860 and the deposit of identical sums back into those same accounts on 31 October 1861. The department, for example, charged the account of the Abenakis of Odanak $14.40 on 20 December 1860 before crediting it the same amount on 31 October 1861. The ledger describes the first of these transactions as "Amount paid Hon. Chas. D. Day acc. Of loan to McGill College, Montreal" and the second as "transferred from Investments."[55] In the decades that followed, no deduction of this amount would occur, which suggests that the 1861 credit was not an error but was in fact the reimbursement of the amount provided to McGill.[56] Furthermore, once the sum had been restored to the Abenakis, it produced interest as part of the community's capital account.[57]

This analysis applies to each of the other eight Indian Fund accounts that financed the McGill loan. For example, the Moravians of the Thames, the community that contributed the most to McGill, had funds placed in other investments when the Indian Department moved to the model of paying 6 per cent annual interest into the Indian Fund from the consolidated revenues of the province. In October 1861, the department credited their account a total of $17,100 "transferred from Investments," an amount that included $7,100 in other investments along with the $10,000 loaned ten months earlier to McGill.[58] The comparatively complicated case of Six Nations, where the funds loaned to McGill ($8,000) formed only a small fraction of all investments transferred to their land account in the Indian Fund in 1861 ($625,234.25), shows the same pattern.[59] The books of the Indian Department make it clear that the full amount taken for the McGill loan was restored to the Six Nations' account on 31 October.[60]

Other evidence that the debt had been transferred from the Indian Fund to the province is found in correspondence from Canadian financial authorities. In April 1862, nearly six months after the accounts in the Indian Fund were credited with the exact amount they contributed, the deputy receiver general made the loan's home clear for the superintendent general of Indian Affairs. "The Bond [from McGill] belongs to the Recr. General … it was *lent* to the Indian Dept. by me, and now I want it back."[61] Documents produced in the context of arbitration between Quebec, Ontario, and the Dominion of Canada over the state of public finances immediately after Confederation suggest the same reading. In late 1868, the auditor general, John Langton, who had held the same post in the Province of Canada from 1855, described the 1857 and 1860 loans as McGill College's "debt to the late Province," all of which had been "transferred to [the] Consolidated Fund Investment Account."[62] Langton characterized the loans to McGill as "doubtful" and treated them, along with a handful of other assets on the Dominion's books, "in the same way as the Railway Debts." Since the value of these could not be gauged "with any accuracy," Langton simply wrote them off.[63] Two months later, the minister of finance in the new Dominion, John Rose, would echo Langton's analysis.[64]

Between December 1860, when the debt was contracted, and October 1861, when it was transferred from the Indian Fund to the province, the loan generated interest at an annual rate of 6 per cent. For the smallest account, the Abenakis of Odanak, this totaled $0.43 paid for the six-month period through 30 June 1861 and the same amount again for 1 July through 31 December 1861.[65] The other accounts received interest payments at the same rate, though given their more diversified investment portfolios, the amount arising from the McGill loan is included with interest earned on other investments, making these cases less straightforward than that of the Abenakis.[66] In an April 1861 letter to the auditor general, the Indian Department's accountant confirms this reading of the departmental ledgers, noting that the Receiver General's Office held nearly $1.2 million of invested Indian Fund capital, including "the loan to McGill College ... upon which interest has been paid to the 31st Decr. 1860."[67] While the capital invested produced interest, it is unclear whether any of this money came from McGill itself or whether it was simply paid by the province from its revenues or withheld from the province's Grant for Superior Education.[68]

McGill's ledgers, like Chancellor Day and the board of governors, all indicate that the university repaid the loan in full under an agreement with the Dominion of Canada signed 17 June 1873. In Day's words, "The Government discharged and released the Royal Institution from its indebtedness for the sum of $40,000."[69] This aligns with correspondence found in the archives of the Department of Indian Affairs. In May 1873, Senator James Ferrier, former president and then member of the Board of Governors of McGill University, forwarded the notarized agreement discharging McGill from the $40,000 loan to the Department of Justice.[70] Under the agreement, the university was to repay $28,000 while also transferring to the Dominion Montreal's Crystal Palace, built on college property to host an exhibition in 1860. While the title to the building had been involved in ongoing legal disputes since its construction that year, the Crystal Palace itself was valued at $12,000, meaning that McGill did indeed reimburse the $40,000 it had borrowed thirteen years earlier.[71]

Although I have not found a copy of the agreement, the deputy minister of justice referred in 1877, as Day had done a few years earlier, to "a release & discharge dated 17th June 1873 from Her Majesty to the Royal Institution for the Advancement of Learning."[72]

In the words of William Dawson's biographers, by the late 1860s "McGill College had become a thriving, steadily growing institution, which was beginning to make a name for itself in eastern North America."[73] This had much to do with the loan it received from the Province of Canada. States throughout the English-speaking world gave endowments to institutions of higher learning consisting of dispossessed Indigenous lands. Although its administration desperately wanted and felt that it failed to receive similar treatment, McGill's loan was not so different from these other arrangements. While the Province of Canada did not grant the college ownership of the $40,000, but only lent it, the sum itself was generated by the sale of dispossessed Indigenous lands. Moreover, these monies did not belong to the colony, but were only administered by it. In this sense, the McGill loan is a clear example of fiduciary colonialism, one in which provincial authorities used their newfound control of First Nations financial resources to prop up an ailing colonial institution. They did this, as trustees had done for centuries, without consulting the Indigenous nations whose property was invested.[74] While McGill's use of the Indian Fund was of short duration and was proposed by elected rather than the college officials, this case should serve as an indication that we need to examine more than just the land on which settler institutions are built. We also need to consider the ways in which Indigenous lands and resources, spread over the entire continent, were financialized as a means of supporting the settler nations and states born of colonialism.[75]

NOTES

1 Memorial of the Governors of McGill College to Sir Edmund Walker Head, s.d. [8 March 1860], Library and Archives Canada (hereafter LAC), RG4-C1, vol. 747, no. 497, reel H-2739.

2 Although the board of governors asked for funds using British North America's pound-based monetary system – generally referred to as "Halifax currency," "pounds current," or simply "currency" – by 1860, most everyone in Canada expressed monetary values in dollars. Under

this system, one "pound current" was worth four dollars. In what follows, I use dollar notation wherever possible.

3 Robert Lee et al., "Land-Grab Universities," accessed 12 June 2023, https://www.landgrabu.org/. On the entangled history of settler colonialism and universities in the English-speaking world, see Caitlin Patricia Alma Harvey, "Bricks and Mortar Boards: University-Building in the Settlement Empire, 1840–1920" (PhD diss., Princeton University, 2021). For works focused on Canada, see Caitlin Harvey, "University Land Grabs: Indigenous Dispossession and the Universities of Toronto and Manitoba," *Canadian Historical Review* 104, no. 4 (2023): 467–93 and Richard Yeomans, "Land Rich, Cash Poor: The Settler-Colonial Beginnings of the University of New Brunswick, 1785–1829," *Acadiensis* 52, no. 2 (2023): 11–44.

4 Harvey, "Bricks and Mortar Boards," 158–9.

5 Memorial of the Governors of McGill College to Sir Edmund Walker Head, s.d. [March 1860], LAC, RG4-C1, vol. 747, no. 497, reel H-2739. On the establishment of the Royal Institution and early francophone resistance to its claims to material support from the state, see Bruce Curtis, *Ruling by Schooling Quebec: Conquest to Liberal Governmentality – A Historical Sociology* (Toronto: University of Toronto Press, 2012), 84–7.

6 "The nine years between 1846 and 1855 were years of continuous financial perplexity during which the Governors had great difficulty in keeping the College in operation." Cyrus MacMillan, *McGill and Its Story: 1821–1921* (Toronto: Oxford University Press, 1921), 186.

7 Dawson as quoted in Stanley Brice Frost, *McGill University: For the Advancement of Learning, Volume I: 1801–1895* (Montreal and Kingston: McGill-Queen's University Press, 1980), 188.

8 John William Dawson, *Fifty Years of Work in Canada, Scientific and Educational*, ed. Rankine Dawson (London and Edinburgh: Ballantyne, Hanson & Co., 1901), 102, http://archive.org/details/fiftyyearsof workoodawsrich; "William Dawson, the aggressive new principal of McGill University, spent the 1855 Christmas recess in Toronto discussing university financing with Cartier." Brian Young, *George-Etienne Cartier: Montreal Bourgeois* (Montreal and Kingston: McGill-Queen's University Press, 1981), 89.

9 Peter R. Eakins and Jean Sinnamon Eakins, "DAWSON, Sir JOHN WILLIAM," in *Dictionary of Canadian Biography*, vol. 12 (University of Toronto/Université Laval, 1990), accessed 9 June 2023, https://www.biographi.ca/en/bio/dawson_john_william_12E.html.

10 Frost, *McGill University*, 1:188 and 214–19.

11 These were the *collèges classiques* since the Université de Montréal would not be founded until 1878, while Université Laval, established in 1852, initially did not receive public funding. Instead, it was fully funded by the Catholic Church, which sought to affirm its institutional independence and educational leadership. Jean Hamelin, *Histoire de l'Université Laval: les péripéties d'une idée* (Sainte-Foy, Quebec: Presses de l'Université Laval, 1995), 44.

12 Frost, *McGill University*, 1:218–9.

13 Frost, *McGill University*, 1:166.

14 An Act to make better provision for promotion of superior Education and the establishment and support of Normal Schools in Lower Canada and for other purposes, 19 June 1856, Canada, Statutes, 19 Vic., cap. 54, 229–34. For a brief description of the distribution of monies from the Fund for Superior Education in Lower Canada, see Jean-Philippe Croteau and Robert Gagnon, "Les débats sur le partage de la taxe scolaire à Montréal (1869–1899): enjeux et rivalités," *Historical Studies in Education / Revue d'histoire de l'éducation* 20, no. 1 (2008): 48–9.

15 Quoted in Frost, *McGill University*, 1:219.

16 Frost, *McGill University*, 1:218–21.

17 MacMillan, *McGill and Its Story*, 232–3; Frost, *McGill University*, 1:200.

18 Frost, *McGill University*, 1:48 and 54.

19 Frost, *McGill University*, 1:165. For the legislation limiting McGill's debt, see An Act to Amend Two Certain Acts Therein Mentioned, and for Other Purposes Connected with the Administration of McGill College, 10 November 1852, Canada, Statutes, 16 Vic., cap. 58, 214–15.

20 An Act Further to Amend the Acts Relative to the Royal Institution for the Advancement of Learning and to the University of McGill College, 27 May 1857, Canada, Statutes, 20 Vic., cap. 53, 249–51.

21 McGill's chancellor wrote that despite the existence of the Fund for Superior Education in Lower Canada, "no such special appropriation could be made and the University was thus left with this debt upon it, and the resource from which relief might probably have been derived was unexpectedly cut off." Charles Dewey Day to T.L. Terrill, 13 July 1857, LAC, RG4-C1, vol. 417, no. 1664, reel H-2708.

22 George-Etienne Cartier, Report on Application of the Governors of McGill College for a Loan of £2000, 3 August 1857, LAC, RG4-C1, vol. 417, no. 1664, reel H-2708.

23 The loan was to be made from "any funds now or hereafter to be available for investment as the proceeds of the sale of public lands made to raise an income for Common School Education under the 12th Vict. Cap. 200;

and that if no such funds be at present available, the above sum be paid out of the Consolidated Revenue Fund." Order-in-Council, 6 August 1857, LAC, RG1-E8, vol. 63, no. 1502, reel H-1797. See also, Provincial Loan Account, 30 September 1857, MUA, RG6, container 6, p. 335.

24 Chs. D. Day to Dr. Dawson, 18 February 1860, MUA, RG2, container 4, bundle 11, item 129.

25 R.T. Pennefather to the Governor General, 15 October 1856, LAC, RG10, vol. 517, 420–1, reel C-13347.

26 Chantal Stebbings, *The Private Trustee in Victorian England* (Cambridge: Cambridge University Press, 2002), 169. Chancery had accepted the principle that the trustee was responsible for any losses to the trust by 1774 at the latest. Michael Chestermen, "Family Settlements in Trust: Landowners and the Rising Bourgeoisie," in *Law, Economy and Society, 1750–1914: Essays in the History of English Law*, eds David Sugarman and Gerry R. Rubin (Abingdon, Oxon: Professional Books, 1984), 159. Upper Canada, however, did not have a court of equity between its creation in 1791 and 1837, something that caused at least theoretical problems for enforcing standard British understandings of the liability of trustees in the colony. Elizabeth Brown, "Equitable Jurisdiction and the Court of Chancery in Upper Canada," *Osgoode Hall Law Journal* 21, no. 2 (1983): 275–314.

27 On the company, see B.E. Hill, "The Grand River Navigation Company and the Six Nations Indians," *Ontario History* 63, no. 1 (1971): 31–40; Susan M. Hill, *The Clay We Are Made Of: Haudenosaunee Land Tenure on the Grand River* (Winnipeg: University of Manitoba Press, 2017); Blair M. to Merritt W.H., 10 April 1838, LAC, RG10, vol. 796, 181–4, reel C-13,500.

28 Canada, "Report of the Special Commissioners Appointed on the 8th of September, 1856, to Investigate Indian Affairs in Canada," Appendix 21 in *Journals of the Legislative Assembly, Sessional Papers*, 6th Parl., 1st Sess., vol. 16 (25 February–16 August 1858), n.p., 40–1.

29 Emilie Connolly, "Fiduciary Colonialism: Annuities and Native Dispossession in the Early United States," *American Historical Review* 127, no. 1 (2022): 227, https://doi.org/10.1093/ahr/rhac012.

30 Thomas E. Blackwell to R.T. Pennefather, 25 August 1859, in Canada, *Second Report of the Financial and Departmental Commission: February 1864* (Quebec: J. Blackburn, 1864), lii–liii. For an overview of Blackwell's proposal, see T.S. Brown, W. Bristow, and George Sheppard, *Second Report of the Financial and Departmental Commission*, 67.

31 Order-in-Council, 26 August 1859, in Canada, Second *Report of the Financial and Departmental Commission*, li; and Ann M. Carlos and Frank D. Lewis, "The Creative Financing of an Unprofitable Enterprise: The Grand Trunk Railway of Canada, 1853–1881," *Explorations in Economic History* 32, no. 3 (1995): 273–301, https://doi.org/10.1006/exeh.1995.1012.

32 Jean-Pierre Kesteman, "GALT, Sir ALEANDER TILLOCH," in *Dictionary of Canadian Biography*, vol. 12 (University of Toronto/Université Laval, 1990), accessed June 20, 2023, http://www.biographi.ca/en/bio/galt_alexander_tilloch_12E.html.

33 A.A. den Otter, "Alexander Galt, the 1859 Tariff, and Canadian Economic Nationalism," *Canadian Historical Review* 63, no. 2 (1982): 153.

34 Emphasis in original. John Ross to A.T. Galt, 30 September 1859, LAC, MG27-ID8, vol. 1, 319–25.

35 J.-C. Bonenfant, "CARTIER, Sir GEORGE-ÉTIENNE," in *Dictionary of Canadian Biography*, vol. 10 (University of Toronto/Université Laval, 1972), accessed 7 April 2022, http://www.biographi.ca/en/bio/cartier_george_etienne_10F.html; Young, *George-Etienne Cartier: Montreal Bourgeois*, 108–18.

36 The members of the Executive Council who were present were: John A. Macdonald (chair), George-Étienne Cartier, Philip Michael Vankoughnet, Narcisse-Fortunat Belleau, Charles Joseph Alleyn, Alexander Tilloch Galt, and John Rose. Order-in-Council, 14 June 1860, LAC, RG1-E8, vol. 72, no. 176, reel H-1802.

37 Emphasis in original. John Ross to A.T. Galt, 30 September 1859, LAC, MG27-ID8, vol. 1, 319–25.

38 A.T. Galt to Thomas Baring, 12 October 1859, LAC, MG27-ID8, vol. 10, 26–9.

39 C.D. Day to Charles Alleyn, 8 March 1860, LAC, RG4-C1, vol. 747, no. 497, reel H-2739.

40 [Charles Day] to Alexander T. Galt, 8 March 1860, LAC, RG4-C1, vol. 747, no. 497, reel H-2739.

41 Chs. D. Day to [John William Dawson], 31 March 1860, MUA, RG2, container 4, bundle 11, item 131.

42 Copy of a Report of a Committee of the Executive Council, 14 June 1860, LAC, RG10, vol. 711, p. 210, reel C-13410.

43 An Act Respecting the Management of the Indian Lands and Property, 30 June 1860, Province of Canada, *Statutes*, 23 Victoria, cap. 151.

44 Edmund Head to the Duke of Newcastle, 18 May 1860 in Great Britain, *Indian Department (Canada): Copies or extracts of correspondence*

between the secretary of state for the colonies and the governor general of Canada respecting alterations in the organization of the Indian Department in Canada ([London]: House of Commons, 1860), 37.

45 *Journals of the Legislative Council of the Province of Canada*, 6th Parl., 3rd Sess., vol. 18 (Quebec: Queen's Printer, 1860), 118.

46 R.T. Pennefather to the Attorney General Canada East, 21 June 1860, LAC, RG10, vol. 520, p. 37, reel C-13348; R.T. Pennefather to T. Doucet, 9 July 1860, LAC, RG10, vol. 520, p. 49, reel C-13348; Minutes, Meeting of the Governors of McGill College, 25 July 1860, MUA, RG37, container 306, 300–1; R.T. Pennefather to T. Doucet, 10 August 1860, LAC, RG10, vol. 520, p. 86, reel C-13348; T. Doucet to R.T. Pennefather, 11 August 1860, LAC, RG10, vol. 255, part 2, 153771–2, reel C-12645; extract from the minutes of the Royal Institution for the Advancement of Learning, Governors of McGill College, 16 August 1860, Bibliothèque et Archives nationales du Québec – Montréal, CN601, S208, no. 5802; Minutes, Meeting of the Governors of McGill College, 16 August 1860, MUA, RG37, container 306, 301–3; C.T. Walcot to T. Doucet, 19 October 1860, LAC, RG10, vol. 520, p. 150, reel C-13348; and T. Doucet to C.T. Walcot, 20 October 1860, LAC, RG10, vol. 256, 154281–2, reel C-12645.

47 Chs. D. Day to [John William Dawson], 7 December 1860, MUA, RG2, container 4, bundle 13, item 10.

48 Obligation by the Royal Institution for the Advancement of Learning to Her Majesty Queen Victoria, 14 December 1860, Notary Joseph Petitclerc, LAC, RG10, vol. 257, 155050–62, reel C-12646.

49 The other contributions were: Saugeen and Owen Sound ($5,000), the River Desert ($3,135.38), the Mississaugas of Alnwick ($3,000), and the Wyandotts of Anderdon ($1,000). The River Desert – now known as Kitigan Zibi – was the only one of these communities not located in Upper Canada.

50 Kanesatake is recorded in the ledgers as Lake of Two Mountains and Odanak as the Abenakis of St Francis. "Loan to the University of McGill College, Montreal, Order-in-Council 14 June 1860," 20 December 1860, LAC, RG10, vol. 1003, f. 131, reel C-9061.

51 T.D. Harington to R.T. Pennefather, 29 January 1861, LAC, RG10, vol. 257, 155420–7, reel C-12646.

52 While rosalind hampton discusses the case briefly, her analysis does not include any archival research, relying entirely on media sources instead. rosalind hampton, *Black Racialization and Resistance at an Elite University* (Toronto: University of Toronto Press, 2020), 40–1.

53 Report of Committee of the Executive Council, 16 January 1861, LAC, RG10, vol. 257, 155358–9, reel C-12646. For the 1859 order-in-council, which initially explicitly did not apply to the Indian Fund, see Report of an Executive Committee, 22 November 1859, LAC, RG10, vol. 1025, file E, 551–2, reel T-1460.

54 Order-in-Council, 25 August 1859, LAC, RG1-E8, vol. 70, reel H-1800.

55 Abenakis of St Francis, Land Fund, 14 November 1860 to 1 July 1862, LAC, RG10, vol. 1004, f. 68, reel C-9061.

56 I have verified through 30 June 1877, well after the McGill loan had been terminated. Abenaki of St Francis, 30 June 1875 to 30 June 1877, LAC, RG10, vol. 1008, f. 62, reel C-9062.

57 Abenakis of St Francis, Land Fund, 14 November 1860 to 1 July 1862, LAC, RG10, vol. 1004, f. 68, reel C-9061.

58 Moravians of the Thames, Land Fund, 10 January 1860 to 2 May 1862, LAC, RG10, vol. 1004, f. 26 and 71, reel C-9061 and Investment Account, 1 April 1860 to 30 April 1862, LAC, RG10, vol. 1004, f. 47, reel C-9061.

59 Six Nations, Land Fund, 30 June 1861 to 30 April 1862, LAC, RG10, vol. 1004, reel C-9061, f. 81.

60 Adding the $8,000 to McGill, the $21,778 in "Amount of Sundry Investments the property of Six Nations" recorded on 1 January 1861 (which includes the $10,000 invested on 1 May 1861 in the "Investments Account"), and $595,456.25, the amount recorded as invested on 1 April 1860, yields the total invested capital in the Six Nations' account as $625,234.25 – the exact amount transferred to the land fund on 31 October 1861. Investment Account, 1 April 1860 to 30 April 1861, LAC, RG10, vol. 1004, reel C-9061, f. 47 and Six Nations, Land Fund, 3 October 1860 to 30 June 1861, in LAC, RG10, vol. 1004, reel C-9061, f. 67.

61 Emphasis in original. T.D. Harington to Spragge, 14 April 1862, LAC, RG10, vol. 296, 198355–6, reel C-12672.

62 John Langton to C. Dunkin, 17 November 1868 in "Return To an Address of the House of Commons, dated 2nd April, 1869, for Copies of all Correspondence between the Governments of the Provinces of Ontario and Quebec and the Dominion Government, relative to the settlement of accounts with and between the same," Appendix 46 in Canada, *Sessional Papers*, vol. 5 (1869), 30.

63 John Langton, "Memorandum upon the doubtful points which will have to be decided in determining the net debt of the late Province of Canada," n.d. [7 July 1868] in "Return To an Address of the House of Commons, dated 2nd April, 1869, for Copies of all Correspondence between

the Governments of the Provinces of Ontario and Quebec and the Dominion Government, relative to the settlement of accounts with and between the same," Appendix 46 in Canada, *Sessional Papers*, vol. 5 (1869), 8–12.

64 John Rose, "Principles upon which the Statement of Affairs of June 30, 1867, is to be revised in preparation for the Arbitration between Ontario and Quebec," n.d. [15 September 1868] in Canada, *Sessional Papers*, vol. 5 (1869), 14–16.

65 Abenakis of St Francis, Land Fund, 14 November 1860 to 1 July 1862, LAC, RG10, vol. 1004, f. 68, reel C-9061.

66 For example, Chippewas of Saugeen and Owen Sound, Land Fund, 14 January 1860 to 15 June 1861, LAC, RG10, vol. 1004, reel C-9061, f. 32 and 79, and River Desert Indians, Land Fund, 27 September 1860 to 1 July 1862 in LAC, RG10, vol. 1004, reel C-9061, f. 66.

67 C.T. Walcot to John Langton, 15 April 1861, LAC, RG10, vol. 520, p. 285, reel C-13348.

68 In 1861, the Province of Canada provided McGill College with $2,591.21 along with an additional $671.07 for "one year's salary to the Secretary of the Royal Institution, and the messenger and for casual expenses." This amount would have been sufficient to cover the annual payment of $2,400 required under the loan (6 per cent interest on $40,000). "Table of the Distribution of the Grant for Superior Education for the year 1861 …," in "Report of the Superintendent of Education for Lower Canada for the Year 1861," in Canada, *Sessional Papers*, 25 Vict., no. 34 (Quebec: Hunter, Rose & Lemieux, 1862).

69 Charles Dewey Day et al., *Statement of the Royal Institution for the Advancement of Learning: Addressed to the Benefactors and Friends of McGill University* (Montreal: Lovell, 1874), 4–5.

70 [James] Ferrier to [?], Department of Justice, 21 May 1873, LAC, RG13-A-2, vol. 30, file 1873-962.

71 Elsbeth Heaman, *The Inglorious Arts of Peace: Exhibitions in Canadian Society during the Nineteenth Century* (Toronto: University of Toronto Press, 1999), 91–2.

72 Z.A. Lash, Memorandum, 22 January 1873, LAC, RG6, vol. 673, file 290.

73 Eakins and Eakins, "DAWSON, Sir JOHN WILLIAM."

74 Several historians have studied early trusts in New England, for example Daniel R. Mandell, *Behind the Frontier: Indians in Eighteenth-Century Eastern Massachusetts* (Lincoln: University of Nebraska Press, 1996); Jean M. O'Brien, *Dispossession by Degrees: Indian Land and Identity in Natick, Massachusetts, 1650–1790* (Cambridge: Cambridge University

Press, 1997); Wendy B. St Jean, "Inventing Guardianship: The Mohegan Indians and Their 'Protectors,'" *New England Quarterly* 72, no. 3 (1999): 362–87; Amy E. Den Ouden, *Beyond Conquest: Native Peoples and the Struggle for History in New England* (Lincoln: University of Nebraska Press, 2005).

75 Angela C. Tozer, "Universal Nation: Settler Colonialism and the Canadian Public Debt over Mi'kma'ki, 1820–1873" (PhD diss, McGill University, 2020); Angela Tozer, "Democracy in a Settler State? Settler Colonialism and the Development of Canada, 1820–67," in *Constant Struggle: Histories of Canadian Democratization*, ed. Julien Mauduit and Jennifer Tunnicliffe (Montreal and Kingston: McGill-Queen's University Press, 2021), 87–115; Angela Tozer, "Racial Capital, Public Debt, and the Appropriation of Epekwitk, 1853–1873," *Journal of Canadian Studies / Revue d'études Canadiennes* 57, no. 2 (2023): 233–54.

5

Willie McDonald's McGill

A Student's Experience in the Late Nineteenth Century

DON NERBAS

It was September 1896 and the train journey from Sydney, Nova Scotia, to Montreal was long. Willie McDonald arrived at the Grand Trunk Railway's Bonaventure Station a few days before classes were to commence. He was met at the station by his father, Senator William McDonald. Having just turned nineteen years of age, Willie McDonald was about to embark on his first year in applied science, engineering, at McGill University. The professional opportunities in engineering were conspicuous in Willie McDonald's home community, the fast-expanding coal town of Glace Bay, where the Dominion Coal Company had recently established itself as a dominant force on the coalfield and an exemplar of the new corporate capitalism of Canada's "Second Industrial Revolution."[1] The senator, without doubt, had his own ambitions for his son too. Willie's elder brothers, Allan Joseph and Dan Lewis (Dannie), had pursued careers in law and medicine (with mixed success), and thus there was perhaps a logic in the combination of professional careers among the McDonald boys. Willie arrived at Bonaventure Station with family support and expectations that propelled him to McGill, like so many other students.

But as a Catholic, Willie was set apart from most of the student body and the "broadly Protestant character" of the McGill environment.[2] He was of a Highland Catholic family, and both his parents were native Gaelic speakers. His father, a powerful political broker to the Highland Catholic population in the Glace Bay area and in the outlying rural districts of Cape Breton County, was first elected to the House of Commons as an Independent Conservative in the 1872 Dominion election. The elder McDonald became a stalwart of the Conservative Party and was re-elected three more times before his appointment to the Senate in 1884. Willie, born in 1877, grew up as a member of a locally prominent family. The importance of his family was also evident at St Francis Xavier College (St FX) in Antigonish, where Willie obtained a bachelor of arts degree prior to his arrival at McGill. His brothers had studied at St FX, an uncle had been a math professor there, and his father was on the college's board of governors. As in Glace Bay, the Highland Catholics were a plurality of the population in Antigonish, where home and family influence were nearby.[3] The move to McGill, and Canada's largest city, was an abrupt transition.

This chapter tells the story of Willie McDonald's year at McGill in 1896–97. Centred on the letters Willie wrote to his father during his time in Montreal, it offers a snapshot of late nineteenth-century McGill and the day-to-day attitudes, impressions, and travails of a student. Letters of this kind have seldom been incorporated into histories of McGill, though they can offer revealing insights about the interior lives of students, both on campus and off, and the social and cultural milieu of the university.[4] While the particularities of Willie's experience were indeed significant and shape much of what follows, this chapter also seeks to explain the broader aspects of the university's development that attracted Willie to McGill, and to explore other historical trends revealed by his unique experience.

The very fact that Willie travelled from Nova Scotia to attend McGill exemplified the university's significant presence in the Maritime region and its links to Nova Scotia's coal country during a post-Confederation era of national integration. When Willie arrived, his father's status and political friends gave him access to some of the grand Square Mile mansions that encircled McGill campus. Meanwhile, the prominent place of engineering at McGill and the hyper-masculine student culture Willie encountered were indicative of new career paths, class identities and attitudes that were being embraced by the urban bourgeoisie and those who sought entry into its ranks. Yet, if – as seems likely to have been the case – Willie's aim was to become an engineer in order to access the growing opportunities in Cape Breton's burgeoning coal mining industry, his time at

McGill did not quite produce the desired outcome. By the winter of 1897, tense exchanges with a patriarchal father over money and Willie's selective account of his academic performance revealed problems. He appears to have operated as a relatively solitary figure; the McGill environment may have produced disinterest and alienation in Willie. Though he had once assumed he would attain a McGill degree, he failed to return for a second year.

MCGILL – INSTITUTIONAL TRANSFORMATION AND EXPANSION

When Willie arrived at McGill in September 1896, he encountered a campus that, in many respects, was new. The Macdonald-Workman Engineering Building, the Macdonald Physics Building, and the Redpath Library had been erected only a few years earlier, and the Redpath Museum had been built little more than a decade before then. These new campus buildings also revealed the prominent place of science and engineering within the university. This was the legacy of another Nova Scotian from the province's coal country, William Dawson, the famed geologist who had retired as McGill's principal in 1893.

The Pictou-born Dawson had been appointed principal nearly four decades earlier, in 1855, at a particularly decisive moment in the university's history. In the wake of John Bethune's failed efforts as principal in the 1830s and 1840s to pattern McGill College after the Oxbridge model, a series of changes placed the college on a new path. James Ferrier became president of the Royal Institution, the body responsible for overseeing the college, in 1847. Mayor of Montreal, a founder of the Bank of British North America, and railway promoter, Ferrier was joined on the Royal Institution board by other "new men," leading commercial figures of the city such as Peter McGill, Robert Armour, and Hew Ramsay.[5] Members of the Royal Institution succeeded in amending the college's charter in 1852 so as to make themselves governors of a reconstituted McGill College board. The new board was empowered with the authority to make statutes for the college and to appoint the principal and professors, while oversight responsibility was transferred from the Royal Institution to the Governor General. The governors themselves led these reforms and mobilized to secure funds for the college's development. Led by Charles Dewey Day, as chair of the board's Education Committee, they also oversaw the design of the university's governance structure with the passage of statutes in 1854 that created a bicameral organization and made provision for faculty representation. In pursuing these reforms, the governors advanced a vision of the college that emphasized "practical" education – including an emphasis on science and the professions – and was non-denominational but also decidedly Protestant.[6] William Dawson, still in his thirties, was their man. Already a major scientific figure by 1855, he was "the first British North American trained to be an exploration geologist" and had worked with Sir Charles Lyell. He had also published a volume on the geology of his coal-rich home province, had championed agricultural chemistry as Nova Scotia's superintendent of education, and was a fellow of the Geological Society of London.[7] Dawson's experience and outlook were in close alignment with the vision and priorities of the college's governors.

The campus that Willie encountered in 1896 was a legacy of the productive years that followed Dawson's appointment, as was the applied science degree program Willie entered. But the path there had not been smooth. In 1857, Dawson hired Mark Hamilton as a professor of civil engineering and road and railway engineering, and a civil engineering diploma was made available to students in arts. The railway boom that buoyed interest in engineering, however, went bust. Only one student chose engineering in 1863; Hamilton's position was terminated.[8] Nearly a decade later, in 1871, Dawson recommenced efforts to establish engineering studies at McGill. Daniel Torrance and George Moffatt committed funds to the initiative, and J.H.R. Molson, Peter Redpath, and G.H. Frothingham supplied the money to guarantee the salary of a professor; a lecturer in assaying and mining, Bernard James Harrington, was appointed in the new Department of Practical Science. G.F. Armstrong was also appointed a professor of civil engineering in 1871. The renamed Department of Applied Science became a separate faculty in 1875, and two years later Armstrong was replaced by another Cambridge graduate as professor of civil engineering, Henry T. Bovey.[9] Bovey had become dean of applied science by the time of Willie's arrival.

The number of students in applied science climbed slowly but unevenly in the 1870s and 1880s before a jump in the early 1890s. The gifts of major benefactors played an important role in this development, securing an enhanced status for engineering and science on campus. In 1890, McGill governor and tobacco magnate

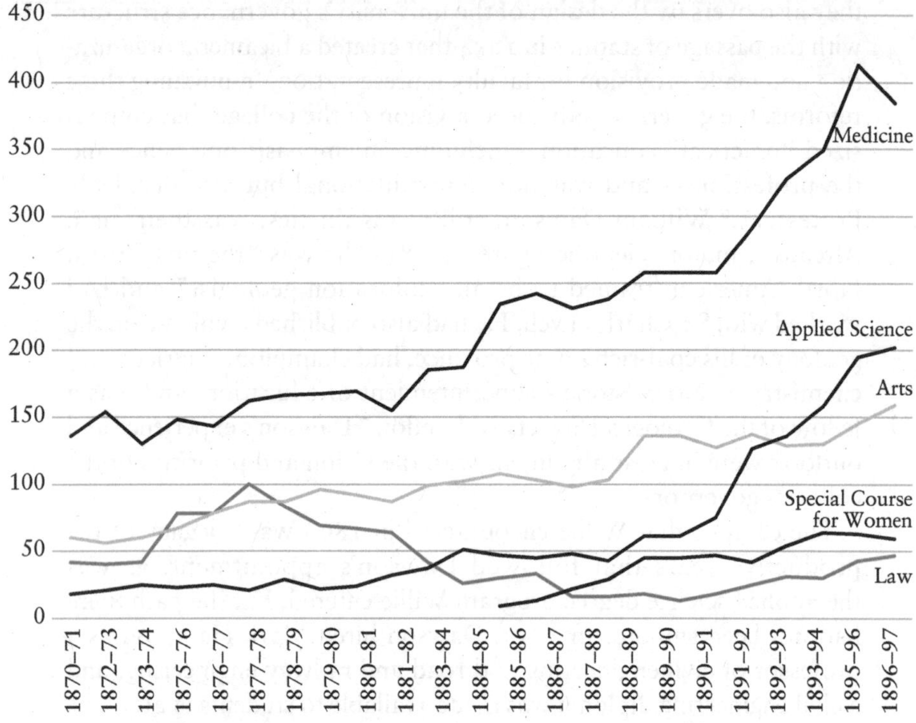

Figure 5.1 Student enrolment, 1870–97

Source: Compiled from McGill University *Calendars*. Partial students were not included in calculation of totals. It should be noted that inclusion of partial students would significantly elevate the number of female students in the later years represented in this graph. For instance, in the 1896–97 session there were more partial students registered in the Special Course for Women (ninety) than regular undergraduates (fifty-nine).

William C. Macdonald gave the university funds for the construction of the engineering building and physics building.[10] Electrical engineering was added to the fields of specialization – civil, mechanical, mining, and practical chemistry – on offer to applied science students in 1891–92, which included intensive work in the electrical engineering laboratory in year four.[11] By the 1892–93 academic year, undergraduate student enrolment in applied science exceeded the numbers in arts for the first time, a trend that would persist in the coming years (see figure 5.1). And architecture was added to the Faculty of Applied Science in 1896.[12] This was a very different institution from the Oxbridge-style college Bethune had imagined more than a half-century earlier.

ENGINEERING AND MARITIME CONNECTIONS DURING THE POST-CONFEDERATION ERA

Lacking professional licensing, engineering work had occupied an uncertain place in the social order, and its persisting association with the trades and manual labour damaged its social status; engineers "were not quite gentleman like doctors and lawyers." The limited presence of engineering education within Canadian universities reflected the ambiguous status of the engineer's work.[13] Despite this, industrialization had elevated the importance of the engineer and had made engineering an increasingly attractive field of study for young men who sought positions of influence in Canada's rapidly industrializing economy of the late nineteenth century.

No equivalent of the bachelor of applied science was offered in Nova Scotia at the time, which may have been a factor that attracted Willie to McGill from his home province.[14] The earlier scions of leading Cape Breton families who became mine managers, such as Charles Archibald and David McKeen, had received training to become mining engineers at the Boston Institute of Technology; they were men of an earlier generation. Willie's generation came of age in a world more directly influenced by the new, national networks of the post-Confederation era, and McGill's expansion coincided with Montreal's growing metropolitan influence within the Maritime region during the period. A university education was, by the end of the nineteenth century, also becoming a more common credential in the world of Canadian business, especially for engineers.[15] In Cape Breton, Hiram Donkin took charge of the development of the Dominion Coal Company's colliery railway in 1894 before replacing McKeen as the company's resident manager. Donkin, like many other engineers of his generation, had not attended university. His son, Frank W. Donkin, was a first-year applied science student at McGill in 1893–94.[16]

McGill had developed an especially strong presence in the Maritime region by the late nineteenth century, exemplified by the arrival of students such as Frank Donkin and Willie McDonald. The university's presence in the Maritimes was an aspect of the region's integration into a Canadian political economy in which Montreal was positioned as a dominant metropole. The case of C.H. "Bunty" McLeod is suggestive. Born in Strathlorne, Cape Breton, the son of a merchant, McLeod began work on the Intercolonial Railway with Sandford Fleming's engineering staff in 1868 before he arrived at McGill to become among the first graduates from the Department of Applied Science in 1873. McLeod returned in 1888 to take up an appointment as professor in the Faculty of Applied Science, and in 1891 succeeded Henry Bovey as secretary of the Canadian Society of Civil Engineers (CSCE).[17] This important professional association, established in 1887, later gained the reputation of being run by a "McGill Clique," a belief that stemmed from "the major organizational and administrative role that McGill engineers played during the early history of the CSCE."[18] In the 1890s, on the cusp of Canada's second industrial revolution, it was already clear that McGill would play an important role in training the growing cadre of engineers who would assume an increasingly important role in Canada's economic life.[19] Applied science was an attractive option, and drew many students from the Maritime region and beyond.[20]

The university calendar advised students to complete the first two years in arts to gain admission to applied science; Willie was admitted to the program on the basis of his St FX degree.[21] In 1896, he joined a student body at McGill where for roughly every two students from Montreal there was one from the Maritime provinces, and where more students came from Charlottetown than Toronto (see figure 5.2). Willie remarked upon the presence of Maritime students in his letters and passed along personal information about known individuals from St FX and his home community (see below); Maritimers were ubiquitous.

Medicine had the highest enrolment (384) and the largest proportion of students from the Maritimes of any faculty. One in four medicine students were Maritimers and they even outnumbered local students from the Island of Montreal (92 to 83). Law drew almost all its students from Quebec (45 of 47), 114 of 159 undergraduate arts students (72 per cent) were from the province, and nearly the same proportion (66 per cent) of female undergraduate students enrolled in the special course for women were from Quebec. Arts and the women's course drew relatively small numbers from the Maritimes. Applied science had the second highest enrolment (202), and only medicine drew a higher proportion – over half – of students from out of province. Twenty-eight applied science students, or nearly one in seven, were Maritimers. Interestingly, 81 per cent of the applied science students from within Quebec were from the Island of Montreal, whereas in the arts this figure was only 61 per cent. That scions of Montreal's industrial elite – Molson, Ogilvie, Redpath, and Sise – were registered in applied science suggests a recognition within elite circles

Figure 5.2 Home communities of McGill students, 1896–97

Source: Compiled from McGill *Calendars* and maps generated by Palladio, https://hdlab.stanford.edu/palladio/.

of the growing significance of engineering education in Canadian business life, and perhaps explains the disproportionately urban social origins of applied science students.

The combination of these various factors helps explain Willie McDonald's decision to enrol in applied science at McGill. His migration to Montreal was also decidedly part of a longer history of McGill's relationship to the Maritime region and Nova Scotia's coal country.

LIVING IN THE SQUARE MILE AND STUDYING AT MCGILL

By 1896, Montreal was a burgeoning industrial metropole; the semi-rural character of campus at mid-century was gone, and McGill stood at the centre of a maturing and moneyed residential district, the Square Mile. Major benefactors of the institution – men such as Donald Smith, William C. Macdonald, and Peter Redpath – lived in the neighbourhood and played a major role in supporting and shaping the university. And Square Mile families sent their children to McGill. This included J.S. McLennan, whose father, Hugh McLennan, was a McGill governor and a leading Montreal merchant and shipping magnate. J.S. McLennan obtained BA degrees from McGill and Cambridge in the 1870s before relocating to Cape Breton to manage a coal mine that his father had acquired with a small group of Montreal capitalists, including Donald Smith. He eventually played a leading role in the establishment of the Dominion Coal Company.[22]

Because his father was a Conservative senator, Willie had a pathway into Square Mile society during his time at McGill. "Yes," he reported to his father in November, "I received a note a couple days ago from Senator Ogilvie asking me to call at his place ... I also got a note from Senator Drummond asking me to his house."[23] Andrew Walker Ogilvie and George A. Drummond sat in the Senate with Willie's father as fellow Conservatives. Willie had dinner at Senator Ogilvie's and "found the people very nice and kind" and returned for dinner again in December.[24] "Senator Ogilvie wished to be remembered to you," Willie wrote to his father. "Do you think I should give him any kind of present on Xmas?"[25] Willie appears to have kept in touch with Senator Ogilvie during the academic year. Before his return to Cape Breton in the spring, he asked his father whether Senator Ogilvie was in Montreal: "If he is," wrote Willie, "I shall go to see him."[26] Willie carried with him his father's status and connections, which opened some exclusive doors.

Yet, these gilded interludes were hardly characteristic of Willie's day-to-day experience as a student living in Montreal. There were no campus residences for male students at McGill until 1936, when

Douglas Hall was built. Dawson had not favoured them when he first arrived but later changed his mind. In 1882, the Faculty of Applied Science observed cases of illness and even death among undergraduate students caused by "unhealthy conditions of their lodging houses and of the places at which they take their meals."[27] That year, Dawson spoke in favour of college residences in his annual address.[28] By 1896, the majority of students travelled from outside Montreal to study at McGill, and thus Willie's preoccupation with housing would have been common among students. Before his arrival in mid-September, he asked his father – in Ottawa on parliamentary business – to locate for him a place to live.[29]

His first residence was at 60 University Street, the block between Burnside Place (now De Maisonneuve Boulevard) and St Catherine Street. The landlady, Mrs Radford, was a widow who lived with her son, an architect. That a medical doctor and bookkeeper lived there around that time suggests it was a comfortable boarding house.[30] Though Willie found the people "very nice," the food did not suit him. He corroborated his judgment for his father: "I might mention that two of the boarders here are leaving in a couple of days. Their names are Patterson – mother and son –; + they told me that the food did not suit them. The son is head book-keeper in one of the leading stores + seems to be well off."[31]

By October Willie had moved to 43 Hutchinson Street, just north of Sherbrooke Street, and was taking his meals at a boarding house run by "Mrs. James Robb" at 83 Union Avenue.[32] It cost him $8 a month for the room, and $12 for his meals. However, while looking at rooms he had found something better: a second-storey room at 116 University Street. The room "was well heated and lighted and was in a very good locality being on the corner of Sherbrooke and University Sts." The rent, however, was no less than $22.50 per month, substantially more than what he was already paying. He wrote to his father that he might be able to get it for $20 if he could find another person to take it with him.[33] In November, Willie moved again. "I am now at 113 Union Avenue for about a month," he wrote to his father on 13 December, "and I find the place the best I have been in. It is warm + comfortable."[34] He later sent his father a photograph of the house. "You can see it is a very nice one," he reported. "My room is on the top flat."[35] And he had continued to take his meals – "very good and wholesome" – at Mrs Robb's at a cost of 12¢ per meal. "I am paying $10.00 a month for my room, so that the whole thing amounts to $20.00."[36] Willie stayed at 113 Union Avenue, just south of Sherbrooke, for the rest of his time in Montreal. Though he moved three times from September to November, he stayed in the locale adjacent to the university – on the fringe of the Square Mile – and was quick to become familiar with the area. "I ... know the part of the city that I live in pretty well," Willie asserted in September.[37]

The gender dynamics of Willie's boarding arrangements are worth noting. "Miss P. Gladstone" is listed in the city directory at 113 Union Avenue, and a woman appears in the city directory as head of household at all three locations Willie lived. This is suggestive of the fact that women inherited and managed significant family assets and were indeed consequential property owners in the Square Mile.[38] Renting rooms was also a common strategy for widows to generate income.[39] Widows appear as household heads at as many as sixteen of seventy-four addresses on Union Avenue, and single women appear as household heads in six instances. In total, then, nearly one-third of the residences on Union Avenue alone (twenty-two of seventy-four) were headed by women.[40] For Willie and other McGill students boarding in Montreal, this likely produced a sharp division between female authority figures at boarding houses off-campus, and the male authority and hyper-masculine student culture at McGill.

Most of Willie's waking hours were likely spent on campus. All first-year applied science students had a common curriculum before course requirements varied based upon area of specialization. Students were in class Monday to Friday, from nine to five, with a lunch break at midday, as well as Saturday from nine to noon. "I have not much spare time," Willie commented at the beginning of the term.[41] Classes in mathematics, chemistry, and drawing occupied most of his schedule. And shopwork sessions were scheduled Tuesday afternoon and Saturday, "to give the Student some knowledge of the nature of the materials of construction, to familiarize him with the more important hand and machine tools, and to give him some manual skill in the use of the same."[42] Willie wrote about his work in these sessions. "I am enclosing you in this letter," he reported to his father, "a sample of what we do in the workshops. This is what I did yesterday, that is made three joints (sash) as shown in the cuts. You have to be very particular + have every thing perfect, else you won't get the highest marks. Every one has to sharpen his own tools +c."[43]

Outside the classroom, as a Catholic at McGill, Willie clearly felt himself in the minority. "I am getting on pretty well now with my classes," he wrote barely a week into the term. "I know six or seven Medical Students, all Catholics + from the lower Provinces. [But] [o]f all the Science men that I know so far, none are Catholics."[44] The enumeration of Catholic students was likely done by Willie for the benefit of a curious father, interested in his son's new environment in Montreal. Willie's first letter from the city to his father was indeed about church. He reported on his visit to the nearby Church of the Gesù on Bleury Street for morning mass: "I was to the Jesuit Church this morning to Mass, but as the sermon was in French, I can not say anything about it. The service lasted some two hours, too long for one sitting in a cold place."[45] He was similarly disappointed the following week: "This morning being very rainy, I did not go to Mass. I went to the Jesuit Church to-night expecting to hear an English sermon, but was disappointed. The Sermon there in the evenings is usually English, but for the past two weeks it has not been so."[46] While Catholicism may have brought Willie into contact with francophone Montreal, the experience was an unfamiliar one and he expressed his preference for St Patrick's Church, just around the corner on Dorchester, where "the sermon is [in] English, [and] only lasts half an hour or so."[47] His attitudes were symptomatic of McGill's place in a world of two linguistic solitudes.[48] Yet, within the McGill context Willie viewed Catholicism as a social disadvantage that he shared in common with French-Canadian students.[49]

Willie also admitted to his brother, Dannie, that he found the pace of the coursework fast. The first six books in geometry were covered in six one-hour lectures: "I found it extremely hard as I had not seen a [*sic*] Geometry for three years."[50] Willie's one preserved letter to his brother, dated 16 November 1896, was more candid than the letters addressed to his father – he did not admit to feeling challenged by the coursework in letters to his father. The letter to Dannie also provided a candid account of student life.

MASCULINITY AND STUDENT CULTURE

The glimpse of campus life offered in Willie's letter to Dannie reveals physical confrontation as a regular aspect of the student experience. Groups of first-year students were subject to "rushes" by more advanced cohorts on campus. This was a ritualized and tolerated hazing practice. Willie wrote to his brother: "The Second + 4th yr. Science tried to rush 1st yr. the other day, but as we outnumbered them, they got the worst of it. A pane of glass worth about $\$2^{00/100}$ Two Dollars was broken. For this the 1st + 2nd years were fined $\$2.^{\underline{00}}$ a piece. Whole fine amounts to $\$190^{00/100}$. Pretty dear glass, eh?" This is muted language – "rush" and "they got the worst of it" – to describe a violent encounter. The nature of these student melees is made clearer in another episode Willie alluded to in the letter: "I suppose you have heard of the scrap that occurred in the McGill Arts Building a couple of weeks ago. It was between 1st + 2nd yr. Arts. In it one poor fellow got crushed so badly that he died last Thursday. He had been bleeding from the lungs since the scrap."[51] The deceased was J.T. Stewart, a second-year arts student training to enter the Presbyterian ministry and the son of a prominent farmer in Athelstan, Quebec.[52] That Willie's letter to his brother ended up with his father's papers suggests that Dannie passed the letter along to his father – Dannie perhaps felt compelled to alert his father to the alarming contents of Willie's letter.

The *Montreal Gazette* published a different account of the circumstances of Stewart's death: "It has been stated that the young man's death was due to his over-exertion in one of the friendly squabbles that occur between the students now and then – sometimes termed a 'rush.' This, however, is quite erroneous, for several of the College authorities and students, who were witnesses of the affair, deny that the deceased took any active part in the affair at all." *The Gazette* thus provided a direct answer to the claim that Stewart had died from an injury sustained in the "rush," a notion that others evidently shared with Willie. Stewart had been in good health, claimed *The Gazette*, but had experienced "several slight hemorrhages from the nose" before the "'rush' took place in the College"; "it is said by his fellow students that young Stewart, not feeling very well, desisted from taking a prominent part in the friendly squabble." The following morning Stewart became quite ill. He bicycled to the hospital and back, unable to see a physician. His condition then worsened dramatically, "a violent hemorrhage of the lungs came on," and he was taken to the Royal Victoria Hospital. His condition deteriorated further. Within a few days the physicians at the hospital concluded there was no hope; his family was telegraphed. "His mother, sister and brother arrived the same day, and were constantly at his bedside until early Friday morning, when he passed away peacefully." A funeral was held on campus at the Presbyterian College in David Morrice Hall before the funeral in Stewart's hometown.[53] The tragedy was, according to *The Gazette*, unconnected to the "rush" in the Arts Building.

La Presse offered a cryptically worded report of the student's death – with "hémorrage causée par les exercises trop violents" indicated as the cause – that seems closer to Willie's account than that of *The Gazette*.[54] Willie's letter was dated two days after news of Stewart's death was reported in the local press. It is evident that *The Gazette* article offered the university's version and reflected McGill influence with the city's English-language daily newspapers.[55] It is impossible to ascertain the precise truth about the episode; no coroner's inquest was conducted. That Willie thought it plausible Stewart had died from an injury suffered in the "rush," however, says something about the intensity and violence of such campus traditions, minimized in *The Gazette* as mere "friendly squabbles" between students.

This was the beginning of an era of "muscular Christianity" and "imperial masculinity," part of a broader antimodern impulse that romanticized and reified physical struggle and aggression as measures of merit in the reconstruction of a new bourgeois manhood in the Anglo-American world. Young McGill students were powerfully exposed to these broader cultural trends, which provided sanction for unruly behaviour and worse.[56]

Other stories of rowdy student behaviour travelled back to Cape Breton as well. Michael T. Sullivan was a first-year medicine student also from Glace Bay. In November, Willie reported home that "Sullivan has become very industrious since coming to McGill. He studies very hard, spends no money, and I don't think there is anyone in first year medicine who studies any harder."[57] Later, Sullivan's father, a merchant in Glace Bay, must have heard news that his son was unwell; he sent a telegram to Willie asking if his son was sick. Willie checked on him and "wired back that he was all right. If he was unconscious + brought to the hospital," wrote Willie to his father in early January, "I did not hear anything of it." Willie then proceeded to recount a story about Sullivan: "The only thing I know derogatory of him is that he was in jail for some hours on Theatre night. I did not mention this before for the reason that he asked me not to, but as Dannie has once told me of it I suppose it is no harm now." Willie was curious to know how Dannie had learned the story, and was worried he would be blamed for spreading it: "Where did Dannie hear of it[?] I should like to know, as I am the only one he can blame here for reporting it. His name appeared in the Herald + Gazette? at the time, but I don't think you could have seen it there. Anyway let me know."

Willie elaborated on the episode that resulted in Sullivan's imprisonment. Sullivan was part of a group of first-year medicine students who were locked up with him. The group consisted of "Lynch, Hughes, Duffy + Almon, Senator Almon's grandson: – all medical first year men. I dare say it was because they were freshmen + kind of green at the business of doing up policemen that they came to grief. One of them Duffy from PEI knocked out six policemen that night." This somewhat unbelievable description of brawling McGill students bringing havoc to the city was capped off with a discordant conclusion: "Although medical men, as a rule, are like this, still there are some respectable fellows among them."[58] Theatre Night, the occasion of this misbehaviour, had emerged a few years earlier as a student night out at the theatre on Sports Day – an event to inaugurate the new academic year. It quickly became an annual focus of riotous student behaviour, which had moved well beyond the control of university officials and become a wider source of embarrassment by the early twentieth century.[59] The tone of Willie's letter suggests that this behaviour nonetheless remained within the boundaries of routine student hijinks and tests of masculinity.

Indeed, his telling of the story of Duffy's handling of the police – surely an exaggerated, if not entirely fabricated, account of pugilistic prowess – suggests that it was meant to circulate as a tale about the demonstration of manliness, not a source embarrassment or shame: "He plays on the McGill III Team of Football," Willie concluded, in reference to Duffy and his presumed physical strength. Likewise, Duffy, Sullivan, and the others ran into trouble, in Willie's telling, because they were "kind of green," though "medical men, as a rule, are like this." The behaviour was unremarkable within the context of McGill student culture and was a brand of masculinity closely associated with the more respectable and ordered pursuits of team sports. Willie thus followed his story about Duffy with a general reflection on the athleticism and social origins of science and medicine students. "Although Science has the best individual athletes," he reported, "it has not so many as Medicine, and they [science students] are more respectable, most of them being very wealthy. Three men on the Hockey Team which won the Victoria Cup from the Winnipeggers last week are science men:– Davidson + Drinkwater of 4th year; and Lea of 3rd year."[60] The progression from discussion of lawless student behaviour during Theatre Night to mention of football, hockey, and general musings about athleticism is made coherent by the overarching subject and thread linking the discussion: elite masculinity.

Though Willie does not appear to have been a direct participant in the masculine displays he described, he was a keen observer and wrote home about noteworthy sporting events and student athletes, whose social origins he was careful to note. In describing a "splendid football match" for the Intermediate Championship of Canada between the McGill and Brockville teams, for instance, Willie observed that "two of the team – Sise + Robertson are 1st year Science. Sise's father is President of the Canadian Bell Telephone Co. + Robertson is from Mexico. Science have good men in all the sports."[61] Having "good men in all the sports" was understood by Willie as a telling indicator – in a broader sense – of capability and merit.

Emergent ideals of elite masculinity placed a new emphasis on physical strength and aggression and was expressed at McGill through a diverse range of student behaviours. Willie's assessments of events suggest that a permissive attitude obtained. However, news of student hijinks that travelled from McGill back to home communities had a different effect. Across this distance – and outside the bourgeois, masculine culture among McGill students – the rowdy behaviour appeared to lose its acceptability. McGill existed as an exceptional space where young men – distanced from the social control of the home – performed ritual expressions of manhood that strained and even defied social norms.

New traditions of student rowdiness would also assume political significance in an era of high imperialism. Within the context of the South African War, on 1 March 1900, McGill students celebrated the victory at Paardeberg by parading through the city streets, engaging in attacks on the offices of French-language papers – *La Presse*, *La Patrie*, and *Le Journal* – critical of Canada's participation in British imperial wars, and then besieging Université Laval de Montréal. In the end, the militia was called to quell the three-day riot. The event, as Carman Miller has written, "shocked public men in Canada and Britain." It was an exercise in "imperialistic excess" that was facilitated by a student culture Willie had observed a few years earlier.[62]

FAMILY MATTERS, MONEY, AND GRADES

While this culture gave considerable scope for bad student behaviour, Willie nonetheless remained subject to traditional forms of social control: his personal resources were restricted by the patriarchal oversight of his father. He was indeed entirely dependent upon his father for money, and this fact was prominent throughout much of his correspondence. "I have had to spend considerable money the last two days," Willie wrote to his father at the beginning of the school year in September; he assured his father that he was buying "as many second hand books ... as I possibly can." The drawing instruments required for first-year students cost $11.50. Willie proposed to purchase a full set for $30 or $40; the full set was required for second-year students anyway, Willie reasoned. The set that Willie proposed to purchase "would be good for all time," though he noted that a full set could be purchased for $19.75. Ultimately, it was his father's decision to make: "In your next letter I wish you would tell me which one to get, + also send me the requisite amount."[63] The senator, it seems, rejected the more expensive option. "Your check for $20.00 I received all right," Willie reported in the subsequent letter. "I am going to get my instruments tomorrow, and will let you know what price I shall pay."[64]

In response to his father's request for a "detailed account of expenses," Willie sent the following account in November:

> [1] ... Fees at College, $178.35 + [$]128. This includes fee of $185.<u>oo</u> which you paid, of course. Gown, overalls + Trencher i.e. (official cap that goes with gown) $10.25; fees Y.MC.A (University) + <u>Undergraduate Society</u>, $4.50; Subscriptions for Janitor 30¢; Subscription to McGill Fortnightly $1.00; Expenses for Theatre night, $3.80. This includes subscription for 1900 Banner, which cost $30.<u>oo</u> and was paid by First Year Science, Uniform Theatre night + admission fee. Four keys rented – one to Locker for gown +c; one for stall in Chemical Laboratory; one for bench in workshops; and one for desk in Drawing Room. Price of four keys amounts to $3.00. This money for keys will be paid back. Dinner for Freshmen 75¢.
>
> [2] The books I got cost $12.22. I will give you a list of them: – Chemistry; Geometry; Algebra; Solid Geometry[;] Geometry + Conic Sections; Geometrical Drawing; Lettering + Freehand Drawing books; Cartridge drawing paper 24 sheets; Dynamics; Mathematical Tables; four books in French – one a Dictionary all in French; two authors in French; and a French Grammar; College Song book; Note + Memo books for class work.

[3] Workshop + Drawing Apparatus. These are: – Set Instruments; two set squares; rule (mille metre); two Sable brushes; two camel hair brushes; one bottle of Higgins' Waterproof India Ink (for drawing purposes); one box of water colors. These amount to $22.06.

[4] Board bill up to Oct 23rd, $25.50, overcoat $17.50, cane 45¢; Cab from station and when coming up here 75¢; for shoes $3.25; for gloves [$]1.25; underclothing [$]2.50. $49.20 ...

Trip from Sydney to Montreal Cost about [$] 28.00

Money spent in paper stamps +c [$]3.50

It was a messy and frankly confusing summary, but it demonstrated an effort to be detailed. And it also communicated Willie's need for more money: total expenses were listed as $296.63 against $305 given to him, which left him with $8.37 in hand.[65] This account reveals the prosaic expenses of a McGill student – undergraduate society membership; books and drawing instruments; cap, gown, overcoat, and cane – but more broadly it reveals that Willie very much remained under the authority of his father, whom he was expected to answer to.

The senator was exacting when it came to his son's expenses, and evidently questioned Willie's spending. On 5 February, Willie wrote to his father and enclosed a list of expenses incurred since November. "As you see, nothing in it was needless; in fact, if I were to go over the last two months again I could but do the same thing." Board and room, rubber boots, gloves, hat, firewood, drawing paper, a class photo: Willie's spending was limited more or less to the essentials. His season pass for the McGill rink, which cost $1.50, was the only item that might have qualified as an expense on entertainment. The back-and-forth between father and son over money became more heated later that month. The senator felt Willie was not writing him frequently enough – and was only writing when in need of money. Willie rejected his father's accusation in a sharp reply:

Your letter, enclosing cheque for 20^{\underline{00}}$, reached me here Friday. Necessary to say that both were opportune. I should have answered sooner but for the fact of having more work to get up during the week than usual.

Speaking about writing letters, you say that my letters home are very unfrequent, and that *I only write you when money is*

> *wanted* [emphasis added]. Well, surely, you can't expect me to write every day or every second day, which I should certainly do if I wanted to satisfy every one. For example ... on Monday, I receive a letter from Dannie; on Tuesday, one from Minnie [Willie's sister] + so on. Do you mean that I am to answer every individual letter? Re money, the last time I wrote you was two weeks ago. The time before that I wrote for money was about the last of October, over four months elapsing between each time. You must have got some letters during that time. In your answer to this, which by the way, I hope will be sooner than last time, I wish you would be more definite + not confuse one by vague and strange references.

The senator had evidently also commented on his son's untidy accounting practices, based on the following from Willie: "Yes, I am afraid I should not impress Messrs Foster or Fielding [ministers of finance] in the matter of Bookkeeping, since the only thing that seems to trouble them is how to obtain a deficit."[66] Willie's response suggests something more than mere annoyance. Discussion of money had become tense and combative – indeed angry.

Sharp words over money and expenses coincided with exchanges about grades; one suspects that the senator was not merely concerned about money but wished to exercise close supervision of his son's activities. The experience of Dannie – Willie's elder brother and his father's middle son – perhaps shaped the senator's thinking. Three years before Willie departed for McGill, Dannie had left to pursue medical training at the Bellevue Medical College in Brooklyn. He quickly squandered the money his father had given him and found himself in a desperate situation. Too embarrassed to write home, Dannie contacted an uncle in Halifax to ask for help. He eventually returned to Glace Bay to manage the family's drug store, having given up on becoming a physician.[67] The big city offered the opportunity for unsupervised leisure that could disrupt academic success. The senator's decision to dole out portions of money to his son during the academic year was likely a deliberate strategy to supervise his son's activities. Montreal was not Antigonish.

Willie does not seem to have been inclined towards the wayward behaviour that landed his brother in trouble. His letters suggest a studious and perhaps even solitary disposition. While he reported in September "I'm getting acquainted with some of the students, some of whom are very nice," he does not appear to have established a circle of friends during the year. He noted concerts, public lectures, and other events, but without mention of particular individuals or friends. "The McGill Arts students, as you probably know, have a Latin play last week in the Academy. All the McGill students attended in a body," Willie wrote in a characteristically distant account of student life.[68] The tight budget he lived on appears to have limited what he could do in Montreal. He attended Seidl's orchestra at the Windsor Hotel Hall with a complimentary ticket – "tickets being worth $1.00" – but otherwise he mostly wrote about events he did not attend.[69] With perhaps a touch of melancholy, Willie wrote: "To-morrow night, John E. Redmond the Irish liberal M.P. will speak at the Windsor Hall, admission is as low as 25¢. *I will not go to hear him*. Yvette Guilbert, the famous French singer is there to night. Her cheapest ticket was $1.50. Harry Furniss, the Caricaturist of Punch gave three lectures at the Windsor Hall this month. *I did not hear him*, however [emphases added]."[70] One suspects that Willie wrote in this manner to make a point about his spartan lifestyle. In either case, his letters suggest that most of his time was occupied by coursework.

The April exam schedule was gruelling. Willie wrote, "The dates of my exams are as follows: – April 5, 6, 7, 8, 10, 12, 13, 14, 15, 17, + 19th."[71] He had reassured his father in early January that he had not failed in anything; in chemistry he attained a Class II rank; in mathematics, Class III; and he did not present himself for the French exam because he was exempted from it and felt he would be "unable to pass in it." "You can see now that I have not failed in anything. [That] list of marks you sent me were not … 1st year Science. The only results in Science which were published was French."[72] Come April, however, Willie did not present himself for the mathematics exam. In letters to his father during this period, there is no mention of this. Rather, Willie boasted that he expected to be awarded first-class honours in practical chemistry and discussed clothes he wanted to buy before his return to Cape Breton.[73] The senator wrote directly to Dean Bovey to inquire about his son's academic standing. Bovey's response is telling:

> In reply to your letter of May 1st I beg to state that your son William McDonald passed in the whole of the subjects in which he presented himself for examination. He did not, however, present himself for examination in French, Mathematics, and Mathematical Laboratory. Mathematics is the most

> important subject of the year, the number of marks awarded for this subject being 400. He will be able to regain his standing by passing a supplemental examination in September next, the date of the examination being Thursday, Sept. 16th. Meanwhile I should advise him to pay special attention to the Mathematics of the First Year and carefully revise the whole of this work. It will not be necessary for him to pass a supplemental examination in French.
>
> As soon as the new announcement is published I shall have the pleasure in forwarding you a copy.[74]

Willie had neglected to tell his father the full truth about his academic standing. Senator McDonald evidently suspected as much. Willie was back in Cape Breton in May; he did not return to take the supplemental exam in September.

CONCLUSION

Shortly after his return to Glace Bay, Willie sought a position with the Dominion Coal Company. He reported to his father on 12 May that he had met with Dominion Coal's resident general manager, Hiram Donkin, "three times. He promises work as soon as he can."[75] But the promised job never materialized. It is likely that the prospect of a career in the mining industry was what initially attracted Willie to applied science. And perhaps Willie's failure to secure summer employment with the coal corporation undermined his apparent ambition to pursue a career in engineering. Or perhaps it undermined the senator's willingness to support his son's ambition. Whatever the case, instead of returning to McGill, Willie became a bank clerk in Glace Bay, and later an accountant.

In Cape Breton, where nicknaming was a common practice to distinguish people with the same name, Willie became known by the nickname "Billy Senator." He died in 1959 at the age of eighty-two. His obituary in the *Cape Breton Post* described him as a prominent Sydney resident from "a noted Glace Bay family," "a kind gentleman with a wide range of interests," "adept in the art of gardening" and a "noted connisseur of of [*sic*] rare and valuable books."[76] It was also noted that he was a graduate of St FX. No mention was made of his time at McGill. This is not surprising. Willie's time at McGill was an aborted project, both academically and socially.

As the son of a senator, one might have expected Willie McDonald to have comfortably carried his privilege. Yet, his letters suggest a more complex story. His father denied him easy access to money that may have allowed him to perform the expected role, and religion, language, and personal inclination appear to have all served as barriers to his social integration into the McGill and Montreal environment.

Nonetheless, his experience was also symptomatic of broader structural forces reshaping McGill at the end of the nineteenth century. The prominent place of engineering at McGill and the masculine student culture Willie encountered were indicative of new career paths, class identities, and attitudes that were being embraced by the urban bourgeoisie and those who sought entry into its ranks. Most people, unlike Willie, could not gain invitations to Square Mile homes or attend McGill, a university whose reach had grown in step with the post-Confederation project of colonial expansion and national integration. Within Canada and Quebec during this period, McGill and its Square Mile surroundings stood as symbols of privilege and social exclusion. The political implications of this would play out in various ways in the century that followed, as will be revealed in proceeding chapters.

NOTES

1 See Craig Heron, "The Second Industrial Revolution in Canada, 1850–1930," in *Class, Community and the Labour Movement: Wales and Canada, 1850–1930*, ed. Deian R. Hopkin and Gregory S. Kealey (St John's: Llafur/Canadian Committee on Labour History, 1989), 48–66.

2 Stanley Brice Frost, *McGill University: For the Advancement of Learning, Volume I, 1801–1895* (Kingston and Montreal: McGill-Queen's University Press, 1980), 157.

3 Don Nerbas, "Family, Society and Highland Identity in an Industrial World," in *Scottish Highlands and the Atlantic World: Social Networks and Identities*, ed. S. Karly Kehoe, Chris Dalglish, and Annie Tindley (Edinburgh: Edinburgh University Press, 2023), 170–93. While at St FX Willie delivered complaints to his father about the dorm accommodations with the understanding that his father could do something about it. See Willie, Antigonish, to Papa, 12 January 1896, item 548, series 26; Willie, Antigonish, to Papa, 19 January 1896, item 552, series 26, MG 9.23, William McDonald fonds, Cape Breton University, Beaton Institute Archives (hereafter BI).

4 An important exception is Suzanne Morton, *Wisdom, Justice, and Charity: Canadian Social Welfare through the Life of Jane B. Wisdom, 1884–1975* (Toronto: University of Toronto Press, 2014).
5 Frost, *McGill University*, 1:106.
6 Frost, *McGill University*, 1:153–7 and 173–4.
7 Peter R. Eakins and Jean Sinnamon Eakins, "DAWSON, Sir JOHN WILLIAM," in *Dictionary of Canadian Biography*, vol. 12 (Université Laval / University of Toronto, 1990), accessed 29 March 2023, http://www.biographi.ca/en/bio/dawson_john_william_12E.html.
8 Frost, *McGill University*, 1:188.
9 Frost, *McGill University*, 1:274.
10 Frost, *McGill University*, 1:244, 274.
11 *Annual Calendar of McGill College and University, Session 1891–92* (Montreal, 1891), 68.
12 Frost, *McGill University: For the Advancement of Learning, Volume II, 1895–1971* (Kingston and Montreal: McGill-Queen's University Press, 1984), 39. On the Scottish networks that shaped architecture at McGill into the twentieth century, see Annmarie Adams, "'Glad of your help': Scottish Architects in Montreal, 1860–1940," in *Montreal's Square Mile: The Making and Transformation of a Colonial Metropole*, eds Dimitry Anastakis, Elizabeth Kirkland, and Don Nerbas (Toronto: University of Toronto Press, 2024), 279–311.
13 See J. Rodney Millard, *The Master Spirit of the Age: Canadian Engineers and the Politics of Professionalism, 1887–1922* (Toronto: University of Toronto Press, 1988), 7–10 (quotation is from p. 9).
14 King's College, Windsor, offered a course in civil and mining engineering in 1871 that was opened to non-Anglican denominations in the 1880s, and in 1895 Dalhousie College began to offer a mining class, but it failed to attract students. See Donald Macleod, "Miners, Mining Men and Mining Reform: Changing the Technology of Nova Scotian Gold Mines and Collieries, 1858 to 1910" (PhD diss., University of Toronto, 1981), 556–7. Dalhousie established a program of mining engineering in 1902. By 1903 Mount Allison students could complete two years in engineering before finishing the last two years of their programs at McGill, and Acadia established the same arrangement with McGill. See P.B. Waite, *The Lives of Dalhousie University*, vol. I (Montreal and Kingston: McGill-Queen's University Press, 1994), 191–4; John G. Reid, *Mount Allison University: A History, to 1963*, vol. I (Toronto: University of Toronto Press, 1984), 235–6.

15 T.W. Acheson, "Changing Social Origins of the Canadian Industrial Elite, 1880–1910," *Business History Review* 47, no. 2 (Summer 1973): 200–1; Millard, *Master Spirit of the Age*; David F. Noble, *America by Design: Science, Technology, and the Rise of Corporate Capitalism* (Oxford: Oxford University Press, 1977). For biographical information on McKeen, see Don MacGillivray, "MACKEEN, DAVID," in *Dictionary of Canadian Biography*, vol. 14 (Université Laval / University of Toronto, 1998), accessed 18 May 2023, http://www.biographi.ca/en/bio/mackeen_david_14F.html. For biographical information on Archibald, see Janet Guildford, "Edith Jessie Archibald: Ardent Feminist and Conservative Reformer," *Journal of the Royal Nova Scotia Historical Society* 11 (2008): 113.

16 *Annual Calendar of McGill College and University, Session 1894–95* (Montreal, 1894), 240.

17 Millard, *Master Spirit of the Age*, 35; "Professor M'Leod Died Suddenly," *The Gazette* (Montreal), 27 December 1917, 4; J.L. MacDougall, *History of Inverness County, Nova Scotia* (Truro: Truro News Print, 1922), 22–4. Suzanne Morton has also revealed the significance of Maritime connections at McGill in her biography of Jane Wisdom. Wisdom would take up a position as C.H. McLeod's assistant with the CSCE in 1911. Jane's elder sister, Katie, had established a friendship with Professor McLeod's daughter, Effie, and the McLeod family prior to Jane's arrival. See Morton, *Wisdom, Justice, and Charity*, 40–2, 78.

18 Millard, *Master Spirit of the Age*, 37–8.

19 See Heron, "The Second Industrial Revolution in Canada."

20 By the early twentieth century, the new buildings on campus were already insufficient to accommodate incoming numbers of applied science students. Frost, *McGill University*, 2:39.

21 *Annual Calendar of McGill College and University, Session 1896–97* (Montreal, 1896), 73.

22 See A.J.B. Johnston, "MCLENNAN, JOHN STEWART," in *Dictionary of Canadian Biography*, vol. 16 (Université Laval / University of Toronto, 2014), accessed 22 June 2023, http://www.biographi.ca/en/bio/mclennan_john_stewart_16E.html.

23 Willie, Montreal, to Father, November 1896, item 611, McDonald fonds, BI.

24 Willie, Montreal, to Father, 16 November 1896, item 609; Willie, Montreal, to Father, 13 December 1896, item 612, McDonald fonds, BI.

25 Willie, Montreal, to Father, 13 December 1896, item 612, McDonald fonds, BI.

26 Willie, Montreal, to Father, 18 April 1897, item 634, McDonald fonds, BI.

27 "Minutes of the Meetings of the Governors of the University of McGill College Situate at Montreal," 25 November 1882, McGill University Archives, quoted in Frost, *McGill University*, 1:288.
28 Frost, *McGill University*, 1:288.
29 Willie, Glace Bay, to Father, 4 September 1896, item 596, McDonald fonds, B1.
30 *Lovell's Montreal Directory, for 1896–97* (Montreal: John Lovell & Son, 1896), 411; *Lovell's Montreal Directory, for 1897–98* (Montreal: John Lovell & Son, 1897), 428.
31 Willie, Montreal, to Father, 20 September 1896, item 603, McDonald fonds, B1.
32 *Lovell's Montreal Directory, for 1896–97*, 410; *Lovell's Montreal Directory, for 1897–98*, 427.
33 Willie, Montreal, to Father, 25 October 1896, item 607, McDonald fonds, B1.
34 Willie, Montreal, to Father, 13 December 1896, item 612, McDonald fonds, B1.
35 Willie, Montreal, to Papa, 7 March 1897, item 624, McDonald fonds, B1.
36 Willie, Montreal, to Father, 13 December 1896, item 612, McDonald fonds, B1.
37 Willie, Montreal, to Father, 22 September 1896, item 604, McDonald fonds, B1.
38 Robert C.H. Sweeny, "Gender and Social Relations in the City above the Hill," in *Montreal's Square Mile*, 219–47.
39 Bettina Bradbury, *Wife to Widow: Lives, Laws, and Politics in Nineteenth-Century Montreal* (Vancouver: UBC Press, 2011).
40 These figures are compiled from *Lovell's Montreal Directory, for 1897–98*, 427. In three instances women household heads appear as "Mrs." without a spouse listed at the household; the assumption was made in these cases that they were in fact widows, and thus they are counted among the 16 widows.
41 Willie, Montreal, to Father, ? Sept. 1896, item 595, McDonald fonds, B1.
42 *Annual Calendar of McGill College and University, Session 1896–97*, 111.
43 Willie, Montreal, to Father, 25 October 1896, item 607, McDonald fonds, B1.
44 Willie, Montreal, to Father, 27 September 1896, item 606, McDonald fonds, B1.
45 Willie, Montreal, to Father, 20 September 1896, item 603, McDonald fonds, B1.

46 Willie, Montreal, to Father, 27 September 1896, item 606, McDonald fonds, B1.

47 Willie, Montreal, to Father, 20 September 1896, item 603, McDonald fonds, B1. Willie later mentioned the rental of a pew. See Willie, Montreal, to Father, 5 February 1897, item 621, McDonald fonds, B1.

48 For Willie, Catholicism facilitated some interaction with Montreal's majority culture, unlike for many Anglo-Protestant students. As Suzanne Morton notes of the experiences of the Presbyterian Wisdom sisters at McGill in the early twentieth century, francophone Montreal was rendered "completely invisible" in their correspondence. See Morton, *Wisdom, Justice, and Charity*, 57.

49 Willie wrote to his brother, Dannie: "Levesque of whom you have heard no doubt, is a med, and a Catholic. Because he is the latter is the reason why he is not Captain of McGill I Team. He is supposed to be the best quarterback in Canada." Willie, Montreal, to Dannie, 16 November 1896, item 608, McDonald fonds, B1.

50 Willie, Montreal, to Dannie, 16 November 1896, item 608, McDonald fonds, B1.

51 Willie, Montreal, to Dannie, 16 November 1896, item 608, McDonald fonds, B1.

52 "A Student's Death," *The Gazette*, 14 November 1896, 3.

53 "A Student's Death."

54 The *Montreal Star* did not indicate anything about cause of death. See "A Student's Death," *Montreal Star*, 14 November 1896, 9.

55 Decades later, in 1930, McGill Chancellor Edward Beatty wrote explicitly in private correspondence to Principal and Vice-Chancellor Sir Arthur Currie about the exercise of this type of influence. A financially embarrassed J.K.L. Ross, a past governor and graduate of the university and son of the influential Square Mile capitalist James Ross, had requested to Beatty that his name be kept out of the press in relation to "the University's application to be reinstated as a creditor." The matter arose from the university's claim upon money that J.K.L. Ross had publicly committed to the university in an earlier fund-raising campaign. Beatty explained to Currie: "I told him at the time that I thought there would be no difficulty in arranging with the English newspapers of Montreal to refrain from reporting what is after all a very formal matter. When, therefore, you know the date the application is to be heard by Judge Panneton, I shall be glad if you will let me know in order that we may arrange with the Star, Gazette and Herald to refrain from making reference

to it." See Beatty to Currie, 10 January 1930, file 853, container 853, RG 2, McGill University Archives. And in the mid-twentieth century, Norman Levine reported, "Everyday a reporter comes from the Montreal Star to the principal's secretary to get some story about the university, to keep it constantly 'in the news.'" Levine, *Canada Made Me* (Toronto: Deneau and Greenberg, 1979 [1958]), 221. Thanks to Suzanne Morton for drawing my attention to Levine's observations.

56 See, for instance, T.J. Jackson Lears, *No Place of Grace: Antimodernism and the Transformation of American Culture, 1880–1920* (Chicago: University of Chicago Press, 1981); Robert H. MacDonald, *Sons of Empire: The Frontier and the Boy Scout Movement, 1890–1918* (Toronto: University of Toronto Press, 1993); J.A. Mangan and James Walvin, eds, *Manliness and Morality: Middle-Class Masculinity in Britain and America, 1880–1940* (New York: St Martin's Press, 1987), 135–59; Clifford Putney, *Muscular Christianity: Manhood and Sport in America, 1880–1920* (Cambridge: Harvard University Press, 2001). See also Keith Walden, "Respectable Hooligans: Male Toronto College Students Celebrate Hallowe'en, 1884–1910," *Canadian Historical Review* 68, no. 1 (March 1987): 1–34.

57 Willie, Montreal, to Dannie, 16 November 1896, item 608, McDonald fonds, B1.

58 Willie, Montreal, to Papa, 8 January 1897, item 616, McDonald fonds, B1.

59 See Camille Queen, "Theatre Night: The Apex of Bad Behavior at McGill University" (undergraduate student essay, McGill University, HIST 437, 2016).

60 Willie, Montreal, to Papa, 8 January 1897, item 616, McDonald fonds, B1.

61 Willie, Montreal, to Dannie, 16 November 1896, item 608, McDonald fonds, B1.

62 Carman Miller, *Painting the Map Red: Canada and the South African War* (Montreal and Kingston: McGill-Queen's University Press, 1993), 443–4.

63 Willie, Montreal, to Father, 22 September 1896, item 604, McDonald fonds, B1.

64 Willie, Montreal, to Father, 27 September 1896, item 606, McDonald fonds, B1.

65 Willie, Montreal, to Father, November 1896, item 611, McDonald fonds, B1.

66 Willie, Montreal, to Papa, 21 February 1897, item 622, McDonald fonds, B1.

67 Nerbas, "Family, Society and Highland Identity in an Industrial World," 182–3.

68 Willie, Montreal, to Papa, 21 February 1897, item 622, McDonald fonds, B1.
69 Willie, Montreal, to Father, 25 October 1896, item 607, McDonald fonds, B1.
70 Willie, Montreal, to Father, 18 January 1896 [*sic*: internal evidence makes clear that the correct year is 1897], item 619, McDonald fonds, B1.
71 Willie, Montreal, to Father, 31 March 1897, item 627, McDonald fonds, B1.
72 Willie, Montreal, to Papa, 8 January 1897, item 616, McDonald fonds, B1.
73 Willie, Montreal, to Father, 15 April 1897, item 633; Willie, Montreal, to Father, 18 April 1897, item 634, McDonald fonds, B1.
74 Henry Bovey, Montreal, to Hon. Mr. McDonald, 3 May 1897, item 637, McDonald fonds, B1.
75 Willie, Glace Bay, to Father, 12 May 1897, item 639, McDonald fonds, B1.
76 "Mourn Passing of Prominent City Resident," *Cape Breton Post* (Sydney), 22 September 1959.

6

"What Is Money?"

Stephen Leacock and Jacob Viner at McGill

E.A. HEAMAN

It was October 1910 and the second-year students in the Faculty of Arts at McGill were listening to Stephen Leacock lecturing on "What is money?" That was a complex question, one that Leacock, with a PhD conferred in 1903 by the University of Chicago, was well-equipped to teach. But the question went unanswered that day because the freshmen "attacked" the class in session. They demolished the door, decimated the class's caution money, destroyed Leacock's dignity, shocked the co-eds, and damaged the "pseudo-economists," according to the happy account written up for the 1914 yearbook.[1] Lacking further details of the incident, I will glean meaning from the context: new economic ideas about money, everyday life on McGill campus, and the way those things aligned on the eve of the First World War. One of the attacking students, Michael Garber (who became a lawyer and founder of the Canadian Jewish Congress), later remembered: "The honours Economics group of Arts '14 considered themselves as the Chosen because they were the Leacock boys (all males). We forsook the venerable courses of honours History or honours English and allowed ourselves to be led by Leacock on the adventurous course which Carlyle called 'the dismal science.'"[2]

Economics was gaining new influence by insinuating its logic into things previously not understood as economic. Theorists such as Werner Sombart in Berlin began to describe capitalism as "not just an economic mechanism for the creation and distribution of land, labor, and capital, but a social and cultural system that shaped every aspect of human existence."[3] The head of the Department of Economics at

Columbia University, E.R.A. Seligman, scion of a German-Jewish banking family enriched by the American Civil War, published a book in 1902, *The Economic Interpretation of History*, which insisted that economics explained everything else, including "political actions, religious movements, or currents of thought."[4] Applied to history, as Charles Beard did in his scandalous 1913 book on the founding of America, Seligman's theory made politics and culture subsets of economics. But no one carried that economic logic further into culture than Thorstein Veblen, an economist at the University of Chicago, whose 1899 book, *The Theory of the Leisure Class*, "struck at the heart of modern culture and revealed its link with the most tawdry of institutions – money."[5] Veblen was appalled by what passed for good taste in his day and described it as crass self-preening, "conspicuous" or "wasteful" consumption intended to show the elite consumer's distance from "sordid" market pressures. Leacock, won over by Veblen's book, carried its lessons into his own. But Veblen had not exempted university culture from his attack. He specially excoriated campus sports and YMCA clubs alongside "higher learning" and economics itself, as corrupted and corrupting vehicles of conspicuous consumption. How to separate the monetary and the non-monetary so that they did not mutually corrupt one another?

McGill students were precociously drawn into debates about the meaning and boundaries of money, which carried into questions of identity. Were identifiable people and institutions especially pecuniary-minded and were they endogenous or exogenous to McGill? More specifically: did *Americans* and *Jews* pose pecuniary threats to McGill's British-Canadian ideals? There was considerable old wine in the new economics bottles. Sombart's account of *The Jews and Modern Capitalism*, published in 1911, argued that, historically, Jews had attacked and undermined old privileges and institutions resistant to both Jews and capitalism. He also warned that, without explicit prohibitions, "all university lectureships and professorships would be held by Jews or Jewish converts," a claim that stirred controversy in the United States as well as Germany.[6] Self-styled "national" universities like Harvard and McGill imposed quotas on professors as well as students.

McGill was a "milieu," a place where "Jew meets non-Jew, if not as political and social equals, then as partners in a ceaseless interaction (e.g. of ideas, practices, and values)."[7] The Arts '14 student who wrote the yearbook entry, Jacob Viner, found his voice in those conversations.

Born in 1892 to Romanian-Jewish refugees, Viner became one of the most prominent economists of his day: an architect of the Chicago school of economics, lend-lease, and Bretton Woods. The McGill yearbook of 1917 joked that he was in Harvard not learning from but coaching the illustrious professors "Taussig and Carver."[8] Already by 1922, the year he defended his PhD, Viner was "world famous" and "'the brightest star in the galaxy' of young and talented economists" at Chicago.[9] This paper reconstructs a kind of conversation between Leacock and Viner about the meaning of money, one mediated and illuminated by McGill campus politics, themselves reflecting wider political, public, and professional debates. It was, and remains, hard to trace the workings of money in motion across different transactions and permutations. Financiers were constructing complicated new monetary instruments, such as trusts, to evade close scrutiny by regulators and taxers. Economists were constructing complicated new theories of money and arguing about what did and did not count as money, in and out of circulation. And both were always in dialogue with popular and *ad hominem* theories of money.

Initially, the fights took shape around the gold standard. Britain, Canada, and the United States had all pegged their currency to gold. Such pledges supposedly stabilized economies by preventing inflationary policies. On David Hume's quantity theory of money, money was like water: it spread naturally and you could not heap it up. The supply of money determined prices, so that where money supply rose, prices did likewise. A government that doubled its money supply (for example, by printing or borrowing from the central bank) would see prices double, causing exports to diminish, a trade deficit, and an outflow of gold. The money supply would then contract until prices had fallen enough to restore the "balance of trade equilibrium."[10] But gold and the quantity theory were both under attack. The founding chair of economics at Chicago, J. Laurence Laughlin, who examined Leacock in 1903 and brought both Veblen and Viner to Chicago, was at the heart of the disputes. Laughlin was a "goldbug," an opponent of Populist demands for either silver or "fiat" money to replace the gold standard. Whereas Populists demanded money as democratic as the American nation, goldbugs replied that the money standard should be as fixed and permanent as the nation.[11] The fights intensified after the 1907 crash that saw the value of the New York Stock Exchange drop by 40 per cent and closed factories in Canada as well as the United States. The crash was precipitated by tightening money policies in England in response to lax regulation of trusts in New York.[12] The Populists saw a "conspiracy of money power against the common people" and "the fiat of organized capital."[13] Some attacked Wall Street, some attacked Lombard Street, and some blamed "Jews, foreigners" and "international financiers, chiefly German in origin and Jewish in race."[14] Jews and money were seen as interchangeable and as "shorthand for capitalist and rationalist": the enemy of local cultures and traditions.[15]

Even Laughlin, a dogmatic liberal distrustful of state intervention, realized something must be done to stabilize money. But he distrusted the quantity theory as much as the state: "Wherever we find discussions in favor of bimetallism, there we shall find the quantity theory of money."[16] Gold, he noticed, never actually moved, because businessmen were everywhere, "always and actively at work to prevent any appreciable differences in the level of gold prices between commercial nations."[17] If neither states nor bankers nor gold could stabilize money, something else must. Laughlin took leave from Chicago to advocate what became, in 1913, a system of Federal Reserve banks in the United States, designed to be responsive to but not controlled by either the bankers or the state and to manage the money supply.[18] "The term 'money' is loosely used," he explained in the fall of 1910. Public (i.e., farmers') demand for "more money" should be ignored much as the Bank of England ignored it; the real need was credit for business.[19]

Laughlin's views on money put him at odds with most other economists. Stephen Leacock later reminisced: "We, the students, did not at the time think much of Laughlin's work on money."[20] Most economists followed Irving Fisher's arguments, published in 1911, which debunked Laughlin's empirical studies with hydraulic and mathematical modelling.[21] Fisher argued for a mechanical and fixed proportional relationship between money supply and prices. But Fisher's model posited a closed economy with non-convertible money and lags between them: "The price level outside of New York City, for instance, affects the price level in New York City only via changes in the money in New York City."[22] Money trailed behind prices internationally but led prices domestically. Laughlin, on the other hand, rejected the theory of non-convertible money as incompatible with real-world facts and events.[23] Jacob Viner's 1922 dissertation would square the circle by making Canadian prewar borrowing an empirical proof of Hume's model.

Laughlin's world, like Veblen's and Viner's, offered scant shelter from inexorable monetary forces. In Leacock's world, by contrast, enlightened statesmanship could resist those forces. Canada and the United States intensely debated the free flow of money, goods, and people during the lead-up to the "Reciprocity election" of 1911, the negotiations themselves a product of inflationary pressure. The tariff was too lucrative, according to labour and farmer parties, and cheaper goods were desperately needed. But what of the huge quantities of money that Canada was borrowing abroad, mostly from British sources but much of it through American banks? Wasn't that influx driving up prices while making Canada a financial colony of the United States? Everywhere, American banks were turning international investment into de facto governing power to make America "a first-class financial power."[24] So, too, they seemed to be buying up Canada. In 1911, Canadian financiers led the attack on American financiers: "The trusts," said Thomas White, vice-president of the Toronto-based National Trust, "were squeezing the people in the United States. The farmer gets low prices and the consumer pays high prices. Do we want this condition of affairs here?"[25] Leacock concurred and he welcomed Robert Borden's election as prime minister, with White as his finance minister. But was it really possible or desirable to slake the flow of foreign investment?

Pace Laughlin, if New York could determine price exogenously, perhaps Canada could do the same, insulating itself against New York. Perhaps it could resist what Charles Conant, a prominent financial journalist, described as the American citizen's "freedom to extend new methods of economy and combination in trade and finance across the continent, untrammeled by local tariffs and State boundaries."[26] Leacock saw the threat. In 1909, he warned that "Monroe's creed of America for the Americans has been altered to mean America for the Americans and as much else of the world's surface as can be obtained at a profitable figure." Canada was being reduced "to the most impotent simulacrum of nationality that it is possible to conceive."[27] As a British immigrant to the Ontario heartland, a Chicago-trained political economist, a McGill professor, and a public intellectual, Leacock sought to shore up McGill, Canada, and the British Empire against foreign, pecuniary threats.

Leacock's intellectual debts to Veblen lent sophistication to his arguments. The two men had much in common: born a dozen years apart to immigrant families, both were farm boys who imbibed as a kind of mother's milk the producerist critique of parasitical urban and financial wealth. Veblen, who followed Laughlin from Cornell to Chicago in 1892, distinguished between "productive" and "pecuniary" activity as reflecting age-old human instincts, one propelled by craftsmanship and curiosity and leading to invention and science; the other more selfish and predatory yet becoming "the controlling factor about which the modern economic process turns."[28] Veblen was attacking the new marginal utility theories that vested value in circulation and consumption, rather than production and labour. He thought finance was hijacking industry, turning productive wealth into unproductive wealth and bending even universities to crudely utilitarian and commercial purposes. Economics should be a science of evolutionary and endogenous change; instead it was reinventing itself as bourgeois culture.[29] Veblen complained "the university is conceived as a business house dealing in merchantable knowledge" pursuing "the largest feasible output."[30] Johns Hopkins was founded by a banker, Cornell by a telecommunications magnate, and Chicago by oil magnate John D. Rockefeller. Chicago was America's mammon-central and so was its university.[31] Leacock shared and popularized Veblen's critique whereby "human industry is not carried on to satisfy human wants but in order to make money."[32] Value now governed cost, not the other way around, and the invisible hand and its social justice now yielded entirely to selfishness.[33] But Leacock put Veblen's radical arguments to reactionary politics. Where Veblen's America was too corrupt to be saved, its universities unable to play saviour, Leacock's Canada could still be saved from American money by a McGill acting as a visible and political hand.

A student who had come to McGill a little earlier would have heard state-of-the-art mathematical economics from Alfred William Flux: a Cambridge wrangler who elegantly mathematized neoclassical theory, first in the Jevons Chair at Owens College in Manchester and then in the William Dow Chair of Political Economy at McGill.[34] But after Flux left in 1908, Leacock took over and erased "higher economics." Leacock's application to McGill boasted of political and economic credentials, but his talents were all in the former.[35] Harold Innis wrote a devastating obituary, while Craufurd Goodwin lamented the damage done to McGill over three decades.[36] Leacock's incompetence had worried Flux who restricted him to politics courses. In December 1904, finding himself among Chicago economists, Flux asked what they thought of Leacock. The results confirmed his suspicions, he told

Principal William Peterson. All of them prevaricated and disavowed "any particular knowledge" of him. "What I learned was far from encouraging, but it was far less what I learned directly than the fact that none of them was willing to say anything that impressed me," not even in "studiously vague terms."[37] In 1906, Flux told Leacock not to teach tariffs and railways in his politics courses. That, Leacock complained to Peterson, reduced his politics classes to mere law.

Peterson made his own inquiries at Chicago. Laughlin was absent, so it fell to Veblen and the dean of arts, H.P. Judson, to answer Peterson's request for "proof that [Leacock] is competent in Economics." Judson, head of political science, testified to Leacock's "brilliant record." Veblen, more measured, described Leacock as "a man of more than ordinary intelligence. Though less widely read in science than some other candidates for doctor's degrees, he had a large fund of general information and a command of the principles of the science."[38] That was good enough for Peterson, who warned Flux to back down or find himself running a one-man Economics Department. Flux compromised "for the sake of peace." A middle ground was found in the appointment, in 1907, of a third economist, J.C. Hemmeon, a recent Harvard PhD working on the history of the British post office, to teach extension classes. In the event, Leacock immediately went on an imperial speaking tour and Hemmeon took over Leacock's classes. Innis's obituary of Leacock observes, "In 1907 an ominous storm of imperialism broke over him and carried him from his moorings." The roots of the tour lay in a 1905 request, by Governor General Lord Grey to Principal Peterson, for someone to lecture on empire to a club founded by his daughter.[39] Delighted with Peterson's choice of Leacock, though regretting his imprudent anti-American tone, Grey arranged the tour through the Rhodes Trust. Thus did Peterson, another imperialist, protect Leacock.

Flux left – in disgust, one suspects – whereupon Leacock demanded the Dow Chair. Peterson turned back to Chicago for warrant for the promotion. We value Leacock, he told Laughlin, as a teacher and political scientist, but the chair was, after all, economics: "What I should very much appreciate from you is an estimate of his standing as an economist, or rather perhaps of what he might achieve in that field if he were to give himself to it wholly." That was a very big if, and it allowed Laughlin to say that it was not *inconceivable* that Leacock *might* acquire standing: "Of course, at present he has no known standing as an Economist; and I can only give an opinion that

I believe he would achieve as much in Economics as he has in Political Science, if he were to give himself wholly to it."[40] Leacock got the Dow Chair without making himself a serious economist. Hemmeon did most of the economics teaching, not without snark. When he lectured that all economists were free traders, a student objected, that "'Dr. Leacock is a protectionist.' 'I repeat,' retorted Hemmeon acidly, 'all economists are free-traders.'"[41]

For Leacock, Canada's history exemplified sovereign autonomy, as spelled out in a 1907 book, *Baldwin, Lafontaine, Hincks: Responsible Government*. Britain had dissolved its corn laws and navigation acts at the same time as it extended self-government to Canada. Liberal economics and politics had reinforced one another. But the more recent evidence for and against state intervention, Leacock's dissertation of 1903 argued, called for a middle ground between the old laissez-faire and the new socialism.[42] This was very much a national-imperial middle ground: Leacock preferred British Dreadnoughts to either a tin-pot Canadian navy or ironic American "protection."[43] "Measure not the price" of self defence, he urged in 1907: "It is not a commercial benefit we buy. We are buying back our honour as Imperial Citizens."[44] The greatness of Greece and Rome, Leacock told the Arts Undergraduate Society in November 1911, was that they "possessed something not to be reckoned in terms of material resources."[45] In Ian Ross Robertson's summary, "Canadians will be elevated in spirit. Money, the claims of the provinces, and the interests of the political parties will have less attraction."[46]

Leacock threw himself into the 1911 campaign to oust the Laurier Liberals and get Robert Borden's Conservatives into power. When he brought Clifford Sifton, formerly a Liberal, now a Conservative political boss, on campus to lecture, students rioted.[47] In 1914, they heard another MP, R.B. Bennett, liken the naval subsidy to a church contribution.[48] Both parties accused the other of selling Canada out to plutocrats. But with millionaire financiers like Borden, Bennett, White, and Sifton running Canada from 1911, prices still rose, and professors and students alike pondered their diminished purchasing power. Among the "many plausible" explanations surveyed in the *McGill Daily* were the tariff, profligacy, stock watering, and excess gold.[49] In November 1913, it predicted that Leacock would chair a promised federal committee of inquiry.[50] Leacock did not join the committee but did lecture and advise on money and prices, always defending the tariff and blaming inflation on gold, profligacy, and immigrants.[51]

Montreal, like Chicago, was an important destination for an Eastern European diaspora that peaked in the years before the First World War, when the influx of immigrants to Canada rose above 400,000, higher than anything seen before. Leacock attacked the Liberal open-door policy early and often. In England in 1907, he described John Bull as a farmer eating "all sorts of foreign stuff, Russian caviar, and Austrian sardines, and Turkish olives," sold to him by sneaking foreign peddlers. John Bull's strapping young sons should "take the whole concern right over" and force farm-grown produce on him.[52] In Ottawa in 1909, he warned the Canadian Club against the "fusion policy" of immigration that would see the "two great races in Canada" mixed up with "Poles, Hungarians, Bukowinians and any others who will come in to share the heritage which our fathers have won." In 1911, his "Canada and the Immigration Problem" rejected the "mere herds of the proletariat of Europe, the lowest classes of industrial society," as "indifferent material from which to build the commonwealth of the future."[53]

Leacock agreed with Veblen in seeing a binary between economic science and economic policy: "In and of itself it is a science; that is, a survey of facts and phenomena made for its own sake, inculcating no precepts and proposing no program."[54] But where Veblen's science debunked "invidious" racial distinctions, Leacock preferred such distinctions to science. He distrusted statistics and facts, denouncing in 1911 "the mere plugger, learning facts and figures."[55] Both threatened the elusive quality of "character" cultivated in Oxford, an important exemplar for Leacock after his 1907 visit there. Where commerce corrupted the ideal university, science rationalized it.

> Oxford is a noble university. It has a great past. It is at present the greatest university in the world: and it is quite possible that it has a great future. Oxford trains scholars of the real type better than any other place in the world. Its methods are antiquated. It despises science. Its lectures are rotten. It has professors who never teach and students who never learn. It has no order, no arrangement, no system. Its curriculum is unintelligible. It has no president. It has no state legislature to tell it how to teach, and yet, – it gets there. Whether we like it or not, Oxford gives something to its students, a life and a mode of thought, which in America as yet we can emulate but not equal.[56]

The classic Oxford professor, for Leacock, was impractical: "Of money he knew nothing; of business, far less … All this is changed in America. A university professor is now a busy, hustling person, approximating as closely to a business man as he can do it. It is on the business man that he models himself."

Marion Fourcade argues that where French economics was more statist, and English economics more "aristocratic," American economics was exceptionally "'market-oriented,' both cognitively and professionally." Americans defined "competitive markets as the single most important principle of economic governance" and imported the principle into the discipline, itself understood as competing in a competitive academic marketplace.[57] Competition was a boon for economic science: the proliferation of competitive schools in the United States drove rivalry amongst them, and – as in nineteenth-century Germany – rivalry drove research and specialization. Thus was the discipline's claim to epistemological authority joined to an intensely commercial outlook in the United States, one that worried both Veblen and Leacock.

Leacock observed that earlier ages treated businessmen as rascals. "In the Middle Ages the businessman, in the form of a Jew, was made use of by unlettered kings and horse-stable princes who occasionally drew his teeth out or boiled him in oil to teach him to know his betters." It was reserved for the moderns "to reverse all this and to enthrone the despised trader in triumph on the debris of broken aristocracies and bankrupt dynasties."[58] But Leacock seemed to be doing much the same thing at McGill by popularizing economics and building up a business school (like Laughlin at Chicago). Where Veblen attacked the monetization of academe, Leacock embraced such things as the price of the Dow Chair. He "relentlessly" pursued money in his university entitlements and his book sales and he pandered to the bourgeois culture that he denounced.[59] Bankers, he complained, seeking higher but still "practical" education for their sons accomplished "such a vacuum-cleaning of modern education as had not been seen in a millennium" to the extent that "a great number of tin-pot institutions and two-penny departments began to turn out a new kind of graduate, who spelt Cæsar with a G and thought that Edmund Burke was the name of a brewer."[60] McGill students observed in 1914 of *Arcadian Adventures of the Idle Rich* that Plutoria University was "supposed to be a thousand miles away, but it reads like it is awfully close to home."[61]

But in pandering to "crude yearnings for culture,"[62] McGill was not so much protecting as diluting culture. The students might insist, as in a *McGill Daily* editorial in February 1914, that "the majority of people do not live in a sordid world but in a sphere where they seek to know the beautiful, the true and the lasting."[63] Veblen-trained economists knew better. The kinds of things that university students most admired were, on Veblen's logic, particularly likely to be sordid and vulgar. Academic gowns and ritual solemnities cropped up, in imitation of ancient mummery, "so soon as wealth begins appreciably to accumulate in the community, and so soon as a given school begins to lean on a leisure-class constituency."[64] Alfred Flux and Ernest Rutherford were scientists' scientists but both left a McGill that preferred vulgarity. The difference between the fake Eastern philosophy peddled by con artists to wealthy women in Leacock's Yahi-Bahi Society and the historic Oxford ideals peddled by Leacock to students and girls' groups, was not easy to define in ways that insulated it from Veblen's corroding logic. All the harder when Leacock's classroom seemed to him populated not just by entrepreneurial young men but also by sexually entrepreneurial young women.

McGill was not yet Chicago. Leacock made that point indirectly, through a McGill student he coached for an intercollegiate debate in 1912 on the topic of big versus small universities. The student, Hugh Farthing, argued that you might produce doctors, lawyers, and scientists like furniture and "sell knowledge the same as in the large department stores" but you could not build up an "aristocracy of thought and feeling in the same manner as commercial manufacturers. In the University of Chicago every piece of printed matter must contain the words 'Founded by John D. Rockefeller['] which is simply an advertisement for the Standard Oil Company." The result was "a tendency to lose sight of the main ideals of a University."[65]

But for Leacock, that corruption had a Jewish vanguard. "Jew" was not a word Leacock bandied about carelessly in his writings, and Margaret Macmillan has said that "one of the few prejudices of his time he seems not to have shared is against Jews."[66] But an attentive auditor at McGill would have heard an antisemitic note mingled into the fear of Eastern immigration. Mainstream economics was riddled with antisemitism. At Harvard, William Ripley's *Races of Europe* ranked Eastern Europeans below Teutons and Jews below them both.[67] Montrealers also feared decivilization from Eastern Europe, a place, Professor H.J. Rose told the McGill Oriental Society in 1914, "where the influences are not wholly those of western civilization."[68]

Jews were particularly likely to emigrate from Romanian-Russian borderlands, where modern antisemitism began to take shape. In 1900 alone, more than 25,000 Romanian Jews walked westward. Where Laurier extended them "a hearty welcome," nativists blamed the pogroms on Jewish refusal to assimilate and tried to close the gates against them.[69] "Eastern European Jews stuck out as particularly foreign. Poor and pious, they clung to their traditions, and spoke Yiddish or Ladino."[70] In Montreal, Jewish "in-migrants married young and lived in extended families, about one-third in streets of very high densities."[71] "Uptown" or established Jews in Montreal often shared in the dismay at the influx. At McGill, the *Daily* observed that the students were growing more "cosmopolitan" every year, with Jews now outnumbering all except the "Canadian" and the "English." In 1913–14, Jews, numbering 112, made up 6.8 per cent of the student body.

Left liberals such as J.S. Woodsworth and Oscar Skelton defended Jews as assimilable. Woodsworth spoke at McGill in 1913, describing a "Russian Jew" who had shed his nihilism and anarchism to settle into university studies and student outreach.[72] A few days later, Oscar Skelton – who had recently spoken on socialism at McGill – gave a paper in Kingston on immigration that the *McGill Daily* reproduced verbatim: Asians could not be assimilated, but Europeans could, *even* Jews in such numbers found in Montreal, who would not convert but were susceptible to liberal Christian influences that could reform Judaism from within.[73]

Leacock, meanwhile, criticized modern Jews as, like their medieval counterparts, a commercial leaven. In February 1912, the *McGill Daily* published a long letter by Leacock that called for an "English" repertory theatre to counter American fare that purveyed

> the unusual and the sensational. It draws enormous crowds to see a man who can make up as a woman or a woman who can imitate a man; it challenges our attention to the negro who can counterfeit a white man almost to the life, or a white comedian who can so black his face as to look absolutely dark. It carries with it its Headliners and its Starts, its First Appearance and its Last, and its Galaxy of Talent in letters eighteen inches high, – the whole of it manufactured on upper Broadway by Jew promoters who run the market for "shows" and "acts" and "attractions" and estimate the aesthetic needs of Montreal in the intervals of chewing the butt end of a forty cent cigar.[74]

Jews were degrading culture in a global marketplace that impinged upon McGill. And Leacock's popularity with students lent his remarks special weight. The *McGill Daily* followed Leacock's lead in denouncing the "New York theatrical manager" and urging civilizing Canadian theatre.[75] The antisemitism was implicit.

Michael Brown argues that English Montrealers were less openly antisemitic than a Goldwin Smith in Toronto, because French Canadians were more openly so.[76] Deep and bitter right-wing French antisemitism was mainstreamed by Catholic newspapers, such as *La Croix de Montréal* and *La Verité*, that railed incessantly against Jews, Freemasons, and liberals.[77] From 1910 to 1914, Quebecers followed the trial of Quebec notary and journalist, Jacques E. Plamondon, who declared Jews "enemies of the Christian faith" and prompted riots and beatings in Quebec City. Two Jewish merchants sued for damages, bringing in as an expert witness Herman Abramowitz, rabbi at the Shaar Hashomayim Synagogue situated on McGill College Avenue just below Sherbrooke Street, and they won their case on appeal.[78] Montreal Anglos had more to lose than to gain from a vituperative antisemitism that might embolden their political rivals. There was also seen to be something very English about tolerance. Antisemitism at McGill, thus, was policed by etiquette as well as by an organized Jewish presence on campus.

But unpleasant incidents abounded, as in November 1911, when the *McGill Daily* called for quiet in the library. Students studying for a Leacock exam were disturbed by a student, who came not to study but "prepared to enter into a lengthy and voluble conversation with a friend, which, to make matters worse, was carried on in abominable French, savoured with a strong Yiddish accent." The *Daily* condemned the "ignorant impropriety." The Jewish students reacted angrily: massed in the library the next night, they drummed their feet upon the floor; they also wrote letters to the *Daily* (that it declared too "puerile" to publish) and one, Jacob Livinson (Arts '11 and Law '14), wrote to Principal Peterson urging "equity, tolerance, and broadmindedness" at a time when "McGill is inevitably becoming cosmopolitan."[79] Peterson glossed over the incident as best forgotten, having "no reference whatever to you personally," and affirmed McGill's treatment of students "on a level and to give equal measure to all, without fear or favour." Another *Daily* article in 1913 warned against shady luring by "Hebrew Speculators": one Israel Finkelbaum (whose "facial characteristics" supposedly revealed his

Semitic "origin") offered to buy deposits at a local bank at seventy-five cents on the dollar.[80]

The trope of the Jewish money-lender was indulged as high culture and as a monetizing threat to that culture. Spendthrift socialites made themselves beholden to Jewish social climbers in Edith Wharton's *The House of Mirth*, published in 1905,[81] and in *The Cabinet Minister*, a play by Sir Arthur Pinero that the graduating students of McGill staged in 1913. It featured a villainous Jewish money lender: "Mr Joseph Lebanon enters – a smartly dressed, unctuous, middle-aged person, of a most pronounced common Semitic type, with a bland manner and a contested smile." Lebanon lends money to another spendthrift socialite, Lady Twombley, who is married to a government cabinet minister. Lebanon does not just demand she introduce him to her friends, but also tries to speculate on cabinet secrets. The portrayal was criticized in 1890s London as too crude.[82] The Arts '14 students may have pushed back in their choice of the senior play. *The Manoeuvres of Jane* was written by Henry Arthur Jones, who argued that Jews were "no more materialistic than their neighbours."[83]

But the *McGill Daily* took the opposite view. In 1914, drama critic Alton Goldbloom (a future professor of pediatrics at McGill) panned two plays based on Dickens novels. A response by Ernest Henson, a Catholic theology student, defended the plays by likening Scrooge and Fagin: "The former was a nominal Christian with distinct Jewish characteristics, whereas the latter was a real Jew only differing in the greater extent of his villainy." Infuriated, Goldbloom asked whether Henson feared "for the safety of himself and his Alma Mater with eighty such 'real Jews' as his fellow students." Was the country endangered by a Jewish postmaster, was justice endangered by a Jewish chief justice? Statistics showed Jews were "singularly free from criminality." Henson defended himself: "When I spoke of Scrooge as 'a nominal Christian with distinct Jewish characteristics, I merely referred to a certain tightness in money matters which is a little weakness that from time immemorial has been laid at the door of the Jews."[84] On David Nirenberg's reading, this was the question of *The Merchant of Venice*: whether commerce was turning Christians into money-grubbing Jews. "Shakespeare seems to suggest, it is only the exceptional knowledge of love that can distinguish the 'gentle' from the 'Jew.'"[85] Henson was accusing Goldbloom, too, of base mindedness. Henson's tedious letters were another thing that Viner mocked in the 1914 yearbook.

Appeals to character, Farthing's "aristocracy of thought and feeling," pervaded McGill culture. The students parroted and also elided discourses denouncing Jewish modernity, much as landlords excluded "Eastern Europeans" as a euphemism for Jews.[86] "Character," on the other hand, was a euphemism for "not Jewish." In February 1912, the week of Leacock's theatre letter, Maurice Hutton, a Toronto classicist, gave a talk at McGill chaired by Leacock that culminated in an appeal to "KNOWLEDGE, ACHIEVEMENT, CHARACTER." Privately, Hutton was given to "gratuitously venomous remarks about the Jews," as when he complained that a Paris dean was "of that race of Jews which is running, if not ruining, the University for the rest of France."[87] The German research ideal that Veblen praised and Leacock criticized seemed disproportionately to benefit Jewish scholars to the detriment of the non-Jewish in Germany and complaints began to mount. Economics lacked the deep antisemitic bias of history, classics, and Oriental studies, not to mention English (which another Montreal transplant to Chicago, Saul Bellow, was told he was too Jewish to grasp). But on that logic, not just money but economics itself was undermining civilization and the "exceptional knowledge of love" animating the campus YMCA.

Nativists sought to block foreign professors as well as goods, money, and labour.[88] But if Viner became effectively unemployable at McGill or Harvard, the new research universities bankrolled by plutocrats were more open. The United States had six research universities in 1890 (Johns Hopkins, Yale, Harvard, Cornell, Columbia, and Clark) with eight more added, including Chicago, by 1900, several of them led by Jews.[89] Numbers of students and tensions continued to rise at McGill and, in 1917, Hemmeon had to "interfere several times when discussion in class became personal" between socialist-internationalist "Hebrews" and patriotic Christians.[90] Jewish student numbers would be capped after the war at 6 per cent, amidst criticisms in the French press in 1919 for preferring "des professeurs allemands ou juifs" over *Canadiens*.[91]

Leacock's arguments culminated in a short book in 1919: *The Unsolved Riddle of Social Justice*, which reworked his PhD by incorporating price theory. He argued that the emphasis on consumption over production, demand over supply, allowed the rich to set prices. That was not justice but mere right of the economically strongest. Socialist ethics were more just but less realistic than liberal ones. But liberalism was too callous to children born in poverty, who were needed, it turned out, for armies. The middle ground was now a national welfare state with the gates closed to everyone outside that state. Strength had seemed, before the war, to rest in "the wholesale import of Austrians, Bulgarians and Czecho-Slovaks. The newer nations boasted proudly of their immigration tables. The fallacy is apparent now. Those who really count in a nation and those who govern its destinies for good or ill are those who are born into it."[92] Canada's essence would flow out like water if not dammed and piled up. The hard lesson: "We must harden ourselves lest we too perish. We feed well while others starve. We make fast the doors of our lighted houses against the indigent and hungry. What else can we do?"[93]

Leacock's lectures on money probably bristled more with prejudice than rigour. If you disagreed with Leacock or with Arts '13, might you want to wage symbolic war by breaking up a lecture? Viner was surely a problem for Leacock and Leacock a problem for Viner. Viner's Romanian-Jewish parents emigrated to Montreal in 1886 and settled in the Jewish quarter around St Urbain, albeit moving around as his father, Samuel, moved up socially from peddling to shopkeeping. Viner shared an anglophile and Conservative political streak with Leacock and complained that the Liberal editors of the yearbook mangled his history. Viner also shared the admiration for Veblen, whom he met and described in 1918 as "*the* American genius."[94] But Viner and Leacock did not share economic theories: Viner knew, when he wrote up his yearbook account, that Leacock could be counted among the "pseudo-economists" in the classroom. Later contacted by a Leacock biographer, David Legate, who confessed to having learned no economics from Leacock, Viner concurred. "In my opinion, then and now, Leacock was simply not qualified as an economist. His graduate work at Chicago was certainly primarily in the Political Science Department, which was, unlike the situation in my time at McGill, a completely separate department" and an undistinguished one. Leacock's "teaching of what he thought advanced economics was a farce, and I'm afraid some of us gave him a rough time, until the girls in the class, out of pity for him, asked us to lay off."[95] Viner's older brother Norman (who did win a medical appointment at McGill) teased him in turn: "The trouble with you, Jake, is that you have the sense of humor of a Hemmeon and the economics of a Leacock."[96]

And yet Viner also found McGill an empowering place, and Leacock and Hemmeon empowering teachers. He praised Leacock's political science as wide-ranging and unbiased, with students offered "full opportunity to state their views."[97] And Leacock helped Viner secure the Chicago position with a "short but emphatic note" to Laughlin in 1916 and also invited him back as an examiner and substitute teacher.[98] Both were iconoclasts in their way. But Viner's iconoclasm was closer to Veblen's: owing more to economic theory and less to reactionary nativism.

Economics allowed a freedom of speech that was often unwelcome in Jews.[99] The *McGill Daily*'s coverage of clubs at McGill shows the gap, in contrast to the yearbook. Yearbooks recorded all official organizations, including fraternities, and the Maccabean Circle formed in 1905 by a handful of Jewish students who "realized the need for some club which would cherish the study of history, thought and ideals of their people." They held literary and social activities and, beginning in March 1913, annually donated volumes pertaining to Jewish matters; the resolution to do so did earn a rare note in the *McGill Daily*. The *Daily* only reported on teams and clubs seen as serving collective cohesion, not fraternities or the Maccabean Circle. The YMCA received particularly lavish coverage in the *Daily*. Jewish content occasionally cropped up in other clubs, as in a paper given to the Philosophical Society in November 1911 on "Jewish Contributions to Philosophy." The author, Abraham Aaron Roback, was a Russian-born philosophy major, who would enjoy a distinguished academic career in the United States. His paper, which posited a Jewish mode of philosophy, provoked debate: "The strength of the Jewish mind, it was suggested, was its analytical and critical and nego-positive, rather than its constructive elements, and it was thus not well suited to synthetic philosophy."[100] Viner was active in the Maccabean Circle and the Shaar Hashomayim Synagogue. In March 1913, he gave a "brilliantly written paper" to the synagogue's Young People's Society (following one on Zionism by Louis Fitch).[101]

But Viner determined to make himself heard at the centre of campus life, not just its margins. In winter 1913, he wrote the yearbook entry and competed for the Reford Cup for public speaking (the topics set by Leacock on classic conservative-imperial questions of the day), only to be eliminated on the first round. In his final year, 1913–14, as his ambitions turned from law school to economics, Viner joined the Mock Parliament run by the Literary and Debating Society and, with Frank Common and L.D. Wilgress, founded a Political Economy Club that "divided the ground between questions of economic theory and social reform." The Political Economy Club met for the first time on

20 November 1913, with a "most satisfactory attendance in point of numbers" (capped at twenty-five). Frank Common was president and Viner treasurer, while Leacock and Hemmeon served as honoraries. The professors claimed to welcome the club, though Hemmeon later referred to Leacock's "disapproval."[102]

In January 1914, during a meeting devoted to John Bates Clark and marginal utility theory, four papers were heard, two by professors and two by students. First, Hemmeon outlined Clark's main arguments, then Frank McDiarmid addressed Clark's theory of distribution showing that distribution depended on "the final productivity of the agents concerned." Next, Viner asked, "Is rent a part of price?" and concluded that rent did enter into cost and price just as wages and interest did, if land productivity had contributed to production. Finally, Leacock gave a satirical talk entitled: "A Little Outing to the Margin of Utility with J.B. Clark." Clark, Leacock, and a "simple person" walked past rich industrial areas to poorer ones and then finally arrived at a barren land with a ramshackle shed that Clark proudly identified as "the place that controlled the wages, profits and interest of the country – there was the margin of utility." Inside the dusty building, one capitalist and one workingman fought to the death. "Prof. Clark exclaimed with horror that prices would immediately rise throughout the country. Dr. Leacock's paper was greatly applauded."[103] Where other students thrilled to hear Canada's "greatest humorist," Viner described the talk to Legate as "utterly fallacious."[104] After Viner's departure, the club abandoned economic theory and focused on reform.[105]

Not everyone welcomed the new club. Jean H. Bieler – a second-year arts student in 1910, now studying law – was "greatly surprised" to see a new club, of which there were too many. Given that "the great majority of the Honor men in Economics belong to the Historical Club, which reserves every year at least one evening to the consideration of economic subjects," the founders should have expanded "social and economic subjects" there. The new club could do "nothing but harm" to the Historical Club.[106] Bieler was treasurer of the Historical Club, and active in the Lit, the French Club, and the Canadian Club. In the Pinero play, Bieler had played a crusty Scottish noble who scolded Lebanon for his lack of manners. Bieler's father was a professor of theology at the Presbyterian College at McGill, having recently emigrated from France, and all the Bielers were active in the YMCA. Bieler probably thought he was on strong ground given that, the

Figure 6.1 Founding executive of the Political Economy Club. Back row: Dana Wilgress and Jacob Viner. Front row: G.D. Burn, Frank Common, Stephen Leacock, and J.C. Hemmeon.

previous month, Principal Peterson had spoken against special studies and urged the study of history: nothing so well counteracted "any narrowing tendencies in the professional career of lawyer, doctor or engineer as to have a wide outlook upon history."[107]

Bieler was on weak ground and Viner, mandated to respond, was brutal. The club had been formed with "but a single object": to give the honours students "presumably" more interested in economics than in history, "an opportunity of discussing in a more informal and detailed manner than is desirable or possible in the lecture room." A new club could not injure an old one that preserved its attractions and usefulness. If decline occurred, "one is inevitably forced to the conclusion that not the evils of the new society, but the defects of the old, are responsible." One economics session at the Historical Club per year was "pabulum for the young." Better the historians stick to history "and leave Economics to the economists." Viner's final salvo attacked the social exclusivity underlying the disciplinary: he doubted that the "great majority" of economists were in the Historical Club but "perhaps Mr. Bieler has inadvertently written 'the great majority' in place [of] 'the majority of the great.'"[108]

New disciplines and specialties always get attacked by the old as privatizing. But Viner was also insisting on economic criteria for judging the worth of a given club or discipline and irreverently dismantling the defences for McGill's "great" things. To be a new discipline was not to be inferior to an old one, just as to be a new Canadian was not to be inferior to an old one. If a quintessentially English history did not know its place in this brave new world, Viner was ready to teach it the hard lessons. Disciplines that could not match the explanatory and popular power of economics deserved to decline. McGill had a reputation as the most conservative and most "English" school of history in Canada with a "sense of power" imbuing many different clubs and teams.[109] Wielding economics like a club, Viner struck at conservative, Anglo-Protestant supremacy. He had precociously imbibed Fourcade's lesson of American economics, "defining competitive markers as the single most important principle of economic governance" and applied it to a bottom-up reconstruction of McGill's governance, understood to rest on student consumer choices and intellectual capital. In Viner's insistence that all things should be priced according to their value, we see hints of nascent Chicago price theory. But we also see a classic novelistic hero, a Tom Jones or an Elizabeth Bennet, finding their way by their wits and their confidence. When Lady Catherine de Bourgh told the protagonist of *Pride and Prejudice* that she should not aspire to marry Mr Darcy, Elizabeth responded: "He is a gentleman; I am a gentleman's daughter; so far we are equal." Being a competent economist in 1913 was like being a gentleman's daughter in 1813: it should open all the doors to which a Viner might reasonably aspire.

Viner's iconoclasm was repudiated by the *Daily* editors, who lamented the twin evils of specialized societies and their clashes. It recommended a McGill version of the Royal Society of Canada, with sections for "literature, art, science and history," and new ones needing approval from the old.[110] But it still reported on the Political Economy Club while ignoring the Maccabean. Political economy had let David Hume do an end run around the clerisy and such heirs as Viner reaped the benefits.[111] Bieler and Viner carried their disputes into the annual student Mock Parliament, where Viner served as the Conservative "Minister of Labour" and called for the abolition of the Senate. But the mock-Conservatives fell and the mock-Liberals rose on that issue, with Bieler made "Minister of Commerce." The clerisy remained in control.

Meanwhile, Viner was stretching his vision in a new course by Leacock on social reform. Leacock invited the students to envision "a Socialistic commonwealth as nearly ideal as it is possible to imagine." Viner's essay, published in the *Daily*, was nothing if not ambitious. Existing economic relations caused too much wealth and poverty, as correctly noted by anarchists and socialists, if not by jobbing economists "perched upon the summit of a mound of textbooks of orthodox political economy, ridden with fallacies and mouldy with age." Anarchy was no solution, nor was a socialism debunked by John Bates Clark and Alfred Marshall: "Labour is by no means the measure of value, for the value of labour itself is determined by the same factors which determine the value of its products, viz.: demand and supply." But Viner also rejected Skelton's liberalism, whose mockery for socialism had only made him ridiculous. Viner reached for something at once more conservative and more radical. He referenced a lecture in 1909 by the retiring professor of physics at McGill, John Cox, to the Montreal Canadian Club: "The words of a staid and sober college professor, delivered before an audience of businessmen," that complained of the "money-making spirit" as encroaching on higher activities, including theatres, newspapers, and universities. Cox blamed high finance for making diplomacy and trade violent and predatory, and recommended national control of resources managed for conservation and universal sufficiency.[112]

Viner likewise predicted that the ethos of competition would be replaced by an ethos of "social utility" that "will begin its work, and will judge land and capital, each on its own merits." Social utility, delivered by market choices, was the argument against a rent-seeking Historical Club and against rent-seeking landlords and financiers. Socialist and single-tax arguments, both of them subjects of Political Economy Club discussions, handed Viner grounds for the abolition of private property in land: "Nationalize all lands and lease them out for a limited period of time, by public auction." Other taxes could be abolished, and the proceeds distributed amongst those unable to work, "not as alms, but as their due." Those who could work, on the other hand, must do so. Compulsory education would be the avenue to universal enfranchisement. The government would monopolize banking and would conserve resources; it would also license all middlemen to the appropriate number. Political parties would persist but corruption would be more aggressively repressed. Viner defended such utopian visions as written not for fine policy but "in the hope that a vivid picture of what might be, placed in contrast to the sad and sordid conditions that were, would stir up the masses to exert the might of their numbers, and to fight their way, by peaceful means if possible, by brute force if not, out of the mire into which in their ignorance they had allowed the privileged classes to push them." Change would come, whether as social catastrophe, provoked by growing inequality, or growing knowledge amongst the working classes that would "lead to the firm but peaceful and gradual exile of the capitalist and non-worker from the direction of government and industry." There would be no end state because ideals always evolved. "And it is well thus."[113]

Viner told Legate that Leacock dealt generously with an essay that "must have contained much that was fit (and perhaps intended by me) to set his teeth on edge."[114] The *Daily* dryly remarked that the proposal was unlikely to win elections. It also lost the socialists: Isidore Boltuck, a Polish Jew and son of a garment worker,[115] immediately penned a rebuttal of "the theories of a pseudo-economist," which Boltuck described as "a patched blanket, made up of Utopian, conservative and revolutionary measures, thrown together in a chop-suey fashion." He defended the labour theory of value while sharing the critique of industrial capitalism. Hugh B. Griffith, another Arts '14 Honours Economics student, replied arguing that Boltuck's socialism was more like anarchism and asked whether he considered himself "an economist, a pseudo-economist, or one who disdains all knowledge of the subject."[116]

Viner was weaponizing the word "economist" to annoy just about everyone else on campus. He made enemies who did much the same with "Christian." What looks like revenge for the attack on Bieler struck at the Faculty of Arts graduation dinner in February of 1914. When the speeches began, the first toast was to the king and the second to the alma mater was supposed to be by Hugh Farthing. But he could not attend and Viner made the toast in his stead, with damningly faint praise in a context where superlatives were usual.

> In the course of his remarks, Mr. Viner pointed out that McGill had developed an individuality which had made her famous all over this continent. "McGill is a factor in the progress of Canada, and the betterment of Montreal."
>
> "I had never known that the McGill YMCA had such contempt for public opinion," said Principal Peterson by way of reply. This remark was occasioned by the fact that during the course of the

> dinner some exuberant youths had started up, "We are, we are, we are the McGill YMCA, etc." There is no greater agency in the Dominion of Canada, the Principal went on to say, "tha[n] McGill, for binding together the different portions of our scattered country."

Peterson was clearly responding to immediate disruptions. He praised McGill's popularity among "the English people," and treasured "that spirit of solidarity which makes McGill a true brotherhood." The next speaker was Ernest Henson, who toasted the Faculty of Arts for encouraging student social and moral life. Dean Charles Moyse replied with an argument for faculty-wide unity and tolerance: "It was composed of men of all shapes, all sizes, all heights and varying degrees of knowledge. Reference was made to the element of cosmopolitanism, which was so large a factor at McGill."[117] I see McGill officers gently disciplining Christian rowdies for disrupting Viner's speech. Peterson knew Viner well enough to recommend him, in May 1914, as "one of our best graduates."[118]

Viner helped to organize the convocation that month, toasted the graduating class, and delivered a speech on "the future of the class of McGill Fourteen," described as a vision delivered through a drinking glass, that depicted every member of the class as "extraordinarily gifted compared to the ordinary run of men." One would become a jobbing politician invoking the "peepul," another would put his smiling countenance on chocolate wrappers, another would write letters in etiquette for young society ladies, while Henson would be haunted from stage to pulpit by the ghost of his "muddled conscience," until he did it to death with a hatpin. The insider jokes do not survive well, any more than in another humorous piece on female suffrage that describes its author as a "pseudo-humourist." They show Viner aspiring to appropriate Leacock's genre as well as his discipline.[119]

Viner did stand in for Leacock one year and also served as an outside examiner. But in 1924, cordial relations ended abruptly after Viner, a notoriously hard grader at Chicago, failed a prize McGill student, then reluctantly, under pressure from Hemmeon and Leacock, allowed a "bare acceptance." Viner wrote two versions of his response, the second tactfully crossing out such remarks as: "But I can never act again as examiner for McGill."[120] The rupture could be tacit, he realized, and equipoise maintained. But deeper hostility lurked beneath the equipoise. Confiding in a writer friend soon after his arrival in Chicago in 1916,

Viner described his new colleague there, James Field, as having a better command of English than anyone but "Stephen Leacock, and he has over Leacock the advantages of being a gentleman, a scholar, and a man of learning besides."[121] Thus did Viner reject Shakespeare's distinction between the "gentle" and the Jew. Unforgivably for Viner, Leacock chose prejudice and a veneer of learning over technical competence that debunked such prejudice and then he led the students on that "adventurous course." Leacock's failure was, and remains, all too common: a failure to follow the trail of money across its complicated transmutations, without taking it into identity politics and beggar-my-neighbour warmongering. Viner spent his life neutralizing such prejudices. He rewrote trade theory and reconstructed international lending institutions so as to make money a productive mechanism of equalization.[122]

Confronted with hostility that might be disciplinary, religious, or racial, young Jack Viner gave as good as he got and made an Anglo-Protestant establishment heed him. Where words of authority – political, social, intellectual – were spoken, he would be in on the conversation: Jewish remarks in his congregation, economics in academe, and a combination of conservative and radical arguments in the student newspaper, itself a compendium of such voices. Viner tested the limits of what could be said in such venues, with brutal criticisms of the old and dazzling projections of the new that, now as then, we see taken to outrageously utopian articles in the *McGill Daily*. And it is well thus.

If Viner called out Leacock, Leacock called out Viner when he as much as asked: Well, then, young prodigy, what are *you* going to do about the extreme wealth and poverty remaking the world in their image? That was inspired teaching. It helped Viner find his voice as a theorist and as another famously inspiring teacher of dissenting students, several of them Nobel laureates. Likewise, both men made themselves policy advocates and champions of the welfare state, but on very different models. Long after Leacock's death, Viner carried on their conversation. In 1958, his inaugural Plaunt lecture at Carleton attacked Canadian economic protectionism and cultural nationalism: all that Canada really needed by way of protection against its giant neighbour, he insisted, was well-funded public schools and open doors to "continental" immigration.[123] Viner, like Leacock, spoke euphemistically while repudiating the closed-door policies that condemned many would-be immigrants to certain death. Where Leacock's loyalty was to an Anglo-Protestant Canadian establishment, Viner's was to an international commonwealth.

NOTES

I gratefully acknowledge support from the Friends of the Princeton University Library and the Seeley G. Mudd librarians. Thanks also to friends for their advice, especially Meg and Andy Seiler, Paul Oslington, Robert Dimand, Seokju Oh, Jean-Philip Mathieu, Jeffrey Kastner, John Zucchi, Judith Szapor, and the late Gershon Hundert, as well as the editors and referees.

1 J.V., "History of Arts 1914," *1914 Yearbook* (1913), 68.

2 Seeley G. Mudd Manuscripts Library, Princeton University, MC 136, Jacob Viner Papers (hereafter JVP) vol. 12, file 18: Michael Garber, 19 January 1970.

3 Nelson Lichtenstein, *American Capitalism: Social Thought and Political Economy in the Twentieth Century* (Philadelphia: University of Pennsylvania Press, 2006), 4.

4 Clyde Barrow, *More than a Historian: The Political and Economic Thought of Charles A. Beard* (London and New York: Routledge, 2017), 39.

5 Morton White, *Social Thought in America: The Revolt Against Formalism* (Boston: Beacon Press, 1949), 78.

6 Götz Aly, *Why the Germans? Why the Jews? Envy, Race Hatred, and the Prehistory of the Holocaust*, trans. Jefferson Chase (Basingstoke: Picador, 2014), 130–1; Emily Levine, *Allies and Rivals: German-American Exchange and the Rise of the Modern Research University* (Chicago: University of Chicago Press, 2021), 184; Alexandra Przyrembel, "Moralizing Wealth: German Debates about Capitalism and Jews in the Early Twentieth Century," in Stefan Berger and Alexandra Pryzrembel, eds, *Moralizing Capitalism: Agents, Discourses and Practices of Capitalism and Anti-Capitalism in the Modern Age* (Basingstoke: Palgrave Macmillan, 2019), 72.

7 David Myers, *Resisting History: Historicism and Its Discontents* (Princeton: Princeton University Press, 2003), 160.

8 McGill yearbook (1917), 140.

9 Simon Leland, quoted in Hugh Murray Grant, *W.A. Mackintosh: The Life of a Canadian Economist* (Montreal and Kingston: McGill-Queen's University Press, 2015), 187; Paul A. Samuelson, "Jacob Viner, 1892–1970," in *Remembering the University of Chicago: Teachers, Scientists, and Scholars*, ed. Edward Shils (Chicago: University of Chicago Press, 1991), 534.

10 David Laidler, *The Golden Age of the Quantity Theory* (Princeton: Princeton University Press, 1991), 26.

11 Jakob Feinig, *Moral Economies of Money: Politics and the Monetary Constitution of Society* (Stanford: Stanford University Press, 2022), 109, 115.
12 Richard T. McCulley, quoted in Roger Lowenstein, *America's Bank: The Epic Struggle to Create the Federal Reserve* (Penguin Press, 2015), 57.
13 Lowenstein, *America's Bank*, 53, 72; Jeffrey Sklansky, *Sovereign of the Market: The Money Question in Early America* (Chicago: University of Chicago Press, 2017), 207–45.
14 Ian Tyrrell, *Transnational Nation: United States History in Global Perspective since 1789* (Basingstoke: Palgrave Macmillan, 2007), 34; Sylvia Nasar, *Grand Pursuit: The Story of Economic Genius* (New York: Simon & Schuster, 2011), 16; Laureen Goodlad, "Moral Character," in *Historicism and the Human Sciences in Victorian Britain* ed. Mark Bevir (Cambridge: Cambridge University Press, 2017), 151.
15 Steven Beller, *Vienna and the Jews 1867–1938: A Cultural History* (Cambridge: Cambridge University Press, 1989), 191; Michela Nacci, "The Present as Nightmare: Cultural Pessimism among European Intellectuals in the Period between the Two World Wars," in *The Intellectual Revolt against Liberal Democracy 1870–1945*, ed. Zeev Sternhell (Jerusalem: Israel Academy of Sciences and Humanities, 1996), 125.
16 In Laidler, *Golden Age*, 163.
17 J.L. Laughlin, "Prices and the International Movement of Specie," *Journal of Political Economy* 10 (September 1902): 526–8, 535.
18 Donald R. Wells, *The Federal Reserve System* (McFarland & Co., 2004), 14; Lowenstein, *America's Bank*, 49.
19 J. Laurence Laughlin, "Banknotes and Lending Power," *Journal of Political Economy* 18, no. 10 (December 1910): 781–2.
20 Stephen Leacock, *My Recollection of Chicago and The Doctrine of Laissez Faire*, Carl Spadoni ed. (Toronto: University of Toronto Press, 1998), 5.
21 Famously, MV = PT: that money, multiplied by the velocity of circulation, is equal to the number of transactions involving money payments times the average price of each transaction.
22 Girton and Roper, "J. Laurence Laughlin and the Quantity Theory of Money," 615–16.
23 Mark Blaug, "Why Is the Quantity of Money the Oldest Surviving Theory in Economics?" in *Not Only an Economist*, ed. Mark Blaug (Cheltenham, England: Edward Elgar, 1997), 116; Justin Fox, *The Myth of the Rational Market: A History of Risk, Reward, and Delusion on Wall Street* (New

York: Harper, 2009), 5; David F. Hendry and Mary S. Morgan, *The Foundations of Econometric Analysis* (Cambridge: Cambridge University Press, 1995); Robert W. Dimand, "Fisher and Veblen: Two Paths for American Economics," *Journal of the History of Economic Thought* 20, no. 4 (1998): 449–65.

24 Sklansky, *Sovereign of the Market*; Tyrrell, *Transnational Nation*, 148; Noel Maurer, *The Empire Trap: The Rise and Fall of U.S. Intervention to Protect American Property Overseas, 1893–2013* (Princeton: Princeton University Press, 2017).

25 E.A. Heaman, *Tax, Order, and Good Government: A New Political History of Canada, 1867–1919* (Montreal and Kingston: McGill-Queen's University Press, 2017), 365.

26 Charles A. Conant, *Wall Street and the Country: A Study of Recent Financial Tendencies* (New York and London: Putnam, 1904), 35–6.

27 Stephen Leacock, "Canada and the Monroe Doctrine," *The University Magazine* 8, no.3 (October 1909): 365–70.

28 Charles Camic, *Veblen: The Making of an Economist who Unmade Economics* (Cambridge, MA: Harvard University Press, 2020), 328; Thorstein Veblen, *Theory of the Leisure Class: An Economic Study of Institutions* (New York: MacMillan, 1899).

29 White, *Social Thought in America*.

30 Emily Levine, *Allies and Rivals: German-American Exchange and the Rise of the Modern Research University* (Chicago: University of Chicago Press, 2021), 177.

31 Lisa Krissoff Boehm, *Popular Culture and the Enduring Myth of Chicago, 1871–1968* (New York: Routledge, 2004), xx, 67; Stephen Edgell, *Veblen in Perspective: His Life and Thought* (Armonk, NY: M.E. Sharpe, 2001), 20.

32 From a later piece, *My Discovery of the West*: see Myron J. Frankman, "Stephen Leacock, Economist: An Owl Among the Peacocks," in *Stephen Leacock: A Reappraisal*, ed. David Staines (Ottawa: University of Ottawa Press, 1966), 53; Leacock, *My Recollection of Chicago*, 6.

33 Stephen Leacock, "What Is Left of Adam Smith?" *Canadian Journal of Economics and Political Science* 1, no. 1 (February 1935): 47.

34 Peter Groenewegen, "Alfred William Flux (1867–1942): A Mathematician Successfully 'Caught' for Economics by Marshall," *History of Economics Review* 48, no. 1 (2008): 63–77.

35 Stephen Leacock to William Peterson 5 May 1900, in *The Letters of Stephen Leacock*, eds David Staines and Barbara Nimmo (Oxford: Oxford University Press, 2006), 12.

36 Margaret Macmillan, *Stephen Leacock* (Toronto: Penguin, 2009), 89–90; Craufurd Goodwin, *Canadian Economic Thought: The Political Economy of a Developing Nation* (Durham, NC: Duke University Press, 1961).

37 McGill University Archives (hereafter MUA), RG2, Principal's Papers, Accession 641, C.17, file 20, Flux to Peterson, 23 March 1905.

38 MUA, RG2 Accession 641, C. 23, file 64, Leacock to Peterson, 31 January 1906; C. 33, vol. 8, p. 463, Peterson to Judson, 26 March 1906; C. 23, file 69: Judson to Peterson, 29 March 1906, Veblen to Peterson, 31 March 1906.

39 Harold Adams Innis, "Obituary: Stephen Butler Leacock (1869–1944)," *Canadian Journal of Economics and Political Science / Revue canadienne d'Economique et de Science politque* 10, no. 2 (May 1944): 219.

40 MUA, Peterson Papers, C. 34, vol. 12, 257–8, Peterson to Laughlin, 16 March 1908; C. 18, file 37, Laughlin to Peterson, 19 March 1918.

41 David M. Legate, *Stephen Leacock: A Biography* (Toronto: Macmillan, 1970), 59; David Lewis, *The Good Fight: Political Memoirs, 1909–1958* (Toronto: Macmillan, 1981), 24–5.

42 See Robert W. Dimand, "Stephen Leacock on Political Economy and the Unsolved Riddle of Social Justice," in *Inequalities and the Progressive Era: Breakthroughs and Legacies*, ed. Guillaume Vallet (Cheltenham: Elgar, 2020), 264–81; Ron Dart, "Stephen Leacock: Walking the Tightrope Between Nationalism and the Market Economy," *VoegelinView*, 20 April 2021, accessed 30 November 2024, https://voegelinview.com/stephen-leacock-walking-the-tightrope-between-nationalism-and-the-market-economy/.

43 Leacock, "Canada and the Monroe Doctrine."

44 Stephen Leacock, "Greater Canada," *The University Magazine* 6 (April 1907): 132–41.

45 *McGill Daily* 1, no. 23 (9 November 1911): 1.

46 Ian Ross Robertson, "The Historical Leacock," in Staines, *Stephen Leacock*, 38.

47 Heaman, *Tax, Order*.

48 *McGill Daily* 3, no. 95 (10 February 1914), 1.

49 *McGill Daily* 3, no. 10 (11 October 1913); 3, no. 67 (8 January 1914), 4; in *Canadian Courier* 15, no. 4 (27 December 1913), 12; 3, no. 109 (14 February 1914), 2.

50 *McGill Daily* 3, no. 51 (29 November 1913), 1.

51 *McGill Daily* 3, no. 51 (29 November 1913), 1.

52 Stephen Leacock, "John Bull and His Grown-Up Sons," in *Canada: An Illustrated Weekly Journal*, 25 May 1907, 230.

53 Susan Bellay, "Pluralism and Race/Ethnic Relations in Canadian Social Science, 1880–1939" (PhD diss., University of Manitoba, 2001), 33–4.

54 Stephen Leacock, "The University and Business," *The University Magazine* 12, no. 4 (December 1913): 546.

55 Dimand, "Stephen Leacock," 268; *McGill Daily* 1, no. 23 (9 November 1911), 1.

56 The *McGill Daily* regularly published such arguments. McGill architecture should emulate Oxford and Tudor architecture made "as pure as possible," so that "the student would breathe in all that is best in the storied past of our race." *McGill Daily* 3, no. 69 (10 January 1914), 4, the article written by W.D. Lighthall.

57 Marion Fourcade, *Economists and Societies: Discipline and Profession in the United States, Britain, and France, 1890s to 1990s* (Princeton: Princeton University Press, 2009), 9.

58 Leacock, "The University and Business," 544.

59 Legate, *Stephen Leacock*, 86.

60 Leacock, "The University and Business," 545.

61 Legate, *Stephen Leacock*, 72.

62 Peter Gilchrist McArthur, *Stephen Leacock* (Toronto: Ryerson Press, 1923), 148.

63 *McGill Daily* 3, no. 99 (16 February 1914), 4.

64 Veblen, *The Theory of the Leisure Class*, 371.

65 *McGill Daily* 2, no. 54 (2 December 1912), 4; *McGill Daily* 2, no. 51 (28 November 1912) and 2, no. 52 (29 November 1912).

66 Macmillan, *Stephen Leacock*, 115.

67 Philippe Broda, "Egalitarianism and Bias: Veblen and the Jewish Question," *Jewish Political Studies Review* 31, no. 1/2 (2020): 245–64; Thomas C. Leonard, *Illiberal Reformers: Race, Eugenics, and American Economics in the Progressive Era* (Princeton: Princeton University Press, 2016).

68 *McGill Daily* 3, no. 112 (3 March 1914), 2.

69 Robinson, *A History of Antisemitism in Quebec*, 53; Peter Price, *Questions of Order: Confederation and the Making of Modern Canada* (Toronto: University of Toronto Press, 2021), 147.

70 Tara Zahra, *The Great Departure: Mass Migration from Eastern Europe and the Making of the Free World* (New York: W.W. Norton, 2016), 41; Götz Aly, *Europe Against the Jews 1880–1945*, trans. Jefferson Chase (New York: Metropolitan Books, 2020), 156.

71 Sherry Olson and Patricia Thornton, *Peopling the North American City: Montreal, 1840–1900* (Montreal and Kingston: McGill-Queen's University Press, 2011), 283.
72 *McGill Daily* 3, no. 15 (17 October 1913), 2.
73 *McGill Daily* 3, no. 21 (25 October 1913), 2.
74 *McGill Daily* 1, no. 69 (17 February 1912), 8.
75 *McGill Daily* 2, no. 59 (7 December 1912), 2.
76 Michael Brown, *Jew or Juif? Jews, French Canadians, and Anglo Canadians, 1759–1914* (Philadelphia: Jewish Publication Society, 1987).
77 Phyllis Senese, "*La Croix de Montréal*: A Link to the French Radical Right," *Canadian Catholic Historical Association, Historical Studies* 53 (1986): 81–95.
78 Joe King, *From the Ghetto to the Main: The Story of Jews of Montreal*, ed. Johanne Schumann (Montreal: Montreal Jewish Publication Society, 2000), 98–9.
79 Peterson Papers, C. 18, 37: Jacob Livinson to William Peterson, 9 November 1911.
80 *McGill Daily* 2, no. 118 (7 March 1913), 3. See John Kalbfleisch, "From the Archives: 1913 Bankers Knew How to Restore Financial Confidence," *Montreal Gazette*, 8 March 2017.
81 Wai-Chee Dimock, "Debasing Exchange: Edith Wharton's *The House of Mirth*," PMLA 100, no. 5 (1985): 783; also Rob Hawkes, "The Descent of Money," *Money on the Left* podcast, 8 December 2022.
82 Meri-Jane Rochelson, *A Jew in the Public Arena: The Career of Israel Zangwill* (Detroit: Wayne State University Press, 2008), 39–40.
83 Henry Arthur Jones, "The Dread of the Jew," *The Spectator* 83 (9 September 1899): 338–9 (reprinted in *Popular Science Monthly*); Deborah Cohen, "Who Was Who: Race and Jews in Turn-of-the-Century Britain," *Journal of British Studies* 41, no. 4 (October 2002): 478.
84 *McGill Daily*, 3, no. 90 (4 February 1914), 2; 3, no. 92 (6 February 1914), 4; 3, no. 93 (7 February 1914), 2.
85 David Nirenberg, *Anti-Judaism: The Western Tradition* (New York: W.W. Norton, 2013), 294; see also Cohen, "Who Was Who," on anxieties of Jewish versus non-Jewish identity in Britain.
86 Robert G. Sachs, on Baltimore, in *Remembering the University of Chicago*, 322.
87 *McGill Daily* 1, no. 70 (19 February 1912), 2; Claude Bissel, *The Young Vincent Massey* (Toronto: University of Toronto Press, 1981), 35–6.

88 For example, Christopher D. Green, "The Hiring of James Mark Baldwin and James Gibson Hume at the University of Toronto in 1889," *History of Psychology* 7, no. 2 (2004): 130–53.
89 Camic, *Veblen*, 195.
90 JVP, Box 14, folder 5, J.C. Hemmeon to Viner, 20 January 1918.
91 *McGill Daily* 3, no. 16 (18 October 1913), 2; 3, no. 68 (9 January 1914), 4; 3, no. 16 (18 October 1913), 2; Peterson Papers, C. 22, file 65, 79; C. 22, file 62.
92 Stephen Leacock, *The Unsolved Riddle of Social Justice* (New York: John Lane, 1920), 141.
93 Leacock, *Unsolved Riddle*, 15.
94 Viner Family Papers, in private possession, Jacob Viner to Frances Klein, 12 February 1916.
95 Legate, *Stephen Leacock*, 53–4; JVP, Viner to Legate, 16 July 1969.
96 Samuelson in Shils, *Remembering*, 534.
97 Legate, *Stephen Leacock*, 53–4; see Myers, *Resisting History*, 160.
98 JVP, Box 17, folder 6, Stephen Leacock to Viner, 6 May 1916.
99 Brown, *Jew or Juif?*, 125.
100 *McGill Daily* 3, no. 112 (3 March 1914), 2 and 1, no. 32 (25 November 1911), 3.
101 *The Jewish Times*, 28 March 1913, 28.
102 *McGill Daily* 3, no. 44 (21 November 1913), 1–2; JVP, Box 14, folder 5, Hemmeon to Viner, 20 January 1918.
103 MUA, RG75, C.50, vol. 2. Political Economy Club, McGill, General Meetings, 1913–1926, 7–9; *McGill Daily* 3, no. 77 (19 January 1914), 1.
104 *McGill Daily* 3, no. 80 (22 January 1914).
105 McGill yearbook 1917, 140.
106 *McGill Daily* 3, no. 43 (20 November 1913), 4. See Philippe Bieler, *Onward Dear Boys: A Family Memoir of the Great War* (Montreal and Kingston: McGill-Queen's University Press, 2014).
107 *McGill Daily* 3, no. 2 (2 October 1913), 3.
108 *McGill Daily* 3, no. 44 (21 November 1913), 2.
109 Michael Perceval-Maxwell, "The History of History at McGill," paper presented to the James McGill Society, 2 April 1981; Carl Berger, *The Sense of Power: Studies in the Ideas of Canadian Imperialism, 1867–1914* (Toronto: University of Toronto Press, 1970).
110 *McGill Daily* 3, no. 48 (26 November 1913), 4.
111 John Robertson, *The Case for the Enlightenment: Scotland and Naples, 1680–1760* (Cambridge: Cambridge University Press, 2009). On Hume's influence extending to Viner: Carl Wennerlind and Margaret Schabas,

A Philosopher's Economist: Hume and the Rise of Capitalism (Chicago: University of Chicago Press, 2020).

112 John Cox, *Canada for the Canadians: Address Delivered to the Canadian Club of Montreal, March 22, 1909* (n.p., n.d.).

113 *McGill Daily* 3, no. 95 (11 February 1914), 2–3.

114 JVP, Viner to Legate, 16 July 1969.

115 Mathieu Houle-Courcelles, "Censure et surveillance de la presse socialiste au Québec (1918–1920): le cas du journal *Labor* et de son éditeur Isidore Boltuck," *Bulletin d'histoire politique* 24, no. 3 (Spring 2016), 37; Benoit Marsan, "'Justice and Not Charity Should Be Your Demand': Montreal's Unemployed and the Workers' Revolt," in *For a Better World: The Winnipeg General Strike & the Workers' Revolt*, eds James Naylor, Rhonda L. Hinther, and Jim Mochoruk (University of Manitoba Press, 2022), 206.

116 *McGill Daily* 3, no. 98 (14 February 1914), 2.

117 *McGill Daily* 3, no. 104 (21 February 1914), 1.

118 MUA, Principal's Papers, RG2, C.20, file 54, Jacob Viner to William Peterson, 23 May 1914; C.35, vol. 23, 98–9, Peterson to Professor V. Dibelius.

119 JVP, Box 1, folder 15, Memorabilia; Box 2, folder 2, papers 1913–1914.

120 JVP, Box 14, folder 5, "J.C. Hemmeon," undated letters.

121 New York Public Library, Genevieve Taggard Papers MssCol 2942, box 34, folder 57, Viner to Robert L. Wolf, 26 November 1916.

122 Sebastiano Nerozzi, "Building up a Multilateral Strategy for the United States: Alvin Hansen, Jacob Viner, and the Council on Foreign Relations (1939–45)," in *American Power and Policy*, ed. Robert Leeson (Basingstoke: Palgrave Macmillan, 2009): 24–68; Sebastiano Nerozzi, "From the Great Depression to Bretton Woods: Jacob Viner and International Monetary Stabilization (1930–1945)," *European Journal of the History of Economic Thought* 18, no. 1 (2011): 55–84; G. William Domhoff, "The Council on Foreign Relations and the Grand Area: Case Studies on the Origins of the IMF and the Vietnam War," *Class, Race, and Corporate Power* 2, no. 1 (2014), 9; see also G. John Ikenberry, "A World Economy Restored: Expert Consensus and the Anglo-American Postwar Settlement," *International Organization* 46, no. 1 (Winter 1992): 289–321; Lionel Robbins, *Jacob Viner (1892–1970): A Tribute* (Princeton: Princeton University Press, 1970), 5–6.

123 Jacob Viner, *Canada and Its Giant Neighbour* (Ottawa: Carleton University Press, 1958).

7

"Risky Business"

Social Sciences, McGill, and the Interwar Years

MARLENE SHORE

The interwar era was a turbulent one for Canadian universities. The First World War and the Great Depression fuelled concerns about the role a university should play in society. The National Research Council of Canada, formed in 1916, supported science fellowships, but research funding for other disciplines was available only through philanthropic organizations, primarily in the United States, or from business communities. At McGill, a private university in Canada's financial capital, these problems were exacerbated by the institution's strong utilitarian tradition and a board of governors drawn from Montreal's largest businesses, including the president of Canadian Pacific Railway (CPR) and director of the Bank of Montreal, Sir Edward Beatty. Although McGill enjoyed a reputation as Canada's premiere university in science and medicine, other fields fared less well. After the First World War, the university took steps to develop the social sciences, persuaded of their practical utility. Within ten years, however, the social sciences were at the centre of a battle over academic freedom at McGill, the legacy of which was to leave them fractured and, with hindsight, perceived as marginal to the university's history. The social sciences had become a target of the administration's attempt to rid the university of a reputation for social and intellectual ferment. It perceived this threat as emanating from the McGill Social Science Research Project, an interdisciplinary program supporting the research of McGill professors and graduate students in several departments, funded by the Rockefeller Foundation (RF) through its connections with the Canadian National Committee for Mental Hygiene (CNCMH).[1]

This chapter explores these twists and turns by examining the concurrence of several developments at McGill in the interwar period – the university's traditions and internal policies, interwar economic and political conditions affecting Montreal, and ideas that shaped the development of the social and behavioural sciences. Accordingly, it is not a standard history of higher education, in which the focus has tended to be on institutional structures, but a study in the history of ideas and, in particular, the subfield of the history of the social and behavioural sciences set within the matrix of a university.[2] Approaching the history of a university in this way entails analysis of internal and external politics, sources of research funding, professional networks, socio-economic conditions affecting the institution's relationship to the communities outside its walls, and the cultural currents of the era it treats. Accordingly, this chapter sets developments at McGill in the wider context of late nineteenth- and early twentieth-century culture and its more radical trends in Canada, particularly in cosmopolitan Montreal,[3] focusing on the interwar period when universities in North America grew more conscious of the need to appeal to the larger populace beyond their walls.[4]

The history of ideas is often dismissed as being centred on elites and too insufficiently grounded in facts to reveal much about the history of a given community. Indeed, writing intellectual history is risky in a discipline where social history has been fashionable since the 1970s and often in conflict with political history.[5] Ideas, however, are also subject to marginalization and erasure. In their power to effect change, control of their direction is extremely important. There is no better place to see this at play than in a university's history. Not only is it evident that McGill faculty were powerfully buffeted by the university's actions during the interwar years but that McGill's status as a private university favouring certain disciplines over others exposes the roots of a deeper Canadian problem – the weak reputation of its thinkers and cultural producers.

Is the part of McGill's history not connected with science or medicine therefore worthy of attention? In 1931, McGill political economist (and renowned Canadian satirist) Stephen Leacock, while serving on the university's Arts Survey Committee, opined that perhaps one reason for the Faculty of Arts' lower standards and weak reputation was that unlike its scientific and medical faculties, it drew students from the local community. Commenting that these students were from families with impoverished cultural backgrounds, many from the refugee population of Europe, he suggested that the university look outside for material. As was only natural in a manufacturing metropolis, he continued, that part of the community that was not French belonged to "the less fortunate ranks of mankind, people close to the poverty line and with scarcely any of the home traditions of books and education which, in other lands, like Scotland, have redeemed and illuminated poverty."[6] Indeed, in the 1930s, the McGill administration took steps to reduce Jewish enrolment.[7]

Counter to Leacock's disparaging comments hinting at the superiority of British traditions, through the 1920s and 1930s professors and graduate students in McGill's Sociology Department focused their research on efforts to understand the many immigrant communities within Montreal, following the model of the pioneering Chicago School of Sociology whose theories, rooted in ecological and environmental ideas, have been revived in recent immigration history scholarship. A larger discussion of this work can be found in my book, *The Science of Social Redemption: McGill, the Chicago School, and the Origins of Social Research in Canada*. Whereas that study dealt with McGill's history and tradition of utility, and the powers and policies of its board of governors as these affected social work, sociology, and sociology's participation in the Social Science Research Project, this chapter focuses on developments in the discipline of psychology. It reveals how McGill University – its academics and the institution – withstood, affected, and engaged in a variety of challenges in the tumultuous interwar period. The analysis unfolds in four sections: a discussion of the ideas of efficiency and modernism that arose in the wake of social unrest in the interwar period; the establishment of psychology at McGill and its popular reception; efforts of McGill psychologists to wrestle with luck, magic, and probability in an era of uncertainty; and the political implications and consequences of research funding.

POSTWAR UNREST, EFFICIENCY, AND MODERNISM

By the 1920s, two major ideas shaped McGill's development – the tradition of utility, which was a distortion of the philosophy of utilitarianism, and the concept of efficiency – human, social, and national. Religious connotations infused the latter – the idea that society could be redeemed through the social sciences. These ideas became interwoven after the disillusioning experience of the First World War. In an era in which tremendous faith in science remained, the vestiges of the pre-war social gospel and social reform movements were channelled into scientific pursuits and into the newly formed social sciences. This constituted part of a more general emphasis on economic productivity. A widespread conviction that such productivity would ensure national and international stability contributed to the belief that industrial efficiency would solve all social ills, and that notion, combined with fears of unrest stemming from the post-war economic depression, changed the shape of university education.[8]

Immediately after the First World War, there was a widespread belief in Canada, Britain, and the United States that the key to international stability was economic productivity, which would produce a wider distribution of wealth and goods and minimize chances for future conflict. This required mobilizing a large part of a nation's resources for industrial development, eliminating wastefulness and inefficiency, and encouraging productivity. The belief arose from a conviction that the war's length and higher-than-anticipated casualties had heavily drained human and material resources. In Canada, the war had initially fostered an almost militant nationalism, bringing together military men, patriots, social gospellers, and reformers. Wartime propaganda reflected their rhetoric that the great struggle would mark the birth of a new society. When enthusiasm for the war dissipated, these groups pledged to achieve their societal goals once the conflict ended. In an atmosphere stressing the importance of productivity and social and economic reconstruction, attention was focused on child welfare, prevention of mental disorder, charity organization, and relief. The cult of scientific management flourished, and universities, following a vogue to produce "trained human doers," implemented programs in applied science and vocational and industrial training.[9]

In Canada, the drive for efficiency, which also fostered the development of the social and behavioural sciences generally, found its strongest impulse at McGill, where it was infused with the notion of service – that it was McGill's duty to make Canada a front-ranking industrial nation – and was reflected in the appointment of Sir Arthur Currie, commander of the Canadian corps in France, as principal.[10] The war had created severe economic problems in Montreal, hampering the university's recovery from wartime disruption. Inflation and widespread unemployment caused social unrest. McGill University officials feared the problems that the high cost of living were creating in their midst, particularly that young professors might turn to socialism and communism. "Bolshevism was in the air," one prominent Montrealer remarked.[11] One of the university's initial attempts to deal with the problems of unrest and create social efficiency, especially in charity organization, was to establish a department of social service, which evolved into the Department of Sociology.[12] Another was to establish and expand a psychology department.

An account of the beginnings of industrial psychology in Montreal, published in 1935, summed up the hope that existed after the Great War that psychology could be applied to the business and educational life of Montreal. It also evoked the image of Moses delivering the Ten Commandments. The account explained that in the winter of 1919, Dr W.D. Tait, head of the Department of Psychology at McGill University, returned from the war and, believing that psychology had a real contribution to make to industry, decided to take it "down the hill from the University to the business world which lies at the foot of Mount Royal by offering a University Extension Course in business psychology. The class was attended by about fifty business men and women," including the author of the piece, F.R. Clarke. Six years later, then engaged to supervise unemployment relief in Montreal, an activity that led to the development of the Protestant Employment Bureau, Clarke contacted Tait about the lectures he had given in 1919 dealing with intelligence testing for work placement. "Dr. Tait immediately 'came down the hill' again with the result that the employment bureau was started with a definite psychological cast." Clarke surmised this was the first time anywhere that a free employment service used tests of intelligence and other abilities for the placement of workers.[13]

Although the early-twentieth-century drive for human and national efficiency might explain psychology's growing acceptance as an academic discipline, its phenomenal rise is also attributable to its entwinement with the emergence of modernism beginning in the late nineteenth century. Modernism arose from industrialization and technology, but emphasized flux and contingency, and the role of chance and risk in human society.

Modernism constitutes a set of beliefs, values, and modes of perception that came into being in the late nineteenth century as part of the processes associated with modernization – industrialization, rationalization, and efficiency – as well as in response to new findings in the biological and physical sciences that led to the collapse of linear conceptions of time and space, and to the development of such notions as streams of consciousness. This interpretation differs from treatments of modernism equating it with modernity or with the avant-garde movement of artists and intellectuals who expressed hostility to modernization or, as in the United States, celebrated technology.[14] The 1913 New York Armory Exhibit is usually identified as the first example of cultural modernism in North America but intellectual developments in physics, biology, philosophy, psychology, and other fledgling social sciences had already established forerunners of modernist thought. In the nineteenth century, a group of social thinkers centred in universities asked questions about human nature and the workings of society resembling what later was labelled modernism. Their ideas no longer reflected a Victorian outlook, one grounded in belief in a predictable universe, a conviction that humans could arrive at a unified and fixed set of truths about all aspects of life, and a dichotomy that separated what was deemed animal from what was regarded as human, thereby polarizing so-called "civilized" and "primitive" societies. Partly influenced by Darwinian ideas, they questioned the notion of the fixed and final, gradually abandoning nineteenth-century positivism in exchange for a view of a more open universe governed by change and chance, and laden with risk. They also rejected hereditarian theories of human nature in favour of environmental ones.[15]

While inseparable from the processes of scientific and economic rationalization occurring throughout the West, modernism, at its heart, was also concerned with the impact of these processes on history, community, and memory.[16] This tension was evident in the social sciences in the late nineteenth century, especially in "the new psychology": it dealt with the function of sensory processes and consciousness through laboratory experimentation rather than through introspection, which had been psychology's approach earlier, as a branch of philosophy dealing with mental life.[17] The 1920s saw the birth of another "new psychology" movement engendered by a postwar desire to understand the roots of social and international problems. It turned against the dry academic approach of the earlier movement, which had largely eschewed practical application.[18] Inheriting some ideas from progressivism and social reform, it focused on the treatment of large numbers of people through mental hygiene, psychiatric social work, mental testing, personnel selection, and welfare practice. The new psychology also provided techniques for modern bureaucratic society. Supplementing wartime ideas of control through propaganda and advertising, control could now be exercised by manipulating inner need and individual desires.[19]

Immediately after the Great War, many psychologists turned their attention to social unrest, echoing Tait's comments to the audience at a well-attended evening talk at Montreal's Emmanu-El Temple in March 1920, where he attributed the period's strikes, lockouts, economic competition, and monopolies to "inner" drives.[20] This suggested that one of psychology's purposes was to prevent the inner self from disrupting the predictability of so-called civilization. Such notions were products of other ideas shaping the new psychology of the 1920s, including biological conceptions of the mind, interest in psychopathology, and attention to the role of unconscious motives in human actions. Before the Great War, psychogenesis and psychotherapeutics were terms used to suggest that the mind was responsible for bodily states, but during the war medical practitioners increasingly recognized the role of consciousness. As hospitals became crowded with soldiers whose troubles did not appear to be physical, many physicians focused on the issue of mental well-being and started ascribing emotions with a variety of powers, often using hypnotic suggestion or mental healing, rather than drugs or surgery, as treatment. Dalhousie University physiologist Dr David Fraser-Harris commented on the irony – that "the Armageddon that produced such brutal force and suffering demonstrated the beneficent action of mind over the ills of the body."[21] Before the war ended, medical publications reporting on treatments acknowledged the interaction of mind and body. A special journal, *Psyche*, devoted to non-material things, regularly advertised in the leading scientific journal, *Nature,* which reported on activities of metaphysical societies.[22]

As psychology moved outside of the academy, however, it came up against postwar fascination with spiritism and the occult. When speaking to public audiences in Montreal, psychologists found themselves answering questions about these subjects, though they disparaged them.[23] Historians now recognize that Western modernity is characterized by enchantment and that the spectres that haunted North America and Europe in the late nineteenth and early twentieth centuries – magicians, mesmerists, invisible worlds, interest in the irrational – were part of a Janus-faced modernity.[24]

PROPHETS OF THE PSYCHE: THE POPULAR RECEPTION OF PSYCHOLOGY

In Canada, psychology was as old as its universities, though taught as philosophy well into the twentieth century. McGill and the University of Toronto established the first psychology departments after the First World War but elsewhere philosophy and psychology were not severed until the 1940s. The head of McGill's department was W.D. Tait, who trained in experimental psychology at Harvard with leading scientific psychologist Hugo Münsterberg. When he first arrived at McGill for the 1909–10 academic session, Tait established a psychological laboratory, the second in Canada.[25] During the war, he joined the armed forces and went overseas, returning to establish the separate department of psychology in 1924. Arriving the same year was Chester Kellogg, an American with a PhD from Harvard. Enlisted in the American army's medical department, Kellogg was a development specialist in testing and grading with the War Department Field Service, and worked as a psychological examiner at Camp Devens in 1917, and at other camps between 1920 and 1921. (During the war, the army developed intelligence tests for the placement of recruits – the Army Alpha and Beta Examinations, with the latter designed for foreign speakers and the non-literate.[26]) Kellogg remained at McGill until 1947, where he also played a major role in the Canadian Psychological Association, founded in 1939. Tait retired in 1946. Others came and went but Tait and Kellogg together shaped psychology at McGill.[27] A separate but short-lived Department of Abnormal Psychology (1924–30) was established in McGill's Faculty of Medicine to provide psychiatric training for medical students, for which there had been little in Canada until the 1940s. However, this was the start of a rift between two types of psychology that would develop at McGill after the Second World War. Rather than work with Tait, under the leadership of C.F. Martin, McGill professor of medicine, the CNCMH provided for the appointment of their own psychologist, J.W. Bridges, along with his wife, Katherine Banham-Bridges, also an academic psychologist. (Banham-Bridges was the first woman to receive a PhD at the Université de Montréal, in 1934, after earning an MA at the University of Toronto in 1923, where she studied with psychologist George S. Brett.)[28]

In the 1920s and 1930s, professors in the social sciences sought to establish the legitimacy of their fields and funding for their work. This involved appealing to university officials and business interests. For psychologists, it also meant dealing with contenders – popularizers – and public misconceptions about psychology. After the First World War, fascination with myriad psychology topics exceeded the popular interest that existed during the wartime mental hygiene and intelligence testing crusades. Abraham Roback, a McGill graduate who went on to become an eminent psychologist, noted in his widely acclaimed book *Popular Psychology* (published in 1928) that it was impossible to read a newspaper without coming across the term. On stage, psychological plays were performed; in front of their fireplaces, people read novels and pondered the psychology of the hero or heroine.[29] Hugo Münsterberg's wish, expressed twenty years earlier, that psychology might become the scientific basis of modern culture, seemed near fulfillment. Leading scholars in an array of fields had become devotees of the discipline.[30] Presidents, congressmen, and parliamentary representatives commonly diagnosed their country's ills as psychological.[31] In an address to local Canadian Clubs, Sir Auckland Geddes, British ambassador to the United States (and former professor of anatomy at McGill), said that peace was a mental state – the recognition of law and justice – and unwillingness to accept it was persistence of a mental condition.[32] Stephen Leacock quipped about "an outbreak of psychology." Where success literature had once been concerned with "honor, dependability, and courage," it had become obsessed with inferiority complexes, neuroses, and conditioning. A great wave of "mind culture" swept through the community, and psychology professors were now "wearing overcoats lined with fur and riding in little coupé cars like doctors."[33]

Taking stock of psychology's postwar advances, an article published in *Atlantic Monthly* in 1933 was more critical. The author, Grace Adams, a psychology professor who had left the discipline because of the lack freedom at a teacher's college in Baltimore where she worked, commented that instead of "the Decade of the Dollar," the 1920s should be labelled "The Period of the Psyche." Pioneering late nineteenth-century psychologists could not have imagined how the meaning of science would change by the 1920s, "symbolized in the popular mind by the washing machine, the telephone, the motor car, or that the test of a 'scientific fact' would have changed from 'Is it true?' to 'Will it get me anywhere?'" During the expansive postwar years, she continued, "the high priests of the youngest science set forth to save the world by making it psychological." American professors, "eager to save democracy through their tests and tabulations," decided that the new psychology should be as practical and as helpful as the new physics. They expounded on subjects ranging from A to Z, as reflected in only a few of the titles of books published between 1919 and 1928: Athletics, Arithmetic, Alcoholism, Beauty, Buying, Bolshevism, Business Success, Christian Life, Citizenship, Coaching, Death, Dress, Fasting, Golf, Group Insurance, Jesus, Leadership, Learning, Marriage, Murder, Package Pabels, The Poet Shelley, Selling Life Insurance, and Psychology of Your Name.[34] That psychology was increasingly equated with the ability to manipulate others was manifested in Dale Carnegie's bestseller, *How to Win Friends and Influence People*, which appeared in 1936.[35]

In the 1920s, academic psychologists were already wary of the "army of charlatans" parading their wares, promising to improve memory, enhance personality, or tell character. University of Manitoba psychologist Henry Wright called them "unscrupulous spell-binders" offering in the name of psychology "to drive forth the demons of disease and unhappiness – for monetary compensation."[36] The source of psychologists' greatest concern was popular interest in the sensational – suggestion, hypnotism, spiritualism, extra-sensory perception, and telepathy; the existence of these phenomena was confirmed for many of the public by the invention of the wireless.[37] There were efforts to communicate not only with "the other side" but with other planets, especially Mars.[38]

Psychologists of the 1920s confronted a dilemma. As J.W. Bridges explained, the public initially held psychology in high regard, accepting it as a science with practical applications. When it failed to provide panaceas, pseudo-science stepped in and psychology grew in popularity as a study of psychic phenomena, hypnosis, telepathy, and the subconscious. Equating psychology with miracles and cures, the public looked for practitioners who promised results.[39] The psychics, phrenologists, character analysts, mediums, and spiritualists to whom they turned were like yesteryear's fortune tellers, observed Abraham Roback. They could perhaps infer the mental level of their consultants but could not predict the future and had to be disclaimed as once were palmists, crystal gazers, and clairvoyants.[40]

Desire to communicate with the spirit world was heightened by the slaughter of the First World War.[41] Nearly 61,000 Canadian soldiers, primarily the nation's youth, were killed in the war and thousands more were wounded. In 1917, more than 1,600 Nova Scotians died when a munitions ship exploded in Halifax Harbour. Through 1918–19, the influenza epidemic killed 50,000 people in Canada.[42] For McGill, there were financial and psychological effects. Enrolment declined as more than 2,500 of its students and 90 faculty enlisted in the armed services: 522 were wounded and 341 were killed in action. In the fall of 1918, the university shut its doors for six weeks when influenza cases reached epidemic proportions in Montreal. As the death rate rose, schools, theatres, and law courts were closed by civic order.[43]

After the war, the public's interest in spiritism and the occult did not dissipate. A wave of psychic literature appeared. Publication of *The Twentieth Plane: A Psychic Revelation* (1918), presenting psychical research undertaken by a Canadian, Albert Durrant Watson, was an overnight sensation with its accounts of famous figures, such as Martin Luther and Abraham Lincoln, delivering trance addresses through a local medium.[44] Appetite for tales of psychic phenomena was aided by the public proclamations and addresses of Sir Arthur Conan Doyle, author of the Sherlock Holmes books, whose speeches to large audiences in Canada, the United States, Britain, and elsewhere on the subject of spiritism drew wide attention.[45] Conan Doyle and Oliver Lodge – whose book, *Raymond, or Life and Death* (1919) prompted belief in the possibility of communicating with soldiers killed in the war by means of seances – were perhaps the most famous exponents of modern spiritualism after the First World War, but there were others.[46] Spiritism also posed a threat to religious institutions. In 1919, addressing the St James Literary Society of Montreal, Grand Trunk Pacific Railway passenger traffic agent G.T. Bell, a member of the American Society of Psychical Research, suggested that the church pay attention to the phenomenon and encourage friends in the other world to communicate rather than be treated as devils. Conan Doyle told an audience at Montreal's Mount Royal Hotel that communication with the dead aligned with early Christianity's communion with saints.[47]

Resurgence of popular interest in the occult was only matched in the 1920s by psychologists' efforts to stamp it out.[48] In 1920, Arthur Stanley Eve, Macdonald professor and chair of the Department of Physics at McGill, and a distinguished scientist who was made a commander of the Order of the British Empire for his work directing secret submarine detection research at the Admiralty Research Station in Harwich, took aim at the phenomenon.[49] Speaking to the Women's Canadian Club at Montreal's Ritz-Carleton Hotel, he told the large audience that the utterances of Lodge, Doyle, and others on the subject of physics, popularly known as spiritism, did not rest on scientific evidence. Distinguished physicists and biologists had been led astray partly by grievous personal bereavement.[50] Some months later, Tait, in a talk entitled "Gateways of Knowledge" (part of a psychology lecture series he gave at the Montreal YMCA on Drummond Street), slammed spiritism, telepathy, and clairvoyance, challenging the audience to find one reputable psychologist or physician who believed in them. He was responding to a class member who asked him why he distinguished between spirit, spiritism, and spiritualism.[51]

In the 1920s, city officials and law courts also wrestled with the issue of spiritism's status. Was it a science, trade, or calling that fell within the purview of city by-laws requiring practitioners to obtain a licence? The question was debated in the Superior Court of Montreal, regarding practitioners who had been fined twenty-five dollars for illegally exercising "the profession of spiritism" without a licence. A female petitioner argued that spiritism was not a trade but a science, and therefore did not require a city licence.[52] In 1921, Chief Judge Decarie heard a case in Montreal's Court of Special Sessions involving a hypnotist who had defrauded a woman, claiming he could use telepathic suggestion to get truant husbands, like hers, to love their wives. Decarie retorted that he did not believe in telepathic suggestion and considered it an immense fake.[53]

MAGIC, LUCK, AND PROBABILITY AMIDST INTERWAR UNCERTAINTY

Professional psychologists' battle with popularizers continued in the 1930s. In an article on luck for the Canadian Credit Institute, University of Alberta psychologist John Macdonald explained that magic and modern science both arose from uncertainty: science sought to control events by discovering their causes and using experiments; magic was a shortcut, a human trick pretending to accomplish the required result.[54] Grace Adams observed that because the popular conception of science equated it with magic, the public expected psychologists, whom they regarded as scientists, to exercise the same kind of magic on the human mind that surgeons worked on the human body, or engineers on steel.[55] The ongoing Depression, however, belied the fact that psychology could offer miracle cures. During the 1930s, Chester Kellogg worked to dispel popular misconceptions about psychology by disproving claims of the existence of telepathy and extra-sensory perception, which he saw arising from the work of

J.B. Rhine. The latter had precipitated a major controversy that reverberated in statistics and psychology and then captured wider public attention when his 1937 book, *New Frontiers of the Mind*, was widely heralded as the selection of the Book of the Month Club. In it, Rhine presented the results of investigations he had been conducting at Duke University since 1930 on ESP and clairvoyance.[56]

Since Kellogg found fault with Rhine's experiments and would test them through experiments in his own McGill lab, as discussed below, a more detailed description of Rhine's work is necessary. Throughout the 1930s, Rhine, a botanist who had established a parapsychology lab at Duke, as well as the *Journal of Parapsychology*, tested many students as volunteer subjects for ESP in card-guessing games. The card-guessing games involved a pack of twenty-five cards, each bearing one of five designs on its face – a circle, a rectangle, a star, a cross, or a set of wavy lines; each design was on five cards in the pack. (These were named Zener Cards, and incidentally appeared in the movie *Ghostbusters*). Once a subject was made familiar with the designs and a pack thoroughly shuffled, an experimenter turned the cards up in order, with the face of each card concealed from the subject, who then had to name the symbol on as many cards as possible without looking at them. A certain percentage of success was expected by chance – the average was one card right for every five. The goal was to determine whether anyone could name enough cards to prove that something more than chance or luck was at work – a significant percentage of successes was considered evidence of telepathy or clairvoyance. These experiments claimed to show amazing results: a score of men and women regularly named so many of the cards correctly that there was not one chance in many millions that it was by luck or accident. Kellogg was skeptical about the methods and results of Rhine's tests because he had become acquainted with the scientific approach to parapsychology as a member of Hugo Münsterberg's graduate seminar at Harvard in 1912–13 and later read John Edgar Coover's report of his psychic research investigations at Stanford that involved treatment of numerical data, partly dealing with card-guessing experiments like Rhine's. Coover found no evidence of occult power. The public's ardour for card guessing had diminished after a psychic test led by Oliver Lodge, with the BBC's assistance, went awry: there were 20,000 replies, mostly wrong – a finding that captured headlines. Rhine's studies, however, revived popular interest when he and his Duke associates conducted more than a hundred thousand card tests.[57]

Kellogg was dismayed that publicity surrounding Rhine's utterances had stimulated further investigations. He also lamented that the founding of the *Journal of Parapsychology* had diverted young men and women in vital years of training into a side issue, with funding that could have supported research on topics of real social significance. Kellogg conceded that popularizers had fostered public appreciation of science as germane to human welfare, something that research published in the difficult language of professional journals could never achieve, but was startled when Professor Ernest Hunter Wright, chairman of the Department of English Literature at Columbia, became yet another recruit to the ranks of popularizers. Based on Rhine's preliminary studies, Wright decided that the existence of clairvoyance and telepathy had been established and wrote two articles for *Harper's* in 1936 presenting proof.[58] Kellogg charged that the results were sweeping generalities based on a few striking cases that had public appeal but proved nothing.

Kellogg conducted experiments with card tests at McGill because he believed in quantitative techniques and considered Rhine's work to be an example of bad method with conclusions unsupported by data.[59] Kellogg found that Rhine's basic error rested in his argument on a supposed difference between the test's actual results and those occurring by chance. In each of Rhine's packs, over 623 trillion different arrangements were possible, making tabulation and comparison beyond human capacity. The tests completed at McGill during the 1937 academic year, using higher mathematical methods, provided the solution.[60] They explained why ordinary methods yielded higher scores.[61] Instead of publishing complete reports of scores from his experiments, Rhine selected only more fortunate results. "The unusual always attracts attention and is the source of mystery," Kellogg said, recalling a hand he once had in bridge consisting of all the spades in the pack, something that could be expected only once in 779,737,580,160 times. Since the same was true for every hand, it meant that in card guessing, a perfect score was no more rare than many other ways of getting an average score. Kellogg charged that Rhine underestimated the chances of high scores, paid no attention to internal inconsistencies in the results, and selected portions of evidence that assumed truth of the theory he sought to prove.[62] Instead of impartially abiding by the results of his experiments, Rhine published only data that confirmed his existing belief in ESP,[63] though Kellogg also thought that Rhine had been misinformed by mathematicians he consulted regarding techniques.[64]

S.N.F. Chant, a University of Toronto psychologist, applauded Kellogg for exposing the elusiveness of the theory of probability. Rhine calculated the most likely number of correct calls that would occur according to chance, and then compared his subjects' calls with this prediction. However, Kellogg's bridge example showed that probability could cut both ways: anything may happen, and invariably, it is the unusual. In bridge, there are millions of chances against getting any single bridge hand, and yet getting some kind of bridge hand is an ordinary occurrence. Because anything may happen by chance, to claim an occurrence does not happen by chance requires a statement of why it did happen. Rhine, instead of meeting that requirement and establishing scientific significance, postulated a power of clairvoyance or telepathy. Chant observed that this was like saying that music comes from a radio because there are little men inside who sing and play. When the question is raised as to how we know the men are in there, we are told that they must be there because we can hear them.[65]

It is telling that psychologists devoted so much attention to disproving the results of card-guessing experiments in the 1930s, in their labs and in print. Exposing fraud was their motive, but they were also reckoning with probability and the role of chance. Moreover, Chant's appeal to reason underlying his caustic reference to how sound came out of a radio, provides affirmation that it was inventions like the wireless that had led so much of the public to believe in the sensational.

POLITICAL IMPLICATIONS AND CONSEQUENCES OF RESEARCH SUPPORT

While competing with popularizers for public attention, McGill psychologists found work within Montreal's business community. For years after Tait's initial assistance to the Protestant Employment Bureau, McGill provided training for the bureau's staff with extension courses in employment, vocational, and industrial psychology. These grew popular through newspaper coverage, as did public lectures sponsored by Montreal businesses. In addition to his regular column for *The Gazette*, "Practical Psychology in Business and the Home," Tait delivered many addresses in the wider Montreal community advocating the study of psychology.[66] In 1925, the Psychology Department established the School Service Bureau to assist businesses and schools with intelligence tests and standardized tests for the classification of students and remedial treatment.[67] At the same time, two of Montreal's largest companies employing thousands of people, including Sun Life Assurance, introduced psychological testing in their personnel departments. Other businesses conducted extensive studies on guidance, personnel management, time-work management, and advertising. Throughout the 1920s and 1930s, large businesses in Montreal and Toronto hired psychologists not only for placement purposes but for dealing with customers who fell behind in deferred payments, or for reviewing and reconstructing advertising methods. This activity reached a crescendo in 1935 when executive officers in Montreal and Toronto's largest firms met weekly to discuss the benefits of industrial psychology. The result was the creation of the Montreal and Toronto Personnel Associations, which included representatives from Bell, Eaton's and Simpsons department stores, Canadian National Railways and the CPR, Sun Life Assurance, Canadian Industries Limited, and Dominion Tire and Rubber. These were influenced by similar associations formed in the northeastern United States from 1912 onwards, and by publicity given to Harvard researcher Elton Mayo's studies in industrial psychology in the mid-1930s. The year 1935 also saw John L. Lewis and his followers leave the American Federation of Labor to form the more radical Committee for Industrial Organization.[68]

It was against this backdrop that McGill received a large grant of $110,000 from the RF in December 1930 for the development of research in the social sciences.[69] Prior to 1958 and the creation of the Canada Council, and later the Social Sciences and Humanities Research Council, very little funding was available for social scientists' research in Canada, compelling them to seek it from American philanthropy.[70] McGill's attainment of the RF grant was facilitated by Charles Meredith Hincks, a physician and psychiatrist who had worked with Dr C.K. Clarke to open the first psychiatric clinic in Canada. Described by one journalist as "the only generalissimo who [could] lead economics and the applied physical and chemical sciences, education and preventive medicine and the social sciences in the vitally necessary struggle for a resurrected civilization," Hincks (a nephew of McGill University physiologist T. Wesley Mills) had served as a public school medical inspector for the Toronto Department of Health from 1912 to 1917, introducing the Binet-Simon tests in Ontario schools. He founded the Canadian National Committee for Mental Hygiene (which had a research division in Montreal) in 1918, serving as its general director and was also appointed general director of the American organization of the same name in 1930.[71] Hincks had cultivated close ties with RF trustees who, in turn, regarded him as someone who could put their objectives into practice in Canada. In the 1920s, the RF shifted from funding medical schools to promoting research on immigration policies, human relations in industry and education, and problems stemming from unemployment, delinquency, dependency, and government administration.

Hincks worked with C.F. Martin, by then McGill's dean of medicine, to obtain the grant for McGill, hoping it would stimulate developments in social science research throughout Canada. RF officials envisioned McGill creating something akin to the interdisciplinary social research projects at the University of Chicago or Yale University. In late 1929, Hincks, Martin, and Edmund E. Day of the Rockefeller's Social Science Division met with Arthur Currie to explain McGill's appeal. It was a university with a national outlook, a private corporation "unfettered by the strictures of government control," and its close cooperation with the Canadian National Committee for Mental Hygiene would facilitate contact with governments, industrialists, and other organizations necessary for research and application of its findings. RF trustees regarded Canada as a young country, in the process of development, less bound by tradition than others, meaning that it offered an unrivalled laboratory for McGill's social scientists.[72] Once the grant was achieved, Leonard Marsh, a London School of Economics graduate who had worked with Sir William Beveridge on a similar project in England, was hired to serve as director.[73] Initially interested in the project, Currie and a few prominent Montreal businessmen, including Beatty, were included on the executive committee.

In ways possibly not fully grasped in these deliberations, the ideas that underlay the mental hygiene movement, some of whose leaders and participants ascribed to eugenics, were in collision with the McGill Social Science Research Project. By the early 1920s, most American (and American-trained) social scientists, particularly the social psychologists, had rejected hereditarian ideas and regarded human nature as flexible, subject to change in response to environmental conditions.[74] These convictions were evident in the McGill project's research program. For the focus of their research, McGill social scientists chose unemployment (some preferring to call it employment) and immigration in Montreal as topics that lent themselves to interdisciplinary investigation. Because Montreal was an industrial city with a multitude of ethnic groups, manufacturing plants, seaport associations, and pronounced seasonal unemployment, it presented a cross-section of Canadian life not found elsewhere.[75] Marsh drew up a large-scale project involving several departments, among them economics, sociology, psychology, and education. Graduate students were drawn upon for research assistance; where considered preferable, salaried assistants were employed for short periods.[76] The plan was to conduct an employment survey with detailed studies of major industries, their employment problems, and the possibility of stabilization, considering sources of labour supply from schools and immigrants. Kellogg, as a member of the executive, was interested in whether unemployment stemmed from failure to employ people in accordance with their abilities and temperament, or lack of vocational education because of child labour, or adjustment difficulties of immigrants, or fluctuations in economic conditions and overproduction. Overproduction struck him as a problem that was senseless to tolerate. If there was a need for goods, he argued, everybody should be busy producing them; if there was a surplus, no one should have to suffer for lack of them. Any system treating surplus as the property of employers while only giving employees sufficient wages to cover subsistence augured trouble. "Can we find a way out," he asked, "or shall we wait for an insane solution by communists?"[77]

In the 1930s, another stream of RF funds channelled through the CNCMH supported psychology at McGill University, University of Toronto, University of Alberta, Queen's University, and the University of Saskatchewan. At McGill, as at the University of Toronto, these were used to establish a nursery school and child centre that would enable longitudinal studies providing insights on conditions that ensured the adjustment of individuals to society. (At the University of Toronto, it became the Institute of Child Study, the first in North America. The McGill nursery school, however, did not thrive.) While at McGill, J.W. Bridges and K.M. Banham undertook psychological studies on juvenile delinquency but the Psychology Department's faculty members and students showed little interest in collaborating or conducting research at the nursery, leaving Banham and Bridges to work alone. When the RF ended its support for the nursery school in the 1930s, both Banham and Bridges lost their jobs.[78]

Within the Social Science Research Project, following Marsh's suggestion that psychologists study the qualitative character and industrial aptitudes of unemployed and employed groups comparatively,[79] Kellogg, along with his student Nelson Whitmore Morton, McGill's first PhD graduate in psychology, and W.C. Webster, worked on industrial psychology and vocational guidance for maladjusted adults. (In the 1930s, the term "maladjustment" connoted the inability to react successfully to the demands of one's environment.) They undertook extensive comparative studies of unemployed and employed men and boys during the Great Depression, publishing articles on these subjects in technical magazines and books. Kellogg and Morton also revised the US Army "Beta" examination intelligence tests, published by the American Psychological Corporation in 1935, and thereafter used in the army as well as for civilian purposes to measure ability in skills for employment and for placement of college students.[80]

Kellogg's expertise in psychological testing had been highlighted in McGill's Rockefeller grant proposal but greater emphasis was given to the business qualifications of the Montreal industrialists participating – Edward Beatty, Sir Charles Blair Gordon, Julian Smith, and Thomas Bassett Macaulay.[81] When the topic of employment/unemployment was proposed in 1930, no one was thinking about the Great Depression; seasonal unemployment, a chronic problem in Montreal, was the issue. By January 1931, when research got underway, unemployment was widespread in Montreal and around world. At McGill, there were serious budget deficits and salary reductions.[82] Within a few years, as the Social Science Research Project studies were published as books, they drew the ire of McGill officials who fought many battles against what they perceived as political radicalism during the 1930s.[83] They watched carefully the activities of League for Social Reconstruction members, some of whom were employed at McGill; they were alarmed at the attachment of Christianity to socialist – or what they perceived as Marxist – principles; they eased J. King Gordon out of the United Theological College; and they redefined tenure and promotion policies so as to rid the university of individuals like political economist Eugene Forsey. However, according to Stanley Frost, the Social Science Research Project was a greater embarrassment to the board of governors because it was conceived and sponsored by the university itself. He also suggested that its publications, with titles like *Employment Research*, *Industrial Diagnosis*, *The Railway Worker*, and *The British Immigrant*, gave the appearance of being more socialistic than they were to those who knew them only by title.[84] McGill officials nevertheless considered the whole project to be tainted with collectivist thought. Currie found it developing along lines different from what he had imagined, and the industrialists withdrew early on, disliking Marsh's "memo-harangues." That left the executive, scathingly labelled the "socialist-sociologist-psychologist-group," to their own devices. Their work was tolerated until the late 1930s, when A.E. Morgan, Currie's successor as principal, was forced to resign and was replaced by Lewis Douglas, who was determined that McGill not become a centre for socialist thinking.[85]

In addition to the dissatisfaction of McGill officials, other problems portended for the Social Science Research Project. By the late 1930s, the mental hygiene connection to psychology was eroding. At Toronto, E.A. Bott, head of the Psychology Department, grew increasingly resentful that its agenda was determining the shape of psychological research. The RF decided that funds would be better allocated to research offering solutions to immediate economic problems, as in banking. By the end of the 1930s, the RF grant to McGill was terminated; university officials did not want it renewed, and Leonard Marsh was let go. As a result, Frost wrote, "The thrust of social science research in the university was dissipated and never again achieved the same sense of a unified purpose."[86]

The lancing of the social sciences at McGill in the 1930s constituted a loss to Canadian research scholarship. People and ideas were forced to the margins; the publications of the Social Science Research Project were criticized, and largely left unread for decades. The study of Canadian intellectual traditions is sometimes blind to all there once was, or to the origins of many major ideas and theories. In 1938, sociologist Everett Hughes, who had begun his book, *French Canada in Transition* (1943) under the aegis of the Social Science Research Project, left McGill for an appointment at the University of Chicago.[87] He went on to introduce a social science research program in Quebec's francophone universities, particularly at Laval, through his acquaintance with Father Georges-Henri Lévesque, which subsequently influenced the work of Jean-Charles Falardeau, a leader in French-Canadian sociology until the 1960s.[88] When John Porter wrote *The Vertical Mosaic* in the 1960s, he was unaware of Marsh's book, *Canadians In and Out of Work* (1940), a compendium of the Social Science Research Project's investigations, which showed the vast discrepancies in wealth and income that separated Canadians, using the same metaphor as Porter.[89] Marsh hoped that the book's detailed account of the Canadian socio-economic strata would provide a foundation for the creation of a national welfare policy.[90] In 1941, after his departure from McGill, Marsh was appointed to the federal government's Committee on Reconstruction as research director.

He said that his *Report on Social Security for Canada* (1943), putting forward the idea of "a social minimum" to be secured through social insurance, social assistance, and children's allowances, saw a decade of social research studies on the McGill campus come to fruition and make a national impact.[91] But what of McGill University itself? A silence seemed to fall over its significant legacy in social science research, while the institution enjoyed renown for its achievements in science and medicine for decades thereafter.

NOTES

1 See Marlene Shore, *The Science of Social Redemption: McGill, the Chicago School, and the Origins of Social Research in Canada* (Toronto: University of Toronto Press, 1987).

2 The list of university histories, some officially commissioned, is too vast to include here. Robin S. Harris, *A History of Higher Education in Canada, 1663–1960* (Toronto: University of Toronto Press, 1976) is a standard history of higher education. Books dealing with the history of universities from the perspective of the history of ideas – exploring theories and currents of thought that shaped the institutions and disciplinary developments – include such pathbreaking studies as Laurence Veysey, *The Emergence of the American University* (Chicago: University of Chicago Press, 1965); A.B. McKillop, *A Disciplined Intelligence: Critical Inquiry and Canadian Thought in the Victorian Era* (Montreal and Kingston: McGill-Queen's University Press, 1980).

3 Molly Pulver Ungar, *The Last Ulysseans: Culture and Modernism in Montreal* (London and Washington: Academica Press, 2020); Marlene Shore, "'Overtures of an Era Being Born': F.R. Scott: Cultural Nationalism and Social Criticism," *Journal of Canadian Studies* 15 (Winter 1980–81): 31–42.

4 Veysey, *The Emergence of the American University*, 3, 221–33, 342–60; McKillop, *Disciplined Intelligence*, 229–30.

5 Geoff Eley, *A Crooked Line: From Cultural History to the History of Society* (Ann Arbor: University of Michigan, 2005); Marlene Shore, ed., *The Contested Past: Reading Canada's History* (Toronto: University of Toronto Press, 2002), 1–62; 196–205; Clarence Karr, "What Happened to Canadian Intellectual History?" *Acadiensis* 18, no. 2 (1989): 159.

6 Stephen Leacock, quoted in Shore, *Science of Social Redemption*, 245; McGill University Archives [MUA], Principals' Files, 1920–1939

(Sir Arthur Currie, A.E. Morgan, Lewis Williams Douglas), Acc. 641, box 241, Stephen Leacock, Remarks and Suggestions for the Principal's [Survey] Committee, 18 February 1931.

7 In the interwar years, Jewish immigrants constituted the largest ethnic group in Montreal and their children enrolled at McGill in increasing numbers. In the 1920s, 25 per cent of the students in the Faculty of Arts were Jewish; 15 per cent in medicine; 40 per cent in law. Towards the end of the 1920s and '30s, a quota system was implemented in medicine, and a higher matriculation standard required for arts. By 1939, these restrictions, which were dropped during the Second World War, had succeeded in reducing the number of Jewish students to 12.1 per cent in arts, 12.8 per cent in medicine, and 15 per cent in law. See Shore, *Science of Social Redemption*, 244; Stanley Brice Frost, *McGill University: For the Advancement of Learning, Volume II, 1895–1971* (Montreal and Kingston: McGill-Queen's University Press, 1984), 128.

8 These ideas and developments are more fully treated in Shore, *Science of Social Redemption*, introduction, xii, chapters 1, 2, and 3.

9 Henry Chellew, *Human and Industrial Efficiency* (London: University of London Press, 1919), 41, 68, 136; Sara Z. Burke, *Seeking the Highest Good: Social Service and Gender at the University of Toronto, 1888–1937* (Toronto: University of Toronto Press, 1996); James Pitsula, "The Emergence of Social Work in Toronto," *Journal of Canadian Studies / Revue d'études canadiennes* 14, no. 1 (1979): 35–42; John Graham, "The Haven, 1878–1930: A Toronto Charity's Transition from a Religious to a Professional Ethos," *Histoire sociale / Social History* 25, no. 50 (1992): 283–306.

10 Shore, *Science of Social Redemption*, 30; "Changes in the Academic Side of the University," in *McGill Annual Report* (1919–20), 4; Report of the Principal, in *McGill Annual Report* (1924–5), 49–50.

11 Wood, *The Storied Province of Quebec*, vol. II (Toronto: Dominion Publishing Co., 1931), 764; A.P.S. Glassco and W. Vaughan, *A Greater McGill*, McGill Centennial Endowment booklet (Montreal: The University, 1920), 7–8, 14–16, 18; *McGill Annual Report* (1918–19), 12–13; "Family Welfare in Montreal," *Social Welfare* 4 (1 July 1922): 219–20; Marcus L. Hansen and J.B. Brebner, *Mingling of the Canadian and American Peoples* (New Haven and Toronto: Yale University Press, 1940), 252; Terry Copp, *Anatomy of Poverty: The Condition of the Working Class in Montreal, 1897–1929* (Toronto: McClelland & Stewart, 1974), 30, 34; Shore, *Science of Social Redemption*, 36–8.

12 A full discussion can be found in Shore, chapter 2, "Social Service and the Origins of Sociology," *Science of Social Redemption*, 24–67.
13 F.R. Clarke, "Industrial Psychology in Montreal, *Human Factor (Occupational Psychology)* 9 (May 1935): 281–4.
14 See for example, Cecelia Tichi, *Shifting Gears: Technology, Literature, Culture in Modernist America* (Chapel Hill: University of North Carolina Press, 1987).
15 John Dewey, *The Influence of Darwinism on Philosophy and other Essays in Contemporary Thought* (New York: Henry Holt, 1910), 1–11. The literature on modernism is vast. See Marlene Shore, "Psychology and Memory in the Midst of Change: The Social Concerns of Late-19th-Century North American Psychologists," in *The Transformation of Psychology*, eds Christopher D. Green, Marlene Shore, and Thomas Teo (Washington, DC: American Psychological Association), 78; Daniel Joseph Singal, "Towards a Definition of American Modernism," in "Modernist Culture in America," ed. Daniel Joseph Singal, special issue, *American Quarterly* 39 (Spring 1987): 7–26; Stephen Kern, *The Culture of Time and Space, 1880–1918* (Cambridge, MA: Harvard University Press, 1983); George Cotkin, *Reluctant Modernism: American Thought and Culture, 1880–1900* (New York: Twayne Publishers, 1992); Frederick Karl, *Modern and Modernism: The Sovereignty of the Artist, 1885–1925* (New York: Atheneum, 1985); Ian Hacking, *The Taming of Chance* (New York: Cambridge University Press, 1990); William R. Everdell, *The First Moderns: Profiles of the Origins of Twentieth-Century Thought* (Chicago: University of Chicago Press, 1997); Elazar Barkan and Ronald Bush, eds, *Prehistories of the Future: The Primitivist Project and the Culture of Modernism* (Stanford: Stanford University Press, 1995).
16 Shore, "Psychology and Memory," 68–71, 78; Alex Owen, *The Place of Enchantment: British Occultism and the Culture of the Modern* (Chicago and London: University of Chicago Press, 2004); Michael Saler, "Modernity and Enchantment: A Historiographic Review," *American Historical Review* 111, no. 3 (June 2006): 692–716.
17 A more detailed discussion of nineteenth-century psychology be found in Marlene Shore, "'Nebulous Penumbra': James Mark Baldwin and the Borderlands of Psychology," in *Thinkers and Dreamers: Historical Essays in Honour of Carl Berger*, eds Gerald Friesen and Doug Owram (Toronto: University of Toronto Press, 2011), 95.
18 Harold C. Rowse, "Tendencies in Modern Psychology," *Canadian Journal of Religious Thought* 4 (July–Aug. 1927): 334–5.

19 John C. Burnham, *Paths into American Culture: Psychology, Medicine, and Morals* (Philadelphia: Temple University Press, 1988), 70, 92–3; John C. Burnham, "Psychiatry, Psychology and the Progressive Movement," *American Quarterly* 12, no. 4 (Winter 1960): 457–65; J.W. Bridges, "Psychoanalysis, A Contribution to the New Psychology," *The [Canadian] Public Health Journal* 14 (May and June 1923): 205; A.A. Roback, *Behaviorism and Psychology* (Cambridge: University Bookstore, Inc., 1923), 227.

20 "Labour Problems and Psychology," *Montreal Gazette*, 13 March 1920, 4.

21 D. Fraser-Harris, "Science and Faith-Healing," *Dalhousie Review* 2, no. 1 (1922): 65–6.

22 Fraser-Harris, "Science and Faith-Healing," 59–60.

23 "Hope and Promise in New Psychology," *Montreal Gazette*, 13 March 1920, 4; "New Auditorium for Psychologist," *Montreal Gazette*, 22 February 1924, 8.

24 See Michael Saler, *As If: Modern Enchantment and the Literary Prehistory of Virtual Reality* (Oxford: Oxford University Press, 2012); Saler, "Modernity and Enchantment"; Owen, *Place of Enchantment*; T.J. Jackson Lears, *No Place of Grace: Antimodernism and the Transformation of American Culture, 1880–1920* (New York: Pantheon Books, 1981).

25 The first psychological laboratory was established at the University of Toronto in 1890 by James Mark Baldwin. Shore, "James Mark Baldwin," 97.

26 Daniel Kevles, "Testing the Army's Intelligence: Psychologists and the Military in World War I," *Journal of American History* 55, no. 3 (December 1968): 565–81. There is a substantial literature on the history of psychology dealing with the creation, application, and misapplication of intelligence tests. For more detailed reference to this issue in the late nineteenth and early twentieth centuries, see Shore, "James Mark Baldwin," 114–6; Shore, "Memory in the Midst of Change," 73–5.

27 Shore, "James Mark Baldwin," 95; Mary J. Wright and C. Rogers Myers, "Introduction," in *History of Academic Psychology in Canada*, ed. Mary J. Wright and C. Rogers Myers (Toronto: Hogrefe, 1982), 12; W.D. Tait, "Minor Studies from the Psychological Laboratory of McGill University: Communicated by William D. Tait," *American Journal of Psychology* 21 (April 1926): 234–9.

28 Eric Oosenbrug, "Building a 'Cross-Roads Discipline' at McGill University: A History of Early Experimental Psychology in Postwar Canada" (PhD diss., York University, 2020), 32, 39, 48–9; David

McLennan, "Beyond the Asylum: Professionalization and the Mental Hygiene Movement in Canada, 1914–1928," *Canadian Bulletin of Medical History* 4 (Spring 1987): 8; J.W. Bridges, *An Outline of Abnormal Psychology* (Columbus, Ohio: R. G. Adams, 1919).

29 A.A. Roback, *Popular Psychology: With Chapters on Character Analysis and Intelligence Tests* (Cambridge: Sci-Art Publishers, 1928), 15–18.

30 Harry Elmer Barnes, "Dynamic History and Social Reform," *Canadian Forum* 4 (August 1924): 331.

31 "To Set Up New International Psychology," *Montreal Gazette*, 4 January 1919, 1. See also "League of Nations Called Experiment in Mental Hygiene," *Toronto Globe*, 6 March 1928, 13.

32 "'Mental Condition Afflicts World'; Men's Minds Not Ready to Accept Reign of Law, Says Sir A. Geddes," *Montreal Gazette*, 10 April 1922, 2.

33 Stephen Leacock, "A Manual of the New Mentality," *Harper's Monthly Magazine* 148 (1924): 472; "The Human Mind Up to Date" in Stephen Leacock, *The Garden of Folly* (New York: Dodd, Mead, 1924), 34–5, 38.

34 Grace Adams, "The Rise and Fall of Psychology," *Atlantic Monthly* (January 1933): 82–4.

35 Dale Carnegie, *How to Win Friends and Influence People* (New York: Simon and Shuster, 1937 [copyrighted in 1936]).

36 H.W. Wright, "Psychology in Human Life," *Canadian Banker* 36 (July 1929): 394.

37 "Italian Scientist Claims Communication Between Distant Minds," *Toronto Globe*, 21 May 1925, 1; Fraser-Harris, "Science and Faith Healing," 68–9; John C. Burnham, *How Superstition Won and Science Lost: Popularizing Science and Health in the United States* (New Brunswick, NJ: Rutgers University Press, 1987), 93–4, 96.

38 "Proposes to Use Light to Reach Another Planet – American Says Concentrated Rays of 200 Searchlights Would Reach Mars," *Montreal Gazette*, 31 January 1920, 11; "U.S. Scientists to Attempt This Week to Talk to Mars," *Montreal Gazette*, 19 April 1920, 14; H. Borsook, "Old Lamps for New," *Canadian Forum* 8 (November 1927): 433–6.

39 J.W. Bridges, *Psychology, Normal and Abnormal* (New York: D. Appleton and Company, 1930), 506.

40 Roback, *Popular Psychology*, 15–18.

41 J.M. Shaw, "Spiritualism and Immortality," *Dalhousie Review* 1 (July 1921): 151.

42 Stan McMullin, *Anatomy of a Seance: A History of Spirit Communication in Central Canada* (Montreal and Kingston: McGill-Queen's University Press, 2004), 107–8. A more complete account of the influenza epidemic

can be found in Magda Fahrni and Esyllt W. Jones, *Epidemic Encounters: Influenza, Society and Culture in Canada, 1918–20* (Vancouver: UBC Press, 2012).

43 Shore, *Science of Social Redemption*, 26; Cyrus Macmillan, *McGill and Its Story, 1821–1921* (London and New York: J. Lane; Toronto: Oxford University Press, 1921), 262–3; J.A. Nicholson, *McGill's War Record*, Centennial Endowment Booklet (Montreal: The University, 1920), 12.

44 A.S. Ferguson, "The Twentieth Plane," *Queen's Quarterly* 27 (January 1920): 258–9; 261–6; "W.D.W." Letter to the Editor, "Advertising Religion," *Canadian Forum* 2 (January 1922): 258; McMullin, *Anatomy of a Seance*, 117.

45 Owen, *Place of Enchantment*, 223; "Suicide Gives No Relief From Care Says Conan Doyle," *Montreal Gazette*, 11 April 1922, 11; "Spirit Photos Presented by Conan Doyle," *Montreal Gazette*, 22 April 1922, 1; "Etheric Plane Is a Place of Delights," *Montreal Gazette*, 10 July 1923, 4.

46 McMullin, *Anatomy of a Seance*, 108; Owen, *Place of Enchantment*, 103; R.M. MacIver, "The Bookshelf: Metaphysics," review of *Thirty Years of Psychical Research: Being a Treatise on Metaphysics* (Macmillan) by Charles Richet, *Canadian Forum* 3 (December 1922): 23; H.D. Kay, "Experimental Metaphysics," *Canadian Forum* 11 (September 1931): 451.

47 "Psychic Research and the Churches," *Montreal Gazette*, 28 February 1919, 5; "Spiritualism as Primitive Faith," *Montreal Gazette*, 9 July 1923, 3.

48 There were numerous such efforts undertaken by psychologists across Canada, the United States, Britain, and France. For example, see Carl Murchison, ed., *The Case For and Against Psychical Belief* (Worcester, Mass.: Clark University, 1927), publication of papers from the symposium of the same name held at Clark University from 29 November to 11 December 1926; Michael Pettit, "Joseph Jastrow, the Psychology of Deception, and the Racial Economy of Observation," *Journal of the History of the Behavioural Sciences* 43 (Spring 2007): 159–75; Michael Pettit, *The Science of Deception: Psychology and Commerce in America* (Chicago: University of Chicago Press, 2013); Françoise Parot, "Psychology Experiments: Spiritism at the Sorbonne," *Journal of the History of the Behavioral Sciences* 29 (January 1993): 22–8.

49 Frost, *McGill University* 2:104, 178.

50 "Psychics Lacking Scientific Value," *Montreal Gazette*, 24 November 1920, 4.

51 "40,000 Colors are Registered by Eye – Professor W.D. Tait, in Lecture Course, Discussed 'Gateways of Knowledge,'" *Montreal* Gazette, 21 July 1922, 5.

52 "'Does Spiritism Call For License?' – Question to Be Submitted in Its Legal Aspects to Superior Court," *Montreal Gazette*, 29 October 1920, 4.
53 "Hypnotism Failed to Regain Husband: Experiment Having Fizzled, Wife Now Wants Her Money Returned," *Montreal Gazette*, 22 June 1921, 4.
54 John Macdonald, "The Belief in Luck," *Bulletin of The Canadian Credit Institute* 85 (December 1938): 1.
55 Adams, "The Rise and Fall of Psychology," 91–2.
56 J.B. [Joseph Banks] Rhine, *New Frontiers of the Mind* (New York: Oxford University Press, 1937); Elizabeth Ann Bucknell, "The Function of Dependent Probability in ESP Data," *Journal of General Psychology* 19 (1938): 373.
57 Raymond E. Fancher, *Pioneers of Psychology*, 3rd ed. (New York and London: W.W. Norton & Company, Inc., 1996), 264. Kellogg refers to Hugo Münsterberg's book, *Psychology and Social Sanity* (London: T.F. Unwin, 1914); John Edgar Coover, *Experiments in Psychical Research at Leland Stanford University* (Stanford: Stanford University Press, 1917); Chester E. Kellogg, "Dr. J.B. Rhine and Extra-Sensory Perception," *Journal of Abnormal and Social Psychology* 31 (July–September 1936): 190–1; Chester E. Kellogg, "The Statistical Techniques of ESP," *Journal of General Psychology* 19 (1938): 383–4; Chester E. Kellogg, "New Evidence for 'Extra-Sensory Perception,'" *Scientific Monthly* 45 (October 1937): 332–3.
58 Kellogg, "New Evidence for 'Extra-Sensory Perception,'" 331–2.
59 Chester E. Kellogg, "A Note in Reply to Mr. Charles E. Stuart," *Journal of Abnormal and Social Psychology* 33 (October 1938): 526.
60 Kellogg, "New Evidence for 'Extra-Sensory Perception,'" 333–5.
61 Kellogg, "Reply to Mr. Charles E. Stuart," 525.
62 Kellogg, "New Evidence for 'Extra-Sensory Perception,'" 336–7, 341.
63 Chester E. Kellogg, "The Problems of Matching and Sampling in the Study of Extra-Sensory Perception," *Journal of Abnormal and Social Psychology* 32 (Oct.–Dec. 1937): 479.
64 Kellogg, "Statistical Techniques of ESP," 386.
65 S.N.F. Chant, "Clairvoyance, Telepathy, and Psychology," Review of J.B. Rhine, *New Frontiers of the Mind* (Oxford University Press, 1937), in *University of Toronto Quarterly* 7 (January 1938): 265–8.
66 "Labour Problems and Psychology," 4.
67 C.E. Kellogg, "Mental Tests and Their Uses," *Dalhousie Review* 2 (January 1923): 490–500.
68 Anon. ("By One of Seven Founders"), "Montreal Personnel Association," *Personnel Journal* 16 (1937): 81–4.

69 The grant was to cover a period of five years beginning 1 June 1931 and ending 31 May 1936; a four-year extension was subsequently approved by the Rockefeller Foundation. Shore, *Science of Social Redemption*, 214, 222.

70 Further discussion of research funding and sources for Canadian social scientists in this period can be found in Shore, *Science of Social Redemption*, chapter 5; Donald Fisher, *The Social Sciences in Canada: 50 Years of National Activity by the Social Science Federation of Canada* (Waterloo: Wilfrid Laurier University Press, 1990).

71 University of Toronto Archives, acc. A73-00261, 151 (78), Hincks, Clarence Meredith; "Hincks, Clarence Meredith," in *Canadian Who's Who*, vol. 2 (1936–1937), ed. Charles G.D. Roberts and Arthur Leonard Tunnell, 511–2; the journalist was Robert Reade in the Toronto *Star Weekly* (n.d., n.p.), quoted in "Hincks," *Canadian Who's Who*, 512; J. D Griffin, *In Search of Sanity: A Chronicle of the Canadian Mental Health Association, 1918–1988* (London, Ont.: Third Eye Publications, 1989); C.G. Roland, *Clarence Hincks: Mental Health Crusader* (Toronto: Hannah Institute and Dundurn Press, 1990).

72 Shore, *Science of Social Redemption*, 201–2, 204, 211.

73 Shore, *Science of Social Redemption*, 208.

74 Shore, *Science of Social Redemption*, 114–15; see Hamilton Cravens and John C. Burham, "Psychology and Evolutionary Naturalism in American Thought, 1890–1940," *American Quarterly* 23 (December 1971): 635, 656. Rosalind Rosenberg, *Beyond Separate Spheres: Intellectual Roots of Modern Feminism* (New Haven and London: Yale University Press, 1982) treats the important contribution that academics at the University of Chicago and Columbia University made to feminist theories by breaking away from mechanistic philosophies of human nature to stress environmental conditioning.

75 A detailed account of the Social Science Research Project's investigations and publications can be found in Shore, *Science of Social Redemption*, chapter 6, "The Social Science Research Project," 195–223.

76 Shore, "The Social Science Research Project," 219, 221. Throughout its ten years of existence, thirty-eight students were employed in the project, more than half from universities other than McGill. For students interested in pursuing graduate studies in the social sciences in Canada, with grants ranging from $500 to $700 dollars a year in a period of economic depression, the Rockefeller Foundation money was a great boon. See also L.C. Marsh, *Employment Research: An Introduction to the McGill Programme of Research in the Social Sciences* (Toronto: Oxford University Press, 1935).

77 MUA, acc. 641, box 289, C.E. Kellogg to Sir Arthur Currie, Tentative Suggestions for Investigation re Unemployment by an Institute of Human Relations, 8 March 1930; Shore, *Science of Social Redemption*, 207.

78 The CNCMH withdrew its financial support after five years because a wider research program had not been established; the nursery had not been used by psychologists or any other department for research purposes. Deprived of Rockefeller Foundation funds, Bridges and Banham-Bridges lost their appointments at McGill. Oosenbrug, "Building a 'Cross-Roads' Discipline," 49.

79 Shore, *Science of Social Redemption*, 219.

80 C.E. Kellogg and N.W. Morton, "Revised Beta Examination," *Personnel Journal* 13 (June 1934–April 1935): 94–100; C.E. Kellogg and N.W. Morton, "Abilities and Unemployment," *Personnel Journal* 13 (June 1934–April 1935): 169–81; W.D. Tait and N.W. Morton, "Industrial Psychology in Canada," *Occupational Psychology* 12 (Summer 1938): 224–32; N.W. Morton, with an introduction by C.E. Kellogg, *Occupational Abilities: A Study of Unemployed Men*, McGill Social Research Series, no. 3 (Toronto: Oxford University Press, 1935); George Humphrey, *The Story of Man's Mind*, rev. ed. (New York, Dodd, Mead; 1932; orig. pub. 1923), 233–4; Frost, *McGill University*, 2:147–8.

81 A governor of McGill, Sir Charles Blair Gordon was president of the Bank of Montreal and the Royal Trust, and a member of the board of directors of both the Dominion Textile and Dominion Glass Companies; Julian Smith was president and general manager of the Shawinigan Water and Power Company, vice-president of Dominion Engineering Works, president of the Quebec Power Company and the Montreal Tramway Company, as well as director of Montreal Light, Heat and Power; Thomas Bassett Macaulay was president of the Sun Life Assurance Company of Canada, director of Dominion Glass, Montreal Light, Heat and Power, and the American Superpower Corporation. Shore, *Science of Social Redemption*, 211–2.

82 MUA, acc. 641, Box 289, copy of L.C. Marsh's address, "Unemployment. An International and Community Problem," delivered at the Montreal Forum, 25 January 1931; Shore, *Science of Social Redemption*, 217–18.

83 Michiel Horn, *Academic Freedom in Canada: A History* (Toronto: University of Toronto Press, 1999), 128–44.

84 Shore, *Science of Social Redemption*, 263.

85 Horn, *Academic Freedom in Canada*, 138–41; Shore, *Science of Social Redemption*, 211, 225, 239–42.

86 Shore, *Science of Social Redemption*, 277n36; Frost, *McGill University*, 2:202.

87 Horn, *Academic Freedom*, 144; Shore, *Science of Social Redemption*, 266–7, 270.

88 David Nock, "History and Evolution of French Canadian Sociology," *Insurgent Sociologist* 4 (Summer 1974): 21; Marlene Shore, "Religion, science et autorité dans le développement des sciences sociales en Amérique du Nord," *Revue d'Histoire de l'Amérique Française* 57, no. 3 (Winter 2004): 385–7; Shore, *Science of Social Redemption*, 270.

89 Shore, *Science of Social Redemption*, 260–1, 271; Leonard C. Marsh, *Canadians In and Out of Work: A Survey of Economic Classes and Their Relation to the Labour Market* (Toronto: Oxford University Press, 1940).

90 Marsh, *Canadians In and Out of Work*, xvii.

91 Shore, *Science of Social Redemption*, 269; Leonard Marsh, *Social Security for Canada*, report prepared for the Committee on Postwar Reconstruction and presented to the Special Committee for Social Security, House of Commons, Apr. 1943 (Ottawa: King's Printer 1943; Toronto: University of Toronto Press, Social History Series, 1975); see Marsh's introduction for the 1975 edition of *Social Security for Canada*, xx.

8

"A Distinct Blow to Our Esteem of That Outstanding Institution"

McGill University's Racial Exclusion of Japanese Canadians, 1943–45

TESS ELSWORTHY

On 24 February 1942, three months after Canada declared war on Japan, the Canadian Cabinet approved Order-in-Council PC 1486, decreeing the expulsion of all "persons of Japanese Racial Origin" from the Pacific Coast.[1] That spring, the federal government forcibly displaced nearly 22,000 Japanese Canadians from their homes, beginning a period of internment and incarceration that would last until 1949. At the time of uprooting, seventy-six second-generation Japanese Canadian students, known as "Nisei," were registered at the University of British Columbia (UBC) in Vancouver.[2] Fourteen would graduate that spring; the rest were left to transfer elsewhere or abandon their degrees.[3]

By the fall of 1943, Nisei students were enrolled at the University of Alberta, the University of Saskatchewan, the University of Manitoba, Queen's University, and the University of Toronto. Exiled Nisei had applied to McGill University as well, but that October McGill distinguished itself by passing a senate motion that declared, "it is inadvisable to admit any students of *Japanese racial origin* to the undergraduate courses of the University during the present war."[4] Principal Frank Cyril James,[5] McGill's board of governors, and a faction of senate members had devoted substantial energy to the project of passing the policy of excluding Nisei and would vigorously defend it over the next two years.[6]

McGill's leadership disagreed over the admission of Nisei students. As applications from Nisei began to arrive in 1942, the registrar, Thomas Matthews, encouraged Principal James to admit as many as possible.[7] James, however, acquiesced to faculty members and governors who demanded their exclusion. On 30 September 1943, the senate voted for a restrictive but not totally exclusive admissions policy towards Japanese Canadian applicants. The exclusionist faction remained unsatisfied, so James orchestrated another vote at the following senate meeting three weeks later. On 20 October, the McGill senate overturned the decision and narrowly passed a motion to ban all undergraduate students "of Japanese racial origin." Thus began a fierce struggle over McGill's principles as an elite educational institution.

This understudied event in McGill history offers an essential case study in white supremacy in Canadian higher education.[8] The policy's architects insisted that accepting Japanese Canadian applicants would deny opportunities to applicants of British ancestry. The senate motion emphasized racial origin, positioning Nisei as inherently different from the White Anglo-Saxons they believed to be racially superior.[9] While it continued a long pattern of exclusion at McGill, the explicitly racist policy met fierce opposition. Japanese Canadian activists and hundreds of allied students protested, and at least four undergraduate and three graduate students "of Japanese racial origin" remained on campus during the exclusion period, defying the senate. McGill community members contested the policy, linking the ban on Japanese Canadians to longstanding unofficial restrictions on Jewish enrolment.[10] The backlash against McGill's racial exclusion of Japanese Canadians accordingly offers an example of resistance to white supremacy in higher education in the 1940s.

With the help of the principal, McGill's governors had traditionally succeeded in isolating radical and leftist faculty members, and in 1943, the early opponents of official racial exclusion were easily outmaneuvered. James's faction, however, eventually found a formidable challenger in law professor Frank Scott, a long-time thorn in the governors' side. In addition to supporting labour organizers and serving as national chairman of the Co-operative Commonwealth Federation (CCF), the predecessor of the New Democratic Party, Scott openly criticized McGill's governors; in a 1934 issue of *The Canadian Forum* he wrote about some governors' alleged recent investment of university money in their own companies.[11] After being elected to the senate to represent his faculty, Scott would deploy his knowledge of McGill statutes to help defeat the policy. In the 1940s, student government, campus newspaper the *McGill Daily,* and student clubs held limited autonomy; pushback against the ban on Japanese Canadians would surprise and offend James and the governors.[12] Using files from McGill's archives, the Canadian Department of External Affairs, the Canadian press, the student press, the Nikkei National Museum, the Japanese Canadian Cultural Centre of Montreal, and an interview with McGill alumna Betty Kobayashi Issenman, this chapter outlines how the racial exclusion policy was passed, resisted, and repealed.

~~~

On 8 December 1941, the day after Japan attacked Pearl Harbor, Principal James telephoned a local RCMP inspector to discuss "enemy students" on McGill's campus. The two men differentiated between Japanese nationals and Japanese Canadians. They decided that McGill would bar Japanese nationals from the Canadian Officers' Training Corps (COTC) but impose no restrictions on Nisei.[13] No Japanese nationals were enrolled that fall. Three Nisei were studying at McGill: second-year science student Kiyokazu Jack Momose, and first-year medicine students George Shimotakahara and Satoru Watanabe.[14] Shimotakahara and Watanabe both completed basic training in the McGill Reserve Training Battalion that year.[15] Momose would join the McGill COTC in May 1942.[16]

Back in their home communities in British Columbia, the families of these three students faced a common experience of dislocation and removal. In the spring of 1942, Shimotakahara's family was forcibly removed from Vancouver to Kaslo,[17] Watanabe's family was relocated from Vancouver to Slocan and Lemon Creek,[18] and Momose's family was uprooted from Vancouver to Chase.[19]

Other Nisei soon tried to join these three students at McGill. At UBC, the International Student Service surveyed forty-six soon-to-be-displaced Japanese Canadian students about plans to continue their education. The respondents named seven Canadian universities to which they would like to transfer. Five students, James Hasegawa, Hajime Kagetsu, Koei Mitsui, Yoshito Takahashi, and Koichi Tsujimura, listed McGill; Kagetsu had already applied.[20] Some displaced Japanese Canadian families chose to resettle in Montreal because of McGill's reputation as a respected university. Fumiko
~~~

Figure 8.1 Japanese Canadian McGill medical students George Shimotakahara (with snowball) and Satoru Watanabe, outside the Acadia Lodge on Prince Arthur Street in Montreal, circa 1942.

Taguchi remembers, "We came to Montreal, and it was McGill University which made us decide."[21] Medical student George Shimotakahara's uncle, prominent merchant Toryaru Shimotakahara, arrived in Montreal with his family of seven in the spring of 1942. He told the *Montreal Gazette* that "present plans call for three of the children ... entering McGill University next term."[22] In a context of tremendous uncertainty, displaced Japanese Canadians believed a McGill degree would expand their children's career opportunities.

The first application from an exiled Nisei reached Matthews, McGill's registrar, in April 1942. In early July, he wrote to James, "I think we should admit as many [exiled Nisei] as we possibly can and decide to do so quickly." Matthews had referred the applications to the dean of arts and science and Liberal member of Parliament for Queen's County, Prince Edward Island, Cyrus Macmillan.[23] Residency regulations provided a convenient pretext to reject exiled third-year UBC students; Macmillan reported that four Nisei had applied for upper years in arts and commerce but "at least two years residence is required."[24]

While federal internment policies emboldened other institutions to discriminate against Japanese Canadians, the Canadian government never ordered universities to exclude them. In August 1942, Matthews wrote to the Department of National Defence to clarify the government's position on admitting Japanese Canadians to universities east of British Columbia.[25] The inquiry was passed on to the Department of External Affairs, which confirmed in early September that the government had "adopted no official attitude on the matter." The undersecretary of external affairs advised, "Your university is free to take whatever stand you wish in this regard without any sanction by the Government."[26] By refusing to affirmatively approve the admission of Nisei applicants, External Affairs gave university administrators permission to discriminate against them. The department's letter nonetheless confirms that McGill officials knew federal authorities had not banned Japanese Canadians from universities. McGill's governing bodies were solely responsible for its exceptional decision to racially exclude Nisei applicants.

James paid selective attention to recommendations regarding Japanese Canadian admissions. For over a year he ignored the registrar's enthusiasm to admit these applicants. In September 1943, G.E. Trueman, an officer from the British Columbia Security Commission (BCSC), visited him to advocate for seven unnamed Japanese Canadian applicants approved by the RCMP.[27] Unmoved, James told him McGill had yet to decide if Nisei would be admitted. There is no evidence that James consulted with faculty members familiar with federal policies against Japanese Canadians. He chose not to consult Forrest LaViolette, for instance, a sociology professor hailed by the *Montreal Star* as an "expert on [the] Japanese Problem," who would go on to publish the definitive contemporary academic text on Japanese Canadian internment.[28] LaViolette would have inconveniently supported Nisei admissions, contradicting the growing exclusionist faction, which included Dean Macmillan and Dean of Engineering John Johnston O'Neill.[29]

Some McGill personnel defied the principal. Matthews discreetly admitted one Nisei, Ryo Otsuki, to begin a science degree in September of 1943.[30] Judging by his surname, French-born Maurice Takeshige, who began his engineering degree at McGill that same fall, may have had Japanese ancestry.[31] The registrar still had no answer for the other Japanese Canadian applicants waiting for an official acceptance or rejection.[32] He urged James to take ownership of university policy by putting it to the senate.[33]

On 29 September 1943, the Faculty of Arts and Science narrowly passed a resolution that "academically qualified Japanese students of Canadian birth who have not been out of school for more than one year be admitted for one year only to courses in the Humanities and Social Science groups."[34] The next day, Dean Macmillan presented his faculty's resolution to the senate but announced his intention to vote against it. He argued that admitting Japanese Canadian students would alienate the public, returning servicemen, and the student body. He claimed that because Japanese Canadians were banned from military service, allowing them to attend university would grant them privileges denied to "students of British ancestry." Finally, he asserted that Japanese Canadians should focus on helping the war effort as agricultural labourers and accused them of being unwilling to do so.[35] Some senate members, including classics chairman William Woodhead and dean of law Charles LeMesurier, advocated for a more lenient approach. Chairman of Physiology Hebbel Hoff proposed that each applicant could be vetted by the RCMP to allay security concerns. His amendment was accepted. The resolution was put to a vote and narrowly passed by a margin of eleven to ten. James echoed Macmillan's arguments for total exclusion but did not cast a vote.

The dean of graduate studies, David Thomson, informed the senate that Japanese Canadian students were already enrolled at McGill, and that the federal government had further proposed sending him "a Canadian student of Japanese extraction to do research work in Pharmacology." Someone proposed a motion to admit Japanese Canadian graduate students "on the recommendation of the Committee on Research." The meeting minutes do not indicate whether this resolution was passed, however the assembled men did pass an amendment to ban Japanese Canadian graduate students from all other McGill faculties.[36]

~ ~ ~

Without officially excluding them, the senate had imposed heavy restrictions on "Japanese students of Canadian birth." Some influential members of the senate and board of governors, however, remained unsatisfied. When the board of governors met on 13 October 1943, they expressed disapproval of any Japanese Canadian admissions; James promised that the motion would be reconsidered.[37] One member of both McGill's senate and its board of governors, president of Sun Life Assurance Arthur Wood, had missed the senate meeting on 30 September. In the first of numerous furious letters to James, Wood urged him to ban all Japanese Canadians.[38]

When the senate met again on 20 October, the exclusionists moved to reverse the policy passed at the previous meeting. Wood claimed wealthy university donors would withhold funds if any Japanese Canadians were admitted. Others repeated Macmillan's arguments, yet they failed to convince all members present. Professor Woodhead and W.H. Brittain, dean of agriculture, defended Nisei inclusion. Woodhead emphasized that "the argument that the motion adopted at the last meeting had been carried only by a small majority would apply equally well if it should be reversed by a small majority."[39] Someone, probably Matthews, announced that a representative from the British Columbia Security Commission had encouraged McGill to admit Japanese Canadian students. Dean Macmillan incorrectly dismissed him as an employee of the YMCA.[40] Law professor Orville Tyndale moved: "In the opinion of Senate it is inadvisable to admit any students *of Japanese racial origin* to the undergraduate courses of the University during the present war." The resolution was adopted by a vote of eleven to nine.[41] The senate traditionally gave local newspapers a mimeographed copy of its meeting minutes, but the resolution barring students of Japanese racial origin was omitted from those of 20 October.[42] Much like their informal efforts to reduce Jewish enrolment, McGill officials evidently intended to keep the racist policy a secret.[43]

~ ~ ~

The use of undemocratic methods to pass the racial exclusion policy alienated some senate members. Professor Woodhead reminded James that the topic had not been added to the meeting's agenda. Consequently, former Kingsford chair of history and financier Charles Colby, Professor Hoff, and the Honourable Adrian Knatchbull Hugessen, all opponents of racial exclusion, had neglected to attend the meeting.[44] Finally, Woodhead highlighted Macmillan's "misstatement" regarding Trueman's status as a government official. In the margins of Woodhead's letter, the principal's secretary scrawled, "this is [Matthews]."[45] It was the second time Matthews had caught James and Macmillan in a lie; in September, James wrote to Matthews that Macmillan's faculty unanimously opposed Japanese Canadian admissions, only for Matthews to conduct his own survey and report that eight faculty members were never consulted.[46] Matthews evidently distrusted James and Macmillan and investigated their claims, communicating his findings to the opponents of exclusion.

James, who had informed the governors of his plans to reverse the first senate resolution, lied to Woodhead, claiming he had not been aware that Japanese Canadian admissions would be reconsidered on 20 October.[47] Woodhead reminded him that the proceedings of that meeting defied the rules of parliamentary procedure.[48] In response, James feigned ignorance of senate rules.[49]

At the senate meeting on 17 November, James sought to pacify critics like Woodhead by proposing a special committee to clarify the rules of procedure.[50] On 19 January 1944, the committee presented its new rules, which stipulated that all items be explicitly described on each meeting's agenda and that "the minimum vote required for the passing of a motion to reconsider [previous resolutions] shall be two-thirds of the members present."[51] The senate's new rules conveniently did not retroactively apply to the reconsideration of the first admissions policy passed on 30 September 1943. The proponents of racial exclusion had passed their policy with eleven votes; their opponents would require fourteen votes to reverse it.

~~~

After passing its policy excluding Japanese Canadian undergraduate students, McGill expelled one Nisei science student, Ryo Otsuki, whom Matthews had admitted during the summer of 1943. Otsuki was in high school when his family was forced from their Surrey home in 1942.[52] They moved to Winnipeg, where his older brother, Juko, having been exiled from UBC, finished his bachelor of science at the University of Manitoba. Despite the stresses created by federal policy, Ryo Otsuki graduated with high enough marks to enter McGill. Although he is listed in the Directory of Students, it is unclear if he managed to complete the 1944 winter term before being forced to leave.[53] In 1945, Otsuki started over once more at the University of New Brunswick, receiving his bachelor of engineering in 1949. In the yearbook, Otsuki's UNB classmates described him fondly: "Possessed of a keen mind and a sense of responsibility, we will ever be proud to claim him as one of our own."[54] While Otsuki was cruelly forced to leave McGill, other Japanese Canadian students managed to remain there.

Kiyokazu Jack Momose, George Shimotakahara, and Satoru Watanabe had been admitted before the era of formal racial exclusion. They were not expelled, but observing Otsuki's abrupt departure may have dismayed them. Watanabe and Shimotakahara graduated in the
~~~

spring of 1944.[55] Momose completed his bachelor of science degree that same spring and notably enrolled in medicine at McGill in the fall while the racial exclusion policy was still in effect.[56] Both the registrar and the dean of medicine, Jonathan Meakins, opposed the exclusion of Nisei and may have quietly organized his admission.[57] Although they were able to continue at McGill, the Nisei students faced racist hostility on campus; Dr Shimotakahara was refused an internship at the General Hospital and recalled fellow students hissing at Watanabe in 1941. Both men nonetheless succeeded in their classes and Shimotakahara ultimately found a position at the Royal Victoria Hospital.[58]

~ ~ ~

McGill's racial exclusion of Japanese Canadians finally captured national publicity the following school year. In October 1944, the Montreal Diocesan Theological College Alumni Association passed a public resolution against McGill's policy. Principal James gave journalists as little information as possible. Newspapers across the country carried the story, repeating the claim that the senate's decision was "in line with the ban against their admission in the armed forces or in war factories."[59] In November, M.J. Coldwell, leader of the CCF, condemned McGill's policies toward Japanese Canadian and Jewish applicants while giving an address at Montreal High School.[60] James declined to comment.

The first documented reaction from McGill's student body appeared in the *McGill Daily* on 24 October. In a letter to the editor, science student Basil Rattray wrote that Japanese Canadian applicants could easily undergo background checks and pointed to the large number of Japanese Americans fighting in the American Armed Forces.[61] The *McGill Daily* editors initially refrained from commenting, telling another letter writer that the principal had not issued any statement.[62] On 27 October 1944, the University of Toronto's newspaper, the *Varsity*, issued the first dissenting student press editorial, noting that their university was also conducting war research, yet it admitted Japanese Canadians.[63] The next day, the national English-language Japanese Canadian newspaper, the *New Canadian*, condemned McGill's policy, pointing to the eighteen Nisei enrolled at the University of Manitoba.[64]

Helmut Richter, editor-in-chief of the *McGill Daily,* visited the principal on 31 October. James cautioned against "[washing] our dirty linen in public through the press," and advised him to encourage the Students Executive Council (SEC) to quietly forward a petition to the senate.[65] The SEC passed a motion the next day for the senate's consideration that "the present blanket measure barring otherwise eligible Canadian-born Japanese students from enrolment at McGill University [is] an unjust criterion of admission to this University."[66] The *McGill Daily* mentioned the motion alongside other items on the SEC agenda. James rebuked SEC President John Costigan, who blamed Richter.[67] James had attempted to quell public student opposition to McGill's racial exclusion policy; the SEC president cooperated but the *McGill Daily* editor refused to obey.

Despite mounting controversy and criticism, McGill's board of governors remained committed to the ban. On 8 November, the governors extended the racial exclusion policy to apply to university employees in response to an attempt by Dean LeMesurier to hire an unnamed Japanese Canadian woman as his secretary.[68]

On 9 November, the Student Labour Club invited "well-known [Japanese Canadian] anti-fascist" and McGill alumna Betty Kobayashi (arts 1940, social work 1942) to speak at the Union Grill. When she learned of the senate's decision, Kobayashi remembers thinking, "This isn't McGill."[69] She had represented McGill at the National Conference of Canadian University Students in 1937, was elected to the SEC in 1938, and served as the vice-president of the Student Christian Movement.[70] The *McGill Daily* reported,

> Miss Kobayashi expressed her conviction that only fighting for tolerance among all the peoples of Canada will vanquish intolerance and make possible the achievement of the common aims of all Canadians. Loyalty, she said, "does not depend on the colour of a person's skin or the shape of the eyes," and she quoted from documents received from young Japanese Canadians in various parts of Canada expressing their desire and determination to fight in every way possible against fascism in every country.[71]

Betty Kobayashi was the only Japanese Canadian who publicly protested McGill's policy on campus. As a recent graduate she was acquainted with members of the student body and safe from potential expulsion. Her sister, Mary Campbell Kobayashi Hecht, was then enrolled in McGill's public health nursing program and may have been afraid to openly criticize the university.[72]

A longtime activist, Betty Kobayashi was personally impacted by unjust federal policies. Her father, Shinsuke Harry Kobayashi, a Canadian First World War veteran, was president of the Montreal branch of the Mikado Company, an import firm. He had been on a business trip to Japan when Canada entered the war in the Pacific. Federal authorities forbade him from returning home until hostilities ceased. Like all assets owned by Japanese Canadians, the Mikado Company was seized and sold by the Custodian of Enemy Property. The RCMP forced the Kobayashi sisters to be fingerprinted, "like we were criminals," reported Betty Kobayashi. Meanwhile, their brother Gordon managed to enlist in the Royal Canadian Air Force (RCAF) after informing the recruiting officer that his father was a First World War veteran. As her brother fought for his country, Betty Kobayashi fought for democracy at her alma mater.[73]

Representatives from the Newman Club, Student Christian Movement, Inter-Varsity Christian Fellowship of Canada, Hillel Foundation, Cosmopolitan Club, British West Indies Society, and Student Affairs Club circulated a petition calling for a meeting of the students' society to discuss the policy.[74] In its announcement of the upcoming students' society meeting, the *McGill Daily* noted that the newly formed McGill Veterans' Society had "gone on record as being in favor of the admission of eligible Japanese Canadians."[75]

Two hundred and fifty students attended the meeting. They passed a motion in support of the previous SEC resolution. The motion highlighted the acceptance of Japanese Canadians at other universities and acknowledged that Canadian Nisei were by then being admitted to the Armed Forces. After a broader discussion of racial and antisemitic exclusion, the students passed an ambitious second motion to establish a committee against racial discrimination.[76] The *McGill Daily* rebuked the second motion, accusing the students' society of forming "an old-time vigilante committee."[77] McGill governor J.W. McConnell's *Montreal Star*, previously silent about the university's racial exclusion policy, finally deigned to mention it, reporting that the alleged vigilantes "were ridiculed today by their own campus paper."[78] The *Montreal Gazette* and other daily newspapers across Canada reported less scornfully on the SEC resolution, and much of the national student press was sympathetic.[79] Possibly under pressure from the principal, SEC President John Costigan issued a press release professing his personal "neutrality" regarding McGill's exclusion of Japanese Canadians.[80]

On 15 November 1944, McGill's senate met for the first time since the ban on Nisei enrolment had provoked national controversy. James perfunctorily shared statements decrying racism from the students' society, the Montreal Diocesan Theological College Association, and the Staff Christian Association. Edward Adair, chairman of history, gave a notice of motion to reconsider the policy at the next meeting.[81]

The *New Canadian* continued to follow developments at McGill. The editors argued that if the sensitivity of war research were truly legitimate grounds for the senate's decision, Shimotakahara and Watanabe would not have been allowed to remain on campus. They asserted that the two Nisei medicine students' presence, "coupled with the policy on Jewish students ... and the fact that other universities admit Nisei students even though war research work is carried on, clearly points to racial discrimination."[82] The editors of *Saturday Night* similarly concluded that "we do not believe that the action of the McGill Senate had anything to do with a desire to reserve the facilities of the university for persons qualifying for the defence plants or the forces."[83] The hollow claim that racial exclusion protected war research had convinced few observers.

Letters from alumni began to arrive: all condemned the policy.[84] In language typical of the alumni messages, Flight Lieutenant H. Russell Ross (MA 1932) wrote to James from his RCAF station in Vulcan, Alberta, "I can hardly believe that a democratic institution with such traditions as McGill could possibly be guilty of such narrow racial action."[85] In his boilerplate response, James assured alumni that the policy had been passed "not on any basis of racial prejudice, as you suggest, but on other considerations entirely."[86] When the senate met on 15 December, Professor Adair moved to reconsider the racial exclusion policy. He failed to secure a two-thirds majority, losing by a single vote.[87] James had cast his vote for the first time to defeat the motion.[88]

~ ~ ~

After Christmas, James finally reached out to his counterparts at ten other Canadian universities regarding their own admissions policies.[89] None had formally banned Japanese Canadian students. Even in Vancouver, then a hotbed of nativist hostility towards Japanese Canadians, the president of the University of British Columbia, Norman MacKenzie, indicated that he expected UBC to admit them when they were allowed to return to the coast.[90] The University of

New Brunswick, Université Laval, Université de Montréal, and Dalhousie University had yet to receive applications from Nisei. All but Dalhousie expressed openness to Japanese Canadians.[91] Dalhousie President Carleton Stanley was sympathetic to McGill's policy because, as he wrote to James, "the treachery of these people is well proven."[92] James thanked him for echoing "precisely my own feeling about this *problem* of Canadian-born Japanese students."[93] Even as the majority of Canadian university leaders expressed willingness to admit Japanese Canadians, McGill's principal offered his solidarity to the one president who repeated racist myths about them.

Two Nisei were enrolled at the University of Saskatchewan[94] and nineteen at the University of Manitoba.[95] The Board of Governors of the University of Alberta had restricted admissions through subtler means. President Robert Newton reported, "All Canadian citizens who are bona fide residents of this province have equal right to register with us, regardless of racial origin. In the case of Japanese [Canadians], bona fide residence was defined as residence in this province prior to the date of Pearl Harbor."[96] Despite this barrier, six Nisei exiled from British Columbia had managed to enrol at the University of Alberta in September 1942.[97]

Ontario universities would have had the strongest excuse to officially ban Nisei students. In the fall of 1942, Premier Mitchell Hepburn, who benefited from exploiting the underpaid labour of displaced Nisei youth on his own farm, had publicly demanded their exclusion from any government-funded university.[98] Several Ontario universities consequently cancelled Nisei students' registrations.[99] Yet both Queen's University and the University of Toronto eventually defied Hepburn's command, admitting Japanese Canadian applicants for the 1943 fall term.[100] Unlike his counterparts at prominent Ontario universities, James had colluded with exclusionist governors despite no political pressure from Premier Maurice Duplessis.

~~~

As James grasped for justifications, public criticism persisted. On 16 January 1945, the *McGill Daily* revealed that a less exclusive policy had originally been passed, only to be reversed a few weeks later. "Undeniably responsible sources" had divulged that the ban was passed to appease "people of high influence whose disfavor with the University's policy might have some effect on its material welfare."
~~~

Sun Life president Arthur Wood and other corporate leaders would have been counted among such "people of high influence" who might withhold donations. On James's copy of the editorial, his secretary scrawled, "who gave them this information?"[101] His efforts to control campus discussion of McGill's racial exclusion policy had failed.

When the senate met on 17 January, James and his allies finally had to contend with law professor Frank Scott. Scott moved to allow reconsideration of resolutions passed in previous academic sessions. His resolution was carried by a vote of twelve to eleven.[102] Going forward, Scott, Adair, and their allies would only require a simple majority to repeal the racial exclusion policy. The board of governors saw the writing on the wall. At their next meeting, they declared their intention to "take jurisdiction if the Senate should wish to make any *recommendation.*"[103] They planned to overrule the senate if it defied their wishes. Scott would later remind James that McGill's statutes did not characterize senate decisions as recommendations.[104]

At the senate meeting on 21 February, Adair moved to reconsider the exclusion policy. Woodhead reported that he had written to eight universities, confirming that McGill was alone in banning Japanese Canadians. Scott announced that the McGill Veterans' Society had passed a resolution supporting Nisei admissions. James and his allies repeated previous excuses for racial exclusion. Echoing McGill's unofficial policy towards Jewish applicants to law and medicine, Dr W.W. Chipman, president of the Royal Victoria Hospital, proposed "to admit Canadian students of Japanese ancestry under some appropriate quota system when peace came." The question to reconsider was put to a vote and carried by a margin of fourteen to ten. Scott finally moved to repeal McGill's racial exclusion of Japanese Canadian applicants. The motion passed with a margin of fourteen to seven. James ordered the assembled members to remain silent about the decision pending review by the board of governors.[105]

On 16 May, the board of governors rejected the senate's decision and announced a joint review committee between the two bodies.[106] The senate appointed five opponents of the policy.[107] The board of governors appointed three supporters of racial exclusion and two opponents.[108] They knew the policy's defenders would be outnumbered; the committee was merely a stalling tactic to appease men like Arthur Wood, who continued writing angry letters to James.[109] On 5 June, the joint committee passed a negatively worded resolution allowing the admission of RCMP-approved qualified Japanese

Canadians if they did not "interfere" with veterans; the board of governors accepted the resolution on 12 September.[110] McGill's registrar had already foreseen the defeat of its racial exclusion policy. While the joint conference committee occupied his opponents for six months, Matthews had admitted five Nisei undergraduate students. In September 1945, Miyoshi Nakashima, George Kobayashi, Henry Satoshi Tamaki, Hazel Shimotakahara, and Margaret Shimotakahara arrived at McGill.[111]

~~~

McGill's exclusion policy had differential impacts on Japanese Canadian students and applicants. For all the effort put into passing it, the ban ultimately proved impractical to implement. Administrators could not identify all students "of Japanese racial origin." McGill's registration cards had never included information about "national extraction." Many students listing residences in Japan were the children of White missionaries. Identifying students by surname proved equally inadequate; Matthews pointed to a student with a Japanese mother and a non-Japanese father whose surname allowed them to escape detection.[112]

While shutting its doors to eligible Nisei applicants, McGill forced Ryo Otsuki, who had already been displaced from his Vancouver home to Winnipeg, to defray the cost of relocating again from Montreal to Fredericton. The senate's racial exclusion policy nonetheless failed to prevent George Shimotakahara, Satoru Watanabe, Kiyokazu Jack Momose, Maurice Takeshige, and at least one other unnamed undergraduate student from finishing their studies.[113] Three Japanese Canadian graduate students enrolled at McGill while it was officially excluding Japanese Canadian undergraduate students and university employees. Mary Campbell Kobayashi Hecht began the public health nursing program in 1944.[114] That same fall, Kimiaki Nakashima started his graduate degree in economics, and George Yamashita enrolled in an evening course in chartered accountancy.[115]

~~~

To pass their racial exclusion policy, Principal James, Dean Macmillan, and their allies in the senate and board of governors emphasized Japanese Canadians' rejection from military service, their alleged refusal to perform agricultural labour, and their purported threat to the security of war-related research.[116] The lived experiences of Nisei students and their families contradict each of these contentions.

Macmillan had emphasized Japanese Canadians' exclusion from military training. Many exiled UBC students, however, had served in the COTC.[117] McGill's COTC records additionally indicate that its male Nisei undergraduate students had completed the requisite training. Momose and Takeshige served in the COTC during the 1944–45 academic year, while the exclusion policy was in effect.[118] Macmillan additionally claimed that Nisei applicants were unwilling to support the war effort through agricultural labour. In 1944, however, Japanese Canadians constituted half of the labour force on Alberta and Manitoba sugar beet farms.[119] Before he arrived at McGill, Nakashima had spent two seasons working at the Broder Canning Company near Lethbridge, Alberta.[120]

Further, the principal's claim that the racial exclusion policy protected war research contradicted his own previous positions on building security. In 1940, the board of governors had restricted building use to registered staff and students, making no mention of race or nationality.[121] Two years later, Professor Otto Maass, special assistant to the director of the National Research Council, tried to ban Jewish refugee "alien" students from the chemistry building.[122] James reminded his staff that they could not authorize the closure of buildings, and that Canadian and American students were more likely to leak information than a handful of RCMP-vetted refugees.[123]

Macmillan had revealed the real rationale for racial exclusion of Nisei alongside such flimsy justifications; he intended to protect students "of British ancestry" from having their postwar positions usurped by "Canadian students of Japanese ancestry."[124] Regardless of their character, conduct, or qualifications, he and his fellow exclusionists believed Japanese Canadians to be racially separate from and inferior to White Anglo-Saxon applicants – the students he presumed McGill was established to serve.

James's acknowledgment of potential leakage from Canadian students proved to be correct. As McGill's senate and board of governors focused their attention on perceived racial enemies, several White staff members broke security protocols. Igor Gouzenko revealed in September 1945 that Raymond Boyer, a chemistry professor and secretary of the Canadian-American RDX Committee, and Philip Durnford Smith, a physicist and assistant research engineer for the National Research Council, had given secret documents to Russian agents. James recommended that Smith be allowed to return to McGill after serving two years in prison, showing more support for a White staff member convicted of passing secrets than Japanese Canadian applicants with clean records.[125]

CONCLUSION

This chapter describes the unscrupulous tactics employed by a committed faction of McGill administrators to deny Japanese Canadians admission on racial grounds. At every turn, the champions of exclusion wilfully ignored contradictory recommendations from the registrar, faculty members, and the British Columbia Security Commission. The principal scolded the students' society for the tone of their dissent while dismissing appeals for change that came through more traditional channels, even from McGill's Veterans' Society.

The men who voted to exclude Nisei chose not to see their action as racist: Arthur Wood insisted that "the University has never indulged in racial discrimination" while defending a policy targeting students "of Japanese racial origin."[126] Students and the broader public, however, were not fooled. The backlash against the racial exclusion of Japanese Canadians is an early example of resistance to institutional racism at McGill. Students, faculty, alumni, and other activists vigorously contested the ban on Japanese Canadians as it was happening. In repeatedly linking the policy to prevailing restrictions on Jewish applicants, these activists recognized and named patterns of discrimination. The exclusionist faction had taken it for granted that their policy would stay a secret; instead it attracted international attention, even receiving mention in *Time* magazine.[127]

In 1949, Thomas Kunito Shoyama, a veteran, president of the Japanese Canadian Citizens Association, and a research economist for the government of Saskatchewan, began graduate courses at McGill, attending James's own macro-economics seminar.[128] After orchestrating the university's racial exclusion policy, James finally found himself teaching one of its targets. It is unclear if James knew that Shoyama had written the *New Canadian* editorials condemning McGill's racism.[129] Having followed events at McGill closely, Shoyama likely understood the principal's role in excluding students like him. Perhaps he was proud to stand before the principal as proof that the racist accusations levied against Japanese Canadian students never had any basis.

NOTES

The quote in the chapter title is taken from "Academic Bigotry," *New Canadian*, 18 November 1944, 2: "The recent announcement of the McGill University Senate to bar Japanese Canadian students from matriculating into that university comes as a distinct blow to our esteem of that outstanding institution."

1 Ann Gomer Sunahara, *The Politics of Racism: The Uprooting of Japanese Canadians during the Second World War* (Toronto: J. Lorimer, 1981), 39; Pamela Sugiman, "Passing Time, Moving Memories: Interpreting Wartime Narratives of Japanese Canadian Women," *Histoire sociale/Social History* 37 (May 2004): 55. As Pamela Sugiman writes, "The government's actions resulted in dispossession, property loss (farms, fishing boats, vehicles, homes, and personal belongings of less monetary worth but great personal value), a violation of human rights, *disruption of education, diminished aspirations*, coerced employment (often highly exploitative in nature and typically for low pay and little recognition), the break-up of families, loss of culture (language, customs, art forms), and continued exposure to racism in its many guises." Emphasis added.

2 *A Degree of Justice, 1942* (Vancouver: n.p., 2017), 10.

3 *A Degree of Justice*, 10–11. In 2012, at the urging of activist Mary Kitagawa, UBC finally granted honorary degrees to the seventy-six Japanese Canadian students exiled in 1942. I describe the experiences of UBC 's Nisei students in chapter 1 of my MA thesis; see Tess Elsworthy, "McGill University's Racial Exclusion of Japanese Canadians, 1943–1945" (MA thesis, McGill University, 2020), 31–55.

4 McGill Senate Meeting Minutes (hereafter Senate Minutes), 20 October 1943, Senate Minute Book 1943 to 1945 (hereafter Senate Minute Book), RG 8, Container 11, File 357, Senate, McGill University Archives (hereafter MUA), Montreal, Quebec. Emphasis added.

5 Stanley Brice Frost, *McGill University: For the Advancement of Learning, Volume II, 1895–1971* (Montreal and Kingston: McGill-Queen's University Press, 1984), 211; Dorothy McMurray, *Four Principals of McGill: A Memoir, 1929–1963* (Montreal: Graduates' Society of McGill University, 1974), 48, 51. James, a London-born economist, began at McGill as head of the Commerce Department in 1939. He became principal in 1940 and remained in office until 1962. His secretary, Dorothy McMurray, emphasizes the force he exerted: "He was the supreme master who … generally won most of what he wanted."

6 In the 1940s, McGill's board of governors was composed of business leaders and powerful alumni; it managed the university's financial affairs and held final authority over university policy. The senate was composed of the deans of each faculty, elected faculty representatives, and several governors. It took jurisdiction over academic affairs including admissions and the granting of degrees.

7 Thomas Henry Matthews was a professor of mathematics at McGill from 1920 to 1929. He served as registrar from 1930 until the late 1950s.

8 R.C. Fetherstonhaugh, *McGill University at War: 1914–1918, 1939–1945* (Montreal: McGill University, 1947); Frost, *McGill University*, 2:211–6. Fetherstonhaugh and Frost both omit the racial exclusion of Japanese Canadian undergraduates from their respective histories of McGill during the Second World War.

9 For more on racial ideology and perceived White Anglo-Saxon supremacy in twentieth-century Canada, see Angus McLaren, *Our Own Master Race: Eugenics in Canada, 1885–1945* (Toronto: University of Toronto Press, 1990). For more on anti-East Asian racial ideology in Canada, see Mona Oikawa, *Cartographies of Violence: Japanese Canadian Women, Memory, and the Subjects of Internment* (Toronto: University of Toronto Press, 2012); Renisa Mawani, *Colonial Proximities: Crossracial Encounters and Juridical Truths in British Columbia, 1871–1921* (Vancouver: UBC Press, 2009); Kay J. Anderson, *Vancouver's Chinatown: Racial Discourse in Canada, 1875–1980* (Montreal and Kingston: McGill-Queen's University Press, 1991); James Cameron, "Canada's Struggle with Illegal Entry on Its West Coast: The Case of Fred Yoshy and Japanese Migrants Before World War II," *BC Studies* 146 (Summer 2005): 37–62.

10 Diary of Frank Cyril James (hereafter James Diary), 1 August 1944, MG 1017, Container 49, Frank Cyril James Fonds (hereafter James Fonds), MUA. See also Ira Robinson, *A History of Antisemitism in Canada* (Waterloo: Wilfrid Laurier University Press, 2015); Pierre Anctil, "Interlude of Hostility: Judeo-Christian Relations in Quebec in the Interwar Period, 1919–39," in *Antisemitism in Canada: History and Interpretation,* ed. Alan Davies (Waterloo: Wilfrid Laurier University Press, 2006), 135–65; Michael Brown, "On Campus in the Thirties: Antipathy, Support, and Indifference," in *Nazi Germany, Canadian Responses: Confronting Antisemitism in the Shadow of War,* ed. L. Ruth Klein (Montreal and Kingston: McGill-Queen's University Press, 2012), 144–82. McGill administrators began restricting Jewish enrolment in the mid-1920s, including a ban on Jewish applicants from outside Quebec,

the requirement of higher high school marks for Jewish applicants to the Faculty of Arts and Science, and a *numerus clausus* quota on Jewish admissions to the faculties of medicine and law. In 1944, Principal James remarked in his diary that he, the registrar, and the dean of engineering had "agreed to apply to the Engineering Faculty the same differential standard of admission ... that now applies in Arts and Science." McGill's antisemitic barriers were never made official by the senate.

11 Sandra Djwa, *The Politics of the Imagination: A Life of F.R. Scott* (Toronto: McClelland and Stewart, 1987), 85, 94, 121, 130, 158, 200, 206, 238. *Montreal Star* owner J.W. McConnell insisted Scott would never be dean of law while he was a member of the board of governors. Scott was especially disliked by Dean Macmillan, whom he had previously nicknamed in a poem "Professor Windbag, Ph.D."

12 For more on academic freedom at McGill in the 1930s and 1940s, see Elsworthy, "McGill University's Racial Exclusion of Japanese Canadians," 59–72.

13 James Diary, 8 December 1941, MG 1017, Container 47, James Fonds, MUA.

14 *McGill University Directory of Students, 1941–1942* (Montreal: McGill University, 1942), 52, 66, 74.

15 McGill University Contingent (148th BN CEF) COTC Names of members of the McGill COTC and those attached with records of service etc, September 1939–March 1946, Volume VIII-A Accession 849/, 1, MUA.

16 McGill University Contingent (148th BN CEF) COTC Historical Record (hereafter McGill Contingent Record), Jan 1, 1942 to Dec 31, 1942, volume IV Accession 849/1, MUA.

17 File "Kozo Shimotakahara," LAC, RG117, c9411, vol. 11773. George Shimotakahara's father, Dr Kozo Shimotakahara, was the first Japanese Canadian physician to practise in Canada.

18 File "Takazo Watanabe," LAC, RG117, c9334, vol. 3287.

19 File "Masae Momose," LAC, RG 117, c9411, vol. 12242.

20 "Information about the Students of Japanese Racial Origin," n.d., Folder Vol 44, Box 10, Docs UBC, Tadashi Jack & Kanaye Kay Kagetsu Fonds, Nikkei National Museum.

21 Interview with Fumiko Taguchi conducted by T. Yoshida, translated by Mariko Ikeda, 1 August 1986, MG 4247, Container 33, Box 25, File 44, Japanese Canadian Cultural Centre of Montreal Fonds (hereafter JCCCM Fonds), MUA. Taguchi's son, Yoshinori Taguchi, enrolled at McGill in 1951, graduating with a bachelor of science in 1955, and his medicine degree in 1959.

22 "Japanese Family Arrives from B.C.," *Montreal Gazette,* 19 May 1942. In Montreal, the Shimotakahara family owned the Clevermaid factory and clothing store.

23 T.H. Matthews to F.C. James, 8 July 1942, RG 2, Container 82, File 1692, Office of the Principal and Vice-Chancellor (hereafter Office of the Principal), MUA. Macmillan served in Parliament from 1940 to 1945. He published the first history of McGill, *McGill and Its Story, 1821–1921* (Toronto: Oxford University Press, 1921).

24 Cyrus Macmillan to James, 15 July 1942, RG 2, Container 82, File 1692, Office of the Principal, MUA.

25 Norman Robertson to K.P.R. Neville, 27 August 1942, File 3464-W-40, RG 25, LAC; Note for Mr Rive, 12 September 1942, File 3464-W-40, RG 25, LAC; James to F.C. Blair, 7 April 1942, RG 2, Container 82, File 1692, Office of the Principal, MUA. In April 1942, James wrote to the Canadian Immigration Branch regarding the admission of Japanese American students but appears to have never contacted the federal government for instructions regarding Japanese Canadian applicants.

26 A. Rive to Matthews, 15 September 1942, File 3464-W-40, RG 25, LAC.

27 James to Macmillan, 3 September 1943, RG 2, Container 113, File 3036, Office of the Principal, MUA. While Trueman advocated for these seven applicants, the BCSC created hardships for other former UBC students. See Elsworthy, "McGill University's Racial Exclusion of Japanese Canadians," 87.

28 "Expert on Japanese Problem Joins Staff at McGill," *Montreal Star,* 27 September 1940; Forrest LaViolette, *The Canadian Japanese and World War II: A Sociological and Psychological Account* (Toronto: University of Toronto Press, 1948); Kunio Hidaka to LaViolette, 29 June 1942, Box 1, Folder 2, Forrest E. LaViolette papers, Manuscripts Collection 295, Louisiana Research Collection, Howard-Tilton Memorial Library, Tulane University, New Orleans, LA (HTML); Matthews to Noby Inamoto, 15 June 1942, Box 1, Folder 2, LaViolette papers, Manuscripts Collection 295, Louisiana Research Collection, HTML. LaViolette describes McGill's racial exclusion policy in an appendix of his book but repeats the administration's baseless claims about building security. At least two of LaViolette's Nisei acquaintances, Kunio Hidaka and Noby Inamoto, asked him about opportunities at McGill. Neither man was accepted.

29 J.J. O'Neill to James, 9 September 1943, RG 2, Container 113, File 3036, Office of the Principal, MUA.

30 *McGill University Directory of Students, 1943–1944* (Montreal: McGill University, 1944), 60.

31 *McGill University Directory of Students, 1943–1944*; yearbook entry, 1947, Maurice Takeshige, accessed 1 December 2024, http://yearbooks.mcgill.ca/viewbook.php?&campus=downtown&book_id=1947#page/153/mode/1up. Matthews may not have recognized Takeshige's possible Japanese heritage.

32 Memo, Matthews to James, 16 September 1943, RG2, Container 113, File 3036, Office of the Principal, MUA.

33 Memo, Matthews to James, 21 September 1943, RG 2, Container 113, File 3036, Office of the Principal, MUA.

34 Resolution of the Faculty of Arts and Science on Japanese Students, 29 September 1943, RG 2, Container 113, File 3036, Office of the Principal, MUA.

35 Senate Minutes, 30 September 1943, Senate Minute Book, RG 8, Container 11, File 357, Senate, MUA.

36 Senate Minutes, 30 September 1943.

37 James, "Summary from Governors," 13 October 1943, RG 2, Container 113, File 3036, Office of the Principal, MUA.

38 A.B. Wood to James, 15 October 1943, RG 2, Container 113, File 3036, Office of the Principal, MUA; Meeting Minutes, 13 October 1943, RG 4, McGill University Governors Minute Book, 22 August 1935 to 13 December 1944, MUA.

39 Senate Minutes, 20 October 1943, Senate Minute Book, RG 8, Container 11, File 357, Senate, MUA.

40 Memo, Matthews to James, 21 October 1943, RG 2, Container 113, File 3036, Office of the Principal, MUA; James to Macmillan, 23 October 1943, RG 2, Container 113, File 3036, Office of the Principal, MUA. When Matthews clarified that Trueman was employed by the Department of Labour, James confided to Macmillan, "I suppose that he is definitely a government official, although I confess that I do not like him anymore on that account."

41 Senate Minutes, 20 October 1943, Senate Minute Book, RG 8, Container 11, File 357, Senate, MUA. Emphasis added.

42 "McGill University Bars Niseis, Manitoba Enrolment Doubled," *New Canadian*, 28 October 1944.

43 Robinson, *A History of Antisemitism in Canada*, 73; Anctil, "Interlude of Hostility," 159.

44 Hugessen received his law degree from McGill in 1914. He was appointed to the Senate of Canada in 1937 and served as president of the federal Liberal Party from 1940–43.

45 W.D. Woodhead to James, 24 October 1943, RG 2, Container 113, File 3036, Office of the Principal, MUA.

46 Memo, Matthews to James, 16 September 1943, RG 2, Container 113, File 3036, Office of the Principal, MUA.
47 James to Woodhead, 26 October 1943, RG 2, Container 113, File 3036, Office of the Principal, MUA.
48 Woodhead to James, 31 October 1943, RG 2, Container 113, File 3036, Office of the Principal, MUA.
49 James to Woodhead, 1 November 1943, RG 2, Container 113, File 3036, Office of the Principal, MUA.
50 Senate Minutes, 17 November 1943, Senate Minute Book, RG 8, Container 11, File 357, Senate, MUA. The Committee was composed of Tyndale, Macmillan, Hugessen, and Woodhead.
51 Senate Minutes, 19 January 1944, Senate Minute Book, RG 8, Container 11, File 357, Senate, MUA.
52 *A Degree of Justice*, 117–18; Elaine Bernard, "A University at War: Japanese Canadians at UBC During World War II," *BC Studies* 35 (Autumn 1977): 53–4.
53 *McGill University Directory of Students, 1943–1944* (Montreal: McGill University, 1944), 60.
54 *Up the Hill* (Fredericton: NB, 1949), University of New Brunswick Archives, Fredericton, New Brunswick.
55 "148 Gain Success in Medical Exams," *Montreal Gazette*, 9 July 1945.
56 Yearbook entry, 1944, Kiyokazu Jack Momose, accessed 1 December 2024, http://yearbooks.mcgill.ca/viewbook.php?&campus=downtown&book_id=1944#page/27/mode/1up; yearbook entry, 1948, Kiyokazu Jack Momose, accessed 1 December 2024, http://yearbooks.mcgill.ca/viewbook.php?&campus=downtown&book_id=1948#page/176/mode/1up.
57 Interview with Cyril Powles and Marjorie conducted by Sandra Kawaii and Melissa Steele, December 1986, MG 4247, Container 33, Box 25, File 16, JCCCM Fonds, MUA. Former Student Christian Movement secretary Marjorie Powles recalls that "[the Nisei students] just couldn't be ordinary. That must have been true about [Momose]. What I remember is people not really wanting to talk about it … most people just wanted to not be noticed."
58 Interview with George Shimotakahara, conducted by Akemi Arakawa, 30 June 1982, MG 4247, Container 19, File 7, JCCCM Fonds, MUA.
59 "Explain Ban on Japs," *Ottawa Journal,* 20 October 1944; "McGill Bars Jap Students," *Vancouver Sun,* 20 October 1944; "Ban Jap Students," *Lethbridge Herald,* 21 October 1944; "McGill Jap Ban Policy Explained," *Windsor Star,* 21 October 1944; "News in Brief,"

Saskatoon Star Phoenix, 21 October 1944; "Jap Student Ban," *Leader–Post,* 21 October 1944; Greg Robinson, *Un drame de la Deuxième Guerre: Le sort de la minorité japonaise aux États-Unis et au Canada* (Montreal: Les Presses de l'Université de Montréal, 2012), 292. Greg Robinson notes that the francophone press ignored McGill's exclusion policy.

60 "Scolds M'Gill For Refusing Jap Students," *Globe and Mail*, 2 November 1944; "Race Restrictions at University Hit," *Gazette,* 2 November 1944. "Coldwell Says Troops Must Be Reinforced," *Montreal Star,* 2 November 1944. The *Montreal Star*, owned by McGill governor J.W. McConnell, omitted any mention of Coldwell's statements about McGill from its coverage of his visit.

61 Basil Rattray, "Letter to the Editor," *McGill Daily*, 24 October 1944. Rattray went on to teach mathematics at McGill.

62 Maurice Lafrance, "Letter to the Editor," *McGill Daily*, 26 October 1944.

63 "Bigotry at McGill," *Varsity*, 27 October 1944.

64 "Montreal: McGill University Bars Niseis, Manitoba Enrolment Doubled," *New Canadian,* 28 October 1944.

65 James Diary, 31 October 1944, MG 1017, Container 49, James Fonds, MUA. Richter went on to serve as president of the McGill union and vice-president of the students' society in 1945–46.

66 "Students' Council Announces Amalgamated Charities Drive to Begin Nov. 20 for One Week," *McGill Daily*, 2 November 1944.

67 James to John Costigan, 2 November 1944, RG 2, Container 82, File 1692, Office of the Principal, MUA; James Diary, 3 November 1944, MG 1017, Container 47, James Fonds, MUA.

68 James Diary, 8 November 1944, MG 1017, Container 49, James Fonds, MUA.

69 Betty Kobayashi Issenman, interview by author, 14 May 2018.

70 "40 McGill Delegates Named to Conference," *Montreal Gazette*, 16 December 1937; "Women of McGill to Aid Red Cross," *Montreal Gazette,* 14 October 1939; Anne Cimon, "McGill Alumnae Through the Decades," *McGill News* (Winter–Spring 1985): 8; Letter to Betty Kobayashi Issenman from John Meehan, 30 September 1999, MG 4247 Box 31 File 56, JCCCM Fonds, MUA.

71 "Miss Kobayashi Addresses SLC In Union Grill," *McGill Daily*, 10 November 1944.

72 Yearbook entry, 1945, Mary Campbell Hecht née Kobayashi, accessed 1 December 2024, http://yearbooks.mcgill.ca/viewbook.php?&campus=downtown&book_id=1945#page/117/mode/1up.

73 Betty Kobayashi, *Application for Japanese Canadian Redress*, 20 December 1988, MG 4247, Box 31, File 56, JCCCM Fonds, MUA; interview with Betty Kobayashi Issenman conducted by Melissa Steele, 3 November 1986, MG 4247, Box 31, File 56, JCCCM Fonds, MUA; Ikuye Uchida and John Endo Greenaway, "Gordon Kobayashi: A Serene Hapa," *Montreal Bulletin* (March 2001): 7, MG 4247, Container 31, Box 6, File 74, JCCCM Fonds, MUA.
74 Peter R.C.V. Hall, "Students to Consider Reasons for Exclusion of Canadian Japanese," *McGill Daily*, 13 November 1944; "Student Opinion," *McGill Daily*, 14 November 1944.
75 "Students' Society Meets in Union Today," *McGill Daily*, 14 November 1944.
76 "Students' Society Supports Council," *McGill Daily*, 15 November 1944; "Banning Canadian-born Japanese from McGill Protested by Students," *Montreal Gazette*, 15 November 1944.
77 "The Vigilantes," *McGill Daily*, 15 November 1944.
78 "Student Paper Scores Jap Bar," *Montreal Star*, 15 November 1944. The *Daily*'s editorial had evidently been shared with the *Star* in advance; both were published on the same day.
79 "McGill Students Would Enroll Canadian-Born Japs," *The Province*, 15 November 1944; "Students Oppose Discrimination," *The Windsor Star*, 15 November 1944; "Students Oppose Bar Against Japs," *Saskatoon Star-Phoenix*, 15 November 1944; "McGill Would Admit Nisei Students," *The Ubyssey*, 16 November 1944; "McGill Men Ask Remove Jap Ban," *Queen's Journal*, 17 November 1944; "Good Work, McGill," *McGill Daily*, 8 December 1944 (reprinted from *McMaster Silhouette*).
80 "Stand on Japs 'Neutral,'" *Montreal Gazette*, 17 November 1944.
81 Senate Minutes, 15 November 1944, Senate Minute Book, RG 8, Container 11, File 357, Senate, MUA.
82 "Academic Bigotry," *New Canadian*, 18 November 1944.
83 "Keep 'Em Out!" *Saturday Night*, 18 November 1944.
84 Rev. C.J.L. Bates to James, 18 November 1944; Gwen R.B. Norman (née Roberts) to the McGill senate, 14 November 1944; Marie Stewart to James, 18 November 1944; Esther Ryan to James, 26 November 1944; Glen Thomson to James, 21 January 1945, RG 2, Container 113, File 3036, Office of the Principal, MUA.
85 H. Russell Ross to the Senate of McGill University, 21 November 1944, RG 2, Container 113, File 3036, Office of the Principal, MUA.

86 James to Bates, 24 November 1944, RG 2, Container 113, File 3036, Office of the Principal, MUA.
87 Senate Minutes, 15 December 1944, Senate Minute Book, RG 8, Container 11, File 357, Senate, MUA.
88 James Diary, 15 December 1944, MG 1017, Container 47, James Fonds, MUA.
89 James to R.C. Wallace, 18 December 1944, RG 2 Container 113, File 3036, Office of the Principal, MUA.
90 Norman MacKenzie to James, 29 December 1944, RG 2, Container 113, File 3036, Office of the Principal, MUA. For more on nativism in British Columbia, see Peter Ward, *White Canada Forever: Popular Attitudes and Public Policy toward Orientals in British Columbia* (Montreal and Kingston: McGill-Queen's University Press, 1978).
91 Cyrille Gagnon to James, 21 December 1944, RG 2, Container 113, File 3036, Office of the Principal, MUA; Olivier Maurault to James, 22 December 1944, RG 2, Container 113, File 3036, Office of the Principal, MUA; Milton F. Gregg to F.C. James, 22 December 1944, RG 2 Container 113, File 3036, Office of the Principal, MUA.
92 Carleton Stanley to James, 27 December 1944, RG 2, Container 113, File 3036, Office of the Principal, MUA.
93 James to Carleton Stanley, 2 January 1945, RG 2, Container 113, File 3036, Office of the Principal, MUA. Emphasis added.
94 J.S. Thomson to James, 23 December 1944, RG 2, Container 113, File 3036, Office of the Principal, MUA.
95 H.P. Armes to James, 30 December 1944, RG 2, Container 113, File 3036, Office of the Principal, MUA.
96 Robert Newton to James, 28 December 1944, RG 2, Container 113, File 3036, Office of the Principal, MUA.
97 "6 Coast Japanese to Attend Varsity," *Edmonton Journal*, 10 September 1942.
98 "Queen's Takes Jap Students," *Windsor Star,* 15 September 1942. On the Japanese Canadian former UBC students who worked on Hepburn's farm, see Elsworthy, "McGill University's Racial Exclusion of Japanese Canadians," 121.
99 *A Degree of Justice*, 41; Ken Adachi, *The Enemy That Never Was: A History of the Japanese Canadians* (Toronto: McClelland and Stewart, 1976), 265. Ken Adachi reports that six students were turned away from Queen's in 1942. This included former UBC student Hajime Kagetsu,

who was accepted into their graduate engineering program but turned away upon arrival. Kagetsu had also applied to McGill.

100 Wallace to James, 20 December 1944, RG 2, Container 113, File 3036, Office of the Principal, MUA; H.J. Cody to James, 22 December 1944, RG 2, Container 113, File 3036, Office of the Principal, MUA.

101 "Canadian-Japanese Students," *McGill Daily*, 16 January 1945, RG 2, Container 113, File 3036, Office of the Principal, MUA.

102 Senate Minutes, 17 January 1945, Senate Minute Book, RG 8, Container 11, File 357, Senate, MUA.

103 Meeting Minutes, 14 February 1945, RG 4, McGill University Governors Minutes, 10 January 1945 to 16 June 1948, MUA. Emphasis added.

104 F.R. Scott to James, 23 May 1945, RG 2, Container 113, File 3036, Office of the Principal, MUA.

105 Senate Minutes, 21 February 1945, Senate Minute Book, RG 8, Container 11, File 357, Senate, MUA.

106 James to Matthews, 19 May 1945, RG 2, Container 113, File 3036, Office of the Principal, MUA.

107 James to Morris Wilson, 17 May 1945, RG 2, Container 113, File 3036, Office of the Principal, MUA.

108 Wilson to James, 18 May 1945, RG 2, Container 113, File 3036, Office of the Principal, MUA.

109 Wood to James, 7 June 1945, RG 2, Container 113, File 3036, Office of the Principal, MUA.

110 Meeting Minutes, 12 September 1945, RG 4, McGill University Governors Minutes, 10 January 1945 to 16 June 1948, MUA.

111 "Old McGill" entry, 1949, Myoshi Nakashima, accessed 1 December 2024, http://yearbooks.mcgill.ca/viewbook.php?&campus=downtown&book_id=1949#page/80/mode/1up; "Old McGill" entry, 1948, George Kobayashi, accessed 1 December 2024, http://yearbooks.mcgill.ca/viewbook.php?&campus=downtown&book_id=1948#page/130/mode/1up; "Old McGill" entry, 1949, Henry Satoshi Tamaki, accessed 1 December 2024, http://yearbooks.mcgill.ca/viewbook.php?&campus=downtown&book_id=1949#page/134/mode/1up; "Old McGill" entry, 1949, Hazel Shimotakahara, accessed 1 December 2024, http://yearbooks.mcgill.ca/viewbook.php?&campus=downtown&book_id=1949 #page/73/mode/1up; "Old McGill" entry, 1949, Margaret Shimotakahara, accessed 1 December 2024, http://yearbooks.mcgill.ca/viewbook.php?&campus=downtown&book_id=1949#page/80/mode/1up.

112 Memo, Matthews to James, 14 February 1945, RG 2, Container 113, File 3036, Office of the Principal, MUA. This student's name remains redacted and their fate at McGill is unclear.

113 Memo, Matthews to James, 14 February 1945.

114 Kobayashi Issenman to Harold Fehr, 23 July 1999, MG 4247 Box 31, File 56, JCCCM Fonds, MUA.

115 George Yamashita to E.H. Morrow, 12 August 1944, Box 1, File 1-6, Japanese Canadian Commerce Students Collection/*Viewpoints* Magazine, UBC Archives; Kimiaki Nakashima, "Economic Aspects of Japanese Evacuation from the Canadian Pacific Coast: A Contribution to the Study of the Economic Consequences of Social Groups and Displaced Persons" (MA thesis, McGill University, 1946); Interview with Kim Nakashima, 21 July 1982, MG 4247, Container 32, Box 24, File 37, JCCCM Fonds, MUA.

116 The senate members and governors who are documented to have voted and advocated for racial exclusion of Japanese Canadians included Chancellor Morris Wilson, Sun Life president Arthur Wood, Dean J.J. O'Neill, professors E.G.D. Murray, O.S. Tyndale, D.A. Keys, and Dr W.W. Chipman.

117 Elaine Bernard, "A University at War: Japanese Canadians at UBC During World War II," *BC Studies* 35 (Autumn 1977): 39.

118 Lt-Col. J.M. Morris, Daily Orders Part II Order no. 32, 19 October 1944, McGill Contingent Record 1 January to 31 December 1944, volume VI, Accession 849/1, MUA. Lt-Col. J.M. Morris, Daily Orders Part II Order no. 32, 26 October 1944, McGill Contingent Record 1 January to 31 December 1944, volume VI, Accession 849/1, MUA. McGill University Contingent (148th BN CEF) COTC Names of members of the McGill COTC and those attached with records of service etc., September 1939–March 1946, Volume VIII-A and VIII-B, Accession 849/1 MUA; War Records, McGill University, accessed 20 August 2019, http://www.archives.mcgill.ca/public/exhibits/mcgillremembers/search.htm, http://www.archives.mcgill.ca/public/exhibits/mcgillremembers/rad.htm. There are no records of Shimotakahara, Watanabe, Momose, or Takeshige in the digital War Records database. According to the administrative history of the collection, "the War Records office solicited information from individuals and their families to create files concerning their participation in the war." There is no evidence that the office contacted any of the aforementioned four cadets; if they offered their own files, those records were not included.

119 Oikawa, *Cartographies of Violence*, 174. For more on the exiled former UBC students whose families worked on sugar beet farms, see Elsworthy, "McGill University's Racial Exclusion of Japanese Canadians," 154.

120 Interview with Teizo Nakashima, n.d., MG 4247, Box 24, Container 32, File 39, JCCCM Fonds, MUA.

121 "Resolutions Regarding Use of Buildings," 8 November 1940, Board of Governors, RG 2, Container 86, File 2401, Office of the Principal, MUA.

122 D.L. Thomson to James, 6 October 1942, RG 2, Container 115, File 3094, Office of the Principal, MUA.

123 James Diary, 8 October 1942, MG 1017, Container 47, James Fonds, MUA.

124 Senate Minutes, 30 September 1943, Senate Minute Book, RG 8, Container 11, File 357, Senate, MUA.

125 Frost, *McGill University,* 2:241–242.

126 Wood to James, 7 June 1945, RG 2, Container 113, File 3036, Office of the Principal, MUA.

127 Pearl Buck, Letter to the editor, *Time* 45, no. 25, 18 June 1945.

128 Macro-Economics Seminar List of Students, 1949, RG 2, Container 130, File 3736, Office of the Principal, MUA; Sunahara, *The Politics of Racism,* 5. Shoyama would go on to hold several senior civil service positions, including deputy minister of finance, deputy minister of energy, mines and resources, and special adviser to the Privy Council on the Constitution.

129 "Montreal: McGill University Bars Niseis, Manitoba Enrolment Doubled," *New Canadian*, 28 October 1944; "McGill University Policy on Niseis Scored by CCF Leader," *New Canadian,* 11 November 1944; "Bigotry at McGill Says U. of Toronto," *New Canadian*, 11 November 1944; "Academic Bigotry," *New Canadian*, 18 November 1944; "McGill Senate to Consider Student Protest on Ban," *New Canadian*, 25 November 1944; "Students Aroused by Bigotry of McGill Exclusionist Stand," *New Canadian*, 3 February 1945.

9

Beyond the Headlines

Heinz Lehmann and the History of McGill Psychiatry

ANDREA TONE

In 1942, an institutionalized patient named Dorothy wrote of the demons that haunted her, of days indistinguishable from nights, and of her fear of permanent confinement. "Another day has gone by," she wrote from Montreal's Verdun Protestant Hospital (hereafter the Verdun). "I came here to get the days straightened out and there [don't] seem to be any ... God has sent an awful curse on my life ... I don't feel sick but something is awfully wrong."[1]

When Dorothy penned these words, psychiatric hospitals across Canada and the United States were in crisis. Underfunded and overcrowded – in 1950 more than 570,000 people resided in US asylums alone – they were populated by patients such as Dorothy, whose hopes for improvement on admission soon descended into protracted despair. In the 1940s and early 1950s the advent of "wonder drugs," beginning with penicillin in 1944, began to vanquish illnesses that had plagued humankind for centuries. But psychiatry lacked the heroic success stories and therapeutic advances of other fields. After centuries it remained rooted in asylums, derogatively referred to as "snake pits," the title of a 1948 Hollywood film showcasing the horrors of asylum life.[2]

Although she had no way of knowing, Dorothy would be among the last generation of psychiatric patients to feel the ennui and despondency of therapeutic and institutional intransigence. A pharmacological revolution was at hand, and it would begin at the Verdun – the same hospital where Dorothy had prayed for deliverance – because of a trial of the drug chlorpromazine run by McGill psychiatrist Heinz Lehmann (1911–1999). Lehmann's findings inaugurated the deinstitutionalization of patients in North America, mainstreamed pharmacotherapy as the gold standard for patient care, and encouraged wide-ranging research on the properties and applications of other psychotropic compounds. Lehmann's work in psychopharmacology, a field he is credited with pioneering, did not end with chlorpromazine. In 1957 he conducted the first successful North American trial of the antidepressant imipramine, extending pharmacotherapy to a larger population. Lehmann was not the only influential member of McGill Psychiatry, but he was instrumental in solidifying its reputation as one of the world's leading centres of pharmacology and neuropsychiatry.[3]

That Lehmann remains an understudied figure is not altogether surprising given the infamy shrouding his more famous colleague, psychiatrist (Donald) Ewen Cameron (1901–1967). Recruited in 1943 to head McGill's new Psychiatry Department and the Allan Memorial Institute (hereafter the Allan), a psychiatric hospital and research unit at the base of Mount Royal, Cameron held both positions until he left the university in 1964.[4]

After Cameron's death in 1967, medical contemporaries praised his leadership and contributions to the field. His decision to open the first day hospital at the Allan garnered widespread acclaim, reversed a centuries-old precedent of locked-door asylums, and inspired like-minded reforms around the world, while his presidencies of the American Psychiatric Association, the Canadian Psychiatric Association, the Quebec Psychiatric Association, and the World Psychiatric Association (among others) reflected and reinforced his professional stature.[5] During his two-decade term, Cameron brought grants, faculty, conferences, and visibility to McGill Psychiatry and to Montreal. His pedagogical initiatives were equally influential. When he left the university, McGill Psychiatry had one of the largest and the most internationally diverse training programs in the world (in North America, only the psychoanalytically oriented Menninger Clinic was larger), affiliated with six Montreal hospitals, including the Verdun.[6]

An early commitment to biological psychiatry was another of the program's distinguishing features. In an era when academic psychiatry was enamoured with psychoanalysis, Cameron disparaged "talk therapy" as too slow and too costly to help heal the masses and urged clinicians to embrace the "realities of active treatment" instead.[7] In a speech at the Allan's opening, he pledged to prioritize "the development of rapid and effective methods of treatment."[8] Cameron built a department that privileged this goal, giving McGill Psychiatry an intellectual axis that distinguished it from other programs. As Robert Cleghorn, Cameron's successor, explained, "Psychoanalysis had filled the vacuum in leadership and biological work was relatively static" but at McGill "the results of Cameron's efforts [were] that nowhere during the forties and fifties in Canada, if not North America, were biological studies receiving so much encouragement in psychiatry."[9]

A decade after Cameron's death, positive assessments of Cameron's legacy were shattered by scandal when journalist John Marks shared documents revealing that the Central Intelligence Agency (CIA) had operated a Cold War mind control program named Project MKULTRA (hereafter MKULTRA) and that Cameron had accepted a grant from an MKULTRA front organization in 1957. Marks's revelations sparked outrage and catapulted Cameron, the Allan, and McGill into the glare of the public spotlight. In the tsunami of media reports that followed, Cameron was vilified as a mad scientist practising medicine at the margins, the Allan the "crime scene" where he had conducted secret experiments at the CIA's behest. His documented misdeeds – accepting CIA funds, using patients as research subjects without their informed consent, and subjecting them to aggressive, injurious experimental treatments that included LSD, all flagged in a *New York Times* cover story – revealed Cameron to be a physician so unprincipled that, according to Marks, "he didn't need the CIA to corrupt him."[10] Time has not attenuated the frustrations and fury fuelling this backlash. As I write, almost fifty years after Marks's revelations made headlines, a class-action lawsuit representing the families of Cameron's patients is making its way through the courts.[11]

The longevity and incendiary character of the scandal are understandable, especially for the relatives of patients Cameron harmed rather than helped. But the scandal has also reduced Cameron's long and variegated career to the 1957 grant, one that continued a research program previously funded by a Canadian grant, and tarnished the reputation of McGill's Psychiatry Department, as if its history and Cameron's MKULTRA grant are, *ipso facto*, one and the same.[12] This conflation is unfortunate because it has caused historians to overlook other events and individuals who imparted different but equally consequential legacies to psychiatry and McGill.[13] Among them is Heinz Lehmann. This contribution goes beyond the headlines to take a closer look at Lehmann's life and work. It explores the paths that led him to the Verdun, his ideas about the discipline, as well as his research priorities and medical experiments, paying particular attention to the organization and impact of his 1953 chlorpromazine trial. A preliminary rather than exhaustive accounting, this piece seeks to restore one facet of McGill Psychiatry's past while contributing to the larger histories of McGill, Montreal, psychiatry, and twentieth-century medicine.

~~~

Born in Berlin in 1911, Heinz Lehmann's interest in psychiatry was kindled by his first episode of depression at age twelve. His misery was compounded by doctors' bafflement about his condition. Because physicians at the time did not believe children could suffer from depression, Lehmann's went undiagnosed. "Nobody knew what to do," he recalled.[14] Unable to concentrate or complete assignments, he quickly fell behind. Lehmann's teachers urged his parents to withdraw him from school; their son "just wasn't made for it," they insisted.[15]

Lehmann's mother ignored their counsel. She did not understand what was vexing her twelve-year-old son but was certain that stifling his dreams and aspirations was not the answer. Instead, she hired a tutor, a university student interested in psychology. The tutor steered Lehmann, a vociferous reader with a capacious curiosity, toward the work of Sigmund Freud. Several books later, Lehmann was hooked. By age fourteen he was back on academic track, had mastered Freud's publications – in his seventies, Lehmann could still visualize pages of text he had memorized as an adolescent – and had decided to become a psychiatrist. His malaise had vanished as mysteriously as it had materialized. He later recognized it as his first bout of depression. There would be others, but none so debilitating or enduring.[16]

Lehmann's surgeon father could not contain his disdain when he learned of his son's chosen career, proclaiming psychiatry and Lehmann's interest in it "ridiculous." In the hierarchy of medical specialties, surgery enjoyed pride of place. Psychiatry did not: in an era when medicine's rising respectability was tied to its scientific credibility, psychiatry was the subjective outlier, a field predicated on one individual's interpretation of another's distress. Psychiatrists' embrace of psychoanalysis, particularly in Germany, where Freud's books would be banned and burned by the Nazis, further stained the discipline's reputation. Lehmann later explained that in the 1930s,
~~~

psychiatry was "a rather derelict career." The perception at the time was that "medical students only went into it if they couldn't do anything else – or they were alcoholic."[17]

Lehmann persevered, earning his MD in 1935 from the University of Berlin. He had hoped to practise psychiatry in Germany's capital, but Hitler's rise and the dangers he faced as the child of a Jewish parent redirected his attention to plotting an escape. He wanted to emigrate to the United States, as his father did, but immigration laws, licensing restrictions, disciplinary quotas privileging other specialties, and organized medicine's opposition to refugee physicians foreclosed this option.[18] By 1936 he had become desperate, at one point considering forsaking medicine and moving to South Africa to work as a magician, indulging a childhood hobby. Fortunately, a German friend had an uncle in Montreal who interceded and extended Lehmann an invitation to go skiing in the Laurentians. Using the fake invitation, borrowed skis, and a round-trip ticket as props, Lehmann convinced the Gestapo that he was travelling to Canada for a winter vacation. Instead, he left Nazi Germany for good, albeit with only enough clothing and cash to last two weeks, also part of the ruse.[19]

Relieved to have escaped, Lehmann was unsure of what awaited him in Canada. He knew almost nothing about the country, believing it to be a frontier society that produced apples and canoes and where "bears and wolves" roamed the streets.[20] Montreal's cosmopolitanism was a welcome surprise, and he quickly decided to make the city his permanent home. An unforeseen obstacle delayed the realization of his plan. Although Lehmann was a refugee, his German citizenship raised security concerns, especially after war broke out. Designated an "enemy alien," Lehmann had to report to the Royal Canadian Mounted Police every two weeks to prove he was not a German spy. So, too, did his French-Canadian wife, Annette Joyal, a nurse Lehmann married during the war. Although her ancestors had lived in Quebec since the 1600s, laws at the time required wives to assume their husbands' citizenship.[21]

Days after arriving, Lehmann made his way to the Verdun, founded in 1881 to serve Montreal's English-speaking population. Historically, psychiatric institutions in Quebec were organized by language and religion; in 1965 the Verdun Protestant Hospital would be renamed the Douglas to reflect its diversity. Located ten kilometres from McGill's downtown campus, the Verdun was Montreal's largest English asylum and the first in the city to offer medical students training in psychiatry.[22] Lehmann continued this pedagogical tradition after his hire in 1937. That he never left – he continued to work at the Verdun in his eighties as a consultant – was a point of tremendous personal and professional pride.[23]

Like most public asylums, the Verdun was stretched beyond capacity. Lehmann began as one of only three psychiatrists assigned to care for an institutionalized population that had mushroomed from 345 in 1900 to more than 14,000 by 1940.[24] Lehmann was shocked by what he saw: patients confined to small rooms with cots infested with bed bugs, others restrained in seclusion rooms, some "literally freezing to death," wards with insufficient sheets, toilets, and bathing facilities.[25] In one area, chronically regressed patients smeared feces on the walls; in another, hallucinating patients yelled at the ceiling.[26] Because of government underfunding, exacerbated by the Great Depression, Lehmann was assigned only one registered nurse for assistance; the remaining hospital personnel were security guards employed to break up patient fights. Lehmann's own starting salary was a paltry fifteen dollars a month and, he recalled, "it took a long time until I made much more."[27] Understaffing was also an offshoot of psychiatry's exclusion from formal medical training. Before McGill established a psychiatry department in 1943 (the Université de Montréal would follow in 1955), there was no steady stream of students, residents, or postgraduates available to help. Lehmann wanted to ameliorate the terrible patient and hospital conditions he encountered, but underfunding, understaffing, and institutional isolation proved formidable barriers to systemic reform. Any changes Lehmann made would have to take place in the one arena he controlled: clinical treatment.

Lehmann's father had derided psychiatrists as lazy slackers who made brief appearances at asylums and, with nothing else to do, spent the rest of their days playing golf.[28] But as psychiatrist and historian Joel Braslow has shown, even during the height of asylum psychiatry's "custodial age," many psychiatrists turned to somatic interventions to try to assuage patients' despair.[29]

Lehmann was among them. He regarded psychiatry as less of a joke than an enigma that, by the 1930s and 1940s, had become a humanitarian crisis. As rife with uncertainty and subjectivity as the discipline was, its common thread was the unimpeachable reality of patient suffering. In his view, ignoring institutionalized patients-in-need contravened the psychiatrist's obligation to help. As Lehmann told Don Bates, MD, historian of medicine and founder of McGill's Department of Social Studies of Medicine, it was incumbent on practitioners to act, "to do something."[30]

Lehmann's clinical work at the Verdun in the 1937–57 period was born of circumstance and conviction. It incorporated three tenets central to Lehmann's views. The first was the necessity of doctor-patient engagement, which Lehmann considered as essential in the 1940s as it was after pharmacotherapy became front-line treatment. A psychiatrist should spend "1000s [*sic*] of hours with patients ... before you finally give them a pill," he told psychiatrist and scholar David Healy in 1994.[31] Lehmann lived in a house on hospital grounds and spent most of his days with patients, often playing cards or checkers with them before finishing rounds at ten or eleven at night. He organized an annual holiday celebration, greeting patients by name. Although physicians were schooled to establish professional boundaries with patients, Lehmann believed psychiatrists should adopt a more personal approach. By treating those under their care as people first and patients second, psychiatrists not only humanized those society had marginalized but increased their odds of getting help. After all, unlike other medical practitioners, psychiatrists could not diagnose or treat patients using blood pressure, laboratory tests, and other biomarkers. They were limited to what they could glean from individual conversations, communications enhanced by patients' comfort and trust. But earning their trust did not happen overnight. It took patience and time. Psychiatrists had to get to know each patient, to learn "when to smile and when not to smile, [and] what kind of tone to use."[32]

According to long-time colleague Tom Ban, Lehmann's dedication to patients was sincere, respected in the profession and, notwithstanding Lehmann's unsuccessful efforts to convince colleagues to reside on hospital grounds too, unrivalled. The implications of Lehmann's actions extended beyond the profession. At a time when institutionalized patients were stigmatized as dangerous and deranged, Lehmann defied stereotype by living alongside them.

Lehmann's second tenet, advocated by a growing number of psychiatrists mid-century, was that mental illnesses fell into one of two categories: neurosis (mild, transient disorders) and psychosis, which included more serious disorders, such as schizophrenia, mania, and acute depression. Caused by life events, neurosis was responsive to psychodynamic therapy. Psychosis, in contrast, was not. Lehmann's third precept followed the second. A proponent of biological psychiatry, he believed that major psychopathologies were of physical origin, rooted in the body, and not the by-product of a person's character or upbringing. They possessed an organic substrate, a biological component that could potentially be altered by the right biochemical agents. Identifying these compounds to engineer effective treatments was the engine driving Lehmann's research.

Some asylum therapies existed, but Lehmann deemed them inadequate: too risky, ineffective, costly, or impractical to administer to the volume of patients in need. None afforded long-term relief, never mind a cure, and many were despised by patients. The most common intervention was shock therapy, used on an estimated 75,000 patients in the United States between 1935 and 1941: largely insulin coma therapy (hypoglycemic comas induced by intravenous insulin) and electric convulsive therapy or ECT (seizures induced by electrical charges to the brain).[33] No one understood precisely why shock therapy worked, only that for many patients, symptoms subsided immediately after treatment. Lehmann used both at the Verdun – their efficacy buttressed his hypothesis that physiology and psychopathology were linked – but their limitations, including the impossibility of predicting which patients would respond favourably, were a constant frustration. Administered six times a week, insulin coma therapy required round-the-clock monitoring by a medical team the Verdun lacked and could not afford to employ. This impracticality, compounded by patients' terror at the prospect of "daily entrance[s] into states of almost death,"[34] ensured that insulin coma "hardly made an impact" at the Verdun.[35] ECT had become more prevalent in psychiatric facilities by the late 1940s, but Lehmann found its very premise repulsive. Likening it to torture, he told Bates that "when I first heard about electric shock I said I would never give this ... It was like the electric chair."[36] And yet Lehmann would go on to administer hundreds of electric shock treatments for want of better options. No less feared by patients before the adjunct use of anesthetics and muscle relaxants became routine, ECT was characterized by Lehmann as "cumbersome, invasive and dangerous"; seizures alone could cause fractures. The procedure was also associated with high relapse rates. Within three months, the 70 to 80 per cent of Verdun patients whose symptoms had initially subsided were fully symptomatic.[37] While its short-term efficacy justified ECT's continued use, its myriad drawbacks fortified Lehmann's resolve to identify something better.

The trajectory of Lehmann's research was shaped by North American and especially European publications, accessible to a physician fluent in German, English, and French. After daily rounds, Lehmann would adjourn to the hospital library and pore over medical case studies, searching for leads to guide his quest. The frequency of his late-night visits gave rise to the rumour that "I was a heroin addict," Lehmann later mused. "Nobody else would walk around the hospital at 3 a.m."[38]

Lehmann did not create the compounds (caffeine, vitamins, hormones, psychedelics) or treatments (from sleep therapy and pyrotherapy to pharmacotherapy) he studied, but he explored their potential in novel ways. At a time when therapeutic progress in psychiatry was measured by incremental gains, and case reports featuring three or four patients were common, Lehmann tested substances on a handful of Verdun patients he believed might benefit. He also tried several on himself.[39] Lehmann was not the only clinician with a penchant for self-experimentation. As historian Erika Dyck has shown, many Canadian psychiatrists in the 1940s and 1950s took LSD hoping that the psychedelic experience it elicited would provide insights into what it meant to have schizophrenia.[40]

Lehmann's small-scale, informal approach to experimentation was a by-product of its time. Today, the organization of clinical trials is a systematized process requiring randomization, third-party review, the use of placebos, informed consent, multi-year phasing, and other protocols intended to produce impartial metadata and to protect human subjects. But before the advent of large-scale trials in the 1960s and informed consent in the 1970s made each a fixture of medical research, trying new treatments on hospitalized patients with the hope of making them better was a common and accepted practice, as long as the clinician's actions were bounded by therapeutic intent. Indeed, what most drew the ire of critics of institutional psychiatry in the 1940s and 1950s was not the absence of informed consent but the charge that asylum patients were being warehoused and ignored by lackadaisical physicians. Had contemporary research protocols existed at Lehmann's time, his experiments, including his chlorpromazine trial, would not have proceeded as they did. Instead, what contemporaries deemed valid, ethical, and necessary medical research authorized his ad hoc approach.

Lehmann proceeded by trial and error. In one experiment he administered "large amounts of caffeine" to "one or two stuporous catatonic patients," hoping it would stimulate a response. (It did not.)[41] Because nitrous oxide (laughing gas), an anesthetic introduced in the 1800s, often induces a state of euphoria, Lehmann studied it as a treatment for depression. Patients inhaled "pure nitrous oxide" until they lost consciousness. Lehmann tried this technique, concluding that while nitrous oxide possessed no antidepressant properties, it had produced "the most significant dream of my life."[42] In one study, he dispensed nicotinic acid (vitamin B3) to depressed patients; in another, he administered ammonium sulfate and sodium carbonate to alter the pH level of patients with manic depression, hypothesizing that manic episodes were triggered by fluctuating pH levels that rendered sufferers excessively acidic or alkaline. Another experiment, in which several schizophrenic patients received a pituitary gland extract, seemed to show promise until Lehmann realized that the patient whose behaviour had markedly improved was responding to the solution's high alcohol content, not the hormone.[43] That none of these compounds worked did not derail Lehmann's search for one that would.

Lehmann was familiar with the research of Austrian physician Julius Wagner-Jauregg, the first psychiatrist to win a Nobel Prize for treating general paresis of the insane (GPI), a disorder caused by late-stage syphilis.[44] Combining pyrotherapy (the purposeful elevation of a patient's temperature) and injections of malaria parasites, Wagner-Jauregg waited for malarial fever to attack the syphilis of afflicted patients (causing GPI symptoms to recede), and then administered antimalarials to eradicate the "therapeutic" malaria he had introduced. That a treatment in which patients were intentionally infected with a potentially lethal disease was celebrated as a medical breakthrough is a telling indicator of the fraught character of medical experimentation and psychiatric treatment in the interwar era. When the putative inventor of the lobotomy, an irreversible psychosurgery performed on more than 40,000 psychiatric patients in Canada and the United States, won a Nobel Prize in 1949, it indexed medical scientists' continued acceptance of heroic measures as acceptable treatments for the institutionalized ill.

With neurosyphilis on the rise during the war, Lehmann sought to replicate Wagner-Jauregg's research using the blood of malaria patients as a vector for infection, but the blood was so scarce that it had to be specially transported from another Montreal hospital.[45] This shortage, the decline of syphilis with the availability of antibiotics, and studies touting the benefits of pyrotherapy for a wider range of psychiatric disorders prodded Lehmann to experiment with "all kinds" of fever- and infection-inducing agents. At a 1985 symposium in Quebec City, he recounted the desperation undergirding this work:

> I injected sulfur in oil which was painful and caused a fever; I injected typhoid antitoxin intravenously which produced pyrexia in schizophrenic patients. Nothing helped. I even injected turpentine into the abdominal walls which produced – and was supposed to produce – a huge sterile abscess and marked leucocytosis [an elevated white blood cell count, often signalling infection]. Of course, that abscess had to be opened in the operating room under sterile conditions. None of this had any effects, but all of this had been proposed in mostly European works.[46]

Lehmann's comments indicate his awareness of the discomfort and dangers to which he subjected patients, yet he did not consider his experiments unethical at the time. In an era when institutionalization regularly condemned the mentally ill to a life of suffering and squalor, Lehmann saw his experiments as necessary steps toward more effective treatments and the possibility of discharge. ECT also had limited efficacy, risks, and adverse side effects and yet it had become a staple of asylum therapy. Lehmann wanted better options. In his eyes, forsaking patients by doing nothing – accepting the status quo – would be the greater calamity. He regarded himself as an agent of change when other psychiatrists "wouldn't experiment [because] they had given up."[47]

Lehmann characterized Verdun patients and staff as willing, even eager, participants. "Anything was better than just being left as they were," he insisted.[48] Unfortunately, we do not know if patients exuded the experimental fervour Lehmann ascribed to them or if they shared his view that experiments were ethical in the context of the time. Patient voices have been muted by time and privacy laws that veil their identities and keep their medical records beyond the historian's reach. Desperate missives penned by patients such as Dorothy register an unequivocal desire to live outside the confines of institutions, but say nothing about the risks or discomfort they were willing to assume to realize this goal. In the early 1970s, awareness of the horrors of the Tuskegee trial cultivated a critical view of medical experimentation and encouraged research that revealed the power inequities intrinsic to its history, but in the 1940s and 1950s these concerns had not yet seeped into the public consciousness. The ethos of the Cold War reified applied science and medical progress and lauded citizen involvement as a patriotic act; it was in the 1950s that national science fairs were established to enlist the participation of young students and to recognize the best ideas and most promising "experimenters." Still, when Lehmann later characterized the 1950s as a time when "everybody ... was anxious to volunteer" and the Verdun as a place where patients, "the relatives of patients, as well as the nurses" were "overjoyed [to try] something new and experimental," he likely glossed over the varied meanings "participation" imparted to different constituencies.[49]

Lehmann's 1953 chlorpromazine experiment would be the most impactful of his career, introducing a categorically new therapy to North American psychiatry. Although the results helped mainstream pharmacotherapy, Lehmann had not previously considered prescription drugs a likely outcome of his research. In 1952, a McGill student despondent by the suffering he had witnessed at the Verdun asked Lehmann if psychiatry would "ever get a pill to help these poor people." The psychiatrist shrugged off the query as "science fiction." The treatment of psychiatric patients, he quipped, "would never be as simple as 'just a pill.'"[50]

A year later, Lehmann proved this prognostication wrong. We often imagine medical innovations to be the outcome of carefully choreographed events but some of the greatest turning points in medical history have occurred largely by accident. Such was the case here. It was during a Sunday bath that Lehmann stumbled across an article left by a sales representative from the French pharmaceutical company Rhone-Poulenc promoting its new sedative, chlorpromazine.[51] Lehmann was intrigued but skeptical of the author's claim that the drug operated as a "chemical lobotomy," calming patients while stopping their hallucinations. He decided to conduct an experiment to explore chlorpromazine's full therapeutic range.[52]

Lehmann's fluency in French positioned him to be the first North American psychiatrist to do so. Other psychiatrists had also received Rhone-Poulenc's promotional materials, and many had more time, funding, and staff than Lehmann to conduct clinical research. Indeed, the expansion of McGill's psychiatry program increased Lehmann's workload exponentially. In 1946 Cameron had merged the program with the Verdun, making it McGill's largest teaching hospital in 1947, and appointed Lehmann a faculty lecturer. In addition to teaching medical students, residents, and postgraduates, Lehmann served as the Verdun's medical director and by 1953 maintained a personal caseload of some six hundred patients. Besides his workload, what most separated Lehmann from his peers was his multilingualism. In 1950s Montreal, English remained the primary language of psychiatry. "Anglophones just wouldn't speak French," Lehmann recalled.[53] Although Cameron worked as a clinician and hospital director in Montreal for twenty-one years and headed the Quebec Psychiatric Association, he did not speak French or try to learn. Lehmann, in contrast, had read Rhone-Poulenc's materials with ease. Under his wife's tutelage, his French had been polished to perfection; at home, it was the only language the couple spoke. Reviewing European publications for research leads was also integral to Lehmann's routine. While his bath-time decision to study chlorpromazine was made in haste, it continued a pattern of trans-Atlantic knowledge translation decades in the making.

Lehmann organized the chlorpromazine trial employing the same haphazard approach he had used in previous experiments: "I simply did what I thought I should." He worked quickly; it took less than two weeks to begin. As he subsequently explained, with "no written protocols, no stated criteria for selecting patients, no placebo or other controls, no government permission (not required then) and, it seems incredible today, no informed consent of patients from the patients or their families ... the work was simply folded into our clinical routines." McGill's establishment of an Institutional Review Board in the 1970s would alter the pace and organization of clinical trials but according to Lehmann, in 1953 he and his colleagues had "only the Hippocratic oath to guide us."[54]

The morning after his bath, Lehmann contacted Rhone-Poulenc for supplies and asked "the first resident I saw," Gorman Hanrahan, for help. He agreed. Hanrahan's assistance was invaluable, allowing Lehmann to run his largest clinical trial to date. Still, the experiment was largely a homegrown operation. Lehmann had asked Rhone-Poulenc for medication but not funding, and because the Verdun remained cash-strapped he did not "have the heart to ask the hospital for a secretary." Instead, he handwrote cards to track the responses of each participant.[55] All told there would be seventy-two, mainly patients with schizophrenia.[56]

Lehmann tested the drug on eight nurse volunteers first. To determine if its effects differed from those of other sedatives, he administered barbiturates and chlorpromazine to nurses on different days and ran functionality tests on each. Both drugs made the nurses drowsy but under the influence of chlorpromazine, their psychomotor and cognitive functioning improved. It appeared that the claim that the drug induced a "new kind of sedation" was more than marketing hype.[57]

Lehmann administered chlorpromazine to patients next. They varied in age (eighteen to eighty-one) and diagnosis, and their doses changed over time, but all were treated exclusively with chlorpromazine.[58] The results were so extraordinary that Lehmann initially dismissed them as a fluke, as "improbable as winning one million dollars in a lottery twice."[59] Within weeks, patients who had previously entertained no hope of recovery or discharge were symptom-free. Chlorpromazine had not cured them but by containing the symptoms of their illnesses, it had achieved something no compound in the annals of psychiatry had done. "We saw the unthinkable – hallucinations and delusions eliminated by a pill!" Lehmann told Healy, excited by the memory decades later.[60] Equally astounding was that the drug had preserved patients' functionality, making many eligible for discharge.[61]

Lehmann and Hanrahan were quick to recognize the drug's significance. "We knew we had something very unique," Lehmann averred. "In fact, we had never seen anything like it."[62] In 1954, they transfixed the medical world when they published the results of their study. The press hailed chlorpromazine as "psychiatry's penicillin," the discipline's first wonder drug.

Even before the article came out, word of its miraculous findings had made its way across North America, aided by the circulation of the unpublished article by Rhone-Poulenc and Smith, Kline, and French (which had acquired the right to sell chlorpromazine in the United States under the trade name Thorazine). Other asylums, including New York's Pilgrim State – with more than 13,000 patients, one of the continent's largest – administered chlorpromazine without further study or FDA approval, granted in 1954. By then, Lehmann's "lottery-like" results had been replicated in hospitals around the world.[63]

Assessments of a drug's therapeutic value are shaped by the contexts in which communities encounter it. The celebratory encomium chlorpromazine engendered reflects this. For patients, chlorpromazine offered a one-way ticket out of the asylum, free of the shackles and shame of institutionalization. The response of the medical community was equally sanguine. Although the drug was neither a curative nor a one-time treatment – its efficacy depended on the willingness and ability of patients to take it daily for the rest of their lives – clinicians deemed it preferable to existing therapies. The drug was less invasive, easier to administer, and seemingly safer and more humane than ECT or psychosurgery. For psychiatrists, the availability of a successful and reversible treatment ended centuries of therapeutic nihilism, delivering psychiatry into the modern age. Long denigrated as overeducated caregivers, psychiatrists could finally be integrated into mainstream medicine as "full-fledged physicians who can help their patients and not just listen to their problems."[64] The drug's efficacy also furnished an exciting new research agenda. If biochemical imbalances caused mental illness, then surely other chemical cocktails could be concocted to recalibrate the "broken brains" of those suffering from other disorders. Treating schizophrenics would be just the beginning.[65]

The positive rhetoric transcended the immediacy of the clinic. More than a treatment for patients, chlorpromazine promised to elevate society itself. Families torn asunder by the ravages of psychiatric illness would be healed and made whole; couples driven to divorce could (and did) remarry.[66] Workplace productivity would soar as thousands returned to and retained paid employment, able to work "in spite of [their] underlying affliction."[67] Chlorpromazine also offered a convenient, low-cost solution to the spiralling mental health crisis, a financial burden asylums had failed to rectify but one that was costing taxpayers annually an estimated $30 million in Canada and $1 billion in the United States.[68] While policymakers praised the drug's affordability, activists outraged by the "shame of the asylums" saw chlorpromazine as both a humanitarian alternative to medical incarceration and the dawn of a more enlightened age of outpatient care.

Chlorpromazine fell short of being a one-pill panacea, but its rapid uptake left an indelible imprint on the organization of psychiatric care, reducing the size and number of asylums.[69] In 1955, admission rates in US psychiatric facilities declined for the first time in twenty-five years. The deinstitutionalization of patients followed. Many facilities closed, others merged with general hospitals, while asylums such as New York's notorious Pilgrim State were transfigured into community clinics providing short-term or transitional services.[70] At the Verdun, deinstutionalization proceeded slowly and was supported by several initiatives: a family care program in 1956 to help those requiring medical care but not hospitalization, a transitional centre in 1961 to facilitate patients' reintegration into the community, a day hospital in 1965, and in 1966, the launch of a pre- and post-hospitalization home visitation program. In 1973, the hospital also established a community mental health clinic. By then, its outpatient population exceeded the number of patients receiving inpatient care.[71]

Lehmann, the architect of the deinstitutionalization movement, was also responsible for introducing a new term to the language of psychiatry when he called chlorpromazine an "antipsychotic" in a 1956 address to the Canadian Medical Association. (Its ability to calm patients without excessive sedation had led many to refer to it as a "major tranquilizer.") Although Lehmann invoked the term "more as a metaphor than a designation," the label stuck. As psychiatric medications began to proliferate in number and kind, the term "antipsychotic" helped distinguish one drug family from the next.[72]

By 1963, ten years after Lehmann's trial, chlorpromazine's global use had translated into an astounding 50 million prescriptions, delivering lucrative profits to Rhone-Poulenc and companies licensed to sell it under different brands.[73] In a medical field in which pharmacotherapy had historically made few inroads, chlorpromazine's commercial success set the stage for the boondoggle that followed, one in which industry would play the definitive role in the development of psychiatric medications. From a business standpoint, a pill people took daily for life was a coveted market few medications had achieved. In an era when a succession of "wonder drugs," from penicillin and the Salk vaccine to corticosteroids, had changed the lives of millions, what made chlorpromazine uniquely "wonderful" was the predictability of profits from daily use. On the heels of chlorpromazine, companies hoping to benefit from psychopharmacology's commercial potential prioritized the development of new psychiatric medications.

By 1960 their gamble had paid off. The market had expanded to include not only new antipsychotics but antidepressants and minor tranquilizers too, medications companies encouraged doctors to prescribe routinely. As physicians' prescribing options grew, chlorpromazine was marketed as a multi-tasking dynamo, a pill that could simultaneously treat an expanding list of therapeutic indications that by 1964 included postpartum anxiety, alcoholism, agitated depression, hyperactivity, nausea, vomiting, and even hiccups.[74] Heinz Lehmann was an anti-materialist who disliked industry-sponsored junkets and the bountiful freebies – from clocks and leather binders to paid vacations for high-volume prescribers – companies could legally gift North American physicians in the 1950s and 1960s. And yet, ironically, his clinical trials were instrumental to this industry's growth.

Chlorpromazine had confirmed Lehmann's hypothesis that psychotic disorders possessed a biological correlate, invigorating his research on the therapeutic properties of other compounds. Among those he studied were psilocybin, mescaline, and lysergic acid diethylamide (LSD), psychedelics whose criminalization would halt research on their therapeutic uses for decades. Before criminalization closed the curtain on psychedelic experimentation, Lehmann was one of many eminent Canadian psychiatrists who had treated patients with LSD and supported its continued availability.[75]

Lehmann's study of imipramine, a tricyclic antidepressant developed by Swiss firm Geigy, was more fruitful. Geigy had hoped that the compound, patented in 1951 and known as G22355 before it was marketed as imipramine in the late 1950s, would become a successful treatment for schizophrenia. When psychiatrist Richard Kuhn, a clinician at a Swiss asylum, advised Geigy that it was ineffective for schizophrenia but unexpectedly beneficial for treating depression, Geigy ignored his findings. There was, as yet, no market in antidepressants and the company was unsure if the drug could be commercially viable. After amassing more evidence, Kuhn urged the company to reconsider: "Since depression is not only one of the most frequently occurring mental illnesses but one of the most frequently occurring illnesses in general, I see an immense potential here."[76]

Lehmann read Kuhn's paper on imipramine, written in German, on a return flight from a 1957 conference in Zurich. Kuhn's talk on imipramine had not drummed up much excitement there; Lehmann remembered the conference room being almost empty. But Lehmann was excited about the implications of Kuhn's findings: "I had told the various drug representatives [that] after we had antipsychotics, it shouldn't be so difficult to find an antidepressant."[77] With ECT remaining the primary treatment for severe depression, Lehmann hoped an antidepressant could help a patient population chlorpromazine had left behind. By the time his plane landed in Montreal, Lehmann had decided to run a trial of imipramine.

Once again, Lehmann proceeded quickly. He called Geigy's Montreal branch to procure supplies only to be told that they had never heard of the drug. After contacting company headquarters in Europe, where imipramine had been available for a year, the Montreal office quickly made things right and within weeks Lehmann and staff psychiatrists Charles Cahn and Roger Louis De Verteuil began the first North American trial of imipramine on eighty-four Verdun patients. The results, published in the *Canadian Psychiatric Association Journal* in October 1958, corroborated Kuhn's findings and introduced antidepressants to North American psychiatry, where they would find their largest and most profitable market.[78] Sold as Tofranil, imipramine's commercial success spurred rivals Merck, Pfizer, and Lily to develop their own antidepressants, all precursors to today's SSRIS (selective serotonin reuptake inhibitors including Prozac) and SSNRIS (selective serotonin and norepinephrine reuptake inhibitors including Effexor). As historian Edward Shorter has noted, imipramine's arrival meant that "for the first time in history, serious depression acquired a pharmacotherapy of its own."[79]

In the brave new world of psychopharmacology he helped create, Lehmann would go on to oppose the political stigmatization of "street" drugs while criticizing physicians' overuse of prescription medications. As a member of Canada's Le Dain Commission (1969–73) on the recreational use of drugs, he supported the decriminalization of cannabis and, in the 1980s, scolded the media for publishing stories sensationalizing the hazards of mild tranquilizers (Miltown, Valium), reports Lehmann believed did more harm than good. At the same time, he worried that psychiatrists' uncritical prescribing patterns had run amok. In the twilight of his career, he reflected on his contributions to the rise of pharmacotherapy, wondering if "it was a good thing that I [got] drugs into psychiatry." Seduced by diagnostic manuals and prescribing guidelines privileging aggregate data over individual needs – "laundry lists and cookbooks," Lehmann called them – psychiatrists had sacrificed empathy on the altar of scientific medicine. Quick to prescribe, they had forgotten how to listen. "You have to help individual patients," Lehmann told Healy in 1994. "You have to help as a psychiatrist and not a neuroscientist."[80]

~~~

An overview of Lehmann's career, however preliminary, inevitably invites comparisons to Cameron's. Colleagues but not friends, Lehmann and Cameron inhabited similar institutional and clinical realms. Both directed local psychiatric hospitals, albeit institutions that differed in size, patient demographics, organization, and funding. Before the biological paradigm eclipsed the psychoanalytic, each insisted that major psychiatric disorders were physiologically based and ontologically real. Both believed in the need for biological treatments, but the experiments they conducted to develop them bequeathed different legacies. While Lehmann's chlorpromazine trial anointed him a venerated father of psychopharmacology, Cameron's therapeutic legacy is one of notoriety and shame. Cameron died as the anti-psychiatry
~~~

movement was gaining momentum, while Lehmann later tasted its full fury when a naysayer smeared cream on his face during a campus debate on psychiatry and social control. Unfazed, Lehmann wiped the cream away and continued speaking.[81]

Similarities in Cameron and Lehmann's approach to experimental medicine attest to the need to study both physicians in a larger historical context attentive to the work of other psychiatrists. That both conducted experiments on patients without informed consent is suggestive but not conclusive.[82] If we want to know if Cameron and Lehmann's actions were normative, we must compare them to those of other asylum psychiatrists in Montreal, Quebec, Canada, and North America in the 1940s and '50s.[83] Indeed, one of the pitfalls of characterizing Cameron as a mad scientist who acted alone is that it negates the epistemic need for comparison while offering a comforting narrative that conveniently blames "one bad apple" for myriad misfortunes.

Cameron's litigated legacy, his MKULTRA grant, the injurious interventions it supported, and US and Canadian government funding of Cold War medical experiments are important and newsworthy topics (the history of which I recount elsewhere) but they do not tell the full story of the department's past. While not exhaustive, this accounting of Lehmann's life and work illustrates what can be gained by reframing the history of McGill Psychiatry to include historical actors sidelined or silenced by the Cameron scandal. McGill Psychiatry's metamorphosis from a fledgling unit into an international powerhouse with strengths in neuropsychiatry, psychopharmacology, transcultural psychiatry, psychosomatic medicine, and more involved a panoply of individuals, ideas, and events.[84] Put differently, the making of McGill Psychiatry was a collective endeavour, the complexities of which cannot be captured by a singular focus on Cameron. Highlighting the work and contributions of Heinz Lehmann, this piece seeks to contribute to the unfinished restoration of McGill Psychiatry's multi-faceted history.

NOTES

Research for this article was funded in part by the Canada Research Chair program and by an Open Operating Grant from the Canadian Institutes of Health Research. The author acknowledges with gratitude their support, and thanks Daniel Hirschkorn, Elke Kluge, and especially Brian Lewis, George Weisz, and two anonymous reviewers for constructive feedback,

Suzanne Morton and Don Nerbas for timely research guidance, and Lana Povitz for invaluable research assistance.

1 Archives of the American College of Neuro-Psychopharmacology, University of California at Los Angeles, Heinz E. Lehmann Papers (hereafter Lehmann Papers), box 41, folder 10, "Patient Writings and Correspondence"; Andrea Tone, "Heinz Lehmann: There at the Revolution," *Newsletter of the Collegium Internationale Neuro-Psychopharmacologium* (March 2004): 16–17.

2 Andrea Tone, *The Age of Anxiety: A History of America's Turbulent Affair with Tranquilizers* (New York: Basic Books, 2009), 78.

3 Because academic and clinical activities were intertwined, I use the term McGill Psychiatry as an amalgam of both.

4 Located in a mansion built as the residence for shipping magnate Sir Hugh Allan and his family, the Allan Memorial Institute opened and operated as part of the Royal Victoria Hospital.

5 American Psychiatric Association, Donald Ewen Cameron Papers (hereafter Cameron Papers), folder 1, "World Psychiatric Association."

6 Cameron Papers, folder 59, "The McGill Postgraduate Diploma Course in Psychiatry: A Report on its State of Affairs in February 1965." Affiliated hospitals included the Allan Memorial Institute, the Douglas, St Mary's Hospital, the Montreal General Hospital, the Montreal Children's Hospital, and the Jewish General Hospital.

7 Cameron advocated somatic interventions long before he was hired at McGill. See Ewen Cameron, *Objective and Experimental Psychiatry* (New York: Macmillan Company, 1935).

8 Cameron Papers, folder 15, "Address on the Opening of the Allan Memorial Institute."

9 Robert Cleghorn, "The Emergence of Psychiatry at McGill," *Canadian Journal of Psychiatry* 29 (1984): 551–5; Extracts from Dr Robert A. Cleghorn's private papers, Appendix 36 in George Cooper, *Ewen Cameron, Allan Memorial Institute, and United States Central Agency. Opinion of George Cooper Q.C. Regarding Canadian Government Funding of the Allan Memorial Institute in the 1950's and 1960's* (Ottawa: Communications and Public Affairs, Department of Justice, 1986), hereafter *Cooper Report*; Emile Legrand and George E. Reed, "Psychiatric Facilities in Montréal and Quebec," *American Journal of Psychiatry* 105, no. 10 (1949): 782–5.

10 "Drugs Tested by CIA on Mental Patients," *New York Times*, 3 August 1977: 37; John Marks, *The Search for the "Manchurian Candidate": The CIA and Mind Control* (New York: Times Books, 1978), 150.

11 The class comprises mainly the families but also the dependants and successors of patients subjected to psychic depatterning at the Allan between 1948 and 1964. Cameron sought to "depattern" patients through sleep therapy, intensive ECT, sensory deprivation, and a combination of pharmaceuticals, and to "repattern" them with positive memories and behaviours implanted through psychic driving, in which patients listened to curated excerpts of recorded therapy sessions or brief statements played on a continuous loop. Cameron's therapeutic goal was to erase the pathologies in a patient's brain and to restructure it, *tabula rasa*, to be disease-free. It was a crude theory, an aggressive intervention, and it did not work.

12 A year before he applied to a CIA front organization for funds to support his research program on psychic driving, Cameron published an article on his preliminary findings in the *American Journal of Psychiatry*, the most widely circulated psychiatry journal in North America. See Ewen Cameron, "Psychic Driving," *American Journal of Psychiatry* 112, no. 7 (1956): 502–9. Canadian grants supported Cameron's psychic driving experiments before and after his MKULTRA grant. In response to an Access to Information request, the Canadian government determined in 1985 that Cameron had been awarded more than $495,000 in Mental Health Grants to support nine projects in which he was identified as principal investigator. Established in 1948, the grants were federally funded but provincially administered. The first, spanning 1950 to 1954, supported a research program that included "psychic driving techniques," while the ninth, spanning 1961 to 1964, supported a study of personality changes in "individuals exposed to prolonged repetition of verbal signals. "HWC response to ATI request," Appendix 27, *Cooper Report*.

13 Even McGill's Department of Psychiatry has struggled with how best to portray Ewen Cameron in representations of its past. In a lecture hall at the Allan are framed photos of department chairs, including Heinz Lehmann and Cameron, but when I last visited only Cameron's mug had been stripped of the corresponding plate identifying each chair's name and dates of service. In contrast, Theodore L. Sourkes, Gilbert Pinard, and McGill University's Department of Psychiatry's *Building on a Proud Past: 50 Years of Psychiatry at McGill* (Department of Psychiatry, McGill University, 1995) provides, as its title suggests, a more positive, albeit internal, assessment of the department's history, which praises the contributions of multiple members. Sourkes, the lead author, received his BSc and MSc from McGill and joined its Department of Psychiatry in 1953 after earning a PhD from Cornell University. He would go on

to publish prolifically in the fields of biochemistry, biological psychiatry, and the neurosciences.

14 Lehmann Papers, ACNP interview, William E. Bunney Jr, 12 December 1994, San Juan, Puerto Rico (hereafter Bunney interview)

15 Bunney interview.

16 According to long-time colleague Tom Ban, who was aware of Lehmann's episodic depression, it was almost impossible to detect when Lehmann was suffering from an episode, but Ban surmised that the few occasions when Lehmann left his office early were the best indicator. Tom Ban oral history interview with Andrea Tone, 15 April 2008, Toronto. Transcript in author's possession.

17 Tone, *The Age of Anxiety*; Lehmann quoted in *Untangling the Mind: The Legacy of Dr. Heinz Lehmann* (Alexander Street Press, Filmmakers Library, 2000); interview with Heinz Lehmann in David Healy, ed., *The Psychopharmacologists: Interviews by David Healy*, vol. 1 (London: Taylor & Francis, 2001), 159–86, 171 (hereafter Healy interview).

18 Bernd Holdorf, "Emigrated Neuroscientists from Berlin to North America," *Journal of the History of the Neurosciences* 25, no. 3 (2016): 227–8. Also see in the same volume F.W. Stahnisch, "Learning Soft Skills the Hard Way: Historiographical Considerations on the Cultural Adjustment Process of German-Speaking Emigré Neuroscientists in Canada, 1933 to 1963," 299–319.

19 Joel Paris, "Heinz Lehmann: A Pioneer of Medical Psychiatry," *Canadian Journal of Psychiatry* 44, no. 5 (2006): 441–2; Donald G. Bates oral history of Heinz Lehmann, c. 1984–85, from McGill and Medicine in Montreal Between the Wars Fonds, P206, series 2, folder 16, Osler Library Reading Room (hereafter Bates oral history); Bunney interview.

20 Bates oral history.

21 Joel Paris, "Heinz Lehmann"; Bunney interview; Bates oral history. Surviving records are unclear as to Joyal's citizenship status after marriage; losing Canadian citizenship and acquiring Lehmann's was legal convention but enforcing it would have compelled Joyal to become a German citizen when Canada and Germany were at war. What is clear is that, at the very least, Joyal's marriage subjected her to political surveillance and security checks. After the war, the Canadian Citizenship Act of 1947 created a pathway to citizenship for residents regardless of country of origin, and Lehmann finally became a Canadian citizen.

22 Training was provided through supplementary lectures and grand rounds on hospital wards.

23 Tone, "Heinz Lehmann."

24 The population of institutionalized patients at the Verdun varies by source and by how a patient's length of stay is counted. In multiple oral histories, Lehmann claimed the residential population in 1937 was 1,600, but other sources, including colleague Charles Cahn's *Hôpital Douglas. 100 ans d'histoire et de progrès / Douglas Hospital: 100 Years of History and Progress* (Verdun, Quebec: Douglas Hospital, 1981), place the number closer to 1,300. The hospital's website notes that its institutional population in 1939 was "over 1200." Accessed 18 February 2023, https://douglas.research.mcgill.ca/history.

25 Bates oral history.

26 *Untangling the Mind*; Bates oral history; Heinz E. Lehmann, MD, "Before They Called It Psychopharmacology," *Neuropsychopharmacology* 8, no. 4 (1993): 291–303.

27 Bates oral history.

28 Lehmann quoted in *Untangling the Mind.*

29 Joel Braslow, *Mental Ills and Bodily Cures: Psychiatric Treatment in the First Half of the Twentieth Century* (Berkeley, CA: University of California Press, 1997).

30 Bates oral history.

31 Healy interview.

32 Healy interview.

33 Jack David Pressman, *Last Resort: Psychosurgery and the Limits of Medicine* (Cambridge, UK: Cambridge University Press, 1998), 158.

34 Pressman, *Last Resort,* 157–8.

35 Heinz Lehmann MD, "The Introduction of Chlorpromazine in North America," *Psychiatric Journal of the University of Ottawa* 14, no. 1 (1989): 264.

36 Bates oral history.

37 Lehmann, "Before They Called It Psychopharmacology," 296.

38 Bunney interview.

39 Ban oral history.

40 Erika Dyck, *Psychedelic Psychiatry: LSD from Clinic to Campus* (Baltimore: Johns Hopkins University Press, 2008).

41 Lehmann, "The Introduction of Chlorpromazine in North America," 263. Lehman's caffeine experiment was based on earlier research, including H.L. Hollingsworth, *The Influence of Caffeine on Mental and Motor Efficiency* (New York: The Science Press, 1912).

42 Lehmann, "Before They Called It Psychopharmacology," 296; H. Lehmann and C. Bos, "The Advantages of Nitrous Oxide Inhalation in Psychiatric Treatment," *American Journal of Psychiatry* 104 (1947): 164–170.

43 Lehmann, "Before They Called It Psychopharmacology"; Lehmann, "The Introduction of Chlorpromazine in North America."

44 Also known as paralytic dementia or syphilitic paresis, the neuropsychiatric disorder causes delusions, tremors, seizures, and other symptoms as the illness progresses.

45 Bates oral history.

46 Presented at the International Symposium on the History of Psychopharmacology in October 1985, Lehmann's paper was published in 1989 as "The Introduction of Chlorpromazine in North America."

47 Bates oral history.

48 Bates oral history.

49 Bates oral history; Lehmann, "Before They Called It Psychopharmacology"; Tone, "Heinz Lehmann."

50 Lehmann, "Before They Called It Psychopharmacology."

51 Synthesized by the French pharmaceutical firm Rhone-Poulenc, chlorpromazine was first marketed as an anesthesia potentiator but by 1952 was being used as a sedative in Paris asylums. Tom A. Ban, "Fifty Years [*sic*] Chlorpromazine: A Historical Perspective," *Neuropsychiatric Disease and Treatment* 3, no. 4 (2007): 495–500; Tone, "Heinz Lehmann."

52 Ban, "Fifty Years Chlorpromazine."

53 Healy interview, 160.

54 Lehmann, "Before They Called It Psychopharmacology," 299, 301. Some readers may be surprised that Lehmann omitted referencing the 1947 Nuremberg Code, a ten-point statement enumerating the principles for the ethical conduct of medical experiments on human subjects that enshrined the importance of voluntary, informed consent. But as a spate of scholarship has shown, in the twenty years after the code (part of the US judges' decision in *United States vs. Karl Brandt et al*, also known as the Nuremberg Medical Trial) was drafted, North American physicians viewed it as guidelines intended for barbaric Nazi physicians, not ordinary physicians such as themselves. See, for example, David Rothman, *Strangers at the Bedside: A History of How Law and Bioethics Transformed Medical Decision Making* (New York: Basic Books, 1994) and Jay Katz, "The Nuremberg Code and the Nuremberg Trial: A Reappraisal," *Journal of the American Medical Association* 276, no. 20 (1996): 1662–6.

55 Bunney interview.

56 Lehmann, "Introduction of Chlorpromazine," 264.

57 Lehmann, "Before They Called It Psychopharmacology," 299.

58 H.E. Lehmann and G.E. Hanrahan, "Chlorpromazine: New Inhibiting Agent for Psychomotor Excitement and Manic States," *Archives of*

Neurology & Psychiatry 71, no. 2 (1954): 227–37; H.E. Lehmann, "Therapeutic Results with Chlorpromazine (Largactil) in Psychiatric Conditions," *Canadian Medical Association Journal* 72, no. 2 (1955): 91–9.

59 Lehmann, "Before They Called It Psychopharmacology," 300.

60 Healy interview, 168; Tone, "Heinz Lehmann."

61 F.J. Ayd, Jr, "Chlorpromazine: Ten Years' Experience," *Journal of the American Medical Association* 184, no. 1 (1963): 173–84.

62 Heinz Lehmann, "Reflections on a Career in Psychiatry," *Canadian Psychiatric Association Bulletin* 12, no. 4 (1980): 14–16; Healy interview; Tone, *The Age of Anxiety*, 79.

63 Tone, *The Age of Anxiety*, 78–80; Tone, "Heinz Lehmann," 17.

64 Tom Ban, "Fifty Years Chlorpromazine," 498.

65 Tone, *The Age of Anxiety*, 80.

66 Healy interview, 168.

67 Ayd, "Chlorpromazine: Ten Years' Experience," 173.

68 Annual hospital maintenance costs in Canada estimated by the Dominion Bureau of Statistics (DBS), in *Memorandum to the Hon. Paul Martin, January 19, 1949*, Appendix 33, *Cooper Report*. The DBS also noted that annual operating costs had tripled in the preceding fifteen years, although the hospitalized population had increased by only 60 per cent in the same period. Because the $30 million cost was reported in 1949, it is likely that the amount had increased by 1953. In *Every Other Bed*, published in 1956, mental health activist and author Mike Gorman characterized the psychiatric crisis in the United States as a billion-dollar-a-year problem, insofar as "every other bed" in public hospitals was occupied by the mentally ill. Mike Gorman, *Every Other Bed* (Cleveland: The World Publishing Company, 1956); Tone, *The Age of Anxiety*, 81. A comparable ratio existed in Canada, where the DBS reported that "there are almost as many beds in the mental hospitals as all the hospitals for the acutely ill physically, in Canada." Appendix 33, *Cooper Report*.

69 My focus here has been on positive perceptions of chlorpromazine and deinstitutionalization in the 1950s and 1960s, but by the 1970s the closing of psychiatric hospitals had created a new humanitarian crisis, as thousands of discharged patients were left without adequate medical care, social support, and housing.

70 The role that privatized health care in the United States played as an impetus for closures relative to closures in countries with public health care, such as Canada, is unknown.

71 On deinstitutionalization at the Douglas, see Madness Canada, "Verdun/Douglas," in L. Baker, L. Beckman, M. Davies, C. Dooley, and E. Dyck,

The Last Asylums Exhibit, 2022, accessed 25 February 2025, https://madnesscanada.com/after-the-asylum/policy-and-practice/the-last-asylums/verdun-douglas/, and "Douglas Sheds 'Snake Pit' Image," 8 January 1981, in Lehmann Papers, box 47, folder 29, "Evolution of Verdun."

72 Healy interview; Tone, "Heinz Lehmann," 16.

73 Ayd, "Chlorpromazine: Ten Years' Experience"; Smith, Kline, and French Laboratories, *Ten Years' Experience with Thorazine* (Philadelphia: Smith, Kline, & French, 1964).

74 Smith, Kline, and French Laboratories, *Ten Years' Experience with Thorazine.*

75 When Swiss pharmaceutical firm Sandoz conducted a survey in May 1962 of LSD use in Canadian psychiatric facilities, Lehmann was one of ten medical directors who responded. All ten supported LSD's continued availability for medical research; all had treated patients with the psychedelic. Neither Lehmann nor Ewen Cameron, another respondent, had used LSD as frequently as others; at the time of the survey, Saskatchewan psychiatrist Albert Hoffer had treated 500 patients with LSD for alcoholism alone. Appendix 10, *Cooper Report.*

76 Kuhn quoted in Edward Shorter, *A Historical Dictionary of Psychiatry* (New York: Oxford University Press, 2005), 141.

77 Bunney interview.

78 H.E. Lehmann, C.H. Cahn, and R.L. DeVerteuil, "The Treatment of Depressive Conditions with Imipramine (G22355)," *Canadian Psychiatric Association Journal* 3, no. 4 (1958): 155–64.

79 Shorter, *A Historical Dictionary of Psychiatry*, 140.

80 Healy interview, 171.

81 David Healy, "Pioneers in Psychopharmacology," *International Journal of Neuropsychopharmacology* 1, no. 2 (1998): 193.

82 Complicating matters is that institutionalization in Quebec in the 1940s and '50s necessitated written consent authorizing admission *and* treatment. In his analysis of the use of informed consent in Canadian psychiatric facilities in the 1950s, Fred Lowy, psychiatrist and dean of medicine at the University of Toronto at the time, determined that informed consent for separate experimental treatments was not routine partly because the original written consent required for admission was often "considered adequate to permit a wide range of therapeutic procedures." Expert Opinion and CV of Dr Fred H. Lowy, Appendix 6, *Cooper Report.*

83 Historians have undertaken groundbreaking scholarship on French asylums in Quebec and psychiatric training in Montreal, but histories of English-speaking institutions and comparisons of institutions,

psychiatrists, policies, and practices have been understudied. See, for example, Karine Aubin, "En quête de financement pour la création d'une clinique externe et d'un service social comme parachèvement de la désinstitutionnalisation à l'Hôpital Saint-Michel-Archange de Beauport, 1961–72," *Canadian Bulletin of Medical History* 36, no. 2 (2019): 281–307; Isabelle Perreault, "La folie, c'est de n'avoir pas d'autres normes que soi-même: la psychiatrie au cours de l'après-guerre au Québec," *Santé Mentale au Québec* 40, no. 2 (Summer 2015): 51–63; Alexis Thibault, "Cinquante ans de résidence: nécessité et pertinence de l'ARPUM," *Santé Mentale au Québec* 40, no. 2 (Summer 2015): 303–13.

84 Cameron Papers, folder 59, "The McGill Postgraduate Diploma Course in Psychiatry: A Report on Its State of Affairs in February 1965," 2.

10

A Perfect Storm

Operation McGill Français, 28 March 1969

JEAN-PHILIPPE WARREN

As long as McGill remains the way it is, an increasing number of Quebecers will regard it as a menace to their development and an obstacle to their liberation.

Stanley Gray[1]

The last years of the 1960s witnessed increased social mobilization in Quebec in the wake of the Quiet Revolution (1960–70), which triggered a vast array of reforms in the province.[2] Since students are less attached to the established social order and are generally more open to revolutionary ideas, several groups demanding radical changes were recruiting in high schools, colleges, and universities; and many of the proposed radical changes they were advocating for aimed to transform education. Still, it may be surprising to learn that the March 1969 Operation McGill français march, which demanded the complete, or at least partial, francization of the university situated in the heart of Montreal, was one of the largest student rallies in Canadian history. What made this demonstration so attractive?

Three factors combined to give the Operation McGill français march its appeal. First, for leftists and nationalists, McGill University was a symbol of the "Anglo-Saxon" (a term that in French refers to people of English and Welsh descent and, more generally, to British civilization) establishment that ruled over an impoverished working class. Quebec's francophones had just learned from the Royal Commission on Bilingualism and Biculturalism that they occupied the bottom rungs of the revenue ladder, ahead only of the Italians and Indigenous peoples. They were concerned with the predominance of the English language in most domains, including at every level of the education system, something that the linguistic school conflict in Saint-Léonard had clearly demonstrated.[3] They were increasingly aware that they were not yet "masters in their own house" (*maîtres chez nous*), as the provincial Liberal Party's electoral slogan promised in 1962. But leftists or nationalists were not alone in seeing McGill University in a negative light. Many Quebecers were simply concerned about the lack of places available in universities as the first wave of baby-boomers was preparing to graduate from the newly created CEGEPs. Experts were adamant that the Université de Montréal would not be in a position to accommodate all applicants in the fall of 1969. McGill became the favoured target because it was wealthy, English, and elitist. This prompted three main groups – socialists, nationalists, and would-be university students – to unite around a common struggle. And it was this explosive context that led a group of activists to organize an anti-McGill demonstration on 28 March 1969.

ENGLISH-SPEAKERS AGAINST McGILL

In the late 1960s, radicalism was in the air more than ever.[4] In the fall of 1968, for example, many CEGEPs were occupied for a few weeks in the hope of generating the kind of popular uprising that had shaken France in May of that year.[5] In a similar spirit, on 3 December, the McGill University computer centre was occupied for four hours by student activists denouncing the institution's discrimination against French-speakers (McGill's washrooms were reportedly filled with hateful graffiti against "French bastards" and "frog lovers"). Using whatever furniture they could get their hands on, they set up makeshift barricades, only to be swiftly evacuated after a police intervention.[6] As they were leaving the premises, the expelled students shouted: "We'll be back!" This event would find an echo in the much larger occupation of the Sir George Williams University computer centre two months later, on 11 February 1969, by student activists denouncing the institution's anti-Black racism.[7] Mark Starowicz, editor of the *McGill Daily*, said of the takeover of the McGill computer room: "It's an irrational racist act that cannot be justified. But it can be understood. It's a reaction to English racism."[8]

As the above quote indicates, it is important to emphasize that not all activists who targeted McGill University had French as their mother tongue. Many anglophones and allophones shared the view that

McGill had to be challenged and eventually profoundly reformed. Some of them were students or professors at McGill itself.[9] For instance, Stanley Gray, a twenty-four-year-old political science lecturer, was waging a battle against what he perceived to be a despotic academic administration. Inspired by the American Students for a Democratic Society, the national student activist organization that was instrumental in spreading the ideas of the new left in the United States, Gray had formed a group of about 150 people (mostly students in philosophy, political science, and sociology), tellingly called the Students for a Democratic University, on 23 November 1967. This group was to be the source of many actions against the university administration. On 24 January 1969, for example, Gray disrupted a senate meeting and three days later a meeting of the board of governors with cries of "Revolution." These direct actions outside the framework of established procedures were aimed at radicalizing student life. At the same time, the leaders of the McGill students' society (Robert Hajaly, Peter Poster, and Ian Hyman), armed with a budget of $250,000, sought to foment protest by engaging in a kind of academic guerrilla warfare. The *McGill Daily*, whose editorial board included Stanley Gray, was no less active in fostering political engagement within the university community.[10] If students, faculty, and staff were to listen to Gray and his followers, McGill would be turned into a thriving centre of leftist activism in North America.

Influenced by Marxist ideas, Gray and his followers wanted to hasten the development of socialism in Quebec. The fundamental struggle for them was that of the proletariat against the bourgeoisie. They had little difficulty seeing how McGill was part of the capitalist regime. For instance, they pointed out that the board of governors included several representatives of the business class, but none from the working class. When it was announced in the spring of 1969 that McGill University would award an honorary doctorate to John Ross Bradfield, director of Noranda Mines, student senator Marc Raboy proposed instead French philosopher Jean-Paul Sartre, American philosopher Herbert Marcuse, and Quebec union activist Michel Chartrand. Why, asked Raboy, should the career of a man who serves the interests of an imperialist and reactionary company be honoured? In his eyes, this decision was more proof of McGill's alliance with high finance, and its betrayal of the common people.[11] "The only sure thing about the Board," wrote Raboy, "is its composition and the interests it represents: big – very, very big – money."[12]

In Quebec, the socialist struggle espoused the nationalist cause to the extent that French-speaking Quebecers allegedly formed an "ethnic class."[13] For Gray and his followers, therefore, the fight to end capitalism in Quebec went hand in hand with efforts to decolonize Quebec. At a time when many colonized nations were gaining their independence (including Cuba, which had shaken off the yoke of US imperialism with Castro's revolution ten years earlier), many activists, ardent admirers of Ernesto "Che" Guevara, saw the struggle in Quebec as one pitting an imperialist elite against an oppressed Québécois nation. This was also the reason for their criticism of McGill University. For them, McGill had for too long been complicit in the oppression of francophones. "Queen Victoria is dead," wrote an anonymous student in the *McGill Daily*, "and McGill can no longer function as an isolated English-Canadian bastion, run by English-speaking financiers to produce English-speaking businessmen."[14] It could no longer, in other words, stand "in direct conflict with those of ... the various national liberation movements,"[15] whether in Asia, Africa, South America, or right here in Canada.[16] When student senator Harry Edel was not comparing Montreal's anglophones to the White minority in Rhodesia, Sven Jurhevski was drawing a parallel between the McGill administration and the *pieds noirs* in Algeria, who supported the OAS (an organization that carried out terrorist attacks in an attempt to prevent Algeria's independence from French colonial rule).[17] Meanwhile, Ian Hyman, vice-president of the McGill students' society, convinced that "English Canadians are racist," claimed that McGill had never been a Quebec university.[18] Later that year, in October 1969, six of the eight student members of the McGill senate eventually resigned in protest of their university's alliance with the economic colonialist powers perpetuating, in their view, the exploitation of the Quebec people. "We're taking action," they said. "McGill in French, McGill for the Québécois. Long live a free Quebec."[19]

Far from being marginal views formulated by a handful of hotheads studying or teaching at McGill, the opinions expressed by Gray and his followers reflected those of many English-speaking Quebecers who acknowledged that McGill had distanced itself too much from Quebec society and that some important changes were in order. A McGill graduate, Dr A.J. Roche, stated in a letter to *The Gazette* that McGill "has done virtually nothing to improve the understanding by the English of the culture, the problems, or the aspirations of French-Canadians."[20] He went on to say that "McGill has always and only educated those destined to live in the English ghetto of Quebec."[21] As a remedy, he proposed to promote greater bilingualism by imposing mandatory French exams before granting degrees to McGill graduates.[22] A contributor to the *Canadian Jewish Outlook*, for his part, wrote: "Even today, McGill's ingrown faculty and its exclusive Anglo-Saxon tradition continue to serve as a WASP refuge from the French Fact. ln 148 years McGill has not basically changed, nor has the English-Quebec society of which it forms a part. McGill has failed to adapt itself to the new Quebec that has emerged in recent years; McGill still remains to French Canadians as a prime instrument of domination."[23] For the contributor to the *Canadian Jewish Outlook*, real efforts needed to be made to better integrate McGill into the fabric of the province and, in particular, reconnect it with the reality of the French-speaking community.

JUSTIFYING THE MARCH

If some English-speaking Quebecers were strongly criticizing McGill, one can only imagine how French-speaking Quebecers felt about the institution. It is therefore not surprising that so many groups flocked to join the anti-McGill march announced for 28 March. Besides the McGill students affiliated with the Radical Students Alliance, the organizations that participated in Operation McGill français included the Comité Indépendance-Socialisme (CIS),[24] the Comités ouvriers of Rosemont and of Sainte-Marie, the Front de libération populaire (FLP),[25] the Intellectuels et ouvriers patriotes du Québec (IOPQ),[26] the Mouvement pour l'unilinguisme français au Québec, the Société nationale populaire, the Mouvement pour l'intégration scolaire (MIS),[27] the Mouvement syndicat-politique (MSP),[28] the Université libre d'art quotidien, the Comité d'action de l'Université de Montréal, the Comité d'action École normale Ville-Marie, the Université du Québec à Montréal, the Comités d'action des cégeps (Ahuntsic, Bois-de-Boulogne, de Mortagne, Édouard-Montpetit, Maisonneuve, Rosemont, Vieux-Montréal), and the Union générale des étudiants du secondaire.

This list shows how Operation McGill français rallied the student, socialist, and nationalist movements around a common cause. While Stanley Gray insisted (for socialist reasons) on the racist character of McGill University, and Lemieux (for nationalist reasons) on its integration into the capitalist system, Chaput underscored its isolation as an ivory tower, completely disconnected from Quebec society.[29] As a case in point, at a conference organized in November 1969 under the theme "Le role de McGill au Québec" (The role of McGill in Quebec), people had a chance to hear an interesting "motley crew" of speakers, including the singer Pauline Julien (sometimes referred to as the Pasionaria of Quebec's sovereignty movement), Raymond Lemieux, Stanley Gray, and Robert Aubin (the latter two from the FLP), and Rosie Douglas (who was doing a master's degree at McGill and led the anti-racism sit-in at Sir George Williams University while supporting Charles Gagnon's and Pierre Vallières's struggle for national liberation).

A week before the march, 100,000 copies of a special issue of the *McGill Daily* were printed and widely circulated across the province by students and union members (primarily those of the CSN).[30] Accompanied by a poster (featuring a bullseye with the word "McGill" in the centre), the eight-page document, titled *Bienvenue à McGill*, was written entirely in French. It stated that the *McGill Daily*'s special French edition was published "to let the people of Quebec know what we know about McGill's true role. We are publishing it in support of the 28 March Operation McGill demonstration and thus joining the demands of students and workers. McGill IN FRENCH. McGill to QUEBECERS."[31] The issue clearly conveyed the message that Quebec's cultural and economic liberation required the democratization and francization of McGill University.

For many people, the case was simple: McGill University was located in Quebec, so it had to serve Quebec's interests. It was wealthy, but its wealth was acquired by historically exploiting and oppressing the French-speaking majority. A leaflet distributed at the demonstration argued that "the University must break its ties with the ruling classes that exploit the people. Operation McGill is a step in the liberation of Quebec: it is about liberating McGill, giving it back to the people of Quebec."[32]

Some facts seemed to justify the anti-McGill cause. It was stated that English-speaking universities received approximately 30 per cent of the total subsidies granted to Quebec universities, while non-French-speakers represented only 18 per cent of the province's population.[33] There were three English-language institutions of higher learning in Montreal (McGill, Loyola, and Sir George Williams), while there was only one French-language university (Université de Montréal). French-speaking Quebecers who wanted to study at

McGill were not blocked by the language barrier alone. They also faced financial hurdles, since tuition fees were $200 higher at McGill than at the Université de Montréal, making it less likely for students from poor backgrounds to enrol at McGill.[34] They were also affected by the particular situation created by the opening of CEGEPs. In 1968, McGill accepted English-speaking students straight from high school, since the first English-language CEGEP, Dawson College, only opened its doors in September 1969; a year later, students who had already completed a year at McGill only needed an overall average of 55 per cent to move on to the second year, while CEGEP graduates who wanted to register in the same classes had to boast an average of 70 per cent. This admission policy seemed crafted to deliberately exclude francophones.

Critics of McGill never missed an opportunity to point out that the university was funded to a large extent by the state, and therefore by French-speaking taxpayers, while its research catered to the interests and needs of big international corporations. The faculty did not reflect the fact that McGill was located in Quebec either. Only 8 per cent of professors were French Canadian (22 per cent were American or British),[35] a situation that bordered on the absurd in the French Department, where only three out of forty professors were born in Quebec. The student body profile did not look much better. Only 7 per cent of students enrolled at McGill had French as their mother tongue, including Belgian and French students, while the French-speaking population of Quebec hovered around 82 per cent. A quarter of McGill's enrolment did not even come from the province. Moreover, half of its graduates went on to pursue careers outside Quebec. What was the point, asked many people, of subsidizing such a "foreign" institution?

Education experts insisted that 10,000 new students, mostly francophones, were about to apply to Quebec's universities in the fall and that the Université de Montréal, Université Laval, and Université de Sherbrooke could not accommodate them all. For weeks, Stanley Gray, Raymond Lemieux, and others toured the various CEGEPs to convince students that, given the lack of space at the Université de Montréal, their only chance to enter an undergraduate program was to enrol at McGill. Some people argued that the shortage of university seats for francophones would be resolved by the opening of the newly created (in December 1968) Université du Québec à Montréal (UQAM) in September 1969. But many feared that there would be long delays in setting up UQAM or that this university, given its meagre resources, would not be able to absorb the entire surplus of enrolments. Moreover, the promise of transforming "three or four slums in the lower part of the city"[36] into the premises of Montreal's second French-language university did not excite those with their sights set on the most prestigious educational institution in Canada.

Those behind the anti-McGill march aimed to convince people of the need for redress. Though it is not always easy to pinpoint exactly what the critics of McGill were asking for, their demands can be boiled down to a few key points:

1 Introduction of French as the language of instruction. The francization of the university was to be both progressive and rapid (50 per cent by 1969–70, 75 per cent by 1970–71, and 100 per cent by 1971–72). "The minimum that the University would have to do would be to immediately begin accepting graduates from French CEGEPs and give them instruction in their own language as a transition step to McGill becoming integrated into Quebec society and becoming a French institution."[37]
2 Acceptance of a large portion of the 10,000 students aspiring to pursue university studies in September 1969. To put pressure on the university, the 10,000 CEGEP students graduating in the fall were encouraged to enrol at McGill and overwhelm English enrolment.[38]
3 Establishment of tuition parity with the Université de Montréal.
4 Abolition of the Centre d'études canadiennes-françaises, created in 1963, which studied the Québécois through a folkloric lens.
5 Opening of the McLennan Library to the general public (it contained the largest collection of French-Canadian works in Canada).
6 Prioritization of national interests in research.
7 Tripartite representation on the board of governors: one-third students, one-third faculty and staff, and one-third direct representatives of the people of Quebec.

Most unions and nationalist organizations in Quebec supported these claims. The FTQ and the CSN sent out press statements endorsing the project to convert McGill University into a French-language institution by 1972.[39] Many intellectuals also agreed with the slate of demands.

The Université de Montréal faculty association (Syndicat des professeurs de l'Université de Montréal, SPUM) came out publicly to support the McGill français march's objectives. "When professor Gray speaks of the necessity of McGill becoming primarily a French institution," wrote Charles Prevost (president of the SPUM and leader of the FLP), "it seems evident to me and to many of my colleagues at the university that this is the only solution if the people of Quebec are concerned about remaining French and deciding their own destiny."[40] Many Université de Montréal professors offered to distribute *Bienvenue à McGill* in their classes and encouraged their students to join the march.

BY ANY MEANS NECESSARY

In the 1960s, many activists were convinced that violent conflict was the only way to foster real change in society. At Sir George Williams University, David Orton, a lecturer in sociology who helped form the Movement for Socialist Liberation (MSL), wrote that revolution will only be accomplished by "those who act, not by those who endlessly talk and contribute to left-wing journals, regarding strategy, tactics, objective versus subjective conditions, etc., etc."[41] Inspired by an upsurge in Front de libération du Québec (FLQ) attacks (including the super-bomb on the floor of the Montreal Stock Exchange, on 13 February 1969) and other radical organizations abroad (the [in]famous "Years of Lead"), many activists shared Orton's views. The MSP, among other groups, was not shy about asserting that political awareness required brutal clashes with the forces maintaining a "fascist" law and order. The extremism of some nationalist leaders did nothing to calm the mood. CIS member Mario François Bachand's inflammatory comments were anything but kind to Quebec's English-speaking minority, suggesting that they could be physically eliminated or forced to emigrate if they persisted in speaking their mother tongue outside the home.[42]

Some of the organizers of Operation McGill français did not hide their thirst for confrontation. Out of a sense of provocation or conviction, they made direct threats to McGill University in the days preceding the march. "There are those, definitely," explained a student from the Université de Montreal, "who are going there to burn the university."[43] The bulletin *La Victoire*, published by a supposed FLQ cell, predicted the worst. Mainstream media reports about the organizers' thirst for violence and anarchy fuelled a climate of panic throughout the country. "The Canadian public was being inured to expect hordes of rabid separatists to burn McGill to the ground."[44] According to an article in *The Suburban*, the march promised to attract "every riffraff, every hoodlum itching for a fight."[45] One columnist ironized:

> Want to let off steam? And you don't know how? Poor journalist! He still doesn't know how to democratize himself! It's simple though, and here's my suggestion: get behind Stanley Gray's banner; stuff your pockets with rocks and add a molotov cocktail or two to spice up the fun. March 28 will be the great day of anti-capitalist unleashing, from what I learn from the abundant and daily chronicle of the newspapers.[46]

Some people feared a repeat, only worse, of the events at Sir George Williams, where students had recently caused $2 million in damage. To prepare for the event, some claimed that McGill should put up barbed wire fences around the campus to protect the buildings from the angry pack. There was even a rumour that the premier of Quebec had asked the Canadian army to be on high alert.[47] The *Ottawa Citizen* announced on its front page: "Troops Stand By." The *Toronto Star*: "Police Set for Riot." The *Toronto Telegram*: "McGill Threat: Mounties Move In."

Yet, if some people behind the Operation McGill français march were indeed looking for a fight, a greater number tried to calm the situation, fearing that things could really get out of hand. The organizers of Operation McGill français were talking about a possible gathering of 5,000 people, an impressive number considering that most previous demonstrations had attracted only a few hundred. Since Premier Jean-Jacques Bertrand had refused to ban the demonstration, arguing that, despite its hostile message, it represented the free expression of a popular feeling, participants sought to display a certain level of self-discipline. For example, the Union générale des étudiants du Québec (UGEQ) attempted to "change the atmosphere of the march" on the eve of the fateful day during a meeting with CEGEP students. To prevent the protest from degenerating, the leaders agreed to enlist two hundred students wearing armbands to maintain order and contain the most radical elements.

The march's organizers were particularly keen to downplay the violent nature of their event for fear of a strong reaction from the government. "There was never any question of violence in the preparations for the march," confided Roger Lapone, a student at CEGEP Ahuntsic, "and the current climate was created by the authorities,"[48] who, according to Lapone, wanted to use the opportunity to increase surveillance and repression of the population. In the weeks before the event, volunteers who distributed leaflets about the rally or the *McGill Daily* were harassed.[49] On 18 March, activists returning from a preparatory meeting were arrested (including Stanley Gray, Mark Starowicz, and Robert Chodos, also a McGill student and a member of the CIS). On 21 March, Mario François Bachand, Raymond Sabourin (a member of the CIS and an ex-FLQ member), Yannick Chuit (a Collège Sainte-Marie student and a leader of the MSP), and Daniel Waterlot (a Collège Sainte-Marie student and Maoist militant) were jailed after being accused of seizing police equipment.[50] John Fekete, a McGill student suspected of possessing explosives in his apartment, was also arrested after police discovered a gram of marijuana there. It is because of such actions that union leader Michel Chartrand accused police officers of acting like Hitler's SS troops.[51]

REFUTING THE ORGANIZERS' CLAIMS

In the face of what promised to be a very tense gathering, McGill's allies did not remain silent or inactive; they tried to show the vacuity of the claims made by the march's organizers. Overall, there were three main responses to Operation McGill français, namely a socialist response, a liberal response, and a reformist response.

Staunch socialists opposed the march because it divided the fight against the established order along ethnic lines. For example, the newly elected members of the McGill students' society, otherwise highly critical of the administration, refused to endorse a rally that pitted Quebecers against each other, instead of class against class.[52] Similarly, the Internationalists, a Maoist group active at McGill, believed all nationalist discourses were invariably fascist.[53]

Liberals were also challenging the assumptions made by the Operation McGill français organizers. Robert Shaw, one of McGill's vice-rectors, did not mince words in a 24 March speech to the Montreal Bar Association. His university was under attack "from Stanley Gray and his revolutionaries; from Lemieux and his Ligue pour l'Intégration scolaire; from Chartrand and his violent separatists; from the taxpayers who foot the bills; from restless youth who demand change in society."[54] There was little doubt in his mind that some CEGEP students intended "to destroy society through the destruction of McGill." The director of the Montreal Neurological Institute, Wilder Penfield, expressed similar concerns, if not anger, in a lecture delivered at the Canadian Club. "A small group of disrupters are entering the [university] gates ... They bypass orderly procedure. They interrupt, block, demand and destroy. It comes at times to anarchy ... They are destroyers, anarchists, public enemies, although they commonly use the language of communism."[55] Comparing Stanley Gray to Adolf Hitler, Penfield ended his speech with an evocation of the end of civilization.[56]

Rather than add fuel to the fire, most of McGill's academic officers tried to calm the situation by promising reforms to make French more prominent in research, administration, and teaching. Michael Oliver, McGill's academic vice-principal, proposed that, while continuing to be an English-first institution, McGill could ensure "a strong and flourishing French presence among both its staff and students,"[57] which included an increase in francophone student enrolment from 7 per cent to 20 per cent by 1974, the adoption of a bilingualism policy for the administration, and the incorporation of courses in French in every faculty. Laurier Lapierre, a history professor teaching in the Département d'études canadiennes-françaises (and vice-president of the NDP), favoured the implementation of bilingualism within a dozen years, with courses duplicated in French at every level.[58] H. Rocke Robertson, the principal, refused to go that far but opened the door to offering elective courses in French. He supported the idea of making the administration bilingual, allowing examinations in French, increasing cooperation with other French-speaking institutions, encouraging research on francophones in Canada, and many other such initiatives. "Oui, the times they are a-changing," he might have been heard saying. "Propositions that would have seemed absolutely outrageous a few years ago," he philosophized, "now seem quite reasonable."[59]

Outside McGill, most intellectuals, whether francophone or anglophone, distanced themselves from the organization of the march. In French-language newspapers, editorials were generally far from sympathetic to the demonstration. Lucien Langlois of the *Montréal-Matin* declared that he was fleeing this "new dogmatism" and "intellectual terrorism."[60] Claude Ryan of *Le Devoir* chose to align himself with Laurier Lapierre's attitude, rather than Stanley Gray's.[61] While, as we saw, most unions encouraged Operation McGill français, the response from the major nationalist organizations was more mixed. For fear, presumably, of being seen as too extremist, the St Jean Baptiste Society wanted to eliminate one of Montreal's three English universities, ideally Sir George Williams, and transform it into a French-language institution,[62] but condemned the march. The Parti Québécois also dissociated itself from Operation McGill français. "From the outset," said René Lévesque, "the demonstration has seemed ill-advised. Taking into account the rather disturbing and hopefully inaccurate information on the possible turn of events, we invite all our members to stay away from a demonstration that is contrary to the political orientation, the principle of democratic action and the official program of the Parti Québécois."[63] As one can imagine, the Quebec Liberal Party and the Union nationale made sure to distance themselves from the 28 March protest.

THE DAY OF THE MARCH

The march's organizers wanted the event to be a resounding success. Ensuring that as many people as possible came, buses brought protestors from as far away as Hull, Saint-Jérôme, Quebec City, and Saint-Hyacinthe. Finally, on the evening of 28 March, about 10,000 people (7,000 according to English newspapers, 15,000 according to French newspapers) left from Saint-Louis Square and made their way to McGill University via Sherbrooke Street, arriving at around 9:30 p.m. Waiting for them on the McGill campus were about one hundred police officers wearing helmets and holding truncheons, and three thousand English-Canadian spectators. Thirteen hundred police officers were ready to be deployed in case of emergency. The university had installed speakers and floodlights on the roofs of its buildings.

The demonstrators gathered in front of the Roddick Gates and occupied Sherbrooke Street peacefully, not setting foot on campus. They shouted political slogans, including the favourite "Ce n'est qu'un début, continuons le combat" (This is just the beginning, let's continue the fight). Their banners included figures of FLQ "political prisoners" Pierre Vallières, Charles Gagnon, and Pierre-Paul Geoffroy, as well as Che Guevara. The *fleurdelisé* (Quebec flag), Communist flag, and 1837–38 Patriot flag could also be seen fluttering in the crowd. The slogans were many and diverse: "À bas la CTM [Conseil du travail de Montréal]" (Down with Montreal's labor council), "Y en pu d'police" (There's no more police), "Vive le cab libre" (Long live free cabs), "Lévesque traître" (Lévesque traitor), "McGill français" (French McGill), "McGill aux travailleurs" (McGill for the workers), "McGill aux Québécois" (McGill for the Québécois), "Québec aux Québécois" (Quebec for the Québécois), "Paix" (Peace), "Vietnam aux Vietnamiens" (Vietnam for the Vietnamese), etc.

At around 10 p.m. Lemieux and Gray took a loudspeaker to announce to the crowd that "the march had reached its goal" and that people should now go home. Before leaving, marchers burned flags, threw bottles and field hockey sticks at the police, and lit firecrackers. A handful of angry English-speaking students responded in counter-protest, chanting "God Save the Queen." A few altercations took place, which gave the signal to the police to intervene and disperse the crowd. As they were leaving, some protesters broke store windows at Eaton's and Simpson's on St Catherine and De Maisonneuve streets, and lit fires in public garbage cans. In the end, there were few injuries (thirty-six people were wounded, including police officers), and little vandalism. The day after the march, the English-Canadian newspapers congratulated themselves that the police had handled the threatening rioters so well. For them, in the end, the march on McGill was a superb demonstration of police efficiency. Reflecting on the event, the front page of the 7 June edition of *The Gazette* featured a giant photo of four police officers in riot gear, menacingly wielding heavy clubs. Inside, the stories all revolved around the disaster averted by the discipline and power of law enforcement. "They marched out in three platoons. Keeping together, acting as one, pushing and jabbing with their three-foot hickory riot sticks, they drove the crowd east and west along Sherbrooke and down the side streets. It was a remarkable illustration of how a body of men can control a mob."[64]

THERE WILL NOT BE ANOTHER McGILL FRANÇAIS

Operation McGill français was the largest street protest in Quebec since the Second World War. Its success encouraged members of the FLP and MSP to continue their high-profile actions. "We must develop programs of struggle with a truly revolutionary content," wrote Stanley Gray.[65] To raise Quebecers' political consciousness, Gray suggested the creation of "two, three, four McGills," just as Che Guevara had wished for the creation of "two, three, or more Vietnams."[66]

This call remained largely unanswered. In the weeks and months that followed Operation McGill français, sporadic skirmishes with the authorities made the headlines (including Opération Anti-Congrès in Quebec on 22 June and the beheading of the statue of Saint Jean-Baptiste at the 24 June parade in Montreal), but nothing like a general uprising was taking shape. For example, almost one year after the McGill march, in January 1970, the MSP and LIS organized a demonstration against Bishop's University, following a plan modelled on Operation McGill français.

> LIS finds that Bishop's situation replicates, in a smaller way, that of McGill: substantial subsidies from private sources; large proportion of international students (between 16 and 20 per cent); government subsidies disproportionate to the region's English-speaking population; study of Quebecers as "natives"; university student status granted to 25 per cent of students who are college students, entitling them to more generous government subsidies; and finally, perpetuation of a system that produces the intractable pillars of Quebec's unilingual English-speaking minority that stubbornly opposes integration within the French-speaking Quebec nation.[67]

Despite this inflammatory rhetoric, which had worked so well the previous year, the Sherbrooke demonstration was a complete failure. What was preventing the revolt from success? The problem, Gray wrote, was that the student movement was still floating too much "from crisis to crisis, from mess to mess, without building a structured grassroots organization, without doing any ongoing socialist education with the people, and without developing a coherent strategy. The FLP, for example, does not have a public image as a socialist movement – the population does not understand – but has an identity of extreme nationalists who like violence and organize riots."[68] Gray believed that social movements, if they were to grow, needed more than isolated, spontaneous, anarchist actions. He felt that his comrades' revolt would lead to a dead end if it lacked solid theory and rigorous organization. For that reason, many who had participated in the McGill march (Ian Hyman, Daniel Waterlot, etc.) would soon join Marxist-Leninist organizations.[69] McGill University did not want them anyway: Gray was officially dismissed from his position as a lecturer in the Political Science Department in April, and radical students sitting on the *McGill Daily* editorial board and on the students' society's executive lost re-election and were replaced by more moderate candidates.

Beyond the strategic explanation offered by Gray, other factors explain why Operation McGill français did not lead to a collective uprising, or even a radical transformation of McGill. Among these, the founding of UQAM is probably the most important. The opening of the second French university eliminated francophones' fears of not being able to find a place in institutions of higher learning once they graduated from CEGEP. Moreover, UQAM immediately attracted a large flock of politicized students who had no interest in studying at a bourgeois institution like McGill or Université de Montréal, and soon ensured that the offshoot of the classical Collège Sainte-Marie would become a hotbed of radical activism in the province. As a consequence, the years that followed saw UQAM, much more than McGill, become the locus of innumerable sit-ins, protests, rallies, and strikes.

NOTES

This chapter is an extensively revised version of Jean-Philippe Warren, "L'Opération McGill français. Une page méconnue de l'histoire de la gauche nationaliste," *Bulletin d'histoire politique* 16, no. 2 (2008): 97–115.

1 Stanley Gray, quoted by Herman Buller, "McGill University and an Aroused Quebec," *Canadian Jewish Outlook* (May 1969): 10.

2 Martin Pâquet and Stéphane Savard, *Brève histoire de la Révolution tranquille* (Montreal: Les éditions du Boréal, 2021).

3 In the 1960s, immigrants (mostly Italian) who settled in Saint-Léonard eagerly wanted to send their children to English-language schools and opposed francophones who believed that the language of instruction in this community situated in east-end Montreal should only be French. Marc V. Levine, *The Reconquest of Montreal: Language Policy and Social Change in a Bilingual City* (Philadelphia: Temple University Press, 1990).

4 Sean Mills, *The Empire Within: Postcolonial Thought and Political Activism in Sixties Montreal* (Montreal and Kingston: McGill-Queen's University Press, 2010).

5 Jean-Philippe Warren, *Une douce anarchie: les années 68 au Québec* (Montreal: Boréal, 2008).

6 "Riot Policemen Called to McGill to Halt Sit-In," *Montreal Star*, 4 December 1968, 1 and 4; "McGill ne déposerait pas de plainte contre ses onze 'occupants' francophones," *Le Devoir*, 5 December 1968, 3.

7 Jean-Philippe Warren, "Le défi d'une histoire objective et inclusive," *Bulletin d'histoire politique* 23, no. 1 (2014): 264–91; David Austin, *Fear of a Black Nation: Race, Sex, and Security in Sixties Montreal* (Montreal: Between the Lines, 2013).

8 Quoted in "Unanimous Reaction over Takeover: 'They Have No Business Here,' Angered Students Proclaim," *Montreal Star*, 4 December 1968, 87.

9 See Mills's analysis in chapter 6 of *The Empire Within*, 138–62.

10 The McGill Radical Students Alliance, led by Stanley Gray, controlled the Student Council, the *McGill Daily*, as well as the eight student seats on the expanded sixty-five-member senate.

11 Mark Starowicz, "Why Was This Man Honored?" *McGill Daily*, 10 October 1968, 1, 5.

12 Marc Raboy, "Das Kapital," *McGill Daily*, 27 January 1969, 4.

13 In 1961, Marcel Rioux and Jacques Dofny presented a paper in English at Carleton University that argued that the French-Canadian nation constituted a social class unto itself. Jacques Dofny and Marcel Rioux, "Les classes sociales au Canada français," *Revue française de sociologie* 3, no. 3 (July–September 1962): 290–300.

14 "Out of the Womb and Into the World," *McGill Daily*, 25 September 1967, 6.

15 "McGill: qui sert-elle?" *Bienvenue à McGill* (March 1969): 3.

16 Of course, decolonization movements included Indigenous movements, but this concern was comparably muted. Roberta Lexier, "To Struggle Together or Fracture Apart: The Sixties Student Movements at English Canadian Universities," in *Debating Dissent: Canada and the Sixties*, eds Greg Kealey, Dominique Clement, and Lara Campbell (Toronto: University of Toronto Press, 2012), 81–94. Roberta Lexier, "'The Backdrop Against Which Everything Happened': English-Canadian Student Movements and Off-Campus Movements for Change," *History of Intellectual Culture* 7, no. 1 (2007): 1–18.

17 Lysiane Gagnon, "Teach-in à McGill: Nous sommes entourés d'une mer anglophone," *La Presse*, 5 March 1969, 50.

18 Michel Vadeboncoeur, "Des anglophones crient: McGill français!" *La Patrie*, 16 March 1969, 5.

19 Quoted in "Au cri de 'McGill aux Québécois,' six des huit étudiants du sénat démissionnent," *Québec-Presse*, 26 October 1969, 9.

20 A.J. Roche, quoted by Andrew Allen, "McGill Québécois," *The McGill News* 50, no. 4 (July 1969), 12.
21 A.J. Roche, quoted by Andrew Allen, "McGill Québécois," *The McGill News* 50, no. 4 (July 1969), 12.
22 Anonymous, "McGill à l'Université du Québec?" *Sept-Jours*, 5 April 1969, 16.
23 Herman Buller, "McGill University and an Aroused Quebec," 9.
24 Created in March 1968 by frustrated Rassemblement pour l'indépendance nationale (RIN) militants, including Andrée Ferreri, the CIS flirted with Marxism-Leninism, before splitting a few months later following an internal ideological quarrel. The CIS-left later resolutely adopted a program of Maoist inspiration. The group merged with the FLP in June 1969. Jean-Philippe Warren, *Ils voulaient changer le monde. Le militantisme marxiste-léniniste au Québec* (Montreal: VLB éditeur, 2007).
25 The FLP was created in May 1968, after the project of transforming the RIN into a workers' party was abandoned. Jean-Philippe Warren, "Revue, club, mouvement, parti, cercle. L'histoire du mouvement de libération populaire," in *Avec ou sans Parti Pris. Le legs d'une revue*, ed. Gilles Dupuis, Karim Larose, Frédéric Rondeau and Robert Schwartzwald (Montreal: Nota Bene, 2018), 289–328.
26 A Marxist-Leninist organization, forerunner of the Communist Party of Canada (Marxist-Leninist), CPC (ML), primarily recruiting McGill students.
27 The Mouvement pour l'intégration scolaire (which changed its name to the Ligue d'intégration scolaire [LIS] in March 1969) was formed during the school conflict in Saint-Léonard, under the leadership of Raymond Lemieux.
28 Created around February 1969, the MSP had risen from the ashes of the Union générale des étudiants du Québec, which was dissolved in March 1969.
29 Marcel Chaput, "McGill, Bastille du Québec," *Journal de Montréal*, 27 March 1969, 8.
30 Instead of the usual 14,000 print-run.
31 "[McGill Student Committee supporting the March 28 demonstration]," *Bienvenue à McGill* (March 1969), 2.
32 Anonymous, "L'Opération McGill continue," 28 March 1969, 8. McMaster University, Archives & Research Collections, Stanley Gray fonds, Collection RC0263, Opération McGill collection.
33 "It is the French majority that pays for McGill, out of their taxes," Stanley Gray, "McGill: option ANTI-QUÉBEC," *Bienvenue à McGill* (March 1969), 4.

34 In response to the accusations made in the French edition of the *McGill Daily*, the McGill administration distributed a four-page leaflet in Montreal universities and CEGEPs, written only in French, in which certain figures, stated without comment, give a more nuanced picture of McGill's situation. Among others, tuition fees were said to be closer, on the whole, to those of the other Quebec universities than what the organizers of the march implied.

35 Andrew Allen, "McGill Québécois," *The McGill News* 50, no. 4 (July 1969), 13.

36 "Who's Afraid of a French McGill," *Le Sainte-Marie. Journal des étudiants du collège Sainte-Marie de Montréal* 14, no. 8, 24 March 1969, 2–3.

37 Stanley Gray, quoted by Patrick Nagle, "H. Rocke Robertson: Man in the Middle," *The McGill News* 50, no. 3 (May 1969), 8.

38 Michel Vadeboncoeur, "Des anglophones crient: McGill français!" *La Patrie*, 16 March 1969, 5.

39 Herman Buller, "McGill University and an Aroused Quebec," 10.

40 Charles Prevost, "Gray Is a Quebec Issue," *McGill Daily*, 5 March 1969, 7.

41 David Orton, "In Memoriam: Che Guevara, Communist Revolutionary," *The Georgian*, 20 October 1967, 5.

42 François Bachand, "Can Quebec Win True Independence," *The Review*, 31 January 1969, 2–3.

43 Pierre Bédard, quoted by Robert Plaskin, "McGill Marchers Argue Details Short Hours Before Showdown," *Montreal Star*, 28 March 1969, 33.

44 Mark Starowicz, "Terrorism in the Press: An Analysis of the Press Coverage of 'Operation McGill,'" *McGill Daily* 58, no. 88, 2 April 1969, 6.

45 Sophie Wollock, "March 28 – Will This Be a Day to Remember," *The Suburban* 7, no. 3, 19 March 1969, 1.

46 Madame Untel, "Ce qu'en pense ma voisine," *Montréal-Matin*, 24 March 1969, 6.

47 Federal Justice Minister John Turner declared that he had received a request from Quebec for military and RCMP assistance. Jean-Jacques Bertrand called Turner's statement "disgusting" and denied having made any request of that nature. François Trépanier, "Jean-Jacques Bertrand l'a-t-il demandé?" *La Presse*, 28 March 1969, 1.

48 Roger Lapone, quoted by André Beauvais, "Les étudiants craignent la provocation de la police!" *Montréal-Matin*, 25 March 1969, 10.

49 Anonymous, "La police interdit la vente sur la rue du journal de McGill," *La Presse*, 21 March 1969, 13.

50 Having caught police officers filming and recording their meeting, held in a room at the Cégep du Vieux-Montréal, the organizing committee members decided to seize the "spy equipment," worth $3,000. Bachand was, according to the police, injured while trying to escape, while, according to the students, he was tortured. C.J., "Arrêté en sortant de la cour," *Journal de Montréal*, 25 March 1969, 5. The charges filed against them were eventually dropped.

51 Steve Hendler, "Racism Rears Head at Meeting," *Montreal Star*, 27 March 1969, 6.

52 McGill Students' Council, quoted in "What the Mardet Hears," *The McGill News* 50, no. 3 (May 1969), 4. Leon Harris and David Dent, "McGill March Opposed by Students' Society," *The Gazette*, 27 March 1969, 1. Claude-Guy Jasmin, "Les étudiants de McGill ne sont pas d'accord," *Montréal-Matin*, 27 March 1969, 3.

53 The lnternationalists, "Statement by the lnternationalists Concerning 'Operation McGill,'" 28 March 1969, McMaster University, Archives & Research Collections, Stanley Gray fonds, Collection RC0263, Opération McGill collection.

54 Anonymous, "Under Attack – Shaw Fights for McGill," *The Gazette*, 28 March 1969, 7; Robert Shaw, "Shaw Calls for Support, Protection of McGill University," Information Office, McGill University Press Release, p. 2. McGill University Archives, Opération McGill fonds, RG2 C401.

55 Wilder Penfield, "The University," lecture delivered at the Canadian Club, reproduced in Wilder Penfield, "Université, contestation et violence," *Le Devoir*, 26 March 1969, 5.

56 Penfield, "Université, contestation et violence." "The extremists in the universities of Quebec, and those in the labour organizations, and those in the separatist organization, have a common objective. They are mad and blind only to the extent that Adolf Hitler was mad and blind." See also the 17 March 1969 edition of the *McGill Reporter* (vol. 1, no. 24) where nationalism was compared to Nazism.

57 Michael Oliver, quoted by Andrew Allen, "McGill Québécois," *The McGill News* 50, no. 4 (July 1969), ii.

58 Laurier Lapierre, "McGill et la société québécoise: être du Québec et non plus seulement au Québec," *Le Devoir*, 24 March 1969, 4.

59 H. Rocke Robertson, quoted by Patrick Nagle, "H. Rocke Robertson: Man in the Middle," 9.

60 Lucien Langlois, "N'exagérons rien," *Montréal-Matin*, 14 March 1969, 6.

61 Claude Ryan, "McGill et son avenir," *Le Devoir*, 26 March 1969, 4. See also "Québec a donné des instructions à la police," *La Presse*, 26 March 1969, 1.

62 "Selon la SSJB, rien ne justifie 2 universités de langue anglaise à Montréal," *Montréal-Matin*, 26 March 1969, 4; "La SSJB de Montréal se dissocie de la manifestation de vendredi prochain," *Le Devoir*, 26 March 1969, 9.

63 Daniel Marsolais, "McGill engage 300 gardes privés pour assurer la défense de ses bâtiments," *Le Journal de Montréal*, 28 March 1969, 4.

64 "How the Cops Handled It," *The Gazette*, 7 June 1969, 9.

65 Stan Gray, "Octobre 2 pour les étudiants du Québec," *Le Quartier Latin* 52, no. 4, 1 November 1969, 36.

66 Gray, "Octobre 2 pour les étudiants."

67 Gérald Godin, "Une 'opération McGill' contre Bishop University," *Québec-Presse*, 25 January 1970, 8.

68 Stanley Gray, quoted in "Le mouvement étudiant au Québec (1964–1972)," *Mobilisation* 4, no. 2 (October 1974), 17.

69 Warren, *Ils voulaient changer le monde.*

11

The Queering of McGill

BRIAN LEWIS

PHASE I: QUEER FRAGMENTS

The queering of McGill can be told as a tale in three parts, with notable ruptures or accelerations around 1970 and 2000. The first part is, unsurprisingly, the most elusive.[1] Of all the countless number of queer lives, thoughts, acts, and desires at McGill in the pre-liberation era, only fragments remain.

The story of George Ralph Mines is one such fragment. Mines was a newly appointed physiology professor at McGill, fresh from England, married with children, who died in his laboratory in 1914 at the age of twenty-eight, allegedly as the result of self-experimentation gone wrong. But his friend and colleague, physiologist and nutritionist V.H. Mottram, alleged in his unpublished reminiscences in the early 1960s that Mines had died by suicide. Mottram was homosexual or bisexual. If Mines did indeed kill himself, the link with Mottram has given rise to speculation that a tortured sexuality or a covered-up homosexual scandal might have been the cause.[2] Frank Campbell MacIntosh, professor of physiology at McGill, produced an unpublished report on "The Short Brilliant Career and Strange Death of G. R. Mines" in 1985, noting, "This line of speculation is one I find as distressing as any. But perhaps, all things considered, it is also as plausible as any, and more plausible than most."[3]

Another fragment comes courtesy of the acclaimed gay poet and translator Daryl Hine. He was born in 1936 in British Columbia and came to Montreal in 1954 to study at McGill.[4] In his book-length autobiographical poem, *In and Out*, written in "running accentual anapaests" and privately printed in 1975, he describes living in residence at the Old Presbyterian College (now Morrice Hall) and meeting a fellow student, Mark. Their first sexual encounter came on a skiing trip to Mont Tremblant where they bunked together in a frigid cabin in an attempt to get warm. Hine describes what happened next:

> Now the curious reader will wonder –
> the candid will frankly demand –
> to be told what we did. I don't know.
> What does anyone do at eighteen,
> without special instruction, the like
> of which neither of us had received,
> but the age-old instinctual fumble?
> The temperature of the room,
> had our tastes been more fully developed,
> prevented extensive experiment
> anyway. First, I suppose,
> we pretended to huddle together
> for warmth. Opportunity being
> the mother of liberties, we
> then began to explore our adjacent
> erogenous zones …[5]

We can imagine many such questioning young students, on and off campus, bunking together and exploring their erogenous zones or conducting more chaste relationships.

We also have evidence of the involvement of McGillians in queer social settings. A sociology student by the name of Maurice Leznoff wrote an MA thesis in 1954 titled "The Homosexual in Urban Society." Drawing on interviews, observation, and correspondence, he described in detail the gay male subculture and semi-covert bar scene in "a large cosmopolitan Canadian city" (i.e., Montreal). The study was sympathetic (Leznoff was himself gay, though this was unacknowledged in the thesis) but he framed homosexuality as "a social problem," with the researcher as a detached sociologist/anthropologist observing from the outside. Leznoff reported that gay men in lower socioeconomic groups were willing to talk but most higher-income and professional men were too fearful. He was very careful not to give any indication that McGill students and staff were in any way involved or implicated – though they surely must have been. In a later interview he recounted that some McGill professors strongly pressured him to discontinue his research lest their secret lives be exposed.[6]

Ross Higgins, in his study of collective identity formation among gay men in pre-liberation Montreal, fills in some of the gaps. Among his thirty interviewees there were a number of McGill students in the 1950s and '60s who described their experiences coming to terms with their sexuality and exploring the developing gay subculture. "Donald" (the names are pseudonyms), a Trinidadian who arrived in Montreal in 1952, lived in a rooming house full of other Caribbean students at McGill. He was not out to them, but this did not prevent him from getting spruced up to visit the gay bars on a Saturday night, nor did it stop him from conducting a clandestine love affair with another young man; they would meet in the latter's apartment during his straight roommate's absences. "Harry," the son of a Montreal lawyer, frequented the bar scene in the mid-1960s. He celebrated the completion of his McGill degree in 1966 by going with a friend to a gay dance club, where they fell victim to a police raid. They were both acquitted on a technicality; their status as middle-class university students probably helped as well. The whole ordeal was "a horrible experience," he said. "Trevor," the son of a Montreal businessman, recalled attending many memorable gay parties during the influx of draft-dodging Americans in the sixties, including those hosted by a McGill professor in his capacious two-floor apartment.[7]

Another gay McGill faculty member came to a gruesome end. James Drummond Ross, thirty-six, until recently assistant professor of philosophy, was shot to death at point-blank range outside his apartment building on Pine Avenue in the early hours of 12 October 1967 by Michael Jenkins, a twenty-eight-year-old freelance photographer, in what the *Montréal-matin* characterized as "Une triste histoire d'amour et de jalousie entre homosexuels" (A sad story of love and jealousy between homosexuals). Jenkins had been in a relationship with a twenty-year-old hotel waiter, Henry Bérubé, for some months, but the latter had recently begun an affair with Ross. Jenkins was found guilty of the murder and received a life sentence in June 1968. At McGill, the James D. Ross Prize, awarded each year "to the outstanding student in the penultimate year of the Honours Philosophy Program," commemorates the victim.[8]

Such splinters of information, running the gamut from rapture to tragedy, indicate the involvement of McGill students and faculty in the city's queer socialization. There are also hints of a proto-activism brewing on campus. "Harry" (real name Charles Hill) reported that he and his friends in and around the university lapped up any and all literature on the subject of homosexuality. He described attending a talk by a representative from the New York branch of the Mattachine Society, the leading homophile organization in the US, in the spring of 1966. He was accompanied by fellow McGill student Douglas Leopold. The event, apparently before a capacity crowd in a large auditorium, was sponsored by McGill's Pre-Med Society. Hill was later one of the founders of Toronto's first gay liberation group (the University of Toronto Homophile Association) and Leopold (nicknamed "Coco") gained celebrity as an openly gay radio and television personality in Montreal.[9]

The sixties saw the stirring of gay activism in Canada. The 1957 Wolfenden Report in Britain had concluded that it was safe to decriminalize sex in private between men over the age of twenty-one.[10] Canadian homophile organizations, such as the Association for Social Knowledge in Vancouver, and activists working through the liberal churches (beginning with the Unitarians and the Quakers), plus some elements of the media and the legal profession, drew heavily on Wolfenden to make a claim for a legal private space for homosexuals. The political response came in the form of Justice Minister Pierre Trudeau's Omnibus Bill, which included homosexuality alongside abortion, contraception, gun possession, drunk driving, and much else besides, which passed into law in the summer of 1969. In the sixties context of rising feminist demands, the anti–Vietnam War movement, and the Black civil rights struggle, a limited reform based on a clear public/private distinction seemed an increasingly sensible holding operation against the radical tide: this far and no further. True liberation only began in the wake of the Stonewall riots in Manhattan that same summer, which sparked the setting up of the Gay Liberation Front in New York and imitators elsewhere, including the Front de Libération Homosexuelle in Montreal, with the additional incitement in Quebec of the suspension of civil liberties during the 1970 October Crisis.[11] It is in this new era and context that the second phase of McGill's queer history begins – and comes alive.

PHASE II: MOBILIZING STUDENTS

A key moment arrived in the fall of 1971 when, after noticing a number of letters in the student newspaper, the *McGill Daily*, lamenting the lack of gay organizations on campus, three McGill instructors – Bruce Garside, Linda Page-Hollander, and John Southin – inaugurated a course on "Biology and Social Change" that included a segment on gay liberation. By the following September, a discussion group from this course had morphed into GAY (later Gay McGill), the first anglophone gay organization in Quebec; a crowd of 150 attended the inaugural meeting – demonstrating a real interest and a pressing need.[12] Its mission: "To provide a gay service-oriented organization" open "to all students at McGill University, and also to non-McGill gays."[13] This outreach was important. The university as an institution, with its relative autonomy and its commitment (real or token) to freedom of speech and assembly, was a logical place to begin such a venture, and McGill was not alone. The University of Toronto Homophile Association, for example, had already spawned the Community Homophile Association of Toronto at the beginning of 1971.[14] As Southin, who taught biology and was director of residences at McGill, explained, "Gay organizations are easily founded in a protected environment such as the university, but there are a lot of people off campus who often need it even more than students."[15]

GAY, initially meeting in the Redpath Library Drop-In Centre, organized study groups, consciousness-raising activities, and community services, attracting anglophones from outside the university. The burst of activity at McGill in these early years included the Gay Line telephone information service,[16] a newsletter, a gay talk show on Radio McGill, an eight-page gay supplement in the *McGill Daily* (repeated most years), sponsored lectures (including a talk in the Leacock Building by gay rights activist Frank Kameney, founder of the Mattachine Society of Washington, DC), and gay theatre (a production by the McGill Players of Mart Crowley's Broadway hit *The Boys in the Band* in 1972 and a staging of *Who's Afraid of Virginia Woolf?* in 1973, which featured a gay couple until the playwright, Edward Albee, issued a cease and desist order).[17] Kirk Kelley, who was very active in GAY, opened Gert's, the pub in the University Centre (the student union) named after Gertrude Stein, which became a popular hangout for the queer community.[18] Best of all, GAY hosted the most popular gay dances in Montreal. The first was hastily organized in November 1972, drawing a crowd of over 500, far exceeding expectations and convincing the organizers that a strong desire existed for a safe space "outside the often alienating and oppressive conditions that exist in commercial establishments catering to gays."[19] Subsequent dances drew crowds of up to 2,000 in the University Centre, including many francophones, and the Women's Committee of GAY in 1973 sponsored a women-only dance with the evocative title "Your Mother Wears Army Boots."[20]

Not all of this early activism succeeded. City-wide bodies – the Centre d'accueil homophile / Gay Community Centre and the Association homophile de Montréal / Gay Montreal Association (which were vulnerable to splits along linguistic lines) – soon took over many of the community services and the dances ran into licensing and organizational roadblocks.[21] In common with the gay liberation movement across the Western world, the treatment of women also quickly emerged as a problem. An early indication of the gender divisions within the "community" came with the first special gay issue of the *Daily*. An anonymous writer outlined the reality for women in a male-dominated society, concluding that being lesbian was the only sane and healthy response. But gay liberation, she claimed, was no place for women: it was largely male-organized and male-dominated and included among its members "some of the most incredibly sexist men I have ever met." Gay women had absolutely nothing in common with gay men except for being gay, "and that's just not enough." Women needed to organize *as* women.[22] And indeed they did over the years – through initiatives like the Gay Women of McGill[23] and the Women's Union (later the Union for Gender Empowerment), with its own lesbian caucus – often depleting the female presence at Gay McGill events in the process. As one gay male interviewee explained in the early 1980s when asked why lesbians did not attend Gay McGill meetings: they either felt too intimidated and/or experienced as much if not more chauvinism than from straight men.[24]

In addition to internal tensions, the early movement encountered homophobia. For example, right from the outset, an organization called the Society for the Repression of Homosexuality distributed flyers calling homosexuality a "repugnant mental illness" that needed to be cured through psychiatric intervention. Then there was a lecture by the American psychologist Bruno Bettelheim, who informed his listeners that homosexuals were narcissists driven by fear of the other sex, and was duly barracked by audience members.[25] A third example was the treatment of Bruce Garside, who taught philosophy at McGill. His outspoken gay activism, including pieces in the student press,[26] did not find favour with the university administration and, encouraged to leave, he was paid off with a year's salary. He described his experiences at McGill in a revealing article shortly after this "terminal sabbatical" came to an end. McGill, he wrote, was typical of liberal universities that had learned the lessons of the sixties well: avoid confrontation and ignore disruptive forces as much as possible until they collapse or are quietly terminated. The reality of this "repressive tolerance" was painfully evident: "Why do you suppose that in the entire teaching staff only two people have admitted to being gay and similarly, that among students only a minuscule percentage of gays have come out? Why do you encounter more gay faculty and students at downtown bars than at the meetings or dances of Gay McGill? The reason is clear: gays feel more comfortable off campus." This neatly reversed the initial justification for the dances that gays felt more at ease at McGill than in commercial establishments.

This repressive tolerance was no better in Garside's own department. His colleagues greeted his articles on gay liberation in the *Daily* with embarrassed silence or covert hostility: "Mostly from graduate students I learned that I was regarded by other professors in the department as immoral, self-indulgent and crazy." Only after his gay activism began did voices suggest that his academic performance was unsatisfactory. And one colleague whom he asked for a letter of recommendation said that he would have to distinguish between his academic and moral qualifications. Garside's conclusion was clear: universities, having emerged from the storms of the sixties virtually unchanged, were not going to serve as vehicles for radical social change, and that he was best out of academia. "Despite the loss of some friends, professional status and financial security," he wrote, "I feel that I have emerged from the turmoils of coming out as a gay at McGill with my identity firmly intact. It is unfortunate that one must survive a university."[27]

Garside used his severance money to start a new venture (along with his boyfriend, Will Aitken, and John Southin): the founding in 1973 of L'Androgyne, Quebec's first LGBTQ+ bookstore.[28] Aitken, later a writer, journalist, film critic, and teacher of film studies at Dawson College, had had his own negative experiences at McGill. He arrived from Indiana in 1972 to write an MA thesis in the English Department on the novels of Christopher Isherwood, maybe the first openly queer thesis written in Canada. And there, buried on pages 99–100 of the thesis, in a discussion of Isherwood's alter ego George in the novel *A Single Man*, Aitken outs himself with these words:

> Concerning oneself, there is the awareness of a response to the novel that is as much emotional as it is critical: as a homosexual one repeatedly experiences the delighted shock of recognition on nearly every page of the novel; as an outsider observing an

> outsider observe, one snarls with George at heterosexuals, one is aroused by the tennis match George cruises, one sees one's own experiences and frustrations and gleeful aggressions against the majority confirmed, amplified and magnificently articulated by George. And one feels boundless admiration for him and his creator because they have made it, they are outsiders, observers, exiles from objective reality, and they have survived.[29]

Aitken sent a copy to Isherwood, who wrote back, "I do think that you have found an original approach, and justified it." The internal examiner judged the thesis to be "excellent" but the external examiner, clearly unpersuaded by Aitken's Freudian analysis, deemed it "unsatisfactory" and demanded it be rewritten before it could pass. In his report, the external examiner also questioned the relevance of Aitken's self-outing. This prompted Aitken to respond with a lawyer's letter charging that there was strong evidence that the examiner's judgment "was coloured by his personal bias of our client's admitted lifeview." The examiner fired back with a lawyer's letter of his own threatening legal action if Aitken did not withdraw his "slanderous and libellous" statements.

The tense stand-off, involving multiple meetings and threats to generate adverse publicity for the university, was ultimately resolved by the submission of the thesis to an alternative examiner, who passed it.[30] "They only backed down after I hired a lawyer," Aitken relates in a letter to the *McGill Tribune* in 2018, "and with the help of many friends made their bigoted behavior an issue in the media." He did finally receive his MA. But, he adds, "I never received an apology from the McGill English department or from the university itself."[31] A half century on, the affair clearly still rankles.

Of course, it was not only on campus that McGillians experienced homophobia. The university, with its porous boundaries in a prime downtown location, has never operated in isolation from the city, and the story of Saleem Kidwai is a case in point. He already had a tenured teaching position in medieval and Mughal history at Delhi University, but he took a leave of absence in 1976, at the age of twenty-five, to do a PhD at McGill. His motivation, which he could not divulge to his colleagues at home, was to seek out what he imagined to be the newly liberated gay world of North America. On arrival, he made tentative forays into gay establishments. A university handbook suggested that the Peel Pub was a place for gays, but he found it uncomfortable and unwelcoming. Friends introduced him instead to the bars in the vicinity of Stanley Street, Montreal's queer hub before the development in the 1980s of the Gay Village on St Catherine Street East. One of these establishments on Stanley contained the Mystique bar in the basement and Truxx (catering mostly to the "leather-Levis crowd") on top. Kidwai was in Truxx on the night that it was raided by police in October 1977.

The Truxx raid ranks as perhaps the most shocking and egregious display of institutionalized homophobia and bigotry by Mayor Jean Drapeau's morality police. The 146 men herded up, detained in squalid conditions, processed, and subjected to humiliating rectal swabbing were each charged with "being a found-in in a bawdy house." The queer community erupted onto the streets the following day and, partly in consequence, by the end of the year René Lévesque's Parti Québécois government was to ban discrimination on the basis of sexual orientation. But the persecution of the Truxx "found-ins" continued. Kidwai received $110 from the McGill students' union for his legal defence, which paid for the services of a sympathetic lawyer; but the whole miserable experience of arrest, court appearances, and threats of deportation was profoundly traumatizing. Disillusioned by the promise of Western gay liberation, he returned to Delhi University after three years, abandoning his PhD; he did not find out that the charges had been dropped until 1984. McGill and Canada's loss was India's gain: back home, he carved out a successful career as a scholar of the Mughal Empire, Hindustani classical music, and Urdu literature – and, from the 1990s, he became a leading gay rights activist. He is best known for his ground-breaking anthology (with Ruth Vanita), *Same-Sex Love in India: Readings from Literature and History*.[32]

Kidwai's story is a reminder, if any were needed, that McGill and Montreal cannot be viewed in isolation but rather were part of the broader struggle for gay rights in a deeply hostile environment. Nevertheless, McGill's queer students, with the support of the student press, squared up to this hostility and built on the initiatives of the seventies to create a (usually) vibrant and thriving community (the energy levels fluctuated, as so often happens with student organizations subject to a rapid changeover of people and operating only in term-time). Gay McGill itself addressed the perception that it was a safe space simply for gay, cis males by a phased adoption of a more inclusive name and mission. Gay McGill became GALOM (Gays and Lesbians of McGill) in 1983, which morphed into LGBM (Lesbians,

Gays, and Bisexuals of McGill) in 1992, LGBTM (Lesbians, Gays, Bisexuals, and Transsexuals of McGill) in 1995, and the all-embracing Queer McGill later in the decade, which is where the name rests.[33] To underline its exemplary openness, Queer McGill's most recent mission statement reads, "Queer is a broad term that includes anyone who chooses to identify with it." While disavowing any claim to completeness, it lists no fewer than sixty-four different self-identities, insists that "queerness goes beyond identity categories and therefore beyond what is possible to list," and "welcomes any and all individuals, including those whose identities do not fit into Western conceptions of gender and sexuality, whether or not they identify as queer."[34]

Queer McGill (like its predecessors) has always functioned as a support group blended with political activism, consciousness-raising, and fun. GALOM in the mid-1980s, for example, had four main components: a coming-out group, an AIDS committee, a women's or lesbian caucus, and a dance committee.[35] One initiative, along with other Montreal universities, was Lesbian & Gay Awareness Week[36] to "give straights an opportunity to de-mystify 'queerness,'" and, as GALOM president Paul Hopkirk explained it, "to make gays and lesbians familiar."[37] The lesbian caucus meanwhile aimed to provide a comfortable environment for women thinking of coming out or who were already out.[38] (The arrival on the scene of *Dykes on Mykes* on CKUT campus radio in 1987 was also integral to many young lesbians coming out, with shows aiming to "normalize" lesbianism by interviewing lesbian filmmakers, plumbers, hockey players, business women, and so on.[39]) And the AIDS committee adopted an ambitious mandate to provide counselling, to set up a resource centre, to counteract the mainstream media, to deal with a potentially hostile public, and throughout it all to remain sex positive ("to eroticise other parts of the body").[40]

Each cohort of students, bolstered by discussion forums such as the *Homo Show* (later *Queercorps*) on CKUT radio, brought the pressing concerns of the moment to the table. One such issue was spirited opposition in the 1990s to a "homophobic and discriminatory" question on the Canadian Red Cross blood donor questionnaire that prevented most gay men from giving blood: "If a male, have you ever had sex with another male, even once?"[41] Street-theatre stunts and demonstrations organized by Queer McGill (and, later, by a more radical group with the imaginative name the Second Cumming, which targeted Héma-Québec) succeeded in disrupting and even suspending the blood drives.[42] This is just one indication of the full-throated political activism that has characterized Queer McGill née GAY from its inception until today. To quote again from its current mission statement: "QM shall carry out its workings from an anti-oppressive and intersectional feminist orientation, including, but not limited to, being anti-racist, anti-classist, anti-homophobic, anti-transphobic, anti-cissexist, anti-ageist, anti-ableist, anti-colonial and anti-sizeist, with full respect for, and without discrimination against, individuals who are, but not limited to, queer."[43]

PHASE III: QUEERING THE INSTITUTION

If student-led activism clearly established roots in the early post-Stonewall decades, roots that have grown and proved resilient, the next phase – the institutional queering of McGill – did not make much headway before the turn of the century. The history of LAGEM (Lesbian and Gay Employees of McGill) is instructive here. Richard Cooper and Robert Head founded it in February 1990 to address homophobia on campus and to fight discrimination. Cooper, who taught courses on ethics and alternative sexualities in the Faculty of Religious Studies, was spurred to action by his suspicion that his open sexuality had influenced a decision not to renew his contract. Both he and Head were to lodge complaints against McGill with the Quebec Human Rights Commission for discrimination on the grounds of sexual orientation.[44] Head, who worked in Admissions and was the inaugural chair of LAGEM, claimed that "It was the world's first gay and lesbian staff organization, as far as I know."[45] But, at the outset, he reported negative comments from university administrators and academics. "Traditionally," he said, "universities are not generally receptive to openly gay or lesbian staff, and McGill is no exception." Finding members was a challenge, since people had a "general fear of reprisal from the university if they become involved."[46] McGill did not officially recognize the organization, expressing the opinion that all employees were already adequately represented by general staff associations, and denied LAGEM's request to use the McGill logo or letterhead.

This denial was one of a catalogue of grievances that Carl Wilson, a writer for the *McGill Daily*, marshalled against McGill in the fall of 1990. He claimed that McGill was years behind many other universities when it came to progressive ideas; its failure "to cleanse itself of homophobia" was especially lamentable. Dalhousie, York, Acadia, and the University of British Columbia had introduced anti-discrimination measures for gay and lesbian staff and students; McGill had not. Other universities had extensive course offerings in gay and lesbian studies; where were McGill's? Concordia had an AIDS policy; McGill did not, in spite of its new AIDS Centre. He concluded: "It's almost as though the last two decades of gay and lesbian liberation and increasing social acceptance ... never happened. It's as if ten years of AIDS activism and education had never penetrated the Roddick Gates ... McGill still caters to a shrinking coven of bigots whose ideas haven't changed since they were in bobby sox and Fabian hairdos."[47]

Whether through bigotry or institutional inertia or a combination of both, Official McGill was certainly not at the forefront of change. One issue pushed by LAGEM was the right of members of the McGill community, in advertising with Off-Campus Housing, to state a preference for "gay/lesbian positive" housemates.[48] On legal advice, the dean of students refused to allow this on the grounds that it was "exclusionary." But, as critics pointed out, other preferences – male or female, international, vegetarian, non-smoking – were allowed.[49] Another issue was McGill's refusal to consider extending staff spousal benefits to same-sex couples, including pension plans, life insurance, health and dental care, and tuition assistance afforded to heterosexuals in common-law or other family arrangements. LAGEM lobbied for these from its inception and Sam Noumoff, professor of economics and long-standing thorn in the flesh of the McGill administration, raised the question in senate.[50]

This time the blunt refusal did not hold: within a year the administration relented, demonstrating a capacity for judicious flexibility in the face of strong opposition and, no doubt, the example of peer institutions. Any same-sex employees who had lived as a couple for at least three years were to be entitled to the same benefits as common-law spouses. In spite of the delay, Noumoff welcomed the fact that the university had ultimately responded positively. Head was less charitable: "It's a sick joke on the part of University administrators to claim to be 'pleased' to make such an announcement," he said. "They steadfastly refused to discuss same-sex spouse benefits with LAGEM."[51]

The foot-dragging if not outright reaction of these years is summed up well by Olivia Jensen, professor in the Department of Earth and Planetary Sciences, who was a trans trailblazer at McGill. Oliver, as she then was, had arrived in 1973, married and fathered a family, then transitioned at the end of the 1980s. McGill at the time, she says, was "an insular place that wasn't welcoming to differences amongst its members. It had a very conservative outlook." On her first day at McGill as Olivia, in 1989, her chair could not really talk about it, a colleague invited her to lunch, and the janitor, initially perplexed, quickly accepted the new reality – perhaps a typical range of reactions. "My colleagues at McGill have been proper and good," she recounted in a 1995 interview, "[but] they haven't gone out of their way to accommodate me ... It's a very subtle discrimination." Unlike many of her peers who sought invisibility after transitioning, Jensen's mantra was always "pure defiance and no apologies." In that same 1995 interview, she said, "I want [people] to read a transexual woman that commands immediate respect," adding, "I don't want to be hidden." She joined LAGEM in the early 1990s, recalling it to be a very small group that would meet at Thomson House but enter by the backdoor so as not to be seen. She, by contrast, used the front door: "I refused to be closeted after my transition and wanted to be seen as me." She made a point of being a fixture in the Faculty Club, often seen as the stuffiest and most establishment of McGill's institutions. And, from the mid-1990s, she routinely guest-lectured about her trans identity and personal history in the Psychology Department's "Human Sexuality and Its Problems" course.[52]

This was when I arrived at McGill, in 1995. A newly minted but still closeted assistant professor in history, at the age of thirty I was at last ready to come out. I thought I would meet gay and lesbian colleagues in my department. There were none. I thought I would join the faculty gay and lesbian association. None existed. I was aware of Gay McGill (or whatever it then called itself), but that was principally for students. I came across an email address for LAGEM and sent off a hopeful message. There was no response. The organization was still alive, just about, but clearly struggling and with a limited membership. The then president, Raynald Lapage, lamented that it was still not easy for staff to come out, that employees "tend to keep a low profile," and "I think the higher they go into the hierarchy, especially at McGill, the less you're going to hear about it."[53]

So, over the next few years, while gradually coming out to my McGill friends and colleagues, I found a gay life off campus: the Montreal Gay Village was at its zenith and it became my playground. It is not that I encountered any kind of hostility at the university.

My colleague Suzanne Morton, professor of Canadian history, reports that, whenever she included queer material in her Canadian history survey classes in the 1990s, the jocks at the back of the room would make a show of walking out en masse. But I included queer material in my classes too, and did not get any such reaction. The closest to homophobia I experienced was a remark from a senior history colleague, relayed to me by a leading member of the administration around 2003: "I think the new man, Lewis [I had been there eight years and was chair of the department by then; whatever] is one of the Oscar Wilde sort." Whether he intended it or not, his remark channelled E.M. Forster's eponymous character in his novel *Maurice*: "I'm an unspeakable of the Oscar Wilde sort."[54]

Aside from that, there was very little antagonism. Queer McGill was active and engaged. In corners of the campus excellent queer work was being done, for example by scholars in the English Department, the Women's Studies program, the McGill Centre for Research and Teaching on Women, and the Faculty of Education. Ross Higgins, co-founder in 1983 of the Archives gaies du Québec, was writing his PhD thesis in the Anthropology Department on pre-liberation homosexuality in Montreal.[55] Dr Norbert (Nobby) Gilmore and others in the Faculty of Medicine were doing ground-breaking work studying and helping people with HIV/AIDS.[56] The School of Social Work was undertaking a number of significant initiatives, most notably Project Interaction, the result of student pressure in 1999, which brought faculty, students, and community activists together in a collaborative effort to transform the design and delivery of social services to the LGBTQ+ community while working towards the elimination of oppression. Adjunct Professor Bill Ryan (founder in 1989 of Projet 10 for Montreal youths questioning their sexual orientation and gender identity) and Professor Shari Brotman, scholar of social justice and queer rights, were especially influential in furthering a queer agenda in social work.[57] All this was important. Even so, the queer presence on campus above the level of the students was muted. Endeavours were often isolated, sporadic, short-lived, and ill-funded. The prevailing and complacent mood of straight colleagues and the higher administration seemed to be, with shoulder-shrugging disdain, "We don't necessarily have a problem with homosexuality, but do we really have to talk about it?"

In retrospect, the speed of the change in attitude (or, at least, the new social unacceptability of performative homophobia) in the few years around the millennium is remarkable – something flipped, just as it did around 1970. To borrow from Ernest Hemingway on bankruptcy, it came gradually, then suddenly. Gradually, the radiation of gay liberationist zeal from Stonewall onwards is a vital part of the story: three decades of grassroots organizing, self-help, and consciousness-raising; of militancy and resistance to police oppression;[58] of annual Pride parades; and of mobilization in the face of AIDS. Coming out was crucial in all of this: it was not as easy to demonize dykes and fags when they were family members, friends, colleagues, neighbours, students, or prominent personalities – out, open, and standing proud. But other big factors were at play as well in the slog towards gay equality. To name just a few: the greater liberalization of ideas towards sex since the 1960s; the collapse of organized religion; the rise of tertiary education – a huge expansion in the numbers of those exposed to progressive ideals at university; the incremental introduction of gay civil rights legislation by successive governments after 1977, even before it was a popular or vote-winning cause; the elaboration of a progressive variant on the prevailing neoliberal, meritocratic consensus, preaching that not a single person could be wasted, of whatever gender, ethnicity, or sexual orientation;[59] and the amorality of capitalism – big and small business, gay-owned or straight, coming to realize that there was money to be made from the pink dollar, both in cultivating queer consumers and, increasingly, in branding one's enterprise as tolerant and inclusive.

McGill, too, in sync with most other North American universities (slower than some – like Concordia – faster than others), rebranded itself in the decades-long transition from hostility to unease to tolerance to inclusion – and recognized the need for the brand to be *seen* as inclusive. All this built up gradually. Pinpointing a sudden tipping point to explain the greater queer institutional presence at McGill is more arbitrary, but a plausible contender is a moment in 2000 when PhD candidate and student senator Stephen Déry, spurred on by a number of homophobic incidents including the ripping down of posters advertising a campus gay dance and the off-campus queer-bashing of a McGill student, raised the question in senate as to whether the Joint Senate-Board Committee on Equity (JSBCE) had ever discussed queer issues. It had not. After several months of discussion, an ad hoc Workgroup on Homophobia at McGill, headed by Professor Estelle Hopmeyer from Social Work, was approved. Within a year this morphed into the JSBCE Subcommittee on Queer People, chaired by Gregg Blachford, the director of the Career and Placement Service and a veteran of gay liberation battles in Sydney and London, with the task of addressing "issues of representation, inclusion and support of LGBT students, staff and faculty at McGill University with respect to academic and non-academic life on campus."[60]

Over the next few years, the Subcommittee's successful campaigns included an interdisciplinary Minor in Sexual Diversity Studies,[61] a Safe Space Program, the addition of preferred names on class lists, a change to the employment equity policy to include "people of minority sexual orientations and gender identities," and gender-inclusive washrooms.[62] Such examples of receptivity in the higher administration, both symbolic and substantive, began to come thick and fast. One could point to then Principal Heather Munroe-Blum attending the Queerequity Subcommittee's "Return to the Rainbow" annual Homecoming celebrations, or the setting up of the Office of Social Equity and Diversity Education (SEDE), or the inauguration of the Institute for Gender, Sexuality and Feminist Studies, or the appointment of Robert Leckey, a former chair of the Queerequity Subcommittee and of EGALE Canada, to be dean of law[63] – in effect, queer penetration to the heart of the McGill establishment, unthinkable just a few years before – or the setting up of a dedicated McGill Equity Team, "embracing and championing equity, diversity, and inclusion across our university."[64]

Two communications from the McGill Provost's Office at the time of writing indicate how far we have come. The first was in response to a demonstration just outside campus, in September 2023, by a group calling itself the "1 Million March 4 Children" opposed to the discussion of sexuality and gender identity in schools. Provost Christopher Manfredi wrote, "We realize that this would have caused distress for some. Please know that McGill remains deeply committed to equity and to supporting all the members of its community, including for 2SLGBTQ+ peoples and communities."[65] This followed a fracas at the start of the year when gay legal scholar Robert Wintemute, who advocates the divorce of LGB from T, generated such outrage that a combined protest including trans activists, RadLaw McGill, and Queer McGill prevented him from speaking at the Law Faculty.[66]

The second provostial intervention, in October 2023, drew attention to McGill's Queer History Month, an annual event since 2018. It ended with this affirmation: "While QHM is a time of pride and celebration, it is also a moment to take stock in our efforts to challenge transphobia, biphobia, and homophobia and to foster a robust sense of belonging for all within our campus community, regardless of gender or sexual identity." It acknowledged the important strides forward thanks to the work of the Queerequity Subcommittee, Queer McGill, the McGill Equity Team, and the McGill Queer Alumni Association, but also that "our work is far from done, especially in the wake of protests and political mobilization against gender identity equality, and we are accelerating our efforts to build an inclusive campus environment where persons of all genders and sexual orientations can flourish."[67]

This is all very welcome; but nobody should be complacent. Hard-won progress is not assured, especially in the world's current febrile climate. It is difficult to imagine a return to the homophobia of the 1970s and 1980s or to institutional resistance, inertia, and indifference. But if people of good will, through reason and education, are to prevail, eternal vigilance is required to maintain and extend McGill's new status as a queer-positive space. The queer revolution can, must, and will continue.

NOTES

I am grateful to Gregg Blachford and Ross Higgins for many pointers, leads, and corrections in the research and writing of this chapter, and to Will Aitken, Shari Brotman, Olivia Jensen, Suzanne Morton, Don Nerbas, and Lloyd Whitesell for their helpful feedback. I have drawn freely on "LGBTQIA2S+ McGill Student, Faculty, and Staff Activism," an excellent resource compiled from multiple archives by Alex Ketchum and Jacob Williams, https://airtable.com/apptSAju1uUEdBdq3/shrQucodb9IBIWKhX/tbl9ZpbTTUbXwBZbp, accessed 6 October 2023. Any cited text from this collection is indicated with an asterisk [*].

1 It is notable, for example, that Dominic Dagenais has no references to McGill in his important book, *Grossières indécences: Pratiques et identités homosexuelles à Montréal, 1880–1929* (Montreal and Kingston: McGill-Queen's University Press, 2020). I am grateful to Dagenais for confirming via email correspondence, 24 October 2023, that he found nothing related to McGill in the court records.

2 I owe this information to my MA student, Robert Montalvo-West, "Death in the Archive: Professor Mines and the Sexuality of Secret Institutional Histories" (MA major research paper, Department of History and

Classical Studies, McGill University, 2020). Mottram's unpublished autobiography, quoted by Montalvo-West, is in the Wellcome Collection, London, GC/151/7/1. See also Leon Glass, John Orlowski, and Alvin Shrier, "Historical Note on the Untimely Passing of George Ralph Mines," *Journal of Physiology*, 28 April 2016, accessed 16 February 2024, https://doi.org/10.1113/JP272232.

3 McGill University Archives, CA OSLER P127-1, box 389, folder 2, Frank Campbell McIntosh, "The Short Brilliant Career and Strange Death of G.R. Mines," p. 18, quoted by Montalvo-West, "Death in the Archive," 21.

4 Leslie Kaufman, obituary of Hine, *New York Times*, 24 August 2012.

5 Daryl Hine, *In and Out: A Confessional Poem* (New York: Alfred A. Knopf, 1989), 30 and *passim*. I am grateful to Lloyd Whitesell for alerting me to this text.

6 Maurice Leznoff, "The Homosexual in Urban Society" (MA thesis, McGill University, 1954); Line Chamberland and Catherine Garneau, "Entrevue avec Ross Higgins, anthropologue et cofondateur des Archives gaies du Québec," *Bulletin d'histoire politique* 16, no. 3 (Spring 2008): 28; Ross Higgins, "A Sense of Belonging: Pre-Liberation Space, Symbolics, and Leadership in Gay Montreal" (PhD diss., Department of Anthropology, McGill University, 1997), 318. See also Maurice Leznoff and William A. Westley, "The Homosexual Community," *Social Problems* 3, no. 4 (Apr. 1956): 257–63.

7 Higgins, "A Sense of Belonging," 151, 175, 189–90, 329, 398–9, 401.

8 Kristian Gravenor, "How a Splashy, Hushed-up, Gay Lovers Triangle Changed History," *Coolopolis Montreal,* 27 December 2016, accessed 31 January 2024, http://coolopolis.blogspot.com/2016/12/how-splashy-hushed-up-gay-lovers.html; *Montréal-matin*, 19 October 1967, 3; La *Presse*, 19 October 1967, 6; 7 June 1968, 11; "McGill Undergraduate Scholarships and Awards 2022/23," 44; Alastair McKinnon, obituary of Ross, *Proceedings and Addresses of the American Philosophical Association* 42 (1968–69): 177. I am grateful to Kristian Gravenor for his information and insights regarding this story.

9 Higgins, "A Sense of Belonging," 175, 377–8; Canadian Lesbian and Gay Archives, Charles Hill papers, 82-015/01, quoted by Donald W. McLeod, *Lesbian and Gay Liberation in Canada: A Selected Annotated Chronology, 1964–1975* (Toronto: ECW Press/Homewood Books, 1996), 14; Tommy Schnurmacher, obituary of Leonard, *Montreal Gazette*, 6 April 1993.

10 See Brian Lewis, *Wolfenden's Witnesses: Homosexuality in Postwar Britain* (Houndmills, Basingstoke, UK: Palgrave Macmillan, 2016).
11 See Gary Kinsman, *The Regulation of Desire: Homo and Hetero Sexualities*, 2nd ed. (Montreal: Black Rose Books, 1996), chs. 8–9; Julie Podmore, "From Contestation to Incorporation: LGBT Activism and Urban Politics in Montreal," in *Queer Mobilizations: Social Movement Activism and Canadian Public Policy*, ed. Manon Tremblay (Vancouver: UBC Press, 2015), 188–9.
12 McLeod, *Lesbian and Gay Liberation*, 80, 105; Ralph Elawani, "L'Androgyne: A Gay Place to Be," *Lettres québécoises* 178 (Fall 2020): 41.
13 GAY constitution [September 1972] [*].
14 Jearld Moldenhauer and Bob Wallace, "History: Toronto & Vancouver," *McGill Daily*, gay special edition, 3 [*]; Michael Chervin, Shari Brotman, Bill Ryan, and Heather Mullin, "Transforming Schools of Social Work into Spaces of Social Action: A Critical Exploration of Project Interaction, the Gay, Lesbian, Bisexual and Two-Spirit Initiative of McGill University's School of Social Work," *Canadian Journal of Community Mental Health* (2009): 72.
15 "*Old McGill* talks to Director of Residences John Southin," *Yearbook*, 1974 [*].
16 For the history, see Canadian Association of Education and Outreach Québec, "History of Gay Line & CAEO Québec," accessed 4 February 2024, https://caeoquebec.org/gay-line/.
17 *McGill Daily*, 24 Oct. 1972 [*]; McLeod, *Lesbian and Gay Liberation*, 105–6, 111, 113, 117–8; *Montreal Gazette*, 29 March 1972, 21; Ross Higgins, "Maxim Mazumdar Synopsis for the Montreal Desi Queer History Project," 13 April 2022.
18 Carl Wilson, *McGill Daily*, 28 February 1991 [*].
19 Frank Brayton, *McGill Daily*, 20 November 1972 [*]; "Some Initial Steps Towards Gay Liberation," *McGill Daily*, gay special edition, 24 November 1972, 7 [*].
20 McLeod, *Lesbian and Gay Liberation*, 110, 118.
21 McLeod, *Lesbian and Gay Liberation*, 106, 150, 162–3; *Montreal Gay Times* 1, no. 2, 4 April 1975, 3 [*]; *McGill Daily*, 6 November 1975 [*].
22 [Anon.], "We Are Women First and Foremost," *McGill Daily*, gay special edition, 24 November 1972, 4 [*].
23 *McGill Daily*, 15 February 1978, 3 [*]; Donald W. McLeod, *Lesbian and Gay Liberation in Canada: A Selected Annotated Chronology 1976–1981* (Toronto: Homewood Books, 2017).

24 *McGill Daily*, 10 February 1983 [*]; Gerald Steen, "An Interview with Robby: A Member of Gay McGill," 24 March 1983 (for Field Methods in Sociology, taught by Prof. Prue Rains) [*].
25 McLeod, *Lesbian and Gay Liberation*, 105, 155.
26 For example, Garside, "The Politics of Gay Liberation: Reform or Revolution?," *McGill Daily*, gay special edition, 24 November 1972, 2 [*].
27 Bruce Garside, "Surviving the McGill Philosophy – A Gay Goodbye," *McGill Daily*, 26 September 1974, 3 [*]; obituary, *Montreal Gazette* online, 2 July 2024.
28 Elawani, "L'Androgyne," 40–2.
29 Will Aitken, "Narcissus Observed and Observing: The Novels of Christopher Isherwood" (MA thesis, Department of English, McGill University, 1974), 99–100.
30 The correspondence (including the letter from Isherwood, 9 October 1974), examiners' reports, statements, and lawyers' letters can be found in "Will Aitken's Personal Collection" [*].
31 *McGill Tribune*, 29 October 2018. I am grateful to Will Aitken for clarifying certain points via email correspondence, 9 October 2023.
32 Saleem Kidwai, "Wrong Place Wrong Time: A Brush with Gay History," *Trikone Magazine* 18, no. 2 (June 2003): 9; obituary, *Washington Post*, 2 September 2021; Vanita and Kidwai, eds, *Same-Sex Love in India: Readings from Literature and History* (New York: Palgrave, 2000); Podmore, "From Contestation to Incorporation," 190.
33 GALOM Constitution, 5 October 1983 [*]; Melanie Newton, *McGill Daily*, 13 November 1995 [*].
34 "Constitution of Queer McGill," 7 April 2020, 3–4, accessed 6 October 2023, https://5d45091d-4fd2-4a4a-b44a-76a29e14b1e0.filesusr.com/ugd/108f5d_0a31354c3102420eb506f5ab9a8a1118.pdf.
35 *McGill Daily*, 30 September 1985, 5 [*].
36 Schedule for "Lesbian & Gay Awareness Week," 15–22 October 1983 [*].
37 *McGill Daily*, 4 February 1985 [*].
38 *McGill Daily*, 12 November 1986 [*].
39 Deborah VanSlet, *Statik*, Spring 1996 [*].
40 "Towards a Statement of Purpose," McGill AIDS Committee, [1 January 1985] [*].
41 *Montreal Gazette*, 19 March 2024; QM archive, AIDS flyer by LBGM, c. February/March 1994 [*]; Jérôme Lévesque, *McGill Daily Français*, 8 October 1996 [*].

42 Cheryl Chan, *Montreal Gazette*, 30 September 1997 [*]; Sarah Colgrave, *McGill Daily*, 30 January 2006 [*]; Niall Mackay Roberts, *McGill Tribune*, 7 February 2006 [*].
43 "Constitution of Queer McGill," 7 April 2020, 4.
44 Michael Rottmayer, *McGill Daily*, 15 January 1992 [*].
45 Robin LeBaron, *McGill Daily*, 18 September 1891 [*].
46 *McGill Tribune*, February 27–March 5, 1990 [*].
47 Carl Wilson, *McGill Daily*, 12 September 1990 [*].
48 Robert Head, copy of letter to Ms M. Aikens, coordinator of Off-Campus Housing, *McGill Daily*, 1 October 1990 [*].
49 Kathleen Hickey, *McGill Daily*, 3 December 1990 [*].
50 Neelam Sandhu, *McGill Daily*, 3 December 1990 [*].
51 Robin LeBaron, *McGill Daily*, 7 October 1991 [*].
52 "Conversation with Prof. Olivia Jensen," McGill Blogs: Géoblog, 12 April 2021; Derek Fung, *McGill Daily*, 13 November 1995 [*].
53 Jacqueline Reis, *McGill Daily*, 13 November 1995 [*].
54 E.M. Forster, *Maurice* (RosettaBooks e-edition, 2015), 116.
55 Higgins's thesis, "A Sense of Belonging," was published in French as *De la clandestinité à l'affirmation: pour une histoire de la communauté gaie montréalaise* (Montreal: Comeau et Nadeau, 1999).
56 "McGill Bicentennial: Dr. Norbert Gilmore," accessed 31 January 2024, https://200.mcgill.ca/unsung-heroes/dr-norbert-gilmore/.
57 Chervin et al., "Transforming Schools of Social Work," 73–9, 83n5; Bill Ryan and Shari Brotman, "Queer McGill," *Service social* 66, no. 1 (2020): 31–3; Fraser Hall, *McGill Daily*, 20 March 2000 [*].
58 See, for example, Podmore, "From Contestation to Incorporation," 194–6.
59 See Michael J. Sandel, *The Tyranny of Merit: What's Become of the Common Good?* (London: Penguin, 2021).
60 McGill Subcommittee on Queer People, "The Early History of the Subcommittee on Queer People," accessed 27 March 2025, https://www.mcgill.ca/queerequity/history; Gregg Blachford, "A Gay Man's Story in Snapshots," accessed 6 October 2023, https://greggblachford.com/.
61 For the record, as an openly gay department chair (the first such, at least according to the *McGill Daily*, 16 September 2002, 1, and Hillary Kaell, "History Chair Comes Out with It," 19), I chaired the steering committee for this "queering of the curriculum" (with El Chenier in the first year, before their departure for Simon Fraser University), and then served for

two terms as the first chair of "Sex Div." My seminar, HIST 433: British Queer History, was the first course on campus to have "queer" in its title.

62 Andrea Clegg, "A History of Gender-Inclusive Washrooms," *McGill Reporter*, 27 September 2023.

63 *McGill Reporter*, 22 April 2016.

64 Equity at McGill home page, accessed 5 October 2023, https://www.mcgill.ca/equity/.

65 *Montreal Gazette*, 20 September 2023; email to all McGill staff and students from Provost Manfredi, 22 September 2023.

66 *Montreal Gazette,* 11 January 2023; "Open Letter on McGill's Platforming of TERFS," 10 January 2023, accessed 6 October 2023, https://docs.google.com/document/d/1tRxRwYvrsT4vvYs85ATIzcDCtSIpyoYggpSKAkYDbMc/edit?pli=1; Tynan Jarrett, "On Transgender Demands and Other 'Hysteria,'" Metonymy Press blog, 20 January 2023, accessed 6 October 2023, https://metonymypress.com/transgender-demands-hysteria/.

67 Email to all McGill staff and students from Provost Manfredi, 2 October 2023.

Epilogue

WENDELL NII LARYEA ADJETEY

The history of the elite university is the history of the state. The university – in its modern, neoliberal form – is a microcosm of state authority with its flag and symbols, anthem and fight songs, power politics, capital accumulation for its endowment, urban "renewal" and land dispossession, and stratification along racial, class, gender, and, in McGill University's case, linguistic lines. In a world order in which Western imperialism and (settler) colonialism not only have dominated, but also shaped global politics for centuries, the university and its history are, truly, the history of how ivory tower ideas can sanction militarism, White domination, and other forms of exploitation and inequity. The university also embodies the symbiotic relationship between hard power and soft power. In a liberal democracy, or a society that aspires to democratic ideals, such as the rule of law, constitutional rights of citizens, and public accountability, understanding the rhythms of the university and the ways that its power ebbs and flows during times of peace and war, during times of prosperity and austerity, and during times of social unrest and repression can help unlock historians' most pressing questions. Like other modern global institutions, McGill can be a force of good or source of pain – or both. To these ends, the university is a remarkable capsule of social history, intellectual history, political history, and military history.

McGill in History is a historiographical gem and a fabulous testament to the modern university as a site for historical analysis. As the editors attest, this volume is not intended to provide a comprehensive history of McGill University, but to explore various threads that can illuminate the ways that a powerful institution changes over time and the underlining dynamics and implications of these changes. History, with all its warts and vexing twists and turns, is consequential. The past, present, and posterity of an elite university like McGill are imprinted in the textual archive and on the bodily archive. The trauma of those who bear the effects of McGill's policies is far reaching. So, too, on balance, is the social good derived from rigorous, ethical, humane university research and instruction.

That *McGill in History* is a critical, commemorative work of scholarship, not a work of celebration, underscores the seriousness with which one must confront this volume. For this reason, scholars must not retreat from scrutinizing history that is unflattering. As the contributors have shown, historians – and the institutions in which they work – must not recoil at their own shadow. The imperfections of history abound. In a world where debates wax and wane over the legitimacy of honouring certain monuments and other historical markers, especially in public spaces and on university campuses, *McGill in History* is a timely anthology of how to think carefully and courageously about dilemmas facing the modern university and society in general.

What should institutions do about great benefactors who had feet of clay, whose conduct appears even more inexcusable with the passage of time? Are said individuals exceptional or simply persons "of their times"? Are they liable to endure interrogation that transcends generations? Similarly, is the university that engaged in egregious conduct and violated human rights, contradicting fundamental "Enlightenment" ideals of truth and human advancement on which the Western university is predicated, also exempt from harsh critiques? Furthermore, is the historian more of a curator who merely showcases historical actors and artifacts depending on contemporary moral standards? Or is the historian, true to the dictates of intellectual curiosity and moral courage, duty bound to critique power, especially institutionalized power? Not only are there scholarly questions, but also existential ones on which professional historians must ruminate. Moreover, what are the metrics by which scholarly communities can determine appropriate institutional responses to the difficult questions that arise from research into institutional history? On whose shoulders, put frankly, should accountability – that is, culpability – fall?

The university as a bastion of ideas, a marketplace of sorts where thinkers can reflect on and challenge dominant paradigms, can only maintain this sacrosanct aura if scholars, particularly historians, are willing to excavate the unpleasant chapters of the past, and when institutions encourage this type of open scholarly investigation. Perhaps no subject about twentieth-century McGill is more controversial – yet still relatively unknown – than the university's connections to the intelligence community and war industry, phenomena that reached an apex during the Cold War.

Two cases are especially noteworthy, demonstrating the anti-Black and colonial dimensions of McGill University's support of various Cold War endeavours rooted in white supremacy, imperialism, capitalism, militarism, and authoritarian repression. One of the seminal cases involves a US-Canadian weapons manufacturer and the other experimentations on human subjects using scientific methods of torture. These two examples are not noteworthy because both are representative of the forces that bedevil the modern, neoliberal university, but because the secrecy, audacity, and depravity of these university-sanctioned processes speak to the major geopolitical challenges of our times, especially when universities, feeling a budgetary crunch, are compelled to forge partnerships or pursue returns on investments that could undermine institutional credibility.

It might surprise members of the McGill community that when South Africa brought a formal case to the International Court of Justice (ICJ) on 29 December 2023 accusing Israel of committing genocide on the Palestinian people in Gaza, the matter shone new light on the complicity of Western universities in past and present war crimes and genocides. In this instance, scholarly and activist demands for universities to divest from weapons manufacturers and various stakeholders allegedly aiding and abetting Israel's protracted genocide in Palestine and other crimes against humanity recall McGill's intimate connections to Cold War strategic bipolarity and Ottawa's and Washington's direct involvement in shaping scientific priorities that overwhelmingly benefited North America's integrated war industry. For this reason, the pro-Palestinian encampment that activists erected on McGill's downtown campus in April 2024 is a clear example of the monumental events that catalyze activism on university campuses, calling into question the stewardship of administrations when the university is culpable of funding or benefiting from imperialism, capitalism, and militarism.

As the anti-colonial struggle raged in 1960s Africa and the Caribbean Basin and Black Power activists locked arms across the US-Canadian border, the United States, partly hamstrung by a nuclear brinkmanship with the Soviet Union, explored a multitude of ways to disrupt the fear emanating from global Black self-determination. To achieve this objective in the Atlantic World, US intelligence enlisted the help of McGill University, or, more specifically, one of McGill's most brilliant scientists.

In the summer of 1961, thirty-four-year-old Dr Gerald Bull, McGill University's youngest professor, stood poised to revolutionize artillery warfare. Founder of the US-Canadian arms firm Space Research Corporation, Bull was a master ballistics engineer whose goal between 1961 and 1967 was to create a satellite launcher – a supergun of sorts – that could fire projectiles into space. McGill provided $200,000 in seed capital. The Pentagon was Bull's other investor. McGill's existing projects in Barbados provided an opportunity for Bull to use the island as a launch site. Young, ambitious, and networked, Bull spent a decade helping to build the Canadian Armaments and Research Development Establishment, which collaborated with the US Army's Ballistic Research Laboratory. The Canadian Armaments and Research project was an outgrowth of McGill's Space Research Institute after termination of the High Altitude Research Program (HARP), a joint US Army-Canadian government venture. HARP created modified 16-inch guns that launched missiles.[1]

Gerald Bull founded Space Research Corporation as a joint US-Canadian venture to maximize its potential for Cold War strategic funding. Its headquarters was in the adjoining border towns of Highwater, Quebec, and North Troy, Vermont. By the early 1970s, Space Research Corporation had constructed a 172-foot, 16.4-inch smooth-bore cannon, which successfully fired 140-pound projectiles at 10,000 feet per second. It also manufactured advanced, remote-operated long-range cannons. By April 1976, the Canadian government designated Space Research Corporation a "wartime and peacetime vital point." In other words, Space Research Corporation's weapons technology had become integral to Canadian officials' formulation of foreign policy and national security. This designation was lucrative, for Space Research Corporation test-fired almost 1,000 projectiles at its Antigua artillery site from March to May 1977.[2]

The CIA and Pentagon feared geopolitical rivalry in southern Africa, specifically in Angola, Mozambique, and Rhodesia, and the human and material support Black activists in the Americas rendered these revolutionary movements. Apartheid South Africa was the gateway to smuggle arms to US proxies fighting revolutionary socialist armies in the region. The organization of African Liberation Day across North America in the 1970s by activists in support of anti-colonial revolutions in southern-Africa – which in turn were buttressed by Black Caribbean troops mainly from Cuba, outfitted with Soviet weapons – terrified Washington. In response to the triangulation of revolutionary Pan-Africanism in the Atlantic World, US intelligence enlisted the support of Bull's US-Canadian arms firm to smuggle arms to white supremacists and other US proxies in southern Africa.

As McGill's direct investments in weapons development aided US foreign policy in the Caribbean and Africa, its faculty's experiments on human subjects, specifically Indigenous people, played a vital role in the ways that the state surveilled, captured, manipulated, subjugated, and killed demographics that the state deemed subversive, surplus, and thus disposable. What some have called "enhanced interrogation" in recent years – namely, torture – is intimately connected to McGill's Cold War history in the 1960s and 1970s. Social and behavioural scientists at McGill and other elite North American institutions devised "carceral technologies," in the words of one scholar. These technologies included "sensory deprivation, electroshock therapy, isolation, hypnotism, chemotherapy, psychosurgery, electrode implantation," psychedelic drug manipulation, hyper confinement, and other cruel acts for prison guards and medical professionals to wield in their attempts to break the resolve of Black and other inmates who aspired to social revolution.[3] Hidden from untrained eyes is how these draconian, sadistic forms of penal control remained racialized and gendered, given the historic ways that white supremacist patriarchy marked Black boys and men – whether in bondage or in quasi freedom – as particularly dangerous to the status quo. This logic, of course, served to justify their dehumanization on one hand and violent removal from the civilian population on the other.

These cruel and unusual tactics emerged from collaborations among the US intelligence community, academia, and philanthropic organizations, such as the Rockefeller Foundation. Better known by code name MKULTRA after its 1975 revelation in the US Senate's Church Committee hearings into the intelligence community's unconstitutional domestic operations, this highly classified program was what CIA director Allen Dulles called "brain warfare" or mind control.[4] Flush with Rockefeller research funding in the 1960s, McGill psychologists and psychiatrists partnered with researchers at the University of

Vermont and psychiatric institutions in New York State to advance MKULTRA. At the United Nations and other liberal internationalist, multilateral organizations, Washington bureaucrats publicly denounced torture. Meanwhile, the CIA clandestinely advocated its efficacy, funding behavioural science experiments for controlling inmates and would-be enemy combatants to the tune of $1 billion annually in the 1960s.[5]

In both instances – whether arms development and trafficking overseas or brain warfare domestically – the legacy of McGill University supporting the war industry and shaping the development of scientific torture techniques has eroded legitimacy and follows a pattern that has plagued other Western institutions. Like the university's connections to and windfall from transatlantic slavery, Cold War McGill has yet to receive its proper institutional accounting and redress. That these historical processes seldom generate focused and sustained institutional self-reflection, critique, and contrition is troubling. However, the fact that these same dynamics continue to shape global politics, particularly the ICJ's investigation into Israel's genocide of the Palestinian people and McGill's ongoing investments in a weapons industry implicated in said genocide, suggests that the lessons of history are not having the impact that is necessary for an intellectual community like McGill – which prizes the pursuit of truth, intellectual curiosity, and human advancement for the public good – to exercise moral courage in excavating its past dealings. Moreover, Israel's war machine subjects thousands of Palestinian hostages, many of whom are children and elderly folk, to some of the very same brain warfare techniques that McGill faculty helped devise for the CIA in the 1960s and 1970s.

Like the global resistance against genocidal apartheid South Africa and student demands for divestment and boycott – uphill struggles from start to finish at McGill and countless campuses – cataloguing, chronicling, and reconciling institutional memory accordingly seems more urgent than ever. These lessons illustrate that academic institutions are not merely products of the times, but bastions of state proxy power in which consequences are far reaching. The modern university, indeed, has been in crisis for decades. *McGill in History* is a timely reminder that this powerful, neoliberal entity known as the modern university casts many shadows and harbours even more secrets.

NOTES

The epilogue revisits subjects and themes from a keynote lecture delivered by Professor Adjetey, titled "Cold War Hot Wars: Arms Smuggling, Revolution, and Counter-Revolution in the Atlantic World," delivered at the "McGill in History" colloquium in April 2022.

1 Wendell Nii Laryea Adjetey, *Cross-Border Cosmopolitans: The Making of a Pan-African North America* (Chapel Hill: University of North Carolina Press, 2023), 230–59.

2 Adjetey, *Cross-Border Cosmopolitans.*

3 Orisanmi Burton, *Tip of the Spear: Black Radicalism, Prison Repression, and the Long Attica Revolt* (Oakland: University of California Press, 2023), 183–222.

4 Burton, *Tip of the Spear*, 185. See also Robin W. Winks, *Cloak & Gown: Scholars in the Secret War, 1939–1961* (New York: William Morrow and Company, 1987).

5 Alfred W. McCoy, *A Question of Torture: CIA Interrogations, from the Cold War to the War on Terror* (New York: Henry Holt and Company, 2007), 7.

Contributors

WENDELL NII LARYEA ADJETEY is William Dawson Associate Professor of US and African Diaspora History at McGill University. His book, *Cross-Border Cosmopolitans: The Making of a Pan-African North America*, won the 2024 Governor General's History Award for Scholarly Research, among other distinctions.

TESS ELSWORTHY received her MA in history from McGill University in 2020. Her chapter for this book is a distillation of her thesis, "McGill University's Racial Exclusion of Japanese Canadians, 1943–1945." She is currently a graduate student in the School of Information Studies at McGill.

BRIAN GETTLER is associate professor of history at the University of Toronto, a member of the Montreal History Group, and co-editor of the *Canadian Historical Review*. He has published numerous articles and book chapters as well as a monograph, *Colonialism's Currency: Money, State, and First Nations in Canada, 1820–1950* (MQUP, 2020).

ELSBETH HEAMAN is professor of history at McGill University, where she first came to study – and join student demonstrations ("Divest Now!") at the James Building – in 1985. She is currently writing a biography of Jacob Viner.

BRIAN LEWIS is professor of history at McGill University. His monographs include *The Middlemost and the Milltowns: Bourgeois Culture and Politics in Early Industrial England* (Stanford, 2001), *'So Clean': Lord Leverhulme, Soap and Civilization* (Manchester, 2008), and *Wolfenden's Witnesses: Homosexuality in Postwar Britain* (Palgrave Macmillan, 2016).

ANDREW MACKILLOP is professor of Scottish global histories at the University of Glasgow. His research interests focus on Scotland's simultaneous integration into the British union state and its wider global empire. His latest monograph, *Human Capital and Empire: Scotland, Ireland, Wales and British Imperialism in Asia, c. 169–c. 1820* (Manchester, 2021), uses comparative approaches to assess how areas of "poorer" Europe accessed early modern globalization.

STEPHEN MULLEN is lecturer in history at the University of Glasgow. His monograph, *The Glasgow Sugar Aristocracy: Scotland and Caribbean Slavery, 1775–1838*, was published by University of London Press in November 2022.

DON NERBAS is associate professor and St Andrew's Society/McEuen Scholarship Foundation chair in Canadian-Scottish Studies at McGill University. He is author of *Dominion of Capital: The Politics of Big Business and the Crisis of the Canadian Bourgeoisie, 1914–1947* (University of Toronto Press, 2013) and co-editor (with Dimitry Anastakis and Elizabeth Kirkland) of *Montreal's Square Mile: The Making and Transformation of a Colonial Metropole* (University of Toronto Press, 2024). He is at work on a book on Cape Breton's political economy of coal during the long nineteenth century.

MELISSA N. SHAW is assistant professor of Black Canadian / Black North American history at McGill University. Her first monograph, *Unblemished Citizenship: Black Canadian Women's Fight for Racial Justice, 1919–1939*, chronicles the unknown story of women's activism in Ontario during the tumultuous interwar years. Drawing from her work as a 2020 Provostial Postdoctoral Research Scholar in Institutional Histories, Slavery, and Colonialism, one of her current projects explores the historical implications of institutional power, accountability, and Black Canadian identity.

MARLENE SHORE is professor emerita and senior scholar of history at York University, Toronto. Her major publications include *The Science of Social Redemption: McGill, the Chicago School, and the Origins of Social Research in Canada* (University of Toronto Press, 1987), *The Transformation of Psychology: Influences of 19th-Century Philosophy, Technology, and Natural Science*, co-edited with Christopher D. Green and Thomas Teo (American Psychological Association, 2001), and *The Contested Past: Reading Canada's History* (University of Toronto Press, 2002).

ANDREA TONE is professor of history at McGill University, with a joint appointment in the Department of Social Studies of Medicine and the Department of History and Classical Studies. Her monographs include *The Business of Benevolence: Industrial Paternalism in Progressive America* (Cornell University Press), *Devices and Desires: A History of Contraceptives in America* (Hill & Wang), *The Age of Anxiety: A History of America's Turbulent Affair with Tranquilizers* (Basic Books), and a forthcoming history of mind control experiments in Cold War America. She is currently researching the history and health hazards of the twentieth-century cosmetics industry.

JEAN-PHILIPPE WARREN is professor of sociology at Concordia University, Montreal. He is a fellow of the Royal Society of Canada and co-director of the "Democracy and Pluralism" research axis of the Centre for Interdisciplinary Research on Diversity and Democracy (CRIDAQ). His honours include the Governor General's Literary Award in the essay category, the Canada Prize for the best scholarly book in the humanities and social sciences, and the Georges-Henri-Lévesque Medal.

BRIAN YOUNG, retired from McGill in 2009, is James McGill Professor Emeritus of Canadian History. He is working on a monograph treating the exercise of judicial authority in Victorian Quebec.

Index